1

CREATING HIGH-TECH TEAMS

Creating High-Tech Teams

PRACTICAL GUIDANCE ON WORK PERFORMANCE AND TECHNOLOGY

EDITED BY

Clint Bowers

Eduardo Salas

Florian Jentsch

AMERICAN PSYCHOLOGICAL ASSOCIATION
WASHINGTON, DC

Published by
American Psychological Association
750 First Street, NE
Washington, DC 20002
www.apa.org

To order
APA Order Department
P.O. Box 92984
Washington, DC 20090-2984
Tel: (800) 374-2721
Direct: (202) 336-5510
Fax: (202) 336-5502
TDD/TTY: (202) 336-6123
Online: www.apa.org/books/
E-mail: order@apa.org

In the U.K., Europe, Africa, and the Middle East, copies may be ordered from
American Psychological Association
3 Henrietta Street
Covent Garden, London
WC2E 8LU England

Typeset in Goudy by World Composition Services, Inc., Sterling, VA

Printer: Book-Mart Press, North Bergen, NJ
Cover Designer: Berg Design, Albany, NY
Technical/Production Editor: Genevieve Gill

The opinions and statements published are the responsibility of the authors, and such opinions and statements do not necessarily represent the policies of the American Psychological Association.

Library of Congress Cataloging-in-Publication Data

Creating high-tech teams : practical guidance on work performance and technology / edited by Clint Bowers, Eduardo Salas, and Florian Jentsch.
    p. cm.
  Includes bibliographical references and index.
  ISBN 1-59147-274-1
  1. Teams in the workplace—Computer networks. 2. Virtual work teams. 3. Decision support systems. 4. Group decision making. 5. Groupware (Computer software) I. Bowers, Clint A. II. Salas, Eduardo. III. Jentsch, Florian.

HD66.2.C73 2005
658.4'022—dc22   2005002127

British Library Cataloguing-in-Publication Data
A CIP record is available from the British Library.

Printed in the United States of America
First Edition

CONTENTS

Contributors .... *vii*

Acknowledgments .... *ix*

Introduction: Creating High-Tech Teams 3
Clint Bowers, Eduardo Salas, and Florian Jentsch

I. High Technology to Support Teamwork 9

Chapter 1.   Groupware, Group Dynamics, and
              Team Performance 11
              James E. Driskell and Eduardo Salas

Chapter 2.   Enabling Team Decision Making 35
              Rick van der Kleij and Jan Maarten Schraagen

Chapter 3.   Effects of Data Visualizations on Group
              Decision Making 51
              Sae Lynne Schatz, Janis Cannon-Bowers,
              and Clint Bowers

II. High-Tech Teams in Action 69

Chapter 4.   Cognition, Teams, and Team Cognition: Memory
              Actions and Memory Failures in Distributed
              Team Environments 71
              Stephen M. Fiore, Haydee M. Cuevas, Jonathan W.
              Schooler, and Eduardo Salas

Chapter 5.   Exploration and Context in
              Communication Analysis 89
              Magnus Morin and Pär-Anders Albinsson

Chapter 6.   Enhancing Command and Control Teamwork in
             Operation Enduring Freedom 113
             Janel H. Schermerhorn and Ronald A. Moore

Chapter 7.   Operational Concepts, Teamwork, and Technology
             in Commercial Nuclear Power Stations 139
             John M. O'Hara and Emilie M. Roth

Chapter 8.   Group Performance and Space Flight Teams 161
             Barrett S. Caldwell

III.   The Future of Teamwork: Technology as a Team Member   183

Chapter 9.   Virtual Teams: Creating Context for
             Distributed Teamwork 185
             *Heather A. Priest, Kevin C. Stagl, Cameron Klein,
             and Eduardo Salas*

Chapter 10. Understanding and Developing Virtual Computer-
             Supported Cooperative Work Teams 213
             Lori Foster Thompson and Michael D. Coovert

Chapter 11. Automated Systems in the Cockpit:
             Is the Autopilot, "George," a Team Member? 243
             *Raegan M. Hoeft, Janeen A. Kochan,
             and Florian Jentsch*

Chapter 12. Training Teamwork With Synthetic Teams 261
             *Jared Freeman, Craig Haimson, Frederick J. Diedrich,
             and Michael Paley*

Creating High-Tech Teams: A Conclusion 283
Raegan M. Hoeft, Florian Jentsch, and Clint Bowers

Author Index 289

Subject Index 299

About the Editors 313

CONTRIBUTORS

Pär-Anders Albinsson, Swedish Defence Research Agency, Linköping, Sweden

Clint Bowers, Department of Psychology, University of Central Florida, Orlando

Barrett S. Caldwell, School of Industrial Engineering, Purdue University, West Lafayette, IN

Janis Cannon-Bowers, School of Film and Digital Media, University of Central Florida, Orlando

Michael D. Coovert, Department of Psychology, University of South Florida, Tampa

Haydee M. Cuevas, Institute for Simulation and Training, University of Central Florida, Orlando

Frederick J. Diedrich, Aptima, Inc., Woburn, MA

James E. Driskell, Florida Maxima Corporation, Winter Park

Stephen M. Fiore, Institute for Simulation and Training, University of Central Florida, Orlando

Jared Freeman, Aptima, Inc., Washington, DC

Craig Haimson, Aptima, Inc., Washington, DC

Raegan M. Hoeft, Department of Psychology, University of Central Florida, Orlando

Florian Jentsch, Department of Psychology, University of Central Florida, Orlando

Cameron Klein, Department of Psychology, University of Central Florida, Orlando

Janeen A. Kochan, Department of Psychology, University of Central Florida, Orlando

Ronald A. Moore, Pacific Science & Engineering Group, San Diego, CA

Magnus Morin, VSL Research Labs, Linköping, Sweden

John M. O'Hara, Brookhaven National Laboratory, Upton, NY

Michael Paley, Aptima, Inc., Washington, DC

Heather A. Priest, Department of Psychology, University of Central Florida, Orlando

Emilie M. Roth, Roth Cognitive Engineering, Brookline, MA

Eduardo Salas, Institute for Simulation and Training, University of Central Florida, Orlando

Sae Lynne Schatz, College of Arts and Sciences, University of Central Florida, Orlando

Janel H. Schermerhorn, Pacific Science & Engineering Group, San Diego, CA

Jonathan W. Schooler, Department of Psychology, University of British Columbia, Vancouver, British Columbia, Canada

Jan Maarten Schraagen, TNO Defence, Security and Safety, Soesterberg, the Netherlands

Kevin C. Stagl, Department of Psychology, University of Central Florida, Orlando

Lori Foster Thompson, Department of Psychology, North Carolina State University, Raleigh

Rick van der Kleij, TNO Defence, Security and Safety, Soesterberg, the Netherlands

ACKNOWLEDGMENTS

We would like to extend a special acknowledgment and "thank you" to Ms. Raegan Hoeft, whose collaboration on this project was of critical importance. Ms. Hoeft, who was an ABD student in the University of Central Florida's applied experimental and human factors psychology doctoral program at the time this book was created, became the central point-of-contact for us in interfacing with the authors and with the American Psychological Association's editorial staff. Without her enthusiasm, diligence, technical expertise, and considerable investment of time, the book would not have become the product it is today.

CREATING HIGH-TECH TEAMS

INTRODUCTION: CREATING HIGH-TECH TEAMS

CLINT BOWERS, EDUARDO SALAS, AND FLORIAN JENTSCH

Perhaps one of the most important changes in the workplace in the past several years has been the dependence of organizations on teams. This dependence on teamwork is interesting for several reasons. First, it was insidious. Teamwork, with few exceptions, was neither requested nor planned for. It seemed to just happen, catching many industries and organizations unaware and unprepared. A second, related issue is that no one was prepared to help. Scientists in various disciplines were caught almost as unaware as the industries that they were supposed to help. In fact, the term *team* was not even listed as an index term in psychology until the 1960s. An actual programmatic science of teamwork did not begin until much later—far too late to be helpful. Consequently, the development of interventions to improve teamwork was largely industry driven.

A third observation about our eventual dependence on teamwork in the workplace is that it was a direct result, and probably unforeseen consequence of, technology. In large part, teamwork was required because systems could create and display more information than any one team member could possibly digest. Thus, there was imposed a demand for teams to do cognitively based tasks. This was a new form of "teamwork." For the most part, the sharing of cognitive tasks was largely unheard of. It imposed a new requirement for communication, coordination, and understanding among team members. We learned, sometimes the hard way, that these new requirements were associated with a need for additional training—that a team of experts did not necessarily coalesce to form an "expert team."

Finally, the area of teamwork is remarkable because it represents one of the rare cases where science, industry, and the government have combined forces to respond to a need, each contributing its own special abilities and resources. Unfortunately, the importance of teamwork was driven home by a series of accidents that resulted in horrible loss of life. For example, when the USS *Vincennes* mistakenly shot down a civilian Iranian Airbus, it was revealed that the mistake could, in part, be attributed to faulty communication and coordination. To its credit, the U.S. government responded to this revelation by launching one of the largest funded programs in the history of behavioral science, concentrating formidable resources on the problem of teamwork to "fill in" a largely absent science.

Similarly, there were a few unfortunate mishaps in commercial aviation that also brought attention to the importance of teamwork. The controlled flight into terrain of Eastern Airlines Flight 401 is one of the most commonly cited examples. In this case, a perfectly functioning airplane crashed needlessly because the crew became fixated on a relatively insignificant problem in the cockpit. Again, the government responded with a tremendous investment in aviation teamwork. Furthermore, we witnessed what might be the best cooperation between industry and science in the history of behavioral science. Professionals in the aviation industry not only cooperated but also invested themselves in the problem of improving teamwork in the cockpit. Because of this cooperation, we were able to identify key teamwork interventions that not only improved performance in the aviation setting but also have been adapted to help everyone from oil workers to surgeons to firefighters.

Other examples of industry and science working together to improve team performance abound. Industries such as oil exploration, industrial design, financial decision making, and so forth, have all contributed either by participating in actual studies, sharing lessons learned, or evaluating interventions developed in other settings. In so doing, both science and industry have progressed more than anyone might have thought 20 years ago.

Sadly, however, the news is not all good. Despite the advances in understanding the nature of effective teamwork previously described, there are still very substantial gaps in our knowledge. We know some factors that seem to be associated with effective teams, but we really do not know how well they generalize across tasks. There is a significant need for understanding the role of individual differences and other team composition effects. Furthermore, there is a need for continued research on assisting teams in coping with stressful situations and a host of other environmental effects. Indeed, this area of research will need to persist for several more years before we can provide the level of guidance needed by industry.

Yet, even as we conduct this research, there is an uneasy feeling that the ground is shifting beneath our feet. The level of technology being acquired and deployed in the workplace is changing the nature of teamwork at least as fast as it is being researched. Thus, there is a concern that by the time we figure teamwork out, teamwork will not be the same. It is precisely this concern that motivated this book.

WHAT IS TEAMWORK, AND HOW IS IT CHANGING?

As noted previously, the scientific study of teams is relatively new. Although social psychologists had studied groups for some time, these studies had been limited largely to the study of small collections of students solving novel problems in laboratory settings. Important observations came from this work, to be sure; however, there was a nagging feeling that results collected from these collectives would not generalize to the types of groupings often seen in the workplace. Consequently, it seemed important to arrive at a definition of *team* that would discriminate between collectives seen in the workplace and the informal groupings seen in laboratory studies. A definition that seems well accepted came from Salas and his colleagues (Salas, Dickinson, Converse, & Tannenbaum, 1992). This definition emphasized the notions of shared goals and interdependence, characteristics not usually attributed to laboratory groups.

In executing our research in teams, we have focused largely on the variables discussed in the *team effectiveness model* (Salas et al., 1992). Although this model focuses on many aspects of team performance, our emphasis has been largely on the characteristics of teams and their tasks. Now, however, it is clear that we must pay more attention to the tools with which they do their work. Not only do tools such as decision support systems alter team behavior, but also we have a tremendous opportunity to influence the design of these tools by informing their designers about principles of team performance.

In general, Salas et al.'s (1992) definition of *teams* has served us well over the past 20 years of team research. However, we recently have been confronted by the fact that there might be important differences between *traditional* work teams (e.g., those that are colocated, at least most of the time) and those that seem to be becoming more prevalent in industry today. These *distributed* teams are rarely colocated, if at all. They may exist in different buildings, regions, or even countries. They rely much less on face-to-face communication and are much more likely to communicate through telephone, electronic mail, and chat rooms. We are not certain whether the "known" principles of teamwork fit as well with these kinds of teams, and many scientists are working to understand effective practices for these groupings.

Finally, it seems clear that teams of the future will be composed of both humans and machines working together. This prospect is as exciting as it is frightening. Our experiences with automation have demonstrated that it is difficult to anticipate all of the issues related to human–machine interaction. Unexpected negative consequences are frequent, and it requires formidable front-end work to create a system that is workable. In fact, there are far too many examples of automation leading to degraded, and occasionally disastrous, performance. Indeed, unintended automation effects in complex, multi-operator systems have been responsible for some of the more horrible recent industrial disasters (e.g., Three Mile Island and the Cali plane crash). However, the promise of these systems is formidable, and their presence is inevitable. This will be an important area of science for years to come.

ORGANIZATION OF THE BOOK

As team researchers, we have been awed by the changes that have occurred in a relatively short time. Technology issues seem to spring up much faster than we can investigate them. We became aware of the other scientists and industries that were struggling with similar problems. Often, these problems (and sometimes even solutions) were not of the types that warrant publication in scientific journals. However, it certainly seemed that there would be value in collecting and distributing this information as best we could, leading to the present volume. Our goals for this book were simple: to extract the state of the art in technology and teamwork from our colleagues in science and industry and to translate these lessons into the best possible guidance for practitioners. Toward that end, we contacted colleagues who we knew were working with specific types of technology and asked them to describe their understanding of how that technology affected teamwork and how best to use it.

The book is divided into three parts. Part I is designed to provide readers with a review of the most prevalent tools used today. Chapter 1, by Driskell and Salas, focuses on groupware and provides an excellent review not only of the tools but also of how they have evolved in response to advances in our understanding of distributed teams. In chapter 2, van der

Kliej and Schraagen extend this discussion by discussing technologies expressly designed to support one critical function: decision making. This area has probably received more attention than any other because of the military's interest and investment. The final chapter in this part, by Schatz et al., presents another approach to augmenting team performance through technology–visualization. This approach, although designed with the same goals as the others, achieves its successes through indirectly affecting team performance through altering data presentations. This is a fascinating, and understudied, area of human performance.

Because this book is targeted toward readers who will apply technologies, we have included a rather large section on applications in a number of industries. Part II begins with chapter 4, by Fiore et al., who caution readers about the challenges of adding technology to complex work team environments. Further challenges (and lessons learned) are discussed in chapter 5, by Morin and Albinsson. Their chapter makes clear the difficulty in understanding "what happened" and should be instructive to anyone who must conduct after-action reviews. Many of the issues related to supporting distributed teams are discussed in chapter 6, on tool development, by Schermerhorn and Moore. This chapter illustrates a process that might be useful to others seeking to develop applications to support distributed teams. Also relevant to design issues for these teams is chapter 7, by O'Hara and Roth. These authors discuss the integration of technological elements into the larger workspace, an issue that requires attention to avoid some of the unintended negative consequences of technology previously discussed. Finally, Caldwell brings several of these issues together in chapter 8, on technology and teams in the space program.

Authors of chapters in Part III, provide a glimpse into the future by discussing various applications of "virtual" teammates (and even entire teams). The many challenges incumbent in this area are detailed in chapter 9, by Priest et al. Thompson and Coovert provide a chapter (chap. 10) that discusses an initial attempt to support these virtual teams through software tools. Moving toward even higher levels of automation, Hoeft et al. discuss in chapter 11 the implications of computerized teammates. Finally, in chapter 12, Freeman et al. discuss the use of entire virtual teams as an adjunct for team training programs. This chapter foreshadows developments we can expect in the not-too-distant future.

The issue of technology-enabled teamwork represents a challenging and exciting area of applied psychology. The issues that are important here are many, and we hope that this book will help to bring them to light. We certainly hope that it will not only assist those trying to apply these technologies but also will inspire much more research interest in this very important topic.

REFERENCE

Salas, E., Dickinson, T. L., Converse, S. A., & Tannenbaum, S. I. (1992). Toward an understanding of team performance and training. In R. W. Swezey & E. Salas (Eds.), *Teams: Their training and performance* (pp. 3–29). Norwood, NJ: Ablex.

I

HIGH TECHNOLOGY TO SUPPORT TEAMWORK

In a book on high-tech teams, it is essential that we present some overview of what kinds of technology affect the team setting, and how. As we mentioned in the Introduction, the chapters in Part I introduce readers to technologies that affect team processes and performance. Part I is dominated by groupware as the core technology to facilitate team processes and centers on two specific types of groupware: (a) decision support systems and (b) data visualization techniques.

In a generic sense, *groupware* refers to any type of technology that is designed to (or unintentionally has been found to) support or enhance the performance of groups and teams. More specifically, decision support systems are types of groupware that facilitate decision making in teams, whereas data visualization techniques are types of groupware that alter information presentation to allow for the extraction of more and different patterns of data.

Part I, which focuses on the different types of groupware, thus lays the foundation for the rest of the book. To understand how technology affects teams and team performance, one must first have a firm grasp on the currently available technologies that might be applied to the team setting. The chapters in Part I not only bring readers up to date on groupware in general, and decision support systems in particular, but also present an emerging technology (data visualizations) that has yet to be exploited fully. The possibilities are endless; Part I merely provides an introduction to where we currently stand and hints at the directions we might be taking in the future.

1

GROUPWARE, GROUP DYNAMICS, AND TEAM PERFORMANCE

JAMES E. DRISKELL AND EDUARDO SALAS

Groupware refers to software that supports group performance. At the very broadest level, groupware may include a variety of applications, including electronic mail (e-mail), document-sharing software, electronic meeting systems, videoconferencing, calendar-scheduling systems, decision support systems, and Intranet or Web-based networks. Just to stretch the concept a bit further, if we consider technology that supports group performance, then we would include such old standbys as flip charts, voice messaging, intercoms, and telephones. Thus, the requirement to support collaborative activities and attempts to harness technology to address these needs are certainly not new phenomena. We can distinguish groupware from these earlier efforts in that groupware is digital or software based, and the development of groupware has occurred relatively recently, in the 1980s and 1990s, emerging from the success of individual software applications.

In this chapter, we do not attempt a traditional review of the groupware literature—a somewhat daunting task in itself, given the nature of this very broad and diverse literature. We focus instead on the group dynamics underlying the development of effective groupware. The term *groupware* is a hybrid of the words *group* and *software*. We argue that the groupware development literature has overemphasized the software approach to product development and almost ignored the group dynamics that determine groupware effectiveness. Moreover, we argue that this is a principal reason why groupware has not achieved greater acceptance and success in supporting teamwork.

First, we discuss the current status and limitations of groupware research; then we address challenges in supporting collaborative activities in distributed teams. Third, we develop and elaborate a *group dynamics* model of groupware development that emphasizes the specific functions or activities that teams perform and contextual factors that affect team interaction. Finally, we discuss one area, *distributed* or *distance learning*, in which collaborative-support tools are extensively incorporated.

CURRENT STATUS

It is important to note that some groupware applications have had a significant and extensive impact on how people collaborate. For example, the use of e-mail has ushered in a significant change in how people interact at a distance. Recent surveys indicate that more than 57 million Americans use e-mail at work (Fallows, 2002); however, many researchers argue that, broadly viewed, groupware has fallen short of achieving its potential. Kline and McGrath (1999) noted that there is a substantial gap between what has been promised by various groupware applications and what has been delivered. Grudin (2002) offered a revealing anecdote, recalling that when the Institute for the Future convened a panel of experts in 1990 to discuss groupware, they used an electronic meeting system to coordinate activities. In 2001, this group again convened its expert panel but used pen, paper, and flip charts instead of digital technology. We believe there are several reasons for the failure of groupware to achieve broader acceptance and application as a tool to support team performance.

The first concern that must be addressed is "Where is the *group* in *groupware?*" A substantial proportion of groupware development efforts take place in departments of computer science, management information systems, and industrial engineering. In contrast, the majority of research on group performance, group processes, and group dynamics takes place in departments of psychology, sociology, and social psychology. Grudin (1994) noted that the development of software for individual users relies heavily on the informed intuition of software designers supplemented by input from human factors, engineers, or cognitive psychologists; however, he noted that the "intuition" for the development of multi-user or group applications is not likely to be found in the software product development team: "The pertinent skills of social psychology and anthropology are absent in most development environments, where human factors engineers and cognitive psychologists are only slowly being accepted" (p. 100).

Grudin (1994) further noted that "Visionary writers have stressed the need for designers to understand the functioning and evolution of groups" (p. 103). However, we argue that it takes little vision to suggest that those who develop groupware should understand groups. There are certainly some groupware researchers who have a strong foundation in group dynamics, and there are prominent social psychologists and group researchers who develop groupware. Nevertheless, it remains a unique feature of groupware development that the individuals who are least likely to a have an intimate understanding of group dynamics are those who are most likely to be developing group software.

A second, related concern is the predominant technology and product development orientation underlying groupware applications. Early groupware development in the 1980s grew out of product development efforts for single-user applications, which is not entirely illogical given that both were software-based products. However, Grudin (1994) noted that, rather than first identifying a group problem and developing a groupware solution to address the problem, most groupware has been developed with an off-the-shelf software-marketing approach. It is too often the case that developers build groupware because the technology exists, rather than the need. In fact, Grudin (1994) observed that the push behind the development of much early groupware was that technology costs had declined to the extent that large-system software could be adapted and marketed for groups. One consequence of this emphasis on technology versus an emphasis on group requirements is that developers end up with an application in search of a user. This technology–production emphasis is further reflected in the groupware literature, in which the reader is as likely to run across references to product development and software requirements as to encounter discussions of group processes and performance.

A third reason that groupware has failed to achieve its full potential is because of the failure of groupware developers to fully embrace the conditional approach to understanding group performance. Most groupware is proclaimed to support *group performance*, or *group collaboration*, very broadly defined; however, most group researchers would argue that group performance cannot be very broadly defined without the further specification of input, process, and output variables that define and moderate group performance. To the extent that groupware is "technology for teams" it is important to note that there are many different types of teams, that teams perform many different tasks, and that teams operate under various situational constraints. Moreover, the type of tool or system that will support team performance in any specific context will depend on the type of team, the type of task, and the environment in which the team performs. As Kline and McGrath (1999) noted, though, the importance of these contextual or moderating variables has been essentially overlooked in the groupware literature.

In the following sections we take a decidedly group dynamics perspective on groupware development. We discuss distinctions among different types of distributed teams and different types of activities that teams perform, and we derive a model that incorporates the role of contextual factors into team performance.

SUPPORTING COLLABORATION IN DISTRIBUTED TEAMS

The challenges in supporting collaboration in distributed or virtual teams are many. One challenge is simply that there are a number of different types of distributed teams. That is, although the core feature of a virtual team is that group members work together on a common task while spatially separated, there are significant differences in the type of technology used and the types of communication enabled in various distributed-team environments. Therefore, in terms of providing support for distributed teams, one must remain cognizant of the fact that there are a variety of types of distributed teams. (See chap. 9 for a more detailed discussion of virtual teams.)

First, distributed-team environments differ according to the communication capabilities that are enabled. Therefore, when discussing distributed teams, one must be aware that they may operate in different types of technological environments and that the type of communication environment enabled will have a significant impact on team interaction. In face-to-face interaction, group members share the same physical location; can see and hear one another; receive messages in real time, as they are produced; and send and receive information simultaneously and in sequence. Teams that are distributed over various types of computer-mediated environments lose certain of these capabilities. On the one hand, in a *videoconference* setting, distributed groups may interact over networked computer systems and exchange live video as well as audio and text. On the other hand, what we have termed *computer chat* refers to computer-mediated electronic dialogue between two or more group members in which the users exchange messages via text in real time. Group communication over this type of distributed environment is cotemporal, simultaneous, and sequential, but group members lack the capability to see one another and to hear the timing or intonation of their speech.

Second, just as there are different types of distributed environments, there are different types of teams. Teams may be *ad hoc* (a temporary team assembled solely for a specific task) or *intact* (an existing team in which team membership is stable). Teams may work together on a task over time, or interaction may be short and time limited. Teams may meet initially prior to interaction, or team members may be completely anonymous. Teams may be hierarchically structured in terms of status or authority, or teams may be composed of members who are equal in status. Teams can be composed of many members or few members. We discuss these contextual factors in more detail, but it is important to note that they all play a significant role in determining how teams interact.

A third and final point is that there are a number of different activities or functions that teams perform. That is, teams do not just "perform" in a broad sense; they perform a number of different functions or task-related activities in support of team goals. These functions may include coordination of team member efforts, maintaining smooth interpersonal relations, planning and carrying out tasks, and making decisions. This more detailed perspective on team performance suggests that groupware should not simply support team performance in a broad sense but more effectively support specific team functions or activities. In the following section we present a taxonomy that attempts to classify team performance functions.

Teamwork Dimensions

Fleishman and Zaccaro (1992) developed a taxonomic classification of the primary task-related activities or functions that teams perform. Building on earlier work on the structure of human performance (Fleishman & Quaintance, 1984), they attempted to describe the common team functions that underlie team performance. Major team functions identified include *orientation* functions (e.g., exchanging information), *coordination* functions (e.g., coordination and sequencing of activities), *monitoring* functions (e.g., performance monitoring and error correction), and *motivational* functions (e.g., maintenance of norms, resolving conflicts).

McIntyre and Salas (1995) described a series of studies that adopted a critical-incident approach to identifying critical teamwork behaviors. Researchers worked with real world teams, including naval shipboard teams and aircrews, to identify critical behaviors characterizing effective and ineffective teams. These core teamwork dimensions were further elaborated by Baker and Salas (1992) to include performance monitoring and feedback, communication, coordination, and adaptability.

Cannon-Bowers, Tannenbaum, Salas, and Volpe (1995) integrated these previous research efforts and proposed that the core teamwork activities be conceptualized as encompassing eight broad dimensions (see Table 1.1). According to Cannon-Bowers et al., the following teamwork dimensions are prerequisites for effective team performance across a variety of types of tasks and teams.

TABLE 1.1
Teamwork Dimensions

Dimension	Definition	Subskills
Adaptability	Team members use information from the task environment to adjust strategies through the use of flexibility, compensatory behavior, and reallocation of resources.	Flexibility, compensatory or backup behavior, providing assistance
Shared situational awareness	Team members develop shared knowledge of the team's internal and external environment.	Shared orientation, team awareness
Performance monitoring and feedback	Team members give, seek, and receive task-clarifying feedback.	Performance monitoring, providing feedback, error correction
Team management	Team members direct and coordinate task activities, assign tasks, plan and organize, and motivate other team members.	Resource management, motivation, planning and goal setting
Interpersonal relations	Team members optimize interpersonal interactions by resolving conflicts, use of cooperation, and building morale.	Conflict resolution, cooperation, morale building
Coordination	Team members organize team resources, activities, and responses to ensure complete and timely completion of tasks.	Task organization, response coordination, timing and activity pacing
Communication	Team members exchange information efficiently.	Seeking or requesting information, providing information, acknowledgement and confirmation
Decision making	Team members integrate or pool information, identify alternatives, select solutions, and evaluate consequences.	Assessment, evaluation, problem solving

Note. From "Defining Competencies and Establishing Team Training Requirements," by J. A. Cannon-Bowers, S. I. Tannenbaum, E. Salas, and C. E. Volpe, in R. Guzzo & E. Salas (Eds.), *Team Effectiveness and Decision Making in Organizations*, 1995, San Francisco: Jossey-Bass. Copyright 1995 by Jossey-Bass. Adapted with permission.

Adaptability

Adaptability functions include mutual adjustment among team members, compensatory behavior, and reallocation of resources in pursuit of team goals. Teams must be adaptive by adjusting task strategies in response to changes in the nature of the task or the team. For example, Porter et al. (2003) emphasized the importance of *backup behavior*, compensatory behavior to support other team members who are overloaded or experiencing difficulty.

Shared Situational Awareness

Team members must develop a *shared situational awareness*, also referred to as *mutual knowledge* (Cramton, 2001; Thompson & Coovert, 2003) or *common ground* (Clark & Brennan, 1991). Team members possess contextual task and team information that must be communicated to and understood by other team members. Cramton (2001) noted that mutual knowledge may suffer when team members fail to communicate unique information that they possess, fail to distribute information evenly among team members, or fail to correct misunderstandings. Some research has shown that the accuracy and similarity of shared mental models among team members predict the quality of team processes and performance (Mathieu, Heffner, Goodwin, Salas, & Cannon-Bowers, 2000; Thompson & Coovert, 2003).

Performance Monitoring and Feedback

Performance monitoring and feedback functions include monitoring other team members' contributions as well as monitoring team progress, identifying errors, providing constructive feedback, and offering advice for performance improvement. Members of effective teams must be familiar with each others' roles and accept responsibility for providing and accepting feedback (McIntyre & Salas, 1995).

Team Management

Team management functions include directing and coordinating the task activities of other team members, assigning tasks, and motivating other team members. These are primarily task behaviors oriented toward instrumental goals. One critical management task, planning, is often overlooked in teams (Hackman & Morris, 1978), although research has clearly demonstrated the value to team performance of planning (Janicik & Bartel, 2003; Weingart, 1992) and pretask briefings (Marks, Zaccaro, & Mathieu, 2000).

Interpersonal Relations

Team members optimize *interpersonal relations* by resolving conflicts, encouraging cooperative behavior, and building team morale. These are primarily socioemotional behaviors oriented toward smooth interpersonal relations. McIntyre and Salas (1995) noted that positive or supporting team behaviors are not always apparent in team interactions—at times, task demands may require terse, formal communications—but that a positive team environment supports all task activities. Moreover, research has shown that cohesive groups generally outperform less cohesive groups (Mullen & Copper, 1994).

Coordination

Janicik and Bartel (2003) noted that effective *coordination*—knowing who is going to do what, when, and with whom—is critical to team performance. Behaviors that support effective coordination include matching team member resources to task requirements, regulating the pace of team activities, and coordinating the response and sequencing of team member activities (Fleishman & Zaccaro, 1992).

Communication

Communication is the primary vehicle through which task groups accomplish their goals (Marks et al., 2000). Team members must exchange ideas and information in a clear and timely manner. Effective communication behaviors include exchanging information in a timely manner, acknowledging information, double-checking that the intent of messages was received (*closed-loop communication*), clarifying ambiguity, and the appropriate use of verbal and nonverbal cues (Kanki & Smith, 2001; Stout, Salas, & Fowlkes, 1997).

Decision Making

Team decision making involves problem identification and assessment, information exchange, generation and evaluation of solutions, implementation, and evaluation of consequences (Forsyth, 1990; Hirokawa, 1980). Barriers to effective team decision making may include failure to adequately assess problems (Moreland & Levine, 1992), failure to consider others' input (Driskell & Salas, 1992), failure to disclose uniquely held information (Stasser & Titus, 1995), and undue influence from a single team member (Milanovich, Driskell, Stout, & Salas, 1998).

A Contextual Model

Figure 1.1 depicts an input–process–output framework that provides a contextual model of groupware development. We wish to emphasize three points that are relevant to this representation. In brief, Figure 1.1 presents a perspective in which groupware is targeted to specific *team functions* to support overall *team performance*. The broad and too often observed claim that groupware supports "team activity" ignores the critical question of what type of team activity or what team functions a specific application is intended to support. Although marketing software to support "groups" may ensure

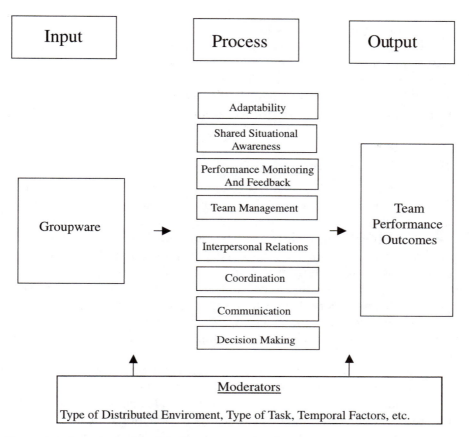

Input	Process	Output

Adaptability

Shared Situational Awareness

Performance Monitoring And Feedback

Team Management

Interpersonal Relations

Coordination

Communication

Decision Making

Groupware

Team Performance Outcomes

Moderators

Type of Distributed Enviroment, Type of Task, Temporal Factors, etc.

Figure 1.1. A contextual model of groupware development.

the broadest audience for a product, it reveals an alarming disregard for the complexities of group dynamics.

A second point of elaboration is that there are a variety of types of team performance outcomes. Outcome measures may include accuracy of performance, speed of performance, variability of performance, number of solutions generated, satisfaction, consensus, confidence, and team member attrition, among others. No specific groupware application would be expected to enhance all types of performance outcomes, yet it is often the case that the particular objectives or goals to be achieved by a particular groupware solution are left undefined. Moreover, groupware may have both positive and negative effects on team outcomes; for example, Kraemer and Pinsonneault (1990) noted that group decision support systems tend to improve decision quality but may increase the time required to make a decision.

Third, there are a number of critical contextual factors or moderators that will determine the effects of groupware on team performance. It is a truism in the group dynamics literature that the effects of almost any type of intervention on team performance will vary according to a variety of task, team, organizational, and environmental variables in which the team is embedded. Yet, as Kline and McGrath (1999) concluded, "Groupware research does not generally include critical contextual variables" (p. 265). In the following sections we discuss several of these potential moderating variables.

Type of Distributed Environment

A large body of research has examined teams that work over various distributed or computer-mediated environments. In a recent review of virtual teams, Driskell, Radtke, and Salas (2003) concluded that, overall, distance seems to matter: Being mediated by technology can have a significant impact on how teams perform. As we noted previously, it is difficult to draw conclusions regarding distributed teams in general, because there are different types of computer-mediated environments (e.g., audio–video vs. audio only vs. chat) that differ considerably in the richness of communications afforded. Thus, the nature of team interaction, and the requirements to support team activities, will vary considerably depending on the type of distributed-team environment.

Two major approaches to understanding the effects of different types of communications media—(a) theories of social presence (Short, Williams, & Christie, 1976) and (b) media richness (Daft & Lengel, 1984)—both hold that the capacity to transmit communicative information (visual, verbal, and contextual cues) is progressively restricted as one moves from face-to-face to audio–video to audio-only to textual modes of communication. This loss of contextual information across various communication modes may lead to weaker interpersonal bonds and loss of cohesion within teams (Straus, 1997), greater difficulty in establishing trust (Bos, Olson, Gergle, Olson, & Wright, 2002), and greater difficulty in establishing mutual knowledge and common ground (Cramton, 2001; Thompson & Coovert, 2003). Overall, less rich communications media exacerbate the effects of technological mediation. Thus, to the extent that technological mediation impairs interaction, it is likely to impair interaction to a greater extent for text-only communications than for text–audio and for audio–video communications.

Type of Task

Perhaps no factor has a greater effect on team interaction than the type of task in which the team is engaged. There have been a number of attempts to classify group tasks along a variety of dimensions, such as the cognitive versus physical requirements of the task or the requirement for cooperation or interdependence (cf. McGrath, 1984; Shaw, 1973; Steiner,

1972). One of the most recent and comprehensive classification systems relevant to teams was offered by Devine (2002), who identified 14 team types based on the type of work in which they are engaged and further classified them along seven contextual dimensions. Driskell, Hogan, and Salas (1987) also classified group tasks on the basis of the primary activities or behaviors required of team members, resulting in six task categories: (a) *mechanical/technical* tasks requiring the construction or operation of things; (b) *intellectual/analytic* tasks requiring generation of ideas, reasoning, or problem solving; (c) *imaginative/aesthetic* tasks requiring creativity or artistic endeavor; (d) *social* tasks requiring the training, supporting, or assisting of others; (e) *manipulative/persuasive* tasks requiring motivation or persuasion of others; and (f) *logical/precision* tasks requiring performance of routine, detailed, or standardized tasks. Gallupe, DeSanctis, and Dickson (1988) used McGrath's (1984) typology of group tasks to classify tasks used in group decision support research. McGrath's (1984) typology outlined four major types of group tasks, with several subtypes within each: (a) *generating* tasks (requiring the generation of plans or ideas), (b) *choosing* tasks (requiring either a correct answer or a preferred answer), (c) *negotiating* tasks (requiring the resolution of conflicts of policy or conflicts of interest), and (d) *executing* tasks (requiring either competing to win or performing against an objective or absolute standard of excellence).

Another way to classify group tasks is by the relative degree of task difficulty. *Task difficulty* refers to the degree of cognitive load, or mental effort, required to identify a problem solution. Task difficulty has been shown to be an important moderator in studies of the effectiveness of group decision support systems. For example, Gallupe et al. (1988) found that group decision support systems enhanced decision quality more in groups that performed a difficult task than in those that performed an easier task.

Tasks may also differ in the degree of *task uncertainty*, or the extent to which they have a verifiably correct answer. For example, a task that requires one to sum a column of numbers has a correct answer. In contrast, a judgment task, such as choosing a candidate for office, does not have a verifiably correct answer. Tasks with no verifiably correct answer emphasize the team's ability to extract a variety of conflicting interpretations and to forge a consensus to yield an agreement on solutions (Samburthy, Poole, & Kelly, 1993).

Finally, tasks may differ in the degree to which they require *interdependence*, or coordination among group members, a fact recognized in the task typologies of Shaw (1973), Steiner (1972), and Herold (1978). Straus and McGrath (1994) and others have argued that to the extent that team tasks require a greater degree of interdependence, coordination difficulties increase. Thus, coordination difficulties are less likely to influence overall performance for tasks that can be accomplished with little interpersonal interaction. Tasks that involve greater requirements for interdependence are more likely to be problematic in a virtual team setting.

Temporal Context

There are several temporal aspects of the team that influence the nature of team interaction and performance. McGrath (1997) noted that research is often conducted with ad hoc groups with no past or anticipated future, in contrast to dynamic groups, which are intact and perform over a longer period of time (see also Hollingshead & McGrath, 1995; McGrath, 1990). Teams that perform over time gain experience with the task and the communications technology, which may reduce performance decrements (Hollingshead, McGrath, & O'Connor, 1995). Although a number of temporal distinctions can be drawn related to the synchronicity, pacing, and sequencing of performance, the simple distinction between ad hoc teams that interact for a single session and dynamic teams that interact over time is an important one.

This distinction is also related to the experience of the team, or the stages of development of a team. Research on group development suggests that a group's interaction patterns change dramatically over time as the group members gain more experience working together (Bales, 1950; Hare, 1976). Time is needed for group members to develop a productive relationship (although time does not guarantee that the group will be productive). A newly formed group, with its lack of structure and cohesion, may be able to perform tasks in which individual members' efforts are pooled; however, tasks that require a high degree of collaboration may prove more difficult.

Instead of launching into productive behavior immediately, most groups seem to progress through a predictable series of stages. Although group theorists differ on the exact delineation, the five basic stages that are included in most models include (a) *orientation*, (b) *conflict*, (c) *cohesion*, (d) *performance*, and (e) *dissolution*. These have been elaborated more precisely in models that describe phases of the group decision-making process. Forsyth (1990) described four stages of team decision making: (a) *orientation*: defining the problem and planning; (b) *discussion*: gathering information, identifying solution alternatives, and evaluating alternatives; (c) *decision making*: choosing solutions; and (d) *implementation*: implementing and evaluating the decision. Kraemer and Pinsonneault (1990) noted that whereas many group decision support efforts focus on the early stages of group development, a large number of task groups in business and industry are intact teams that are more advanced in development with greater experience working together. Although Kraemer and Pinsonneault concluded that the effects of group decision support differ substantially according to the stage of group development, they also noted that this factor is rarely examined in groupware research.

Group Size

Steiner (1972) noted that a team's size may affect its performance in several ways. As a group gets larger, the diversity of its members increases, as do the variety of viewpoints and, potentially, the number of problem solutions available to the team. However, larger teams do not always perform better than smaller ones. Increasing team size makes coordination requirements more difficult, and as groups increase in size and complexity, more group structure (i.e., role differentiation, etc.) is required to coordinate group activity. Larger groups may increase conformity pressures and suppress the expression of minority or conflicting input (Steiner, 1972). As groups increase in size, opportunities for participation decrease and group discussion becomes increasingly dominated by a smaller proportion of group members. It is well established that whereas total group performance may increase as the size of the group increases, group member performance (i.e., performance per person) and satisfaction decrease as a function of group size (e.g., Mullen, 1991; Mullen & Baumeister, 1987). The effects of group size suggest a rather discouraging picture of larger groups, bringing to mind Old's (1946) tongue-in-cheek assertion that the optimal size for a group is approximately 0.7 people.

Vogel and Nunamaker (1990) argued that group size is an important factor in the application of group decision support systems. They suggested that decision support may be particularly valuable for larger groups because it has the potential to encourage more equal participation and increase the efficiency of group discussion. However, it is interesting to note that despite the suggestion that group decision support systems might be especially helpful for large group decision making, most of the research in this field has examined small (three- to four-person) groups.

Status Structure

The *status structure* of a team refers to the pattern of power, prestige, and authority among team members. Some teams are hierarchically structured or stratified, with clearly defined rankings of team members in terms of power and prestige. Examples of hierarchically structured teams include a business team composed of upper managers, middle managers, sales staff, and clerical personnel, or a military squad composed of personnel of varying rank. Other teams may be less hierarchically structured in terms of status and include team members who are of relatively equal status.

The status structure of the team has a significant impact on the nature of team interaction. Different status structures impose different interaction requirements on team members. In a typical work group, individuals with higher status assume a leadership position and command more of the group's resources—they talk more, they direct group activities, and they are more

likely to exert their opinion during decision making. In brief, higher
persons within the group command more of the group's resour
dominate conversation, their ideas are accepted more often, an
more likely to be seen as leaders (Driskell, Olmstead, & Salas

The status structure in a group clearly may have posi
negative effects. Ideally, status processes operate to allo
use its resources more effectively to accomplish a task
hierarchical patterning of interaction may have posir
operates in general accordance with the distribution c
That is, if status differences reflect actual differenc
and competence, then it is desirable for higher st
more active and influential. However, to the ex
within the group are based on cultural stereot
on factors unrelated to ability, this may r
the group and undesirable barriers to equ
ethnic minorities.

Moreover, there are conditions v
structures support group efficiency. F
simple, when one team member is
tion structure, or when the lar
lines of authority, then a hierar
However, there are condition
more efficient. For example
information resides in the
of great consequence ir
important, then a star
equally may be ben

This conditic
examining the e
tems may have
mediated enviro
team member input,
to more equal participatic
Sethna, 1991). In fact, Brenna
of groupware in organizations in
more dynamic, [and] hierarchies flatter
noted, this can be a double-edged sword: A
may lead to more open and equal participation
which the group can draw; in other cases, howeve.
status effects can lead to lower participation by team mem
competence and a disruption of the established chain of comma.
a greater understanding of the operation of status processes in groups,

stress may lead to a neglect of social or interpersonal cues as well. In fact,
Driskell et al. (1999) found that team members were less likely to maintain
a broad team perspective under stress and were more likely to shift to a
more individualistic self-focus, resulting in poorer overall team performance.
These results suggest that, under stress, group members may lose the collective representation of group activity that characterizes interdependent
team behavior.

Other research has examined the effects of stressors on group decision
making (Driskell, Driskell, & Salas, 1997). Formal,
analytic decision-making approaches require the decision maker to carry
out an elaborate and exhaustive procedure characterized by a systematic,
organized information search, thorough consideration of all available al
natives, evaluation of each alternative, and reexamination and revi
the decision-making ideal, some researchers have argued that u
data before a decision is made. Although this procedure is often ta
task demands, decision makers do not have the luxury of adop
consuming analytic strategy. Moreover, encouraging the decis
adopt an analytic model could undermine behavior that may
fit the requirements of the task situation. Johnston et al. (
on a time-pressured, naturalistic task, individuals who
use a less analytic or "hypervigilant" strategy perform
than those who used a formal, analytic decision
emphasize the importance of contextual factors,
making and suggest that any attempt to support
consider the demands under which teams perf

A Successful Application: Distance Lear

One area in which group suppo
researched and applied is the field of
distance learning is typically not
distance learning environments al
interaction to occur at a distanc
tion. Certainly, one reason un
cation of collaborative-suppo
forces driving growth in th
more important is the e
on a conditional appr
influences are a criti
textual influences as the
plications, we
paragraphs, lea
distance lear

Group Size

Steiner (1972) noted that a team's size may affect its performance in several ways. As a group gets larger, the diversity of its members increases, as do the variety of viewpoints and, potentially, the number of problem solutions available to the team. However, larger teams do not always perform better than smaller ones. Increasing team size makes coordination requirements more difficult, and as groups increase in size and complexity, more group structure (i.e., role differentiation, etc.) is required to coordinate group activity. Larger groups may increase conformity pressures and suppress the expression of minority or conflicting input (Steiner, 1972). As groups increase in size, opportunities for participation decrease and group discussion becomes increasingly dominated by a smaller proportion of group members. It is well established that whereas total group performance may increase as the size of the group increases, group member performance (i.e., performance per person) and satisfaction decrease as a function of group size (e.g., Mullen, 1991; Mullen & Baumeister, 1987). The effects of group size suggest a rather discouraging picture of larger groups, bringing to mind Old's (1946) tongue-in-cheek assertion that the optimal size for a group is approximately 0.7 people.

Vogel and Nunamaker (1990) argued that group size is an important factor in the application of group decision support systems. They suggested that decision support may be particularly valuable for larger groups because it has the potential to encourage more equal participation and increase the efficiency of group discussion. However, it is interesting to note that despite the suggestion that group decision support systems might be especially helpful for large group decision making, most of the research in this field has examined small (three- to four-person) groups.

Status Structure

The *status structure* of a team refers to the pattern of power, prestige, and authority among team members. Some teams are hierarchically structured or stratified, with clearly defined rankings of team members in terms of power and prestige. Examples of hierarchically structured teams include a business team composed of upper managers, middle managers, sales staff, and clerical personnel, or a military squad composed of personnel of varying rank. Other teams may be less hierarchically structured in terms of status and include team members who are of relatively equal status.

The status structure of the team has a significant impact on the nature of team interaction. Different status structures impose different interaction requirements on team members. In a typical work group, individuals with higher status assume a leadership position and command more of the group's resources—they talk more, they direct group activities, and they are more likely to exert their opinion during decision making. In brief, higher status persons within the group command more of the group's resources; they dominate conversation, their ideas are accepted more often, and they are more likely to be seen as leaders (Driskell, Olmstead, & Salas, 1993).

The status structure in a group clearly may have positive as well as negative effects. Ideally, status processes operate to allow the group to use its resources more effectively to accomplish a task. This structured, hierarchical patterning of interaction may have positive effects when it operates in general accordance with the distribution of ability in the group. That is, if status differences reflect actual differences in ability, expertise, and competence, then it is desirable for higher status group members to be more active and influential. However, to the extent that status differentials within the group are based on cultural stereotypes (e.g., race or gender), or on factors unrelated to ability, this may result in a loss of resources to the group and undesirable barriers to equal participation for women and ethnic minorities.

Moreover, there are conditions under which different types of status structures support group efficiency. For example, when a task is technically simple, when one team member is centrally located in a group communication structure, or when the larger organization is organized along strict lines of authority, then a hierarchical status structure may be advantageous. However, there are conditions under which a flat group status structure is more efficient. For example, when tasks are ambiguous or complex, when information resides in the hands of many people, or when making decisions of great consequence in which alternative or minority input is especially important, then a status structure in which team members contribute more equally may be beneficial.

This conditional perspective on status is important to consider when examining the effects that some computer-mediated communications systems may have on status in groups. Some research suggests that computer-mediated environments, such as text-based systems or those that structure team member input, may block the operation of status processes and lead to more equal participation (Driskell et al., 2003; Dubrovsky, Kiesler, & Sethna, 1991). In fact, Brennan and Rubenstein (1995) touted the value of groupware in organizations in that "organizational forms can become more dynamic, [and] hierarchies flatter" (p. 39). However, as we previously noted, this can be a double-edged sword: A flattening of the status hierarchy may lead to more open and equal participation and greater resources on which the group can draw; in other cases, however, the dampening of status effects can lead to lower participation by team members with greater competence and a disruption of the established chain of command. Without a greater understanding of the operation of status processes in groups, groupware developers run the risk of imposing structural changes within teams that may lead to greater inefficiency under certain task conditions.

High Stress or High Demand

Most research studies use as participants groups of students in experimental laboratories or workers who operate in relatively relaxed conditions. In contrast, real world teams often operate under vastly different conditions. Often, teams are taxed to make critical decisions under extreme pressures and demands. Emergency or crisis conditions may occur suddenly and unexpectedly, team members must make critical decisions under extreme stress, and the consequences of poor performance are immediate and often catastrophic. There are some occupations—including aviation, military operations, emergency medicine, mining, law enforcement, and firefighting—for which a high-stress, high-demand performance environment is almost the norm. However, even in more everyday settings, such as the office conference room, team members may operate under various stressors—such as noise, time pressure, and task load—that may disrupt task performance.

Stress can lead to a number of effects on team interaction. Stress may result in a reduced tendency to assist others, increased interpersonal aggression, neglect of social or interpersonal cues, and less cooperative behavior among team members (Mathews & Canon, 1975; Sherrod & Downs, 1974). Research suggests that time pressure is likely to inhibit joint problem solving and, specifically, the search for integrative agreements that are beneficial for all parties (Walton & McKersie, 1965). Thus, Yukl, Malone, Hayslip, and Pamin (1976) found that under high time pressure, participants reached agreements sooner, but they made fewer offers and reached joint outcomes of poorer quality. Isenberg (1981) found that team members' participation in interaction became more disproportionate with increasing time pressure. Kelly and McGrath (1985) found that, under time pressure conditions, group members made fewer interpersonal remarks and vocalized fewer agreements or disagreements compared with those members of groups not working under time pressure.

One of the more well-established findings in the research literature is that stress leads to a narrowing of individual focus (see Broadbent, 1971; Easterbrook, 1959). As attention narrows, peripheral (less relevant) task cues are first ignored, followed by further restriction of central or task-relevant cues. To the extent that task-relevant cues are neglected, performance suffers. Driskell, Salas, and Johnston (1999) extended this argument to the group level of analysis, examining the hypothesis that stress results in a narrowing of team perspective or team awareness—that is, they argued that, to the extent that stress results in a narrowing of attentional focus, stress may lead to a neglect of social or interpersonal cues as well. In fact, Driskell et al. (1999) found that team members were less likely to maintain a broad team perspective under stress and were more likely to shift to a more individualistic self-focus, resulting in poorer overall team performance. These results suggest that, under stress, group members may lose the collective representation of group activity that characterizes interdependent team behavior.

Other research has examined the effects of stressors on group decision making (Driskell & Salas, 1991; Johnston, Driskell, & Salas, 1997). Formal, analytic decision-making approaches require the decision maker to carry out an elaborate and exhaustive procedure characterized by a systematic, organized information search, thorough consideration of all available alternatives, evaluation of each alternative, and reexamination and review of data before a decision is made. Although this procedure is often taught as the decision-making ideal, some researchers have argued that under high task demands, decision makers do not have the luxury of adopting a time-consuming analytic strategy. Moreover, encouraging the decision maker to adopt an analytic model could undermine behavior that may more adequately fit the requirements of the task situation. Johnston et al. (1997) found that on a time-pressured, naturalistic task, individuals who had been trained to use a less analytic or "hypervigilant" strategy performed more effectively than those who used a formal, analytic decision strategy. These results emphasize the importance of contextual factors, such as stress, in decision making and suggest that any attempt to support team decision making must consider the demands under which teams perform.

A Successful Application: Distance Learning

One area in which group support tools are currently very actively researched and applied is the field of *distributed* or *distance learning*. Although distance learning is typically not considered a traditional team setting, distance learning environments allow student–teacher and student–student interaction to occur at a distance, and software tools enable this collaboration. Certainly, one reason underlying the widespread acceptance and application of collaborative-support tools in distance learning has been the market forces driving growth in this area in general. However, we believe that even more important is the emphasis in the educational and training community on a conditional approach to training—that is, the belief that contextual influences are a critical determinant of training effectiveness. Thus, contextual influences are as highly emphasized in education and training applications as they are ignored in groupware applications. In the following paragraphs, we provide a brief overview of the use of collaborative tools in distance learning.

Traditional classroom learning environments are *synchronous* (everyone meets at the same time) and *localized* (everyone meets at the same place), with typically one instructor required per class. By contrast, distance learning environments are technology enabled, orchestrated across classrooms or workplaces, and instruction is delivered "anytime and anywhere." Two primary challenges that face the distance learning community are to ensure that online instruction (a) is as pedagogically sound as traditional instruction (so that online students do not learn less) and (b) is as appealing to students as traditional instruction (so that online students do not drop out at a disproportionately higher rate). To address these problems, training researchers have identified several key facets of learning that are assumed to be missing from online instruction, including *collaboration* or opportunities for student interaction. Thus, the research literature has consistently issued calls to increase collaborative support in distance learning. Collaborative-support tools have included the use of e-mail, listservs, and discussion boards; video conferencing; electronic bulletin boards; chat sessions; and collaborative discussions, debates, and projects.

Certainly, collaborative activities can lead to effective learning. However, there is also a clear understanding within the education and training community that there are conditions of learning under which collaborative learning activities may be most effective and conditions of learning under which collaborative learning activities may be less effective. The *conditions-of-learning* approach to instructional design maintains that there are different conditions of learning (i.e., different stages of learning in which similar cognitive activities occur) and that there are different types of instruction required to support learning for these conditions. Therefore, in determining the requirements for collaborative support, many researchers view contextual factors as critical. Gunawardena and McIsaac (2004) asked, "What type and level of interaction is essential for effective learning? Is interaction more important for certain types of learners? Should patterns of interaction change over time when designing a distance education course?" (p. 381). Hartley (1999) noted that "We know that individual study of well-prepared instructional materials can result in substantial learning . . . We need to understand the situations in which particular forms of interaction and their management are effective" (p. 14). Thus, in contrast to the unconditional claim that tools to foster collaboration are effective for all learning environments, researchers have offered a more moderate view that some performances benefit from learning in a collaborative context and some do not (see Anderson, Greeno, Reder, & Simon, 2000; Anderson, Reder, & Simon, 1997). Anderson et al. (1997) concluded that "Instruction need not take place only in complex social situations. There is great value as well in . . . learning that occurs individually. The issue is when and where to use what type of instruction" (p. 18).

The examination of the relevant conditions of learning under which collaborative activity is most effective has addressed several potential moderators, which we describe in the following sections.

Type of Learning Outcome

One potential moderator of the effectiveness of collaborative tools is the type of learning outcome to be achieved. At a broad level of analysis, there is some consensus among researchers regarding the distinction between *declarative* knowledge (knowledge of facts and data), *procedural* knowledge (knowledge about how to apply rules and procedures to specific cases), and *strategic* knowledge (knowledge about problem solving and applying general rules to novel cases; Anderson, 1982; Gist, 1997). Others have offered more detailed classifications of learning objectives. The commonality among these models is that they all represent a continuum of learning, from simple to more complex, from fact to principle, from recall to application.

Ellis et al. (2003) argued that at the declarative stage of learning, cognitive demands are high and the learner must devote a large amount of attentional resources to the task. The addition of greater collaborative demands may tax attentional capacity and may be detrimental to the learning process. Thus, on the one hand, some have suggested that the benefits of collaboration—exploring, elaborating, and challenging ideas—may be more useful for advanced stages of learning. On the other hand, others have argued that interest and motivation may be lower during the initial stages of learning, and the motivational benefits of collaboration may be most evident during this time.

Learner Characteristics

Ragoonaden and Bordeleau (2000) found that "For some students, these collaborative assignments proved to be a frustrating and time consuming process that in no way enhanced their learning. Yet, for other students . . . this collaborative process was a welcome addition" (p. 2). One truism in education is that learning practices should be designed to fit the needs and requirements of varying and diverse types of students. Learner characteristics that may affect requirements for collaboration include age, educational level, learning style, gender, personality, and group composition. Some researchers have argued that low-ability students may benefit more from interacting with peers (a claim supported by Lou, Abrami, & d'Apollonia, 2001), others have suggested that increased collaboration may hinder low-ability students if performance is dominated by higher ability students, and still others have argued that both high- and low-ability learners may benefit from collaborative activity for different reasons.

Type of Task

Some researchers have argued that the value of enhanced collaborative activities is dependent on the type of task that is being learned; suggesting that all instruction should take place in a collaborative environment because virtually all jobs are social in nature, and learning is closely associated with its context. However, Anderson et al. (1997) argued that this case is overstated, that many jobs involve individual tasks, and that it is not necessary to train an individual task in a collaborative learning environment.

It is important to note that many of these questions have yet to be answered satisfactorily. However, the fact that these questions are being raised—that there are conditions under which enhanced collaborative support may be beneficial and conditions under which it may not—is encouraging. Moreover, this perspective contrasts sharply with the "one-size fits-all" off-the-shelf approach that has characterized most groupware development.

CONCLUSION

Because of the complexity and scope of many modern-day tasks, there has been a heightened realization over the past decade of the value of team performance to business, industry, and the military. Furthermore, changes in business practice and advances in telecommunications have led to the increasing prevalence of distributed teams that interact over long distances. It is clear that unprecedented opportunities exist for the development of tools to support team collaboration.

We argue that, on the whole, groupware has failed to exploit these opportunities. If groupware is intended to serve as a tool to support team performance, then groupware development must specify the team activities to be supported, the outcomes to be achieved, and the contextual factors that determine groupware effectiveness. We have attempted to address some of these group dynamics issues by posing a contextual model of groupware development that emphasizes the specific functions or activities that teams perform and the contextual factors that influence team interaction. Our hope is that we have highlighted the complexities of supporting team performance and identified some of the variables that must be considered in developing an effective team support tool.

In most cases, we have raised issues but certainly not fully answered them. For example, consider a real world team such as a management team. A training needs analysis is performed and identifies problems in team management (e.g., resource management, planning, and goal setting). Ideally, groupware could be incorporated to provide support targeted to these team functions. Moreover, our model suggests that the effectiveness of these support activities may be dependent on contextual factors such as the size of the team, the nature of the team task, the experience of the team, and other factors. If one objective is to enhance planning and goal setting, then the researcher or developer must consider how planning and goal setting may differ in large versus small groups, in groups that perform production tasks versus groups that perform negotiation tasks, and so on. This is a formidable task, but this contextual approach is needed to enhance the development of groupware for real world team applications.

REFERENCES

Anderson, J. R. (1982). Acquisition of cognitive skill. *Psychological Review*, 89, 369–406.

Anderson, J. R., Greeno, J. G., Reder, L. M., & Simon, H. A. (2000). Perspectives on learning, thinking, and activity. *Educational Researcher*, 29, 11–13.

Anderson, J. R., Reder, L. M., & Simon, H. A. (1997). Situative versus cognitive perspectives: Form versus substance. *Educational Researcher*, 26, 19–21.

Baker, D. P., & Salas, E. (1992). Principles for measuring teamwork skills. *Human Factors*, 34, 469–475.

Bales, R. F. (1950). *Interaction process analysis*. Cambridge, MA: Addison-Wesley.

Bos, N., Olson, J. S., Gergle, D., Olson, G. M., & Wright, Z. (2002). Effects of four computer-mediated communications channels on trust development. In *Proceedings of CHI 2002* (pp. 135–140). New York: ACM Press.

Brennan, L. L., & Rubenstein, A. H. (1995). Applications of groupware in organizational learning. *Journal of Organizational Behavior*, 9, 37–50.

Broadbent, D. E. (1971). *Decision and stress*. New York: Academic Press.

Cannon-Bowers, J. A., Tannenbaum, S. I., Salas, E., & Volpe, C. E. (1995). Defining competencies and establishing team training requirements. In R. Guzzo & E. Salas (Eds.), *Team effectiveness and decision making in organizations* (pp. 333–380). San Francisco: Jossey-Bass.

Clark, H. H., & Brennan, S. E. (1991). Grounding in communication. In L. B. Resnick, J. M. Levine, & S. D. Teasley (Eds.), *Perspectives on socially shared cognition* (pp. 127–149). Washington, DC: American Psychological Association.

Cramton, C. D. (2001). The mutual knowledge problem and its consequences for dispersed collaboration. *Organizational Science*, 12, 346–371.

Daft, R. L., & Lengel, R. H. (1984). Information richness: A new approach to managerial behavior and organization design. *Research in Organizational Behavior*, 6, 191–233.

Devine, D. J. (2002). A review and integration of classification systems relevant to teams in organizations. *Group Dynamics*, 6, 291–310.

Driskell, J. E., Hogan, R., & Salas, E. (1987). Personality and group performance. In C. Hendrick (Ed.), *Review of personality and social psychology* (Vol. 9, pp. 91–112). Newbury Park, CA: Sage.

Driskell, J. E., Olmstead, B., & Salas, E. (1993). Task cues, dominance cues, and influence in task groups. *Journal of Applied Psychology, 78,* 51–60.

Driskell, J. E., Radtke, P. H., & Salas, E. (2003). Virtual teams: Effects of technological mediation on team performance. *Group Dynamics, 7,* 297–323.

Driskell, J. E., & Salas, E. (1991). Group decision making under stress. *Journal of Applied Psychology, 76,* 473–478.

Driskell, J. E., & Salas, E. (1992). Collective behavior and team performance. *Human Factors, 34,* 277–288.

Driskell, J. E., Salas, E., & Johnston, J. H. (1999). Does stress lead to a loss of team perspective? *Group Dynamics, 3,* 1–12.

Dubrovsky, V., Kiesler, S., & Sethna, B. (1991). The equalization phenomenon: Status effects in computer-mediated and face-to-face decision-making groups. *Human–Computer Interaction, 6,* 119–146.

Easterbrook, J. A. (1959). The effect of emotion on cue utilization and the organization of behavior. *Psychological Review, 66,* 183–201.

Ellis, A. P. J., Hollenbeck, J. R., Ilgen, D. R., Porter, C., West, B. J., & Moon, H. (2003). Team learning: Collectively connecting the dots. *Journal of Applied Psychology, 88,* 821–835.

Fallows, D. (2002). *E-mail at work.* Washington, DC: Pew Internet & American Life Project.

Fleishman, E. A., & Quaintance, M. K. (1984). *Taxonomies of human performance.* New York: Academic Press.

Fleishman, E. A., & Zaccaro, S. J. (1992). Toward a taxonomy of team performance functions. In R. W. Swezey & E. Salas (Eds.), *Teams: Their training and performance* (pp. 31–56). Norwood, NJ: Ablex Publishing.

Forsyth, D. R. (1990). *Group dynamics.* Pacific Grove, CA: Brooks/Cole.

Gallupe, R. B., DeSanctis, G., & Dickson, G. W. (1988). Computer-based support for group problem-finding: An experimental investigation. *MIS Quarterly, 12,* 277–296.

Gist, M. E. (1997). Training design and pedagogy: Implications for skill acquisition, maintenance, and generalization. In M. A. Quinones & A. Ehrenstein (Eds.), *Training for a rapidly changing workplace* (pp. 201–222). Washington, DC: American Psychological Association.

Grudin, J. (1994). Groupware and social dynamics: Eight challenges for developers. *Communications of the ACM, 37,* 92–105.

Grudin, J. (2002). Group dynamics and ubiquitous computing: From "Here and now" to "Everywhere and forever." *Communications of the ACM, 45,* 74–78.

Gunawardena, C. N., & McIsaac, M. S. (2004). Distance education. In D. Jonassen (Ed.), *Handbook of research on educational communication and technology* (pp. 355–395). Mahwah, NJ: Erlbaum.

Hackman, J. R., & Morris, C. G. (1978). Group tasks, group interaction process, and group performance effectiveness: A review and proposed integration. In L. Berkowitz (Ed.), *Group processes* (pp. 1–55). New York: Academic Press.

Hare, A. P. (1976). *Handbook of small group research* (2nd ed.). New York: Free Press.

Hartley, J. R. (1999). Effective pedagogies for managing collaborative learning in online learning environments. *Educational Technology and Society, 2,* 12–19.

Herold, D. M. (1978). Improving performance effectiveness of groups through a task-contingent selection of intervention strategies. *Academy of Management Review, 3,* 315–325.

Hirokawa, R. Y. (1980). A comparative analysis of communication patterns within effective and ineffective decision-making groups. *Communication Monographs, 47,* 312–321.

Hollingshead, A. B., & McGrath, J. E. (1995). Computer-assisted groups: A critical review of the empirical research. In R. A. Guzzo, E. Salas, & Associates (Eds.), *Team effectiveness and decision making in organizations* (pp. 46–78). San Francisco: Jossey-Bass.

Hollingshead, A. B., McGrath, J. E., & O'Conner, K. M. (1995). Group task performance and communication technology: A longitudinal study of computer-mediated versus face-to-face work groups. *Small Group Research, 24,* 307–334.

Isenberg, D. J. (1981). Some effects of time-pressure on vertical structure and decision-making accuracy in small groups. *Organizational Behavior and Human Performance, 27,* 119–134.

Janicik, G. A., & Bartel, C. A. (2003). Talking about time: Effects of temporal planning and time awareness norms on group coordination and performance. *Group Dynamics, 7,* 122–134.

Johnston, J., Driskell, J. E., & Salas, E. (1997). Vigilant and hypervigilant decision making. *Journal of Applied Psychology, 82,* 614–622.

Kanki, B. G., & Smith, G. M. (2001). Training aviation communication skills. In E. Salas, C. A. Bowers, & E. Edens (Eds.), *Improving teamwork in organizations* (pp. 95–127). Mahwah, NJ: Erlbaum.

Kelly, J. R., & McGrath, J. E. (1985). Effects of time limits and task types on task performance and interaction in four-person groups. *Journal of Personality and Social Psychology, 49,* 395–407.

Kline, T. J. B., & McGrath, J. (1999). A review of the groupware literature: Theories, methodologies, and a research agenda. *Canadian Psychology, 40,* 265–271.

Kraemer, K. L., & Pinsonneault, A. (1990). Technology and groups: Assessment of the empirical research. In J. Galegher, R. E. Kraut, & C. Egido (Eds.), *Intellectual teamwork: Social and technological foundations of cooperative work* (pp. 375–405). Hillsdale, NJ: Erlbaum.

Lou, Y., Abrami, P. C., & d'Apollonia, S. (2001). Small group and individual learning with technology: A meta-analysis. *Review of Educational Research, 3,* 449–521.

Marks, M. A., Zaccaro, S. J., & Mathieu, J. E. (2000). Performance implications of leader briefings and team-interaction training for team adaptation to novel environments. *Journal of Applied Psychology, 85,* 971–986.

Mathews, K. E., & Canon, L. K. (1975). Environmental noise level as a determinant of helping behavior. *Journal of Personality and Social Psychology, 32,* 571–577.

Mathieu, J. E., Heffner, T. S., Goodwin, G. F., Salas, E., & Cannon-Bowers, J. A. (2000). The influence of shared mental models on team process and performance. *Journal of Applied Psychology, 85,* 273–283.

McGrath, J. E. (1984). *Groups: Interaction and performance.* Englewood Cliffs, NJ: Prentice Hall.

McGrath, J. E. (1990). Time matters in groups. In J. Galegher, R. E. Kraut, & C. Egido (Eds.), *Intellectual teamwork: Social and technical bases of collaborative work* (pp. 23–61). Hillsdale, NJ: Erlbaum.

McGrath, J. E. (1997). Small group research, that once and future field: An interpretation of the past with an eye to the future. *Group Dynamics, 1,* 7–27.

McIntyre, R. M., & Salas, E. (1995). Measuring and managing for team performance: Lessons from complex environments. In R. A. Guzzo, E. Salas, & Associates (Eds.), *Team effectiveness and decision making in organizations* (pp. 9–45). San Francisco: Jossey-Bass.

Milanovich, D., Driskell, J. E., Stout, R. J., & Salas, E. (1998). Status and cockpit dynamics: A review and empirical study. *Group Dynamics, 2,* 155–167.

Moreland, R. L., & Levine, J. M. (1992). Problem identification by groups. In S. Worchel, W. Wood, & J. A. Simpson (Eds.), *Group process and productivity* (pp. 17–47). Newbury Park, CA: Sage.

Mullen, B. (1991). Group composition, salience, and cognitive representations: The phenomenology of being in a group. *Journal of Experimental Social Psychology, 27,* 297–323.

Mullen, B., & Baumeister, R. F. (1987). Group effects on self-attention and performance: Social loafing, social facilitation, and social impairment. In C. Hendrick (Ed.), *Review of personality and social psychology* (pp. 189–206). Beverly Hills, CA: Sage.

Mullen, B., & Copper, C. (1994). The relation between group cohesiveness and performance: An integration. *Psychological Bulletin, 115,* 210–227.

Old, B. S. (1946). On the mathematics of committees, boards, and panels. *Scientific Monthly, 63,* 129–134.

Porter, C., Hollenbeck, J. R., Ilgen, D. R., Ellis, A., West, B. J., & Moon, H. (2003). Backing up behaviors in teams: The role of personality and legitimacy of need. *Journal of Applied Psychology, 88,* 391–403.

Ragoonaden, K., & Bordeleau, P. (2000). Collaborative learning via the Internet. *Educational Technology & Society, 3,* 1–15.

Samburthy, V., Poole, M. S., & Kelly, J. (1993). The effects of variations in GDSS capabilities on decision-making processes in groups. *Small Group Research, 24,* 523–546.

Shaw, M. E. (1973). *Group dynamics: The psychology of small group behavior*. New York: McGraw-Hill.

Sherrod, D. R., & Downs, R. (1974). Environmental determinants of altruism: The effects of stimulus overload and perceived control on helping. *Journal of Experimental Social Psychology, 10*, 468–479.

Short, J., Williams, E., & Christie, B. (1976). *The social psychology of telecommunications*. New York: Wiley.

Stasser, G., & Titus, W. (1995). Effects of information load and percentage of shared information on the dissemination of unshared information during group discussion. *Journal of Personality and Social Psychology, 48*, 1467–1478.

Steiner, I. D. (1972). *Group process and productivity*. New York: Academic Press.

Stout, R. J., Salas, E., & Fowlkes, J. E. (1997). Enhancing teamwork in complex environments through team training. *Group Dynamics, 1*, 169–182.

Straus, S. G. (1997). Technology, group process, and group outcomes: Testing the connections in computer-mediated and face-to-face groups. *Human–Computer Interaction, 12*, 227–266.

Straus, S. G., & McGrath, J. E. (1994). Does the medium matter? The interaction of task type and technology on group performance and member reactions. *Journal of Applied Psychology, 79*, 87–97.

Thompson, L. F., & Coovert, M. D. (2003). Teamwork online: The effects of computer conferencing on perceived confusion, satisfaction, and postdiscussion accuracy. *Group Dynamics, 7*, 135–151.

Vogel, D. R., & Nunamaker, J. F. (1990). Design and assessment of a group decision support system. In J. Galegher, R. E. Kraut, & C. Egido (Eds.), *Intellectual teamwork: Social and technological foundations of cooperative work* (pp. 375–405). Hillsdale, NJ: Erlbaum.

Walton, R. E., & McKersie, R. B. (1965). *A behavioral theory of labor negotiation: An analysis of a social interaction system*. New York: McGraw-Hill.

Weingart, L. R. (1992). Impact of group goals, task component complexity, effort, and planning on group performance. *Journal of Applied Psychology, 77*, 682–693.

Yukl, G. A., Malone, M. P., Hayslip, B., & Pamin, T. A. (1976). The effects of time pressure and issue settlement order on integrative bargaining. *Sociometry, 39*, 277–281.

2

ENABLING TEAM DECISION MAKING

RICK VAN DER KLEIJ AND JAN MAARTEN SCHRAAGEN

In 1996, a Belgian C-130 Hercules with 37 passengers and 4 crew members aboard crashed and caught fire after colliding with birds while landing at the Eindhoven air force base in the Netherlands. Thirty-four people died in the crash. Because of a misconception in the communication with the air traffic controller, the air force base firefighters assumed that only crew members were on board. As a consequence, the firefighting was aimed at the cockpit of the plane and not at the rear part, where the passengers were located. Because of the nature of the fire and the location of the fire in the front part of the plane, the firefighters were also under the impression that the crew was no longer alive. This assumption, together with the initial misunderstanding, led to the fact that a considerable amount of time passed between the firefighters' arrival at the scene and the attempt at a rescue mission in the rear part of the plane. In all likelihood, more people could have been rescued if the rescue mission had commenced earlier, and questions were subsequently raised regarding shortcomings in team decision making and information distribution (Inspectie Brandweerzorg en Rampenbestrijding, 1997).

The preceding example involved skilled and competent team members interacting with each other and contributing to the final outcome. However, something went wrong, and people died. What could have prevented these shortcomings in team decision making and information distribution? For example, could these shortcomings have been prevented if the on-scene commander of the firefighters had been equipped with a technologically sophisticated support system that provided up-to-date and correctly formatted information about the C-130 Hercules (see Payne, Bettman, & Johnson, 1993, for an overview of how the information environment can improve decisions)? Or, would the miscommunication not have occurred if the on-scene commander had been equipped with a mobile videoconferencing system, allowing him to receive both verbal and nonverbal information, instead of a ramshackle radio? In this chapter, we describe problems that can affect team decision making as well as methods of supporting team decision making. This chapter is primarily concerned with teams, although on several occasions we draw from the more extensive literature on small groups. Where appropriate, specific examples of decision aiding are given, and we finish the chapter with a discussion of principles for applying technologically based decision-aiding tools to team-based work settings.

PROBLEMS THAT CAN AFFECT TEAM DECISION MAKING

Several problems commonly affect team decision making, including biases, loss of individual input in larger groups, and coordination problems. We examine these issues in this section.

Group Biases and Errors

The literature on individual decision making (e.g., Kahneman, Slovic, & Tversky, 1982) has shown that people are subject to numerous biases. To minimize individual cognitive biases, researchers have advised managers to include others in the decision-making process (e.g., Hogarth, 1980). Recent empirical research has shown, however, that teams are just as susceptible as individuals to these biases (Houghton, Simon, Aquino, & Goldberg, 2000). In the case of the *law of small numbers* bias, when one ignores the poor predictive ability of a small sample, teams were found to be even more susceptible than individuals.

Turning to automated-decision environments in commercial aircraft, researchers have found evidence for the existence of *automation bias*, which refers to the use of automation as a heuristic replacement for vigilant information seeking and processing (Mosier, Skitka, Heers, & Burdick, 1998). Mosier, Dunbar, et al. (1998) investigated in two consecutive studies whether the errors due to automation bias also occur in a team context. Using students and professional pilots as participants, the authors demonstrated that despite technological enhancements and explicit training, automation bias persisted in crews compared with solo performers. However, groups that were trained about automation bias, its consequences, and how to avoid them more frequently verified the automated directive against other available information than did groups that were trained only to verify automated directives. In addition, Mosier, Dunbar, et al. found that training had no effect on professional pilots, implying that instruction on automation bias should take place before individuals gain experience with reliable automated systems. Besides training, explicitly establishing procedures, such as *devil's advocacy* (i.e., deliberately bringing up counterarguments), may reduce the occurrence of biases in a business context.

Process Losses

In addition to biases, one must also consider the problems group size may bring about for team decision making. The number of persons in a group or traditional meeting may have several important consequences for group processes, such as decision making and problem solving. For instance, researchers have indicated that larger groups possess a greater range of abilities, knowledge, and skills available to the group (Shaw, 1981). Indeed, considerable research has shown that the skills of individual group members are critical determinants of group success (see Locke et al., 2001, for a review). However, others have indicated that, as group size increases, so-called *process losses* (Steiner, 1972) become apparent. For example, coordination problems become prevalent, subgroups that monopolize the group's time are more likely to form, people spend more and more time waiting for their turn to speak, and the potential for conflict becomes greater. In addition, once group size is increased beyond an optimum, group members become less sensitive in their exploration of different points of view, tend to adopt more mechanistic methods of introducing information, and appear to rush to reach solutions (Hare, 1981). Therefore, although there is potentially a greater amount of knowledge as group size increases, the available knowledge may not always be used because of process losses.

There is widespread belief in the efficacy of brainstorming, probably because people enjoy working in groups much more than working individually but also because of the intuitively appealing maxim "Two heads are better than one." Unfortunately, controlled laboratory research has found that groups often generate only half as many ideas as similar numbers of solitary performers and do not generate higher quality ideas (Diehl & Stroebe, 1987; Mullen, Johnson, & Salas, 1991). The important comparison in these studies is between nominal groups and brainstorming groups. *Nominal groups* consist of *n* participants (with *n* being equal to the size of the brainstorming group), whose nonredundant ideas are summed. Diehl and Stroebe (1991) argued that process losses in brainstorming groups are largely due to the delay between idea generation and verbalization: In groups, one must wait for someone to finish talking before presenting one's idea. While waiting, one is distracted and forgets the idea. This is called *production blocking*.

On the basis of the extant research, an obvious solution to production blocking would be to use electronic-brainstorming tools. With these tools, group members can generate ideas while simultaneously being able to access the ideas of other group members in a manner that neither distracts from nor interferes with the idea-generation process. Indeed, as shown in studies conducted by Gallupe, Bastianutti, and Cooper (1991) and Gallupe et al. (1992), electronic-brainstorming groups of four or more people are more productive and satisfied than are verbal brainstorming groups. Gallupe, Cooper, Grisé, and Bastianutti (1994) tested the hypothesis that the reduction in production blocking inherent in using the electronic-brainstorming tools is one reason for the higher productivity of electronic-brainstorming groups. Gallupe et al. (1994) found that only when ideas could be entered immediately, and in parallel—the conventional procedure used in electronic brainstorming—did the advantage of electronic brainstorming became apparent. When participants were artificially forced to wait 5 seconds before being able to type in their next idea, electronic-brainstorming groups lost their advantage compared with verbal brainstorming groups. These experiments confirm the importance of the production-blocking explanation. They also point to the possible advantages of using electronic-brainstorming tools, at least insofar as the production of a large number of ideas is concerned.

One should be aware that brainstorming hardly ever constitutes a separate task in real life decision-making situations. Van den Herik (1998) carried out four field studies on policy making using GroupSystems, which is a commercial suite of electronic tools to support groups designed to alleviate some of the problems associated with traditional face-to-face meetings. He concluded that the strengths of electronic brainstorming also constitute its weaknesses. For instance, the large number of ideas that were generated frequently led to information overload, superficiality, and ambiguity in interpreting the ideas. The ideas could not easily be internalized in the mental models of participants, and ambiguity could not easily be resolved through immediate feedback. In the end, participants did not commit to and accept the ideas generated through this medium. Subtle and complex ideas could hardly be exchanged, and participants missed the depth of verbal discussions. In addition, some higher ranking participants regretted the lack of opportunity for airing their opinions publicly. Van den Herik concluded that systems such as GroupSystems are useful for problem-solving sessions in which the emphasis is on information gathering; however, these systems are less useful for social interaction sessions in which the emphasis is on problem awareness, consensus building, and creating commitment around a strategy.

In short, increasing the size of the group introduces opposing forces with respect to group performance and productivity. On the one hand, the added resources that are available in larger groups contribute to effective group performance; on the other hand, the increased organizational problems and social psychological aspects tend to decrease the effectiveness of the group. Design considerations for support should focus on combating these negative aspects of increasing group size.

AIDING TEAM DECISION MAKING

Group decision support systems (GDSSs) have been defined as systems that support a group of people engaged in a decision-related process (Finlay, 1989); as systems that combine communication and computing with decision support to help groups solve unstructured problems, to overcome biases and errors, and to reduce process losses (Paris, Salas, & Cannon-Bowers, 1999); and as systems aimed at improving team functioning (Chidambaram, Bostrom, & Wynne, 1991). These are just a few definitions of GDSSs, but common elements are obvious. Currently, the broader term *group support system* (GSS) is also used to refer to a set of techniques, software, and technology designed to focus and enhance communication, deliberations, and decision making in groups (Nunamaker, 1997). Some examples include a naval Command and Information System (CIS), brainstorming, and electronic mail (e-mail).

CISs allow the commanding officer (CO) to view and understand the battlespace, communicate intentions, and distribute pertinent information throughout the chain of command (Rasker & van der Kleij, 2000). Effective CISs help the Combat Information Center members to get the right information to the right location, on time, to allow COs to make quality decisions and take appropriate actions. CISs include personnel, machines, manual or automated procedures, and systems that allow the collection, processing, dissemination, and display of information. These functions cover all aspects of the organization, providing COs with an accurate, relevant, common operational picture and a common situational awareness. In addition, CISs enable the CO to coordinate the activities of his tactical forces.

Benbasat and L. H. Lim (1993) investigated how brainstorming and e-mail contribute to the reduction of group decision-making biases. Both electronic brainstorming and e-mail helped to reduce the *availability bias* associated with the phenomenon in which events that are more available to human memory are correspondingly judged as occurring more frequently or as being more important. In both cases, the reduction in bias was due to increased attention paid to items that were found to have low availability in the absence of these support tools. Electronic brainstorming led to an increase in the total numbers of ideas generated. As a result, more ideas pertaining to low-availability items were generated, which led to lower bias. E-mail helped to reduce bias by enabling the decision-making group to suggest and explore a greater range of possible solutions before reaching a final agreement.

Chidambaram et al. (1991) examined the behavior of face-to-face, same-room groups, assigned to either manual support or GSS support over four sessions. The GSS-supported groups used three separate group decision support tools to generate, review, and evaluate decision alternatives. Manual groups used flip charts for recording and reviewing alternatives and for voting. Their results showed significant differences in development patterns between computer-supported groups and groups that were not supported. After adapting to the support system, computer-supported groups demonstrated more productive conflict management and higher cohesiveness than groups that were not supported.

Dennis and Wixom (2002) investigated several moderators of group performance, such as the tool the group is using or the task the group is performing, and their influences on the overall effects of GSSs. To address the influences of these moderators, Dennis and Wixom conducted a meta-analysis of the cumulative research findings from 1980 up to 1999. The objective of their meta-analysis was to better understand the moderators that affect group performance when using group support systems. Results showed that a GSS improved the quality of the group's decision (defined as the correctness or goodness of the group's choice for choice tasks), compared with groups using no GSS. The structure of the groups, whether a virtual team working in different places or time or working together face to face, was also important for decision-making tasks. Virtual teams made decisions of significantly lower quality compared with groups working face to face, with or without a GSS. There were no significant differences in idea-generating performance. These findings suggest that distributed virtual teams can generate ideas and discuss issues well, but virtual teams are ineffective at making decisions compared with teams that work face to face. It seems, according to Dennis and Wixom, that verbal communication is critical when team members are converging on a decision, and GSSs in general do not have a rich verbal component. Therefore, to facilitate effective performance, organizations need to ensure that distributed teams working on decision-making tasks have some access to face-to-face meetings, teleconferencing facilities, or a series of telephone calls to augment GSSs.

Dennis and Wixom (2002) also found that larger GSS groups took less time and were more satisfied with the process than were smaller groups. As discussed previously, an increase in the number of persons in a group or traditional meeting tends to decrease the effectiveness of the group. Therefore, larger groups working without a GSS should encounter more problems than smaller groups who are without a GSS. Hence, it makes sense that larger groups gain more benefits from GSSs than do smaller groups who can function well without a GSS. However, Dennis and Wixom found no differences between large and small GSS groups in idea-generating performance, suggesting that a GSS can help even small groups to generate more ideas.

Another important moderator of group performance is *process facilitation* (Dennis & Wixom, 2002). In providing process facilitation, the facilitator attempts to help the group in structuring the process by which the group uses the available GSS tools and helps the group respond to problems. GSS groups with a facilitator made better decisions and were more satisfied with the process than GSS groups without a facilitator (Dennis & Wixom, 2002). It seems that the role of the facilitator is to help groups successfully appropriate the GSS into their work processes.

In sum, it appears that the ideal situation in which to use a GSS is for a larger group that is meeting face-to-face to perform idea generation under the guidance of a facilitator. However, this ideal circumstance does not always arise. For example, suppose a virtual team is assigned to a project. In such situations, Dennis and Wixom (2002) advised that the team use the GSS to generate ideas and discuss issues but that team members be brought together face to face or in an audio- or videoconference when the team needs to make important decisions. If the team is small (five or fewer members) and is capable of using the GSS, the team could then use the technology to generate ideas, but it should not be used for decision making because, as discussed previously, the GSS offers little value at the decision-making stage.

SETTINGS FOR GROUP DECISION SUPPORT

Group decision support may take place in a variety of settings. Electronic meeting systems can be used both face-to-face and in settings where the parties are separated temporally or spatially. In this section, we analyze several such settings.

Electronic Meeting Rooms

The most obvious setting where GSSs are found is in electronic meeting rooms or conference rooms that involve individuals working face to face. These systems are typically based on a network of personal computers, usually one for each participant. Electronic meeting systems have tools to facilitate idea generation (brainstorming), idea exploring, idea organization, prioritizing, and voting (Beacker, Grudin, Buxton, & Greenberg, 1995; Nunamaker, Briggs, & Mittleman, 1995). A typical scenario would be one in which group members get together in one large room, with each group member in front of a computer terminal. The facilitator would explain the purpose of the meeting, for example, to generate as many ideas as possible on a policy issue. Each individual would enter their ideas one by one into the GSS. These ideas are pooled and displayed anonymously so that all group members can react to them. By reading the ideas generated by others, group members are stimulated to generate further ideas. Usually, there is no verbal interaction at this stage among the group members. At a later stage, after all ideas have been collected, there may be idea organization. This may involve extensive face-to-face group interaction. Of course, electronic meetings may also be carried out virtually, over the Internet.

Electronic meeting systems have been commercially available since the late 1980s, and at present there are several vendors of electronic meeting systems. Several dozens of published research articles have reported both experimental and field research. From those studies we have learned a great deal about support for decision-making teams. For example, we have learned what features and functions are important and how we should use the tools to overcome process losses, group biases, and errors. Besides supporting information access, electronic meeting rooms can support group interactions by improving communication and by structuring and focusing problem-solving efforts and decision making (see, e.g., Nunamaker et al., 1995, for a summary of important features and functions of electronic meeting rooms).

An important feature of electronic meeting systems is that they permit large groups of people to work together at the same time in parallel (Nunamaker et al., 1995). This means that all stakeholders can participate in the same meeting instead of developing their understanding of the issues in a fragmented series of small meetings. When all interest groups are represented, the group also has access to much more information. In addition, a meeting need not be interrupted or postponed until all information or approval can be obtained from people who are not present. These features should lead to increases in group decision-making effectiveness, decreases in time required to reach a decision, and increases in group member satisfaction.

Furthermore, electronic meeting systems can permit people to make anonymous contributions to the group effort (Nunamaker et al., 1995). This focuses discussion on content and encourages participation from persons who might otherwise be too shy or too intimidated to speak up. The results are shorter, more productive meetings and a freer flow of ideas.

According to Nunamaker et al. (1995), the structure, use, and interface of electronic meeting room application software can also have a great impact on group work. For example, it is very useful to build an electronic meeting system into a collection of special-purpose modules, rather than using a single module. Group members must talk, listen, think, and remember what has been said. An interface that has an overwhelming number of features, or is difficult to comprehend, will harm rather than facilitate group decision making and problem solving. For instance, an idea-generation tool leads to different outcomes when people have a five-line limit per comment for a large number of issues, compared with no limit per comment for a small number of issues. In the former condition, a broad range of ideas can quickly be explored, whereas the latter condition will encourage in-depth examination of issues. Because differences in interface design influence team performance, it is useful to build separate interfaces, each to support a particular performance.

Non-Colocated Group Decision Making

Decision making and problem solving can also take place in situations where decision makers are geographically or temporally separated from each other. The integration of computers and communication technologies allows decisions to be made without regard to temporal and spatial impediments (Dix, Finlay, Abowd, & Beale, 1993; Morley, 1994). These technologies make decision making more convenient and less expensive and time consuming than when group members must travel to meet face to face (van der Kleij, Paashuis, Langefeld, & Schraagen, 2004).

Although the convenience and savings associated with electronic meeting technologies are praised by advertisers, little or no attention is paid to questions about the quality of the decisions made or to differences in the ways in which people interact with each other online versus face to face (Baltes, Dickson, Sherman, Bauer, & LaGanke, 2002). Baltes et al. (2002) addressed these issues in a meta-analysis of research comparing decision making in face-to-face versus non-colocated computer-mediated communication groups. The results suggest that, in general, and compared with face-to-face groups, computer-mediated communication leads to decreases in group decision-making effectiveness, increases in time required to reach a decision, and decreases in group member satisfaction. However, when various moderators were considered, it was found that non-colocated teams could be just as effective as face-to-face decision-making teams. For instance, when team members were anonymous (most text-based computer mediated communication includes a feature that allows members to contribute to discussions without attaching their names), no differences were found on team decision-making effectiveness compared with face-to-face decision-making teams. When non-colocated teams were given unlimited discussion time of the same matter, no decrease in effectiveness was found compared with face-to-face groups. Neither of these circumstances, however, is common in organizations. More common are situations in which time pressure is high and the individuals are chosen for the decision-making team on the basis of their expertise, and thus their identities are quite salient to other team members (Baltes et al., 2002).

Dispersed work could lead to a loss of engagement. The lack of verbal and nonverbal cues appears to reduce the involvement of remote participants (Nunamaker et al., 1995). Furthermore, in face-to-face groups peer pressure keeps people moving. Distributed groups tend to lose momentum. In sum, despite all advantages of computer-mediated communication, such as reductions in travel time and cost, it does not appear to be the most effective means of making group decisions.

Innovative technological solutions could perhaps alleviate some of these negative effects of computer-mediated communication on group decision making. For instance, software features that replace nonverbal cues can lead to more effective decision making and more engagement in meetings with participants separated in both time and space (Nunamaker et al., 1995). An example is the use of telecursors in remote meetings. The use of telecursors, which allow users to electronically point at objects on a public screen, could be seen as a substitute for hand gestures.

Adding communication media that are capable of transmitting rich information, such as videoconferencing systems, could also help combat some of these negative effects of computer-mediated communication on group decision making. Daft and Lengel (1984, 1986) posited that communication media differ in the richness of the information that can be transmitted. *Information richness* refers to how much the information contains emotional, attitudinal, normative, and other meanings, beyond the literal cognitive denotations of the symbols to express it. Face-to-face communication is the richest form of information processing because it provides immediate feedback. With feedback, understanding can be checked and interpretations corrected. In addition, face-to-face conversations allow for the simultaneous observations of multiple cues, including body language, facial expression, and tone of voice. Audio conversations—through telephone, for example— are less rich than face-to-face interactions. Feedback is fast, but visual cues are absent. Group members have to rely on language content and audio cues to reach understanding.

Daft and Lengel (1984, 1986) have argued that task performance will be improved when task needs, which differ in terms of the degree to which effective performance on them requires the transmission of information that is more or less rich in its contents, are matched to the communication medium's richness. Group climate factors, such as cohesiveness and conflict resolution, might also be enhanced in situations of good fit between task and communication medium. If a communication medium does not provide the requisite support, group members may not be able to resolve task issues, which could lead to a negative group climate (Zigurs & Buckland, 1998). For routine tasks that are well understood, media of lower richness, such as Internet chat or e-mail, would provide sufficient information. Emotional connotations about message and source are not required for routine tasks and are often considered to be a hindrance. Media capable of transmitting rich information, such as video communication technologies, are better suited to support equivocal tasks (i.e., negotiations or strategic decision making) for which there are multiple interpretations for available information.

There are still many lessons to be learned when it comes to group work and technology. For instance, empirical data of media effects on temporal group processes are rare. Most studies that have been conducted in this area can be described as single-session experiments with ad hoc groups. Reasons for this failure to deal with temporal issues in past group research can be attributed to methodological and practical difficulties. Empirical research of groups over time is difficult and requires considerable financial resources (McGrath, Arrow, Gruenfeld, Hollingshead, & O'Connor, 1993).

The few experimental studies that have focused on communication media effects on temporal group processes suggest that temporal aspects can have a large impact on group task performance (e.g., Hollingshead, McGrath, & O'Connor, 1993; van der Kleij, Paashuis, & Schraagen, in press). It seems that as dispersed groups gain experience, initial constraints due to technological limitations of the communication medium are compensated for. For example, in a longitudinal between-groups design that compared face-to-face with video-mediated communication, van der Kleij, Paashuis, and Schraagen (in press) tested 22 three-person groups over the course of four test sessions at 2-week intervals. The investigators designed a paper-folding task that had the potential to induce differences in task performance and behavior under different communication conditions. The results showed that at the end of the second test session, initial differences between conditions on task performance in favor of the face-to-face groups had disappeared. These findings were explained in terms of a technological adaptation effect. *Technological adaptation* occurs when people learn how to use the technological tools available despite technological limitations, such as restricted bandwidth (Dourish, Adler, Bellotti, & Henderson, 1996; Olson & Olson, 2000; Qureshi & Vogel, 2001).

The implications of these findings are that researchers run the risk of devoting time, effort, and financial resources to the development of innovative solutions to nonproblems, that is, problems that diminish in time as people learn effective practices to use the technologies available to them (Dourish et al., 1996). In practice, the implication of an adaptation effect is that video-mediated groups are new to the communication medium and must learn to operate it; they must be given some time to adapt the medium's structures into their work processes (van der Kleij, Paashuis, Langefeld, & Schraagen, 2004).

Synchronous or Asynchronous Group Decision Support?

Earlier, we mentioned studies that compared GSS groups with those that are not supported, called *manual groups*. Although these studies are capable of indicating differences between the two modes, Shirani, Tafti, and Affisco (1999) stated that more relevant for comparison is the question of which technologies would better augment face-to-face collaboration. To answer this question, Shirani et al. conducted an experiment to differentiate between two technologies with synchronous and asynchronous group communication support. Those technologies, GroupSystems and e-mail, were used in an experimental setting over a 1-week period as a means of group idea exchange, pooling, storing, and retrieval. A menu-driven DOS version of GroupSystems was used in an electronic meeting room setting with group members sitting in the same room. This setting was compared with a non-colocated setting in which group members used a menu-driven e-mail system to communicate with one another from different locations. Shirani et al. used basic and inferential ideas as dependent measures. *Basic* ideas contained task-related facts and information, and *inferential* ideas went beyond providing factual information about the case to entail a synthesis of a number of basic ideas, use inference, give opinions, or suggest alternatives.

Their results indicated that the synchronous GroupSystems groups generated more total and basic ideas than the asynchronous e-mail groups. The latter groups, however, generated a higher proportion of inferential ideas. An explanation Shirani et al. (1999) offered is that asynchronous communication support allows, and perhaps encourages, greater use of human information processing, resulting in the deeper analysis that is crucial in the late stages of a group decision. Interactive and synchronous communication, on the other hand, may be more appropriate for initial stages of problem solving, when the emphasis is more on generating a large number of new ideas than on generating alternative solutions and strategies.

IMPLICATIONS FOR PRACTICE

We believe that the review we have provided in this chapter enables one to draw several important implications for practice. First, the review allows one to draw reasonable conclusions about the probable impact of the use of support on decision-making effectiveness and on group climate factors, such as user satisfaction. For example, there is ample evidence that

GDSSs can indeed overcome biases and errors and reduce process losses (e.g., Benbasat & J. Lim, 2000). There is also more than enough evidence of GDSS groups outperforming groups that were not supported, the manual groups.

Second, it seems that the ideal situation in which to use GSSs is for a larger group that is meeting face to face; that is, it seems that larger groups gain more benefits from GSS use than do smaller groups, which can function well without a GSS. If a manager has a small team (five or fewer members) that is capable of using the GSS, the team could use the GSS to generate ideas, but not for decision making, as the GSS offers little value at the decision-making stage.

Third, decision-making groups need to be under the guidance of a facilitator. GSS groups with a facilitator make better decisions and are more satisfied with the process than do GSS groups without a facilitator (Dennis & Wixom, 2002). It seems that the role of the facilitator is to help groups incorporate the GSS into their work processes.

Fourth, organizations need to ensure that distributed teams working on decision-making tasks have some access to face-to-face meetings, teleconferencing facilities, or a series of telephone calls to augment text-based GSS (Dennis & Wixom, 2002). In addition, Dennis and Wixom (2002) recommended having the distributed team use the GSS to generate ideas and discuss issues but bringing team members together face to face or in an audio- or videoconference when the team needs to make important decisions.

Fifth, when verbal communication it not possible, interactive and synchronous communication (e.g., Internet chat) is more appropriate for the initial stages of problem solving, when the emphasis is more on generating a large number of new ideas than on generating alternative solutions and strategies. In addition, when the group needs to generate alternative solutions and strategies, which is crucial in the late stages of a group decision, asynchronous communication support, such as e-mail, is more suitable (Shirani et al., 1999).

As a final point, give decision-making groups—in particular, those that are working at a distance—time to gain experience using support tools. Increased experience of a group reduces doubt with regard to distribution of labor and responsibilities. These changes are expected to reduce the degree of interdependence and the level of coordination and information exchange required in dispersed work groups. Moreover, increased experience with a given tool will make collaborating easier in the sense that group members can become more accustomed to the procedures involved in efficient collaboration. This, too, will tend to reduce the degree of coordination required. Furthermore, as a group gains experience using support tools, it will change the ways in which it uses those tools in such a manner that initial constraints caused by the tools will be compensated for (McGrath et al., 1993).

REFERENCES

Baltes, B. B., Dickson, M. W., Sherman, M. P., Bauer, C. C., & LaGanke, J. S. (2002). Computer-mediated communication and group decision making: A meta-analysis. *Organizational Behavior and Human Decision Processes, 87,* 156–179.

Beacker, R. M., Grudin, J., Buxton, W. A. S., & Greenberg, S. (1995). Groupware and computer-supported cooperative work. In R. M. Beacker, J. Grudin, W. A. S. Buxton, & S. Greenberg (Eds.), *Readings in human–computer interaction: Toward the year 2000* (pp. 741–753). San Francisco: Morgan Kaufmann.

Benbasat, I., & Lim, J. (2000). Information technology support for debiasing group judgements: An empirical evaluation. *Organizational Behavior and Human Decision Processes, 83,* 167–183.

Benbasat, I., & Lim, L. H. (1993). The effects of group, task, context, and technology variables on the usefulness of group support systems: A meta-analysis of experimental studies. *Small Group Research, 24,* 430–462.

Chidambaram, L., Bostrom, R. P., & Wynne, B. E. (1991). A longitudinal study of the impact of group decision support systems on group development. *Journal of Management Information Systems, 7,* 7–25.

Daft, R. L., & Lengel, R. H. (1984). Information richness: A new approach to managerial behavior and organization design. *Research in Organizational Behavior, 6,* 191–233.

Daft, R. L., & Lengel, R. H. (1986). Organizational information requirements, media richness and structural design. *Management Science, 32,* 554–571.

Dennis, A. R., & Wixom, B. H. (2002). Investigating the moderators of the group support systems use with meta-analysis. *Journal of Management Information Systems, 18,* 235–257.

Diehl, M., & Stroebe, W. (1987). Productivity loss in brainstorming groups: Toward the solution of a riddle. *Journal of Personality and Social Psychology, 53,* 497–509.

Diehl, M., & Stroebe, W. (1991). Productivity loss in idea-generating groups: Tracking down the blocking effect. *Journal of Personality and Social Psychology, 61,* 392–403.

Dix, A., Finlay, J., Abowd, G., & Beale, R. (1993). *Human–computer interaction.* Hemel Hempstead, Hertfordshire, England: Prentice Hall International.

Dourish, P., Adler, A., Bellotti, V., & Henderson, A. (1996). Your place or mine? Learning from long-term use of audio–video communication. *Computer Supported Cooperative Work, 5,* 33–62.

Finlay, P. (1989). *Introducing decision support systems.* Oxford, England: Basil Blackwell.

Gallupe, R. B., Bastianutti, L., & Cooper, W. H. (1991). Unblocking brainstorms. *Journal of Applied Psychology, 76,* 137–142.

Gallupe, R. B., Cooper, W. H., Grisé, M.-L., & Bastianutti, L. M. (1994). Blocking electronic brainstorms. *Journal of Applied Psychology, 79,* 77–86.

Gallupe, R. B., Dennis, A. R., Cooper, W. H., Valacich, J. S., Bastianutti, L., & Nunamaker, J. (1992). Electronic brainstorming and group size. *Academy of Management Journal, 35*, 350–369.

Hare, A. P. (1981). Group size. *American Behavioral Scientist, 24*, 695–708.

Herik, K. W. van den. (1998). *Group support for policy making.* Unpublished doctoral dissertation, Technical University, Delft, the Netherlands.

Hogarth, R. M. (1980). *Judgment and choice: The psychology of decisions.* New York: Wiley.

Hollingshead, A. B., McGrath, J. E., & O'Connor, K. M. (1993). Group task performance and communication technology: A longitudinal study of computer-mediated versus face to face work group. *Small Group Research, 24*, 307–333.

Houghton, S. M., Simon, M., Aquino, K., & Goldberg, C. B. (2000). No safety in numbers: Persistence of biases and their effects on team risk perception and team decision making. *Group & Organization Management, 25*, 325–353.

Inspectie Brandweerzorg en Rampenbestrijding. (1997). *Vliegtuigongeval Vliegbasis Eindhoven 15 juli 1996. Eindrapport* [Air plane crash at Eindhoven air force base July 15th 1996. Final Report]. Den Haag, the Netherlands: Sdu Grafische Projecten.

Kahneman, D., Slovic, P., & Tversky, A. (Eds.). (1982). *Judgment under uncertainty: Heuristics and biases.* Cambridge, England: Cambridge University Press.

Kleij, R. van der, Paashuis, R. M., Langefeld, J. J., & Schraagen, J. M. C. (2004). Effects of long-term use of video-communication technologies on the conversational process. *International Journal of Cognition, Technology & Work, 6*, 57–59.

Kleij, R. van der, Paashuis, R. M., & Schraagen, J. M. C. (in press). On the passage of time: Temporal differences in video-mediated and face-to-face interaction. *International Journal of Human–Computer Studies.*

Locke, E. A., Tirnauer, D., Roberson, Q., Goldman, B., Latham, M. E., & Weldon, E. (2001). The importance of the individual in an age of groupism. In M. E. Turner (Ed.), *Groups at work: Theory and research* (pp. 501–528). Mahwah, NJ: Erlbaum.

McGrath, J. E., Arrow, H., Gruenfeld, D. H., Hollingshead, A. B., & O'Connor, K. M. (1993). Groups, tasks and technology: The effects of experience and change. *Small Group Research, 24*, 406–420.

Morley, I. E. (1994). Computer supported cooperative work and engineering product design. In E. Andriessen & R. Roe (Eds.), *Telematics at work* (pp. 231–260). East Sussex, England: Erlbaum.

Mosier, K. L., Dunbar, M., McDonnell, L., Skitka, L. J., Burdick, M., & Rosenblatt, B. (1998). Automation bias and errors: Are teams better than individuals? In *Proceedings of the Human Factors and Ergonomics Society 42nd Annual Meeting* (pp. 201–205). Santa Monica, CA: Human Factors and Ergonomics Society.

Mosier, K. L., Skitka, L. J., Heers, S., & Burdick, M. D. (1998). Automation bias: Decision making and performance in high-tech cockpits. *International Journal of Aviation Psychology, 8*, 47–63.

Mullen, B., Johnson, C., & Salas, E. (1991). Productivity loss in brainstorming groups: A meta-analytic integration. *Basic and Applied Social Psychology, 12,* 3–23.

Nunamaker, J. F. (1997). Future research in group support systems: Needs, some questions and possible directions. *International Journal of Human–Computer Studies, 47,* 357–385.

Nunamaker, J. F., Briggs, R. O., & Mittleman, D. D. (1995). Electronic meeting systems: Ten years of lessons learned. In D. Coleman & R. Khanna (Eds.), *Groupware: Technology and applications* (pp. 146–193). Upper Saddle River, NJ: Prentice Hall.

Olson, G. M., & Olson, J. S. (2000). Distance matters. *Human–Computer Interaction, 15,* 139–178.

Paris, C. R., Salas, E., & Cannon-Bowers, J. A. (1999). Human performance in multi-operator systems. In P. A. Hancock (Ed.), *Human performance and ergonomics: Handbook of perception and cognition series* (2nd ed., pp. 329–386). San Diego, CA: Academic Press.

Payne, J. W., Bettman, J. R., & Johnson, E. J. (1993). *The adaptive decision maker.* Cambridge, England: Cambridge University Press.

Qureshi, S., & Vogel, D. (2001). Adaptiveness in virtual teams: Organisational challenges and research directions. *Group Decision and Negotiation, 10,* 27–46.

Rasker, P. C., & Kleij, R. van der. (2000). *Human factors issues and support in combat information centres* (Research Report No. TM-00-C007). Soesterberg, the Netherlands: TNO Human Factors.

Shaw, M. E. (1981). *Group dynamics: The psychology of small group behavior* (3rd ed.). New York: McGraw-Hill.

Shirani, A. I., Tafti, M. H. A., & Affisco, J. F. (1999). Task and technology fit: A comparison of two technologies for synchronous and asynchronous group communication. *Information & Management, 36,* 139–150.

Steiner, I. (1972). *Group processes and productivity.* New York: Academic Press.

Zigurs, I., & Buckland, B. K. (1998, September). A theory of task/technology fit and group support systems effectiveness. *MIS Quarterly,* 313–334.

3

EFFECTS OF DATA VISUALIZATIONS ON GROUP DECISION MAKING

SAE LYNNE SCHATZ, JANIS CANNON-BOWERS, AND CLINT BOWERS

In 1962, mathematician and computer scientist Richard Hamming observed that "the purpose of computing is insight, not numbers" (p. 1). Yet today, many computers are still used primarily to generate enormous quantities of impractical, difficult-to-decipher data. Even experts, such as statisticians and mathematicians, often struggle to comprehend and appreciate these masses of numbers, and nonspecialists are usually unable to do so at all. The obliqueness of these complex data burdens decision-making processes and strains team collaborations. However, complex numerical data can be represented in the form of visualizations, which people—specialists and nonspecialists alike—can glean insight from, use to make better decisions, and draw on to improve team interactions.

In this chapter we present an overview of data visualizations and how they can enhance team task performance. In the first section, we provide a very brief overview of the form and function of visualizations; interested readers are encouraged to see Chen (2003) for a more detailed treatment of data visualizations. In the second section, we introduce the general benefits of, and problems with, data visualizations, and in the last section we discuss visualizations in the context of group performance and communication.

AN INTRODUCTION TO DATA VISUALIZATIONS

Data visualizations are computer-based programs that translate complex numerical data into graphical forms that convey information to their viewers. The art and science of creating visualizations has gradually emerged over the last 20 years out of several other disciplines: computer science, psychology, semiotics, graphic design, cartography, and art (Munzner, 2000).

Basic statistical graphs—such as pie charts, bar charts, time series graphs, and scatter plots—are the predecessors of data visualizations. Graphs' effectiveness stems from their ability to communicate and summarize quantitative information; however, traditional statistical graphs have three major shortcomings. First, modern data have outgrown the capacities of statistical graphs. Despite the need for ever larger data sets, even the most sophisticated examples of traditional graphing techniques can effectively handle only a few hundred or thousand data points (Yang, Ward, & Rundensteiner, 2003). Second, traditional graphs are, generally, not interactive. To make the best choices, decision makers need to have access to all of the pertinent data and have the relationships among the data articulated by the interface. For large or complex data sets, this requires flexible, dynamic interactivity, which most traditional graphing techniques—even the advanced, computerized variety—cannot provide. Third, traditional graphs are limited to specific structures that the user must predefine. In other words, the people who graph the data must have certain relationships in mind before using the graphing tools. This causes only the known or predicted relationships in the data to be graphed, which limits their ability to reveal unexpected structures and the full range of possible relationships.

Data visualizations can meet the challenges that traditional graphs cannot; visualizations are innovative, interactive, robust, and adaptable. Data visualizations can take on many forms and can be applied to quantitative, frequency, or discrete data sets (Friendly, 2000a). Typically, they consist of two- or three-dimensional graphics that use color, shading, special shapes, symbols, scale, placement, and animation to convey complex information to the user.

Data visualizations can relay information in real time. For example, consider an active oil reservoir. The technicians want to monitor the gasses, pressure, chemicals, machinery, and so on, of the oil reservoir simultaneously through one interface. To do this, they use a visualization that consists of a single abstract image that constantly updates and responds to the changing conditions inside of the reservoir. This visualization conveys all of the data the technicians need—immediately and in a readily comprehensible form.

Data visualizations can also be used to navigate "through" information, so that detailed or aggregate information can be explored depending on the task. For example, the data visualization of a large company's finances might resemble a conceptual cityscape—with groupings of "buildings" (that are colored to represent spending areas and whose heights represent spending amounts) on various "city blocks" (that represent company divisions). In this scenario, a senior executive could see the "big picture" (the aggregate information) by looking at the marks and groupings of the "city," or a division manager could zoom in and explore the details of his or her "city block"—in other words, the details of that division's finances.

How effective are data visualizations? More generalizable research on complex graphs, such as three-dimensional and interactive visualizations, is needed, but some findings can be applied. For example, Kumar and Benbasat's (2004) recent experiment showed that three-dimensional visualizations outperform traditional two-dimensional graphs under all conditions with more than two variables—even simplistic situations. In a case study, Munzner, Hoffman, Claffy, and Fenner (1996) found that their visualization of the Internet multicast backbone MBone permitted an "immediate understanding of the global structure unavailable from the data in its original form" and that the resulting visualization displayed the information "more effectively than would be possible with still pictures or pre-made videos" (p. 85). Other groups have also used visualizations to support particular cases. The Netherlands Cancer Institute in Plesmanlaan and Rosetta Inpharmatics successfully used visualizations to study tumor samples from almost 100 patients, and Edward Wegman, a statistician at George Mason University, used visualization methods to explore data on bank customers. He uncovered previously unknown correlations between certain occupations and likelihood of debt; these relationships had not been detected using any of the traditional analysis or graphing methods (Ball, 2002).

USING DATA VISUALIZATIONS: BENEFITS AND PITFALLS

Complex decision making occurs in organizations with great frequency. In fact, most tasks can be conceptualized as a series of decisions aimed at accomplishing a specific goal. Hence, the way people use, understand, and interpret the data around decisions has been the subject of much study. In this section, we address questions related to complex numerical-based decision making, such as the following:

- How do people react to numeric, verbal, or graphical representations of information?
- What types of presentations influence individuals' opinions and assessment of the data?
- How are relationships among elements in the data best revealed?

In the context of these questions we examine the benefits of data visualizations and warn of potential pitfalls associated with them. This is not meant to be an exhaustive treatment of the literature in these areas; our goal is only to familiarize readers with the concept of data visualizations so that the team aspects can be addressed.

Benefits: Insight and Speed

Visualizations reveal a data set's "big picture" and interrelations. They can support people's natural ways of thinking by using their visual, perceptual, and cognitive abilities—instead of just their mathematical capacities—to facilitate their problem-solving skills (Card & Mackinlay, 1997).

Revealing Relationships

Classical communications theory states that sets of numeric data, alone, convey no information. The information is revealed only by differences and associations among the groups of vectors (Wise, 1977). Or, as the mathematician and graph theorist John Tukey (1977) observed, "The greatest value of a picture is when it forces us to notice what we never expected to see" (p. vi). Tukey's statement highlights two fundamental reasons for using graphs and visualizations: (a) to discover overlooked errors and (b) to find unknown relationships.

Pacific Northwest National Laboratory's "Galaxies" visualization, shown in Figure 3.1, illustrates data visualizations' ability to reveal relationships. This visualization uses the image of stars in the night sky to represent a set of documents. Each document is represented by a single "docustar"; closely related documents cluster together, and unrelated documents are separated by large distances. Users can investigate the document groupings, query the document contents, and investigate time-based trends from this visualization interface (Pacific Northwest National Laboratory, 2000).

Creating Compelling Images

Both traditional graphs—and, to a greater degree, data visualizations—tell stories about the data, and when compared with many other communication media, these stories are richer, more memorable, and more compelling. By *compelling* we mean that the information is conveyed to the viewer in such a way that he or she immediately perceives qualitative messages from it, such as urgency or importance. Compelling visualizations do have the potential to exaggerate the qualitative messages, but the benefit of translating confounding numbers into captivating reports outweighs this potential pitfall.

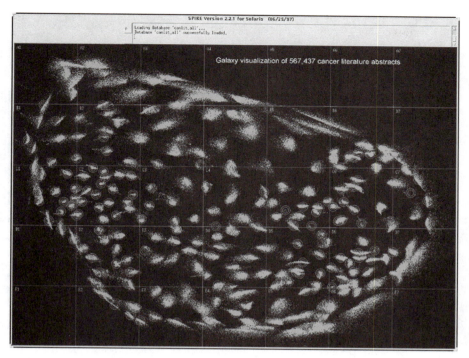

Speed

In business, a new paradigm is emerging that highly rewards rapid responses (Hammond, Koubek, & Harvey, 2001); this coincides with the third overarching benefit of data visualizations: their ability to quickly process gigabytes or terabytes of unstructured data into convincing, communicative graphics. For example, consider that a stockholder may need only glance at a graph of stock performance to grasp trends, whereas the same task would take much longer if he or she were scanning a list of numbers.

In visualizations the outputs are more complex than stock performance graphs, but the increased efficiency is similar. For example, in 2003, the energy company ConocoPhillips was faced with a dilemma: Drill an oil well in a risky location, using a nonfixed drill that had failed in two previous attempts, or give up the location and accept the lost production. They needed to make the decision extremely quickly because the drill was going to be moved to another location. A solution was found using a data visualization program named "Inside Reality," shown in Figure 3.2. Using this program,

Figure 3.2. Two people collaborate using "Inside Reality" software. They are examining oil well data with a reservoir model and seismic data. From "SIS, Inside Reality Screenshots and Event Photos," by Schlumberger Information Solutions, 2004. Retrieved March 29, 2004, from http://www.sis.slb.com/content/software/virtual/screenshots.asp. Reprinted with permission.

the executives were able to evaluate the conditions of the location and the chances of success and plan for possible failures. They were also able to decide to drill and devise a plan to do so in a very short amount of time and, ultimately, succeeded in the attempt. "The value of the project is having production six months earlier than anticipated from this area, representing a value of approximately $18 million dollars" (Schlumberger Information Solutions, 2003, p. 1).

Pitfalls: Distortion, Perception, Cognition, and Interpretation

The most basic function of data visualizations is to translate numeric data into graphical, semantic information. However, like translation between human languages, meanings can be changed, lost, or obscured by the process. Obviously, any graph or visualization will fail if the underlying data are flawed, inaccurate, or insufficient. The challenge of collecting and inputting correct, sufficient data should not be understated, but it is outside the scope of this chapter. So, precluding the problems associated with data integrity, the next most common pitfalls include accidental or intentional distortion of the data, the inability of the viewer to perceive or cognitively understand the visualization, and misinterpretation of the graphic by the viewer. We discuss these next.

Distorting Data

Data distortion problems arise because of errors or overlooked details in the underlying visualization system or program. Two broad categories of distortion errors—(a) incongruity and (b) rhetoric—are most problematic.

Incongruity occurs when different communication mechanisms are used for similar elements. Varying the proportions of a scale is one form of incongruity often found in traditional graphs. Other examples include ambiguous labeling; colors, symbols, shapes, or other elements that represent multiple meanings; and variations of presentation methods between related data sets. For a plethora of data distortion examples, review Wainer's (1997) chapter on "How to Display Data Badly."

Rhetorical problems are more subtle than incongruities. *Rhetoric* accounts for the ways and degree to which the presentation of information influences people's understanding and appreciation of it. Different words, sounds, colors, symbols, proportions, shapes, movements, and so on, can be used to intentionally or accidentally alter—or completely obscure—the connotation of the data's meaning. A common example of rhetorical influence is found in scales that represent temperature. Typically, warm colors (red, orange, and yellow) represent high temperature values and cold colors (shades of blue and cyan) represent low temperature values. However, if a graph or visualization about temperature reversed these color choices (i.e., representing high temperature values with blue shades and low temperatures with red shades), the data would be distorted even if all of the other labels and representations were clear.

Other forms of distortion that can occur include exaggerating the trivial data, hiding the important data, convoluting relationships among the data elements, and obscuring trends in the data. These and similar problems can be minimized by applying meticulous care, domain-specific knowledge, and (if applicable) company-specific knowledge beginning in the creation stage of the visualization.

Perception and Cognition

Perception and cognition difficulties are inherent to some individuals. Examples of perception issues include the ability to recognize color, the ability to distinguish and name different colors, preferences for font and character size, and the ability to accurately perceive lines. Cognition issues include the ability to mentally rotate representations of two- and three-dimensional objects, the ability to recognize and understand patterns in the data, and the user's familiarity and experience with computer interaction (Gutkauf, Thies, & Domik, 1997).

A subset of these issues obviously has biological sources, and the visualization program should make affordances for these issues to the extent possible. Other difficulties can often be resolved through training and experience. Also, almost all perception and cognition difficulties can be mitigated by using teams, whose members can complement each others' knowledge and experiences and expedite the learning and training processes.

Misinterpretation

Data visualizations, by their very nature, are complex and abstract. They represent data in meaningful ways, but those meanings may vary among viewers. Misinterpretation problems may stem from ambiguous semantics in the visualization (which are related to both types of data-distortion problems, previously discussed), or the interpretation discrepancies may result from individual viewer biases.

Viewer biases stem from individuals' past experiences. When people make assumptions and cognitive leaps because of these past experiences, it is called *vertical thinking*. Vertical thinking is a sort of shortcut that helps people to understand new experiences, situations, and input (Patton, Giffin, & Nyquist Patton, 1989). This notion is also consistent with Klein's (1989) theory of recognition-primed decision making. It is a necessary part of analytical thought, but if past experiences are incorrectly linked to new ones, then misinterpretations occur.

One way to alleviate misinterpretation errors is to ensure that all users have a complete knowledge about the goals, functions, and adaptive capabilities of the visualization system (Gutkauf et al., 1997). Another way to reduce misinterpretation is to rely on groups—instead of just individual decision makers. We discuss visualization-based group decision making in the next section.

Summary

Data visualization techniques are a potentially powerful means to support and enhance human decision making. As with other forms of decision support, the effectiveness of the visualization will depend largely on how well it is conceived and developed, especially within the context of the task and user population. We now turn to the central topic in this chapter: how data visualization can enhance team performance.

DECISION MAKING IN GROUPS

An interesting, if unintended, facet of data visualizations is the possibility that they may facilitate team performance. This belief has been reported anecdotally by several groups who have used these technologies in multioperator decision-making environments. Indeed, there are now visualization products that are marketed purely to facilitate team decision making. There is not currently a sufficient body of scientific literature to evaluate these claims. If they are true, however, there appear to be two underlying mechanisms. The first is, simply, that in team situations the benefits of data visualizations are compounded, and some of their potential pitfalls are minimized. The second is that these visualizations may foster *shared mental models*, a condition thought to be associated with effective team performance (Cannon-Bowers & Salas, 1997, 2001; Fiore, Salas, & Cannon-Bowers, 2001).

When to Apply Data Visualizations to Group Decision Making

Obviously, business teams make many different types of decisions. However, only a small subset of these is likely to benefit from visualizations. The conditions under which visualizations are likely to be helpful are those where success is dependent on the ability of the team to function interdependently as a coherent unit. A second condition is the need for various classes of expertise of the team members; that is, visualizations are most likely to be useful when the decision is beyond the capability of a single individual.

Here we limit our consideration to team processes that involve gathering, processing, integrating, and communicating information in support of arriving at a task-relevant decision. These processes do not require that a consensus be reached among members; neither do we suggest that all team members will be involved in all aspects of the decision. Instead, these situations require that team members process and filter raw data, apply individual expertise, communicate relevant information, and make recommendations to other members.

Because of the nature of the tasks to which visualization-based group decision making applies, it is likely that aspects of the visualization interact with other team behaviors—specifically, how team members interact, coordinate, communicate, exchange information, and adapt. Much of our discussion explores this relationship between team behaviors and visualization technology.

Challenges of Complex Decision Making

The challenge with *complex* decision making in groups is that when the task involves complicated data it discourages interaction, at best, and precludes participation from nonspecialists, at worst.

First, studies have shown that complex, technical interactions that are conducted using purely analytic methods can cause team members to perceive that they are overloaded with information. However, if the team shares the same content and amount of information in different forms, it becomes usable to the individuals (Carey & Kacmar, 1997). To mitigate information overload, certain kinds of technology must be used to support effective interactions among teams who are dealing with complex data (Hammond et al., 2001). Visualizations offer one way to accomplish this. Because they translate data into forms that require the use of different types of cognition, they disperse the information load and minimize its perceived burden.

Second, data visualizations facilitate the inclusion of both specialist and nonspecialist decision makers, which is becoming increasingly important as teams continue to be composed of multidisciplinary experts. This means that team members who previously were unable to participate in certain aspects of the decision-making process are enabled by visualization techniques to do so. This enhances potential interaction among team members and can foster more extensive overall participation.

Cultivating Shared Cognitive Models and Cohesion

Much of the literature regarding the facilitation of shared mental models relates to training. According to Rouse and Morris (1986), "one of the purposes of instruction is to provide necessary mental modes" (p. 357). Extending this to teams, it is clear that training should provide mental models that lead team members to form common interpretations of, and expectations for, the task and team. It is not necessary that these models be identical; rather, we suggest that mental models that lead to similar expectations must be developed.

There are several ways that data visualizations might be helpful in this regard. For example, Rouse and Morris (1986) suggested that providing people with knowledge of theories, fundamentals, and principles is not sufficient to ensure effective performance; instead, technology such as visualizations might assist in providing the other necessary types of information to team members.

Consider an experiment involving device operation conducted by Kieras and Bovair (1984). They concluded that effective training must include information about the system or device that allows an operator to infer specific information about the system's operation. Visualization systems can do this very quickly. For example, it is possible to demonstrate interdependencies, cause-and-effect scenarios, and other information that is difficult to relate in other communication modalities. This might be especially evident in helping operators to understand how their actions might affect the system downstream.

Related to this, it appears that presenting conceptual models of a system (i.e., those that make explicit the major objects, actions, and causal relationships) during training can help trainees to develop more accurate mental models (Mayer, 1989). This is particularly true for learners in complex domains (Borgman, 1986) and when the model allows the operator to infer procedures for operating the system (Kieras, 1988). Again, it is easy to imagine the utility of visualization technologies here. Archival (or real time) data can be displayed in a manner that makes clear the interdependencies in the system. By making the system transparent, team members might be much better able to infer the relationships between their roles. The effects of this type of intervention have been demonstrated in experiments on cross-training. Cross-training appears to help team members understand the roles and responsibilities of their teammates (Cannon-Bowers & Salas, 1990; Cannon-Bowers, Salas, Blickensderfer, & Bowers, 1998; Schraagen & Rasker, 2003) and help team members understand information from these other perspectives.

Also, like cross-training, data visualizations may help team members to assess the extent of overlap in their mental models by making concrete and explicit what would normally be assumed or implicit. Hence, if team members could see a common depiction of the data, it might help them to change or adapt their own model if it is different. This may be especially useful in teams that have specialized expertise, where it is more likely that team members' unique perspectives will cause them to develop disparate models of the problem.

Another aspect of developing shared mental models was addressed by Stout and her colleagues; they concluded that preexisting shared knowledge lays the groundwork for effective team performance but must be augmented by compatible dynamic problem representations that are constructed while the problem is unfolding (Stout, Cannon-Bowers, Salas, & Milanovich, 1999). In other words, an infrastructure of some kind is necessary to support shared mental models. Data visualizations seem to be a key method of representing situations so as to support (or create) the team's mental model.

Finally, it seems reasonable to suggest that data visualizations can assist team performance by augmenting, or perhaps replacing, teams' verbal communication. Verbal communication is clearly one of the critical competencies for effective teams (Smith-Jentsch, Baker, Salas, & Cannon-Bowers, 2001). However, communication in complex teams is often quite difficult because of the differing vocabularies used by specialists. Data visualizations might be important in mitigating these vocabulary problems. By creating a "common picture," team members have a shared point of reference. Also, the ability to refer to the visual image (e.g., with a laser pointer) might allow team members to more quickly overcome issues of semantics, jargon, colloquialism, language, and the like.

Facilitating Communication in a Sociotechnical Environment

Some Challenges of Distributed Teams

In the modern era, businesses must deal with ever-larger and more complex tasks whose completion often requires the creation of multidisciplinary, geographically dispersed teams. These groups must depend on computing and telecommunications technology for all forms of interaction. Decision making in these dispersed, sociotechnical teams presents its own set of unique problems (Cuevas, Fiore, Salas, & Bowers, 2004). One such problem is *workspace awareness*, the ability of each team member to monitor the others. It is generally held that workspace awareness is an important aspect of team performance. Team monitoring serves two important roles. First, it allows team members to catch, and prevent, mistakes by others. Second, it allows members to determine when another member is overtaxed so they can provide assistance. Distributed teams are often lacking the cues required to perform these monitoring functions; consequently, there is a need to replace these cues. This is a place where visualization technologies might be of assistance, because (as previously discussed) they can help make team members' roles, responsibilities, and tasks more transparent.

A second issue with distributed teams is *teledata* (the team objects that require collaboration). Complex distributed systems often rely on the transmission of large amounts of data to enable the team to accomplish its tasks. This imposes an additional demand for operators to store and organize these data for later retrieval. It seems likely that distributed teams could benefit from visualization systems that facilitate data storage, retrieval, and associativity.

A third challenge for distributed teams is to create *social presence* (use of technology to generate a sense of social interaction). Distributed teams lack important cues that allow operators to draw accurate inferences about their coworkers. Thus, there is a need to create new cues that might allow operators to work with one another more effectively, such as revealing processes that have traditionally been opaque (e.g., data analysis) or enhancing cognitive sharing through the techniques previously discussed.

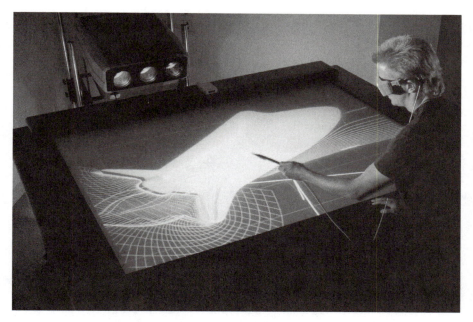

Figure 3.3. This image shows the Distributed Collaborative Virtual Wind Tunnel developed by the National Aeronautics and Space Administration's (NASA's) Advanced Supercomputing. The software enables interactive, three-dimensional visualization of vector and scalar data sets, such as those generated by aerodynamic simulations. As pictured here, active stereo glasses and a workbench are used as an interactive display unit. Photograph by Tom Trower, NASA Ames Research Center. Retrieved March 10, 2004, from http://www.nas.nasa.gov/About/Media/photos.html. In the public domain.

Using Data Visualizations in Distributed Teams

All of these factors—and the team's success as a whole—depend in large part on the team's effective use of technology (Hammond et al., 2001). Although we realize that technology alone cannot solve all of the challenges that face dispersed groups, we do propose that data visualizations can mitigate some sociotechnical team issues.

The newest visualization forms support "same time, different locations" collaborations. Figure 3.3 shows an example of a distributed, collaborative visualization that was created by the National Aeronautics and Space Administration's Advanced Supercomputing division. Programs such as this one operate simultaneously across global, interconnected computer platforms (Brodlie et al., 2002). The theory behind their use is that the simultaneous interactions with the system improve collaboration and the quality of communication among the distributed team members. Instead of simply receiving data, team members can watch and participate in its generation and exploration.

By observing and participating in the translation of the data into information and knowledge, the work of some team members that would normally be obfuscated becomes visible. Also, collaboration over difficult topics is facilitated in a relatively simple, user-friendly manner. During a case study of a distributed visualization system, Brodlie et al. (2002) found that the "group" nature of the distributed visualization systems alters the collaboration away from just individual-to-individual interactions and toward a truly "team" collaboration.

Discussion

Data visualizations seem like the philosopher's stone of data analysis: turning raw, unprocessed numbers into valuable, insightful visualizations. However, it must be remembered that they are merely a tool—one that, used correctly, can have beneficial impacts on groups and group decision making. Still, the advice of data visualization expert Michael Friendly (2000b) should be remembered: Good data visualizations, like good writing, require clear, precise, and efficient communication. Similarly, poor data visualizations, like poor writing, can distort, obscure, or otherwise confound the data's message.

Also, although data visualizations do translate data into forms that nonspecialists can appreciate, their use does not substitute for domain-specific knowledge. In other words, a clear, user-friendly visualization of a company's finances does not imbue that company's executives with understanding of good financial practice, it merely reveals the data to them; they must use their own knowledge to gain insight from the visualization.

The effective use of data visualizations is a many-sided process. The visualizations must be accurate, understandable, efficient, and adaptable. They also must be implemented in an environment where domain-specific knowledge, group dynamics, and good decision-making principles are considered and, in sociotechnical instances, data visualizations must be integrated with other telecommunication devices to achieve the best results.

CONCLUSION

In this chapter, we have briefly reviewed the form, function, benefits, and potential pitfalls of data visualizations. We showed how visualizations can be used to assist decision making, and how, when used effectively, they can provide greater insight into, and speed the analysis of, complex numerical problems. We also showed that data visualizations can provide potentially significant benefits for teams and team decision making. In particular, visualizations may provide the necessary additional information about a system and about team members' roles and responsibilities. They may also increase the amount of shared cognition among the team and enable noncomputational specialists to participate in more aspects of decision-making processes. Finally, distributed visualization technology can be used in dispersed teams to assist distributed communications and extend the same benefits that colocated teams receive from visualizations to the globally distributed environment.

REFERENCES

Ball, P. (2002, July, 4). Data visualization: Picture this. *Nature, 418*, 11–13.

Borgman, C. L. (1986). The user's mental model of an information retrieval system: An experiment on a prototype online catalog. *International Journal of Man–Machine Studies, 24*, 47–64.

Brodlie, K., Wood, J., Boyd, D., Sastry, L., Gallop, J., Osland, C., & Bunn, S. E. (2002, September). *Collaborative visualisation using access grid.* Paper presented at the e-Science All Hands Conference, Sheffield, England.

Cannon-Bowers, J. A., & Salas, E. (1990, April). *Cognitive psychology and team training: Shared mental models in complex systems.* Paper presented at the annual meeting of the Society for Industrial and Organizational Psychology, Miami, FL.

Cannon-Bowers, J. A., & Salas, E. (1997). A framework for developing team performance measures in training. In M. T. Brannick, E. Salas, & C. Prince (Eds.), *Team performance assessment and measurement: Theory, methods, and applications* (pp. 45–62). Mahwah, NJ: Erlbaum.

Cannon-Bowers, J. A., & Salas, E. (2001). Reflections on shared cognition. *Journal of Organizational Behavior, 22*, 195–202.

Cannon-Bowers, J. A., Salas, E., Blickensderfer, E., & Bowers, C. A. (1998). The impact of cross-training and workload on team functioning: A replication and extension of initial findings. *Human Factors, 40*, 92–101.

Card, S. K., & Mackinlay, J. (1997). The structure of the information visualization design space. In J. Dill & N. Gershon (Eds.), *Proceedings of the Symposium on Information Visualization '97, Phoenix, AZ* (92–99). Washington, DC: IEEE Computer Society.

Carey, J. M., & Kacmar, C. J. (1997). The impact of communication mode and task complexity on small group performance and member satisfaction. *Computers in Human Behavior, 13*, 23–49.

Chen, C. (2003). *Mapping scientific frontiers: The quest for knowledge visualization.* New York: Springer.

Cuevas, H. M., Fiore, S. M., Salas, E., & Bowers, C. A. (2004). Virtual teams as sociotechnical systems. In S. H. Godar & S. P. Ferris (Eds.), *Virtual and collaborative teams: Process, technologies and practice* (pp. 1–19). London: Idea Group.

Fiore, S. M., Salas, E., & Cannon-Bowers, J. A. (2001). Group dynamics and shared mental model development. In M. London (Ed.), *How people evaluate others in organizations: Person perception and interpersonal judgment in industrial/organizational psychology* (pp. 309–336). Mahwah, NJ: Erlbaum.

Friendly, M. (2000a, April). *Visualizing categorical data: Data, stories, and pictures.* Paper presented at the 25th Annual SAS User Group International Conference, Indianapolis, IN.

Friendly, M. (2000b). *Gallery of data visualization.* Retrieved March 10, 2004, from http://www.math.yorku.ca/SCS/Gallery

Gutkauf, B., Thies, S., & Domik, G. (1997). *User adaptive chart editing and presentation—Applied through user modeling and critiquing.* Retrieved February 28, 2004, from http://www.uni-paderborn.de/fachbereich/AG/agdomik/arbeitsschwerpunkte/ucmm/idias/root.html

Hamming, R. W. (1962). *Numerical methods for scientists and engineers.* New York: McGraw-Hill.

Hammond, J., Koubek, R. J., & Harvey, C. M. (2001). Distributed collaboration for engineering design: A review and reappraisal. *Human Factors and Ergonomics in Manufacturing, 11,* 35–52.

Kieras, D. E. (1988). Towards a practical GOMS model methodology for user interface design. In M. Helander (Ed.), *Handbook of human–computer interaction* (pp. 135–157). Amsterdam: North-Holland.

Kieras, D. E., & Bovair, S. (1984). The role of a mental model in learning to operate a device. *Cognitive Science, 8,* 255–273.

Klein, G. (1989). Recognition-primed decisions. In W. B. Rouse (Ed.), *Advances in man–machine systems research* (pp. 47–92). Greenwich, CT: JAI Press.

Kumar, N., & Benbasat, I. (2004). The effect of relationship encoding, task type, and complexity on information representation: An empirical evaluation of 2D and 3D line graphs. *MIS Quarterly, 28,* 255–281.

Mayer, R. E. (1989). Models for understanding. *Review of Educational Research, 59,* 43–64.

Munzner, T. (2000). Interactive visualization of large graphs and networks. *Dissertation Abstracts International, 61*(11), 5965. (UMI No. AAT 9995264)

Munzner, T., Hoffman, E., Claffy, K., & Fenner, B. (1996, October). Visualizing the global topology of the MBone. In *1996 IEEE Symposium on Information Visualization* (pp. 85–92). Retrieved March 2, 2004, from http://csdl.computer.org/comp/proceedings/infovis/1996/7668/00/7668toc.htm

Pacific Northwest National Laboratory. (2000, November) *Our technologies—PNNL Infoviz.* Retrieved March 11, 2004, from http://www.pnl.gov/infoviz/technologies.html

Patton, B. R., Giffin, K., & Nyquist Patton, E. (1989). *Decision-making group interaction.* New York: Harper & Row.

Rouse, W. B., & Morris, N. M. (1986). On looking into the black box: Prospects and limits in the search for mental models. *Psychological Bulletin, 100,* 349–363.

Schlumberger Information Solutions. (2003, May). *Case study: Immersive visualization as a decision-making tool.* Retrieved March 7, 2004, from http://www.sis.slb.com/media/software/success/ir_immersivevis.pdf

Schraagen, J. M., & Rasker, P. (2003). In E. Hollnagel (Ed.), *Handbook of cognitive task design* (pp. 753–786). Mahwah, NJ: Erlbaum.

Smith-Jentsch, K. A., Baker, D. P., Salas, E., & Cannon-Bowers, J. A. (2001). Uncovering differences in team competency requirements: The case of air traffic control teams. In E. Salas, C. A. Bowers, & E. Edens (Eds.), *Improving teamwork in organizations: Applications of resource management training* (pp. 31–54). Mahwah, NJ: Erlbaum.

Stout, R. J., Cannon-Bowers, J. A., Salas, E., & Milanovich, D. M. (1999). Planning, shared mental models, and coordinated performance: An empirical link is established. *Human Factors, 41,* 61–71.

Tukey, J. W. (1977). *Exploratory data analysis.* Reading, MA: Addison-Wesley.

Wainer, H. (1997). *Visual revelations: Graphical tales of fate and deception from Napoleon Bonaparte to Ross Perot.* New York: Copernicus.

Wise, J. A. (1977). *Change as a concept in information systems theory.* Unpublished doctoral dissertation, University of Pittsburgh.

Yang, J., Ward, M. O., & Rundensteiner, E. A. (2003). Interactive hierarchical displays: A general framework for visualization and exploration of large multivariate data sets. *Computers & Graphics, 27,* 265–283.

II

HIGH-TECH TEAMS
IN ACTION

Part I provided an understanding of the different types of technology that affect team performance. Following that, it is necessary to explore the different contexts in which the technologies are being used. Thus, the purpose of Part II, High-Tech Teams in Action, delves more into how technologies are being used in the real world to improve team performance and how technologies intentionally or unintentionally change teamwork.

Part II takes up the bulk of this book, as our target audience is made up of practitioners and scientists who want to apply technology to their respective team environments. The goal of the chapters in Part II is therefore to show how technology has been applied in the past and thus to allow the readers to extrapolate these applications to other contexts in which these same methods could be exploited. Furthermore, we hope that readers will develop new methods for applying technology in various team contexts, perhaps being inspired by the variety of creative methods presented here.

The first chapter in this part addresses how technology will unintentionally affect teams. It is important for everyone to understand that the introduction of any type of technology into the team setting will ultimately affect team performance in more and different ways than anticipated. The second and third chapters discuss the development and implementation of tools to aid in analyzing and understanding team processes and performance in complex environments. Finally, the last two chapters present two specific contexts, nuclear power plants and space flight, in which the introduction of technology has significantly affected the performance of teams. Part II shows that technology can be, but is not necessarily always, advantageous both in affecting actual team performance and in helping researchers to analyze and assess that performance.

4

COGNITION, TEAMS, AND TEAM COGNITION: MEMORY ACTIONS AND MEMORY FAILURES IN DISTRIBUTED TEAM ENVIRONMENTS

STEPHEN M. FIORE, HAYDEE M. CUEVAS, JONATHAN W. SCHOOLER, AND EDUARDO SALAS

In the last decade, a merging of disciplinary approaches has produced what is now being called *team cognition* (Salas & Fiore, 2004). It is this increasing commingling of ideas between the cognitive and the organizational sciences on which we base this chapter. Our goal is to more fully integrate facets of cognition yet to be explored in team environments and highlight their relevance to team cognition. We illustrate how memory research can be used to augment our understanding of team process and performance in complex environments. More specifically, dramatic improvements in computer and communication technology have brought about an

The views herein are those of the authors and do not necessarily reflect those of the organizations with which the authors are affiliated. This research was partially funded by Grant F49620-01-1-0214, from the U.S. Air Force Office of Scientific Research to Eduardo Salas, Stephen M. Fiore, and Clint A. Bowers, and by Grant SBE0350345 from the National Science Foundation to Eduardo Salas and Stephen M. Fiore. We thank Douglas J. Herrmann for his guidance and many helpful discussions on this topic.

unprecedented increase in the use of *distributed* environments in a variety of settings (e.g., industrial, academic, military) for individual and group training and for use in collaborative group work (e.g., Harvey & Koubek, 2000; Kleinman & Serfaty, 1989; Wellens, 1993). Often referred to as *distributed* or *virtual* teams, they consist of members who are not constrained by geographical, temporal, organizational, or national boundaries (Townsend, DeMarie, & Hendrickson, 1998; Van Ryssen & Godar, 2000).

We focus on this growing subset of teams and describe how memory theory can be effectively used to better understand team cognition in such environments. First, following a sociotechnical systems approach, we elaborate on how what we have termed *team opacity*, arising from distributed interaction (Fiore, Salas, Cuevas, & Bowers, 2003), can affect team cognition. Second, we review recent theorizing on general memory failures and prospective memory, in particular, and relate these findings to distributed team performance. We conclude with a proposed framework designed to facilitate readers' understanding of memory failures in complex operational team environments, and we offer guidelines for organizational practice.

TEAM OPACITY IN A DISTRIBUTED COORDINATION SPACE

Our theoretical approach is based on a sociotechnical framework we label a *distributed coordination space*, which consists of (a) the sociocognitive factors arising from the group dynamics inherent in team environments (e.g., cohesion, shared mental models), (b) the artificial components that enable interaction among distributed team members (e.g., collaborative information technology), and (c) the dynamic processes associated with distributed team interaction (e.g., coordination, communication; for a detailed discussion, see Fiore et al., 2003). Following this approach, we view a distributed team as an open sociotechnical system that includes the *personnel subsystem* (i.e., the members of the distributed team); the *technological subsystem* (i.e., the technology available to the distributed team); and the *external environmental factors* (e.g., task complexity, time pressure) that both act on, and are acted upon by, the distributed team (Cuevas, Fiore, Salas, & Bowers, 2004).

By setting limits on member actions and group processes, the technological subsystem components, in particular, may have a greater effect on team member interactions in distributed environments than would be expected in traditional colocated task environments. Distribution of team members transforms a data-rich perceptual–cognitive environment into a data-lean and primarily cognitive experience. Former perceptual cues are supplanted entirely or interpreted by means of these technological subsystem components (e.g., video media). Consequently, distribution may decrease awareness of team member actions and thus may potentially alter team interactions due to this loss of the paralinguistic cues typically associated with traditional colocated teams. We refer to this increased level of abstraction and artificiality forced on team members by the distributed nature of their interaction (i.e., the absence of colocation) as *team opacity* (Fiore et al., 2003). The team opacity that manifests during the interaction between cognition and behaviors in distributed environments may create a new factor that potentially contributes to coordination losses in distributed teams.

In short, team opacity may represent a unique form of cognitive workload arising from the lack of colocation, attenuating the efficacy of the distributed cognition normally experienced in colocated teams. Within a memory framework, team opacity can be considered as the manner in which the context of interacting in a distributed environment affects team process and performance. Distributed interaction is essentially a *virtual context*, that is, an amalgam of a real and an artificial environment. In this environment, actual cues (e.g., from systems or colocated team members) and representations of cues (e.g., from task artifacts or distributed teammates) combine to create the context of interaction. Thus, team opacity interacts with this virtual context and will influence cognitive and interactional factors. The lack of colocation alters the cues to which teammates are exposed, regardless of the level of information richness associated with communication channels. Thus, the subjective experience will be modified, resulting in changes in how teammates may think and behave. We next elaborate on how a team's memory actions may be influenced by technological and environmental factors, highlighting how team opacity may negatively affect team cognition and lead to memory failures. In addition, although our discussion focuses on memory actions and memory failures in particular, our goal is to gain a better understanding of both traditional and distributed team performance in general.

MEMORY ACTIONS AND MEMORY FAILURES IN COMPLEX OPERATIONAL ENVIRONMENTS

The complex nature of the team tasks found in today's technologically dependent distributed environments requires team members to integrate sensory input from a variety of modalities (e.g., audio, visual), placing a new form of cognitive load on their information processing ability and potentially influencing the execution of successful memory actions. As described earlier, we refer to this as team opacity. Specifically, in distributed teams, knowledge is conveyed through a particular information technology medium in which the full range of auditory and visual cues normally available to colocated teams does not exist (i.e., paralinguistic cues are not fully present). Because such cues are used by the receiver of a message to facilitate comprehension, their absence may lead to comprehension difficulties. Moreover, by limiting team members' ability to monitor the task-relevant cues provided by their geographically dispersed teammates, team opacity may impose additional workload on the memory processes of teams performing in distributed environments and thus may induce a greater occurrence of memory failures. We use the term *memory failures* to describe failures occurring in the context of teams and team tasks, rather than larger failures occurring at an organizational level (e.g., an institutional memory problem). Because teams have long relied on cues at both the individual and the team level to support memory function, we argue that this new interaction environment may alter and even hinder memory performance for distributed team members.

We propose that the organizational and cognitive sciences must simultaneously explore the impact of team opacity on cognitive processes and the resultant coordination. Specifically, an important issue with respect to performance in these complex environments is the nature of the memory failures associated with such settings. A necessary first step in understanding this phenomenon, therefore, is the development of a classification of the types and causes of memory failures experienced by team members in complex environments. We argue that one must investigate not only the nature of the memory failures but also the proximal (direct) and distal (indirect) causes of these failures associated with complex decision-making tasks.

The overall goals of such an effort are threefold: (a) a classification of memory failures leading to categories of differentiated memory lapses; (b) a taxonomy of causes of memory failures associated with complex tasks; and (c) a set of guidelines instructing operators, system designers, or both, in a given field regarding how to identify and avoid situations that lead to these memory failures. We turn next to a discussion of a portion of the research on memory failures and present a framework that may guide the development of our understanding of the memory failures experienced by both traditional and distributed teams performing in complex operational environments.

Memory Failures in Complex Operational Environments

Relatively little research has been conducted on memory failures outside of the laboratory, particularly in complex operational environments. Specifically, only a limited amount of research has explicitly focused on the nature and causes of memory failures typically experienced in dynamic settings. Among the various investigations that have examined memory failures, some researchers used diary studies to explore absent-minded behavior (e.g., Reason & Lucas, 1984), and others explored prospective memory (e.g., Sehulster, 1988) and the benefits of reminders (e.g., Beal, 1988). Other studies suggest that memory-improvement techniques can reduce memory failures somewhat (e.g., Herrmann, Brubaker, Yoder, Sheets, & Tio, 1999; Herrmann, Buschke, & Gall, 1987).

Recent research has attempted to investigate everyday memory failures to better understand the relation between types of failures and their causes (Fiore, Schooler, Whiteside, & Herrmann, 1997; Herrmann, Gruneberg, Fiore, Schooler, & Torres, in press). This research showed how surveys can reliably collect memory failure data and described a taxonomy that classifies everyday memory failures and their causes. In particular, memory failures can be classified as lapses in either *prospective memory*, which concerns remembering to do something in the future, or *retrospective memory*, which concerns remembering something previously learned. Accordingly, a prospective memory failure would include forgetting to engage an intention, whereas a lapse in retrospective memory entails failing to recall necessary information, that is, forgetting something one knows. Fiore et al. (1997) noted that the majority of reported everyday memory failures were prospective and were caused by either contextual cue failure (e.g., reminder not visible) or interference from some aspect of the environment (e.g., engaged in conversation). The failures in retrospective memory were more likely due to differing states of the participant (e.g., physiological states, such as fatigue). Herrmann et al. (in press) also noted that a majority of the memory errors were prospective, but they found that many could be attributable to multiple causes.

Although some progress has been made, there is a generally modest amount of research relative to the need to better understand this phenomenon. Furthermore, an investigation of actual everyday memory failures in complex operational environments, at both the individual and the team level, has yet to be conducted. This paucity of research is surprising given that such failures can have serious results. Recent applied research, for example, has focused primarily on the aviation domain, and the findings are indeed cause for concern. In investigations of aviation mishaps, memory failures are typically one of the largest categories of causes, accounting for more than 10% of the reported errors (Endsley, 1999). Memory failures can lead to errors in decision making, and such errors have been implicated as the causes of up to 50% of fatal and 35% of nonfatal accidents (Jones & Endsley, 1996). Jones and Endsley (1996) found that memory failures accounted for 11% of the losses of situation awareness reported in the Aviation Safety Reporting System.

Similarly, Federal Aviation Administration officials have stated that memory failures are an increasing concern in the area of air traffic control (ATC). The interaction between the ATC tower and cockpit crews is a cogent example of how a distributed team must coordinate their actions in the absence of colocation. Although their interaction is of relatively short duration, it is a dynamic and complex situation in which team members must rely on each other to provide important data to support their functioning. Federal Aviation Administration officials have stated that they are "disturbed by problems involving memory lapses" and further noted that "memory is perhaps the main mental tool of air traffic control" (Phillips, 1998, p. A1). Yet only a handful of studies have investigated the role of memory in ATC. For instance, some research has explored memory for flight data and demonstrated the impact of aircraft importance (Gronlund, Ohrt, Dougherty, Perry, & Manning, 1998). ATC researchers have recently documented that certain memory processes are very vulnerable to disruption (Garland, Stein, & Muller, 1999; Stone, Dismukes, & Remington, 2001). In light of these findings, it is clear that a better understanding of memory failures in these complex operational environments is critically warranted. In the next section, we attempt to address this issue by reviewing recent theorizing on the causes of memory failures, focusing in particular on prospective memory.

Prospective Memory

Prospective memory has long been recognized as a critical component of everyday cognition, dating back to the writings of Aristotle, who described what he labeled as "memory for the future" (Herrmann & Chaffin, 1988). Although memory failure research has been dominated by the study of retrospective memory, there has been a tremendous increase in the amount of theoretical and empirical research on prospective memory in the last decade. In the 20 years prior to 1996, only 45 articles on this topic were published (Kvavilashvili & Ellis, 1996). From 1996 to 2000, more than 100 articles were published on this topic (Ellis & Kvavilashvili, 2000).

Recent theorizing on prospective memory tasks argues that a multiprocess framework is appropriate to delineate the factors driving successful prospective memory execution (e.g., Einstein & McDaniel, 1996; West, Herndon, & Ross-Munroe, 2000). In particular, two processes, one largely *perceptually driven* and the other largely *conceptually driven*, are thought to be involved. The first process is referred to as the *noticing* component (McDaniel, 1995), whereby relatively automatic processes (McDaniel & Einstein, 2000) are relied on for attention capture (e.g., perceptally salient stimuli in the environment serve as reminders). The second is referred to as a *directed-search* component (McDaniel, 1995) and is a more effortful process whereby, following successful noticing, memory is searched for the intended action (West et al., 2000). Neurocognitive investigations of prospective memory implicate differing neural systems for these phases. West et al. (2000) found, for example, that the noticing component draws on the occipital–parietal region, whereas portions of the frontal cortex may be more responsible for the search component (see also Burgess & Shallice, 1997; McDaniel, Glisky, Rubin, Guynn, & Routhieaux, 1999).

Others attempt to disentangle prospective memory by focusing on the relation between the actual intention to be performed and the concurrent task in which it is embedded. Drawing from transfer-appropriate processing theory (Morris, Bransford, & Franks, 1977), some researchers suggest that the possibility for errors occurring is due to a mismatch between the prospective memory task itself (i.e., the intention) and the context in which it is to occur (Marsh, Hicks, & Hancock, 2000). Indeed, in a series of laboratory studies investigating what was labeled "task-appropriate processing," Marsh et al. (2000) found that prospective memory tasks were facilitated when the ongoing activity required similar cognitive processing. With a similar theoretical approach, Meier and Graf (2000) found that many of the empirical studies conducted on prospective memory fit within what they called a "sequential processing overlap" effect within a transfer-appropriate processing framework. Specifically, prospective memory performance was best when the initial planning phase required processing similar to that in the testing phase (e.g., no switch between semantic and perceptual processes).

From the standpoint of distributed interaction in operational environments, the implications of the aforementioned theoretical approaches are as follows. Prospective memory failures can be due to errors in noticing or errors in search, each potentially influenced by differing factors. When considering distributed interaction, the decrease in perceptual saliency in cues supplied by team members may lead to memory failures. Thus, a noticing failure may be due to factors associated with distractions in the environment, or it may occur because cues are not salient enough. Lapses in attention may be problematic during the early stages of a task because critical cues could be missed, but the perceptual saliency of the prospective memory cues can mitigate this effect (Marsh et al., 2000). Finally, distractions in the environment may be less critical during situations in which there is a match in processing between ongoing and prospective memory tasks (Meier & Graf, 2000), yet attention management problems may be exacerbated when there is a mismatch in processing.

Despite the surge of recent research on this topic, there is still a limited understanding of such memory failures in more complex settings. Furthermore, the aforementioned studies have not addressed how memory failures may affect team process and performance, particularly in complex distributed environments. Thus, failures in memory actions represent an important cognitive component in dynamic coordinated environments. This is especially critical for improving team performance in distributed environments, where such lapses are exacerbated because of the team opacity arising from the artificial technology-mediated nature of team member interactions.

We next discuss the potential application of a previously developed memory failures paradigm (Fiore et al., 1997; Herrmann et al., in press) designed to study memory outside of the laboratory.

Memory Failures Framework

Any cohesive research program to augment system operation in dynamic environments should meet the following criteria: (a) understand and specify memory requirements, (b) understand and specify the nature of memory failures, and (c) understand and specify causes of memory failures. The memory failures framework discussed in a portion of the aforementioned studies (Fiore et al., 1997; Herrmann et al., in press) was developed to encompass a broad range of factors potentially contributing to memory in everyday life. Specifically, the framework is based on the *multimodal* approach to human memory (Herrmann, 1996; Herrmann & Parente, 1994). This approach argues that, to understand memory function in complex environments, one must look at the entire sociotechnical system and account not only for the psychological and physiological factors inherent in the members of the team (i.e., the personnel subsystem) that may contribute to memory failures but also the technological and environmental factors that could impact successful and unsuccessful memory performance (as illustrated in Figure 4.1).

By adopting this framework to the study of memory performance in complex environments, it may be feasible to mitigate the occurrence, or minimize the effects of, memory failures at the individual and team levels. In the next section, we describe the components of this framework in the hope that it may guide research in this area. There are two main objectives to the use of such a framework. First, it may aid in the classification of the types of memory failures experienced in complex operational settings, such as those found with distributed teams. Second, it may help determine what team members' explanations are for such failures through analyses of subjective self-report data.

As discussed, memory lapses may be classified as being either *prospective* failures, which involve forgetting to do something (e.g., an error in the instrument scan process), or *retrospective* failures, which involve forgetting something one knows (e.g., an error in procedural knowledge; Fiore et al., 1997; Herrmann et al., in press). As illustrated in Figure 4.1, we further suggest that causes of memory failures in complex environments must be classified as either *exogenous* or *endogenous* factors, that is, as being either *external* or *internal* to the team member, respectively. Exogenous factors influence memory performance through the operational context and involve limitations imposed by the technological subsystem components available

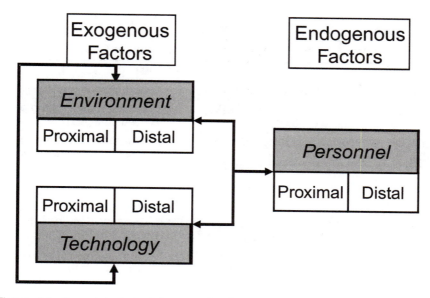

Figure 4.1. A sociotechnical framework of exogenous and endogenous factors affecting memory actions in complex operational environments.

to team members (e.g., computer-mediated communication relied on by distributed teams) as well as constraints due to the environment in which team members operate and interact (e.g., the lack of colocation associated with distributed teams). Following Herrmann and Parente (1994), we describe the endogenous factors as involving psychological or physiological changes (or both) that are internal to the team, that is, the individual team members' internal states (e.g., anxiety, fatigue).

Memory failures must also be classified as being due to either direct (proximal) or indirect (distal) factors (Herrmann et al., in press). *Proximal* factors include causes that directly disrupt encoding, retention, or remembering processes. *Distal* factors involve causes that affect nonmemory processes (e.g., physiological and emotional states, motivation), that in turn disrupt memory processing. Certain forms of interference can be considered direct because they have an immediate impact, and they may be endogenous because they arise within the individual (i.e., something within oneself is interfering with one's performance). Self-reports of memory failure causes such as "too many things on my mind" or "thinking about something else" have been characterized as such (e.g., Fiore et al., 1997; Herrmann et al., in press). Similarly, failures due to some aspect of the state of the individual team member can be considered endogenous and indirect in that the memory

TABLE 4.1
Memory Failures in Complex Operational Environments
Classified by the Directness and Location of Causes

Directness of cause	Location of cause	
	Endogenous (internal)	Exogenous (external)
Proximal (direct)	Interference (too many tasks being conducted)	Context (reminder missing or context changed)
Distal (indirect)	Physiological (fatigue or anxiety)	Social disruption (distraction from external conversations)

system is being compromised from within, but the cause is only distally related to the failure (e.g., "I was too tired").

Exogenous factors affect the team externally; that is, the impact comes from outside the team member and may be direct or indirect. Environment-based distractions, in particular, are external and indirect to team members (e.g., "a teammate was talking to me"). Distractions at the level of the technological subsystem can also be construed as external and either direct or indirect. As an illustration, a direct cause could be task overload, which would occur when team members are monitoring too many parameters on a display. An indirect cause would be illustrated by poor design factors such as system designs that lack affordances. A cross-section of possible causes for memory failures is displayed in Table 4.1. As depicted, the explanation provided for memory lapses can be classified as being due to context, distractions, internal states, or some combination of these. *Context* refers to the presence or absence of cues (e.g., being habituated to cue or cues no longer present). *Distractions* can be either *external* disruptions from the environment (e.g., "a teammate was talking to me") or *internal* interference from cognition (e.g., "too many things on my mind"). *Internal states* include physiological (e.g., fatigue), emotional (e.g., anxiety), and motivational (e.g., lack of perceived importance) changes in the individual team member.

Another relevant distinction for prospective memory in complex environments has to do with disentangling the manner in which the intended action must be accomplished. Ellis (1988) noted that some actions must be *precisely* executed (e.g., a turn-point procedure for a navigator), whereas others can occur over a broader spectrum of time (e.g., monitoring a particular gauge during mission). The former are referred to as *pulses*, and the latter are referred to as *steps*. A similar distinction revolves around the degree to which time is a critical factor. To illustrate this distinction, consider that many prospective memory tasks are time based and must be executed at a given time, whereas others are event based, that is, driven by a need to fulfill some requirement (Herrmann et al., 1999). Although these distinctions overlap somewhat, there is not a perfect concordance between the two. From the perspective of understanding prospective memory in dynamic environments, these distinctions are important because of the potential for differing failure mechanisms as well as differing methodologies to attenuate the potential for failure. For instance, system augmentation may be more appropriate for pulses because they are easily programmable (e.g., time-based reminders that teammates can monitor). Although the degree of system augmentation programming would need to be more sophisticated, event-based prospective memory tasks may also be programmable (e.g., emphasizing mission chronology parameters rather than rigidly relying on a specific time).

Finally, many researchers argue that although human memory is remarkably resilient to failure, when the team is functioning suboptimally (e.g., because of poor internal states) it may be more susceptible to exogenous causal factors. Thus, what becomes important is the co-occurrence of causal factors in that memory may fail more readily when causes are multiple (Herrmann et al., in press). When team functioning is optimal (i.e., no endogeneous, indirect causes are present), the probability of failure may be low regardless of the cause set size. However, when team functioning is suboptimal (i.e., an endogenous indirect cause exists), there is an increasing probability of failure, and it may be proportional to the cause set size. Simply stated, when a team member is fatigued (an endogenous indirect cause), he or she would be more susceptible to either lapses in attention or distractions (a direct causal factor). To the degree that memory failures in operational environments can be classified along these lines, augmentation of the technological subsystem may better target methods to prevent such failures.

IMPLICATIONS FOR TRAINING, SYSTEM DESIGN, AND PERFORMANCE

This proposed memory failures framework can serve as a guide for research to determine the degree to which team opacity hinders the use of memory processes (memory actions and memory failures) in distributed environments. We contend that teams performing in distributed environments may be more susceptible to increases in exogenous and proximal causes to memory failures because of the relatively greater and more direct impact of the external environment (e.g., situational constraints, such as lack of colocation) as well as the inherent team opacity emerging from the technology-mediated nature of team member interactions. In other words, exogenous factors may interact with technological subsystem constraints to produce a multiplicative causal effect resulting in memory failures. In particular, the team opacity associated with distributed environments changes the nature of the contextual cues available to distributed team members (e.g., paralinguistic cues that are filtered or altogether eliminated), potentially influencing both prospective and retrospective memory actions. In distributed environments, cues triggering memory actions are altered or absent (e.g., absence of teammate actions), potentially attenuating prospective memory. Retrospective memory is affected in that cue absence can inhibit recall to the degree that contextual factors associated with learning these cues are different from the actual distributed environment.

From the standpoint of training interventions, team training that facilitates the development of shared mental models or shared situation assessment processes can be used to prevent memory disruption of team functioning. For example, research on transactive memory systems (e.g., Liang, Moreland, & Argote, 1995; Moreland & Myaskovsky, 2000) has shown that teammates are able to rely on one another to scaffold their interaction processes. This body of research suggests that experience with each other may support coordination in that team members develop a shared episodic memory for critical task information. *Episodic memory* describes the autobiographical knowledge one maintains in relation to interactions with one's environment (for recent discussions of episodic memory, see Baddeley, Aggleton, & Conway, 2002). In prior work, Fiore et al. (2003) suggested that, when discussing episodic memory and teams, "episodic memory is composed of interactions with teammates, and the scenarios or situations engaged by the team" (p. 353). Research in transactive memory has found that when training and performing a task as a group (as opposed to training individually and performing as a group), procedural recall increases, and errors decrease (Liang et al., 1995). Fitting such research into the context of this chapter, one could argue that training teams in colocated environments may create a group episodic memory. As such, to the degree that distributed teams are able to develop memories that allow them a sufficient understanding of each others' tasks, they may ameliorate the negative consequences associated with memory failures.

Related to this, if teams are trained in shared situation assessment processes, then prospective memory failures may be identified by teammates familiar with the cues to which a colleague normally attends. For instance, cue recognition training was developed to address the need to link the cognitive components associated with individual situation assessment processes (e.g., Endsley, 1995) to the complex interdependent behavioral components associated with team situation assessment (Stout, Cannon-Bowers, & Salas, 1996). When team members are trained to focus on cues that are relevant to the team's tasks (see Salas, Cannon-Bowers, Fiore, & Stout, 2001), cue recognition training can make critical aspects of the environment salient so as to increase the probability that team members will recognize when a cue for prospective memory may have been missed.

The distinctions in our proposed framework are important specifically because they bear on our understanding of human memory and resultant failures. Once research determines the nature of memory lapses and their suspected causes, it may be possible to develop training procedures on how to overcome them and design systems capable of minimizing them. In particular, the differing degree of prospective and retrospective memory failures will suggest the types of memory aids that are warranted. Prospective memory failures implicate a need for reminding devices, whereas retrospective failures suggest either better training of declarative knowledge or easier access to critical data. Furthermore, identification of particular failure causes may suggest modifications to the design of the technological subsystem components. If failures are due to problems in attention management (e.g., distractions), then displays that more clearly communicate information may be warranted. Last, as discussed, Herrmann et al. (in press) found that memory failures often were the result of multiple factors. Therefore, attempts to modify system design by targeting only a single potential failure cause or a small number of potential failure causes may be inadequate. Only by understanding the complex relation between multimodal factors influencing memory failures (see Herrmann & Parente, 1994) can designers better target the overall distributed team factors in their attempts to ameliorate their occurrence.

Such an approach may have important theoretical as well as practical implications. From a theoretical perspective, such an effort would allow researchers to assess the nature of the memory processes associated with complex tasks in both traditional and distributed teams. Specifically, researchers could (a) investigate the utility of the application of a taxonomy being developed to classify everyday memory failures to an applied setting, (b) determine the proportion of differing types of memory failures associated with complex team tasks, (c) determine the suspected causes of everyday memory failures, (d) determine whether there are different times of day (i.e., circadian rhythm effects) associated with more or fewer memory failures of a particular type, and (e) ascertain the relation between the types of everyday memory failures and various components of complex team tasks in applied settings.

From a practical perspective, an investigation of the memory failures typically experienced within distributed team environments might ultimately lead to memory improvement techniques that could lead to safer and more efficient training procedures. In particular, such research may lead to a variety of future experimental questions, such as the following:

- What identifiable causes of memory failures can be addressed with benign modifications to technological subsystem design?

- What aspect of training may influence the effects on performance of differing memory failures?
- Are modifications to instructional strategies warranted?
- Do practice and feedback strategies alter the occurrence of particular forms of memory failures?
- How can simulation and training systems be better used to investigate such training interventions?

This form of data collection could pave the way for experimental investigations of ways to improve memory performance during the execution of complex tasks and may suggest methods for designing interventions associated with a variety of operational settings, including both traditional and distributed environments.

This aspect of team cognition research is important for a multitude of reasons, both theoretical and practical. By more closely linking theories, concepts, and findings from cognitive science to organizational psychology, we may be able to truly wed the fields to garner a deeper understanding of team performance in general and distributed team performance in particular.

REFERENCES

Baddeley, A., Aggleton, J. P., & Conway, M. A. (Eds.). (2002). *Episodic memory: New directions in research*. Oxford, England: Oxford University Press.

Beal, C. (1988). The development of prospective memory skills. In M. M. Gruneberg & P. E. Morris (Eds.), *Practical aspects of memory: Current research and issues* (Vol. 1, pp. 366–370). New York: Wiley.

Burgess, P. W., & Shallice, T. (1997). The relationship between prospective memory and retrospective memory: Neuropsychological evidence. In M. A. Conway (Ed.), *Cognitive models of memory* (pp. 247–272). Cambridge, MA: MIT Press.

Cuevas, H. M., Fiore, S. M., Salas, E., & Bowers, C. A. (2004). Virtual teams as sociotechnical systems. In S. H. Godar & S. P. Ferris (Eds.), *Virtual and collaborative teams: Process, technologies, and practice* (pp. 1–19). Hershey, PA: Idea Group.

Einstein, G. O., & McDaniel, M. A. (1996). Retrieval processes in prospective memory: Theoretical approaches and some new empirical findings. In M. A. Brandimonte, G. O. Einstein, & M. A. McDaniel (Eds.), *Prospective memory: Theory and applications* (pp. 115–142). Mahwah, NJ: Erlbaum.

Ellis, J. A. (1988). Memory for future intentions: Investigating pulses and steps. In M. M. Gruneberg, P. E. Morris, & R. N. Sykes (Eds.), *Practical aspects of memory: Current research and issues* (Vol. 1, pp. 371–376). Oxford, England: Wiley.

Ellis, J. A., & Kvavilashvili, L. (2000). Prospective memory: Past, present, and future directions. *Applied Cognitive Psychology, 14*, S1–S9.

Endsley, M. R. (1995). Toward a theory of situation awareness in dynamic systems. *Human Factors, 37*, 32–64.

Endsley, M. R. (1999). Situation awareness in aviation systems. In D. J. Garland & J. A. Wise (Eds.), *Handbook of aviation human factors: Human factors in transportation* (pp. 257–276). Mahwah, NJ: Erlbaum.

Fiore, S. M., Salas, E., Cuevas, H. M., & Bowers, C. A. (2003). Distributed coordination space: Toward a theory of distributed team process and performance. *Theoretical Issues in Ergonomics Science, 4*, 340–364.

Fiore, S. M., Schooler, J. W., Whiteside, D., & Herrmann, D. J. (1997, July). *Perceived contributions of cues and mental states to prospective and retrospective memory failures.* Paper presented at the 2nd biennial meeting of the Society for Applied Research in Memory and Cognition, Toronto, Ontario, Canada.

Garland, D. J., Stein, E. S., & Muller, J. K. (1999). Air traffic controller memory: Capabilities, limitations, and volatility. In D. J. Garland & J. A. Wise (Eds.), *Handbook of aviation human factors: Human factors in transportation* (pp. 455–496). Mahwah, NJ: Erlbaum.

Gronlund, S. D., Ohrt, D. D., Dougherty, M. R. P., Perry, J. L., & Manning, C. A. (1998). Role of memory in air traffic control. *Journal of Experimental Psychology: Applied, 4*, 263–280.

Harvey, C. M., & Koubek, R. J. (2000). Cognitive, social, and environmental attributes of distributed engineering collaboration: A review and proposed model. *Human Factors and Ergonomics in Manufacturing, 10*, 369–393.

Herrmann, D. J. (1996). Improving prospective memory. In M. A. Brandimonte, G. O. Einstein, & M. A. McDaniel (Eds.), *Prospective memory: Theory and applications* (pp. 391–398). Mahwah, NJ: Erlbaum.

Herrmann, D. J., Brubaker, B., Yoder, C., Sheets, V., & Tio, A. (1999). Devices that remind. In F. T. Durso (Ed.), *Handbook of applied cognition* (pp. 377–407). Chichester, England: Wiley.

Herrmann, D. J., Buschke, H., & Gall, M. B. (1987). Improving retrieval. *Applied Cognitive Psychology, 1*, 27–33.

Herrmann, D. J., & Chaffin, R. (1988). *Memory in a historical perspective.* New York: Springer-Verlag.

Herrmann, D. J., Gruneberg, M., Fiore, S. M., Schooler, J. W., & Torres, R. (in press). Accuracy of reports of memory failures and of their causes. In L. Nilson & H. Oata (Eds.), *Memory and society.* Oxford, England: Oxford University Press.

Herrmann, D. J., & Parente, R. (1994). A multi-modal approach to cognitive rehabilitation. *Neuro Rehabilitation, 4*, 133–142.

Jones, D. G., & Endsley, M. R. (1996). Sources of situation awareness errors in aviation. *Aviation, Space, & Environmental Medicine, 67*, 507–512.

Kleinman, D. L., & Serfaty, D. (1989). Team performance assessment in distributed decisionmaking. In R. Gilson, J. P. Kincaid, & B. Goldiez (Eds.), *Proceedings of the Interactive Networked Simulation for Training Conference* (pp. 22–27). Orlando, FL: Naval Training Systems Center.

Kvavilashvili, L., & Ellis, J. A. (1996). Varieties of intention: Some distinctions and classifications. In M. A. Brandimonte, G. O. Einstein, & M. A. McDaniel (Eds.), *Prospective memory: Theory and applications* (pp. 23–51). Mahwah, NJ: Erlbaum.

Liang, D., Moreland, R., & Argote, L. (1995). Group versus individual training and group performance: The mediating factor of transactive memory. *Personality & Social Psychology Bulletin, 21*, 384–393.

Marsh, R. L., Hicks, J. L., & Hancock, T. W. (2000). On the interaction of ongoing cognitive activity and the nature of an event-based intention. *Applied Cognitive Psychology, 14*, S29–S41.

McDaniel, M. A. (1995). Prospective memory: Progress and processes. In D. L. Medin (Ed.), *The psychology of learning and motivation* (pp. 191–222). San Diego, CA: Academic Press.

McDaniel, M. A., & Einstein, G. O. (2000). Strategic and automatic processes in prospective memory retrieval: A multiprocess framework. *Applied Cognitive Psychology, 14*, S127–S144.

McDaniel, M. A., Glisky, E. L., Rubin, S. R., Guynn, M. J., & Routhieaux, B. C. (1999). Prospective memory: A neuropsychological study. *Neuropsychology, 13*, 103–110.

Meier, B., & Graf, P. (2000). Transfer appropriate processing for prospective memory tests. *Applied Cognitive Psychology, 14*, S11–S27.

Moreland, R. L., & Myaskovsky, L. (2000). Exploring the performance benefits of group training: Transactive memory or improved communication? *Organizational Behavior and Human Decision Processes, 82*, 117–133.

Morris, C. D., Bransford, J. D., & Franks, J. J. (1977). Levels of processing versus transfer appropriate processing. *Journal of Verbal Learning and Verbal Behavior, 16*, 519–533.

Phillips, D. (1998, June 6). Air traffic errors up 20 pct., FAA says; controller miscues are highest in N.Y. *The Washington Post*, A1, A12.

Reason, J., & Lucas, D. (1984). Absent-mindedness in shops: Its incidence, correlates and consequences. *British Journal of Clinical Psychology, 23*, 121–131.

Salas, E., Cannon-Bowers, J. A., Fiore, S. M., & Stout, R. J. (2001). Cue-recognition training to enhance team situation awareness. In M. McNeese, E. Salas, & M. Endsley (Eds.), *New trends in collaborative activities: Understanding system dynamics in complex environments* (pp. 169–190). Santa Monica, CA: Human Factors and Ergonomics Society.

Salas, E., & Fiore, S. M. (Eds.). (2004). *Team cognition: Understanding the factors that drive process and performance*. Washington, DC: American Psychological Association.

Sehulster, J. R. (1988). Broader perspectives on everyday memory. In M. M. Gruneberg & P. E. Morris (Eds.), *Practical aspects of memory: Current research and issues* (Vol. 1, pp. 323–328). New York: Wiley.

Stone, M., Dismukes, R. K., & Remington, R. (2001). Prospective memory in dynamic environments: Effects of load, delay, and phonological rehearsal. *Memory, 9,* 165–176.

Stout, R. J., Cannon-Bowers, J. A., & Salas, E. (1996). The role of shared mental models in developing team situational awareness: Implications for training. *Training Research Journal, 2,* 85–116.

Townsend, A. M., DeMarie, S. M., & Hendrickson, A. R. (1998). Virtual teams: Technology and the workplace of the future. *Academy of Management Executives, 12,* 17–29.

Van Ryssen, S., & Godar, S. H. (2000). Going international without going international: Multinational virtual teams. *Journal of International Management, 6,* 49–60.

Wellens, A. R. (1993). Group situation awareness and distributed decision making: From military to civilian applications. In J. Castellan (Ed.), *Individual and group decision making: Current issues* (pp. 267–291). Hillsdale, NJ: Erlbaum.

West, R., Herndon, R. W., & Ross-Munroe, K. (2000). Event-related neural activity associated with prospective remembering. *Applied Cognitive Psychology, 14,* S115–S126.

5

EXPLORATION AND CONTEXT
IN COMMUNICATION ANALYSIS

MAGNUS MORIN AND PÄR-ANDERS ALBINSSON

Communication is crucial in the command and control of distributed, safety-critical human activities, such as firefighting, law enforcement, and military operations. In such environments, multiple teams operate at separate locations under hazardous conditions to achieve common goals. Commanders, team leaders, and specialists must exchange plans, procedures, reports, and orders to coordinate and synchronize their efforts (e.g., Rasker, Post, & Schraagen, 2000). Such messages not only are essential to ensure a successful outcome of an operation but also provide an observable trace of how key actors have perceived the emerging situation and what decisions they have made. Therefore, recording and analyzing communication from multiple channels are important means of gaining insight into the processes involved in the command and control of multiple teams.

Unfortunately, communication analysis and other process-tracing methods can generate huge amounts of data (Woods, 1993). Another problem is that analysis of audio data based on transcription is time consuming and tedious (Cooke, 1994). Fisher and Sanderson (1996) indicated a potential solution to the problem based on visual, abstract representations of audio data. The key idea in their approach is to store digitized audio data and postpone any transcription or replay of the data until it is required. Instead, the analyst interacts with an abstract representation of the sequential audio data through a graphical user interface that supports navigation based on speech patterns or annotated keywords. Also, the interface provides random access to all audio sequences.

Another problem in communication analysis is the need for contextual information. To understand the significance of a particular message, it is necessary to take into account information about the dynamic situation. Considering contextual information also makes it possible to analyze why an anticipated message was *not* sent. Additional issues in communication analysis are the need to manage very large data sets, to handle unanticipated and unique elements in such data sets, and to maintain a connection between the original data and the theories constructed in the course of analysis.

To address these problems, which are inherent in communication analysis, there is a need for methods and tools that preserve contextual data, manage large amounts of data, provide access to original data, and support navigation and exploration. In this chapter we present an approach that addresses these needs. We describe a methodology that comprises two main activities: (a) reconstruction and (b) exploration. *Reconstruction* involves several steps for constructing a multimedia model of the course of events of a distributed work session. This model—a *mission history*—incorporates extensive process data, such as audio, video, digital photographs, observation statements, system log files, and position track files, from multiple sources in the operational environment. *Exploration* refers to the rendering of this model in a multimedia tool that supports explorative analysis of the data. We have used this approach together with practitioners and domain experts in multiple tactical domains to support systems development, performance evaluation, and training (Morin, 2002).

In the following section, we characterize a domain of distributed tactical operations and discuss some central problems pertaining to human control of complex sociotechnical systems. Next, we give an overview of a methodology for reconstructing and exploring distributed tactical operations based on data collected in the field. We then describe the MIND[1] presentation tool for exploring such multimedia data and give an example of how we used our approach to analyze communication from an exercise involving a multi-agency emergency response to an underground derailment. In the last section, we summarize the findings and discuss remaining issues and future extensions.

---

[1] MIND is a name, not an acronym.

DISTRIBUTED TACTICAL OPERATIONS

We study distributed human activities in tactical operations. Although the term *tactical operation* has military connotations, it is generally used in various organizations to denote the level of activity that aims at achieving specific goals with a body of personnel and equipment under unified command. We use the term *task force* to denote the collection of teams that conduct a distributed tactical operation.

Distribution and Complexity

Woods (1988) used four dimensions to characterize the complexity of a domain: (a) the *parts, variables, and their interconnections*; (b) the *dynamism* of the system; (c) the inherent *uncertainty*; and (d) the *risks* involved. A task force in a distributed tactical operation consists of several teams, typically drawn from multiple organizations, each with a different culture and *raison d'être*. It operates in a dynamic environment, whose conditions may shift spontaneously, without deliberate interventions of task force elements. Moreover, the task force lacks a persistent physical structure. The number of teams assigned, their location and status, and their means of communication may vary rapidly over time. Both the involved structure of a task force and the dynamism of its environment and structure contribute to the complexity of tactical operations.

Uncertainty is abundant in distributed tactical operations. The status and behavior of distributed teams are not directly observable, and there is usually insufficient information about critical aspects of the environment. Malfunctioning sensors and communication systems are common sources of uncertainty. The existence of a hostile and intelligent adversary capable of concealment and deception can add dramatically to the uncertainty. Flin (1996) reported that not having a complete picture of an emerging situation was a major source of stress for fire commanders. Because many tactical operations take place in safety-critical domains, the personnel face hazardous situations in which the loss of property and lives may be imminent. They operate under arduous conditions that may expose them to extreme heat, cold, dust, and noise. Explosive and hazardous materials are common.

Distributed tactical operations score high in all dimensions of complexity. Next, we examine how advanced arrangements for command and control can reduce this complexity.

Command and Control

Hierarchical decomposition is a standard way of managing complexity in distributed tactical operations. Introducing multiple command levels enables every level to control a smaller number of units. It also makes it possible to address short-term responses to changing conditions in the environment and long-term strategies at different levels (Brehmer, 2000). The division of labor and responsibility rests on the assumption that activities can be decoupled—that is, tasks should be weakly dependent and require synchronization only occasionally.

Pigeau and McCann (2000) provided a general definition of *command and control* that focuses on its role in a distributed activity: "the establishment of common intent to achieve coordinated action" (p. 165). They further distinguished between intent that is publicly communicated (*explicit intent*) and intent that is assumed from the cultural, organizational, and individual context (*implicit intent*). On the basis of this notion, Shattuck and Woods (2000) analyzed command and control in the theoretical framework of a *distributed supervisory control system*, conceived as a hierarchical assembly of remote supervisors and local actors who cooperate to control some process:

> A **remote supervisor** uses a **communication process** to provide **local actors** with **plans and procedures** and to impart his or her **presence**. The **degree of control** established by the remote supervisor influences the ability of local actors to adapt to unanticipated conditions based on the actors' assessments of their local environments. (p. 281, boldface in original)

By specifying the boldface terms, we can characterize generic command and control in distributed tactical operations as a distributed supervisory control system:

- *remote supervisor*: a commander who is responsible for carrying out the task assigned to him or her by coordinating the actions of a number of teams;
- *local actors*: subordinate commanders or leaders who monitor local conditions and respond to the plans and procedures of their remote supervisors;
- *communication process*: the means of exchanging information between the superior commanders and subordinate commanders;
- *plans and procedures*: prescriptions for coordinated action in anticipated situations;
- *presence*: the subordinate commanders' sense of being close to the superior commander despite the physical distance; and
- *degree of control*: the latitude or flexibility a superior commander will give subordinate commanders to adapt plans and procedures in response to unanticipated situations.

Applying these definitions recursively makes it possible to define distributed supervisory control systems with multiple levels. Thus, a commander at a specific level in the hierarchy can be both a local actor with respect to superior commander, who acts as a remote supervisor, and a remote supervisor with respect to subordinate commanders serving as local actors.

Communication

A distributed supervisory control system links the role of command and control to the role of a communication process as a conveyor of plans, procedures, and reports on system status between supervisors and local actors in a hierarchical, distributed organization. In essence, this issue concerns what must be communicated, before and during a mission, and what can be managed at a local level guided by what has been communicated and what can be inferred from the context.

A fundamental question in a distributed supervisory control system is how much latitude and flexibility the remote supervisor is willing to allow local actors (Shattuck & Woods, 2000). The same basic question arises in discussions on military command and control (Keithly & Ferris, 1999) and on emergency incident command (Rogalski & Samurçay, 1993). In *centralized control*, the remote supervisor not only defines what goals local actors should pursue but also prescribes, in detail, how they should attain their objectives. This level of control enables a high degree of coordination but requires detailed plans and procedures and extensive communication during execution, which makes it time consuming and sensitive to failures in the communication process. In *decentralized control*, the supervisor establishes the goals of the operation and explains the rationales for pursuing them. He or she grants the local actors a high degree of latitude and flexibility when it comes to adapting plans and procedures to local and unanticipated conditions. Decentralized control is robust in the presence of communication failures because it defines only a minimal set of synchronization points; instead, much of the coordination relies on shared implicit intent acquired in education, training, and previous operations (Pigeau & McCann, 2000). In practice, the degree of centralization a distributed supervisory control system exhibits may vary over time. This variation may be both a result of deliberate adaptation to shifting operational conditions and an unintended consequence of dynamically evolving circumstances.

Context

What actors communicate and what they do not communicate can provide valuable insights into the processes involved in command and control. However, there is always a need to be able to approach data from different viewpoints, going from one source to another, until reaching tangible conclusions, finding novel problems, or perhaps discovering insufficiencies in the methods and tools used. Thus, to understand the significance of communication or noncommunication, it is necessary to consider the dynamic situation. Analysis of communication in command and control therefore must include contextual information. Albinsson and Morin (2002) provided the following examples of important issues to consider in the context of a distributed tactical operation:

- *Actors*: What individuals and teams are involved, what is their status, where are they, what tasks have they been assigned, and what are they doing?
- *Organization*: How are individuals organized in teams, and what does the chain of command look like?
- *Coordination*: What activities need to be coordinated to ensure effective, efficient, and safe operations? Are there deadlines, and when do activities have to commence and cease?
- *Communication*: What means of communication exist, and how does the communication structure relate to the chain of command?
- *Artifacts*: What is the status of communication systems and other tools for command and control, and how are they used?
- *Environment*: What does the terrain look like, what is the weather like, and how does that affect the operation?

Although communication analysis can provide crucial information pertaining to those issues, other means of process data are required as well, for example, log files from command and control systems, log files from positioning devices, observation protocols from experts, and video recordings from command posts (Thorstensson, Axelsson, Morin, & Jenvald, 2001).

RECONSTRUCTION AND EXPLORATION

We pursue the hypothesis that embedding communication data in rich contextual information, and providing means of exploring these data in a multimedia environment, is a viable approach to communication analysis. In this section, we briefly characterize mission histories and outline a methodology for reconstructing and exploring distributed tactical operations.

Mission History

A *mission history* is an event-based multimedia model of a distributed tactical operation. This model combines data collected in the field during the operation with meta-data provided by subject matter experts. Examples of meta-data are remarks, questions, hypotheses, and conclusions. The model provides a coherent representation of the operation that can be stored in a computer file and replayed in a multimedia replay tool. In this way, the mission history becomes an "operation in a can" that can be opened and digested in portions. Moreover, commanders, managers, and analysts can add their comments to the mission histories and disseminate them to convey lessons learned to a wider audience.

Every piece of data included in the mission history has an associated timestamp. These timestamps define a temporal order over the data set. Establishing and preserving this order is a key to analyzing tactical operations, because it makes it possible to link events at one location to events at other locations, based on the temporal separation of events. Thus, time is fundamental in reconstruction and exploration of distributed tactical operations.

Methodology

This section gives an overview of the main steps required to construct and use a mission history of a distributed tactical operation using the reconstruction–exploration approach. Although Figure 5.1 outlines the steps in sequential order, there are frequent loops in the three first stages of reconstruction.

The goal of *domain analysis* is to determine what aspects of a tactical operation should be represented in the mission history. Analysts and subject

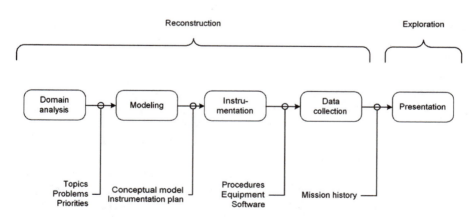

Figure 5.1. Overview of the steps of the reconstruction–exploration approach. Boxes indicate the principal activities, whereas annotated arrows show the artifacts produced in each step.

matter experts collaborate to establish crucial topics in the tactical situation, particular problems of interest, and a tentative prioritization among problems and topics. Examples of topics are objectives, critical procedures, and limiting resources. Methods to this end include semistructured interviews, examination of critical incidents, and scenario structure analysis (Morin, Jenvald, & Thorstensson, 2000).

The purpose of *modeling* is to turn the topics and problems pronounced in the domain analysis into an explicit representation of the domain that is capable of supporting instrumentation, data collection, and presentation. Modeling produces an object-oriented conceptual model that defines the main actors and activities in the domain. Modeling is an iterative process whereby analysts devise and evaluate candidate models until they produce a suitable representation. If the model meets all requirements, it is accepted and submitted for instrumentation. Otherwise, two things may happen: (a) the analysts modify the model to meet the requirements or (b) they find a way to relax requirements and construct a new candidate model. Should all attempts at relaxation fail, modeling cannot proceed, and reconstruction falls back to domain analysis.

The goal of *instrumentation* is to ensure that appropriate equipment and procedures for collecting data are available when the operation takes place. To succeed, instrumentation must balance extensive data requirements with practicable data collection methods. It requires an intimate knowledge of working procedures and operational scenarios and a great familiarity with the advantages and drawbacks of various data collection methods. Furthermore, instrumentation should make sure that appropriate means of presenting the data exist in time for the analysis.

Data collection takes place during a tactical operation. In this step, the procedures and tools devised in the instrumentation step capture the activities in the operational environment. The data collected are converted and combined to build a mission history. Automated procedures facilitate the rapid compilation of data. For example, multiple channels of radio communication can be recorded digitally, time stamped, and imported to the mission history. In other cases, manual preprocessing of the data may be necessary to produce a structured format. One such example is link analysis (Thorstensson et al., 2001), which creates an abstract representation of communication data to facilitate exploration.

Presentation is the final step; it refers to the rendering of the mission history in a form that supports exploratory analysis of the operation. Presentation requires a software tool that can interpret the mission history and present data from multiple sources and locations in a synchronized manner. We use the MIND presentation tool for this purpose. In the "MIND Presentation Tool" section, we describe it in more detail.

Reuse

Performing all the steps of the methodology can be quite time consuming. However, there are significant similarities between different tactical domains that enable the reuse of models, instrumentation procedures, and presentation techniques (Morin, 2002). Reuse can decrease the time and effort required in the reconstruction phase by allowing analysts to concentrate on the topics and problems that are unique to a domain.

MIND PRESENTATION TOOL

MIND is an interactive multimedia tool that can present mission histories in a way that supports exploration. To promote flexibility and extensibility, MIND has a component-based architecture (Orfali, Harkey, & Edwards, 1996). This feature makes it possible to distribute MIND with component sets customized to the needs of different users. In addition, it enables experiments with alternative presentation techniques based on existing data sets.

Architecture

The core of MIND includes managers for *components*, *events*, *time*, and *user interface*. The component manager administrates all components loaded into MIND by managing their creation, destruction, storage, state, lookup, and modification. It loads a mission history, instantiates its components, and keeps a table of all components. The event manager maintains a time-ordered data structure of all events included in a mission history. During replay, it receives specifications of time points or time intervals and retrieves the corresponding events. The time manager keeps track of the mission time. It also provides a clock with a variable tick rate for ordinary and fast-forward replay. Finally, the user interface manager handles user input and routes it to the appropriate manager.

All parts of the system outside the MIND core are replaceable and extensible. Table 5.1 gives an overview of the different types of components in MIND. Standard components exist in all categories to meet recurring requirements. Instrumentation must ensure that there are objects and events in place to represent elements and mechanisms in the tactical domain. In addition, it should check that sources and views required for converting and presenting data exist.

TABLE 5.1

Type	Description	Examples
Objects	Objects model real-world elements of a taskforce in a hierarchical fashion. State variables represent essential aspects, such as location, capabilities, and resources.	Vehicles, ships, aircraft, people, casualties
Events	Events represent time-stamped data. Events define changes in object state variables at particular time points corresponding to time stamps.	Position sample, observation report, sensor sample
Sources	Sources manage collections of events from a particular physical or logical source. Sources are the primary mechanism for organizing and tracing data from an operation. Sources can filter and format data.	Picture source, position source, audio source
Views	Views are presentation windows for particular types of data. Customized views are the primary means of extending the presentation capabilities of MIND.	Map view, casualty view, dynamic timeline, communication link view, Communication Explorer
Maps	Maps encapsulate a model of the earth, a projection method, and the logic necessary to render an image of this model in a generic map view.	Raster map, vector map, generic coordinate system view
Documents	Documents are static data, for example, text, digital photographs, video clips, audio samples, local HTML pages, and Internet URLs. A document can be made dynamic by linking it to an activation event that specifies when it was created.	Text, HTML, digital photograph, video clip, audio clip, URLs

Coordination of Multiple Views

Using multiple views is a well-known strategy to take advantage of the strengths of different presentation styles (Shneiderman, 1998), but it carries costs for user learning, screen space management, and computational complexity (Baldonado, Woodruff, & Kuchinsky, 2000). Therefore, it is important to consider various means of coordinating the contents and interaction between multiple views in a presentation (North & Shneiderman, 2000).

The data collected in a tactical operation define discrete events in the mission history. The objects in the mission history and their attributes capture aspects of the real-world phenomena observed. This relationship between observations in the real world and corresponding changes in object attributes in the mission history is fundamental for understanding playback of mission histories. MIND uses time as the primary navigation and coordination mechanism. Timestamps link the data in the mission history with the time the data were collected. In this way, MIND maps data to time and time to data. When the user selects a time point, MIND constructs the state of the mission at that point from the data available in the mission history. MIND updates all views to reflect this state. It works the other way around, too: The user can select a data item—for example, a communication sequence— and ask MIND to synchronize the state of the mission to that item. MIND then uses the associated timestamp to update and present that state. In replay mode, MIND uses successive time points to animate the corresponding state changes.

To help the user manage multiple views, MIND includes support for *themes* that define the layout, contents, and presentation mode for a sub-set of views. When the user activates a theme, the views included resume their user-defined settings. *Breakpoints* define points of interest in the temporal dimension. Combining breakpoints and themes makes it possible to define *episodes* that highlight particular aspects of the tactical operation in a presentation.

The Communication Explorer

The *Communication Explorer* is a view in MIND for exploring communication (Albinsson & Morin, 2002; Albinsson, Morin, & Fransson, 2003). It applies the explorative techniques introduced in the *Attribute Explorer* (Spence, 2000; Spence & Tweedie, 1998), an interactive data presentation tool that uses the concept of *linked histograms*. It provides one histogram for each dimension (or attribute) of a data set, in which the height of each bar corresponds to the number of data elements that fall under that interval. By applying constraints or selections in one dimension, the corresponding changes are displayed in the other dimensions. Data elements presented in green represent *full hits*—that is, they satisfy all constraints applied, or they fall within all selections, in all dimensions. Shades of gray, from black to white, represent the number of dimensions failing. An element is black if it fails in only one dimension and white if it fails in all dimensions. For each dimension in the data set, a constraint can be violated, and therefore the required number of shades of gray equals the number of dimensions of the data set.

Consider the following example, depicted in Figure 5.2. Suppose that we want to find a certain communication occurrence from a large data set collected during a tactical operation. The communication data set has two dimensions: *sender* and (start) *time* of communication events. Consequently, the Attribute Explorer provides two histograms. The first dimension (1) shows five actors involved in the communication, whereas the other (2) shows

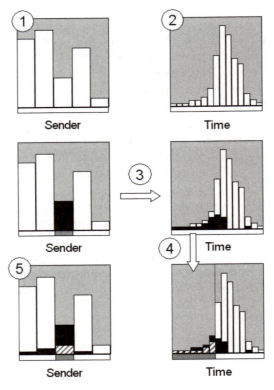

Figure 5.2. An example of the use of the Communication Explorer. The example uses a two-dimensional data set—(a) sender and (b) start time of communication—to explain the basic principles of the Communication Explorer. Note that in this black-and-white reproduction, green elements were drawn with a hatched brush.

the range of start times. There are some early communication events, some late ones, and many in between. At first, all histograms are white, because there are no selections, and thus all elements fail in all dimensions. Changing the constraints for one dimension—for instance, by selecting a certain sender—causes a part of the histogram bar to turn black, which indicates that the data elements (i.e., communication events) in that portion fail in only one dimension. The corresponding change appears in the time dimension (3), where the same elements turn black. Looking at these black elements, we see that most communication events of the selected sender occur relatively early in the operation. Suppose that we look for a communication event early in the operation and apply constraints to the time dimension accordingly (4). We know that the black elements within the new range are going to be full hits (and turn green), because they previously failed only in this dimension. The green elements (hatched in these black-and-white examples in the figure) represent communication events initiated by the selected sender within the time interval of interest. Elements that are black under these constraints represent early communication initiated by *other* actors. Finally, we look at the sender dimension again (5) and see the corresponding green hits. Here, the black elements (failing in the time dimension) tell us who initiated those other early communication events.

APPLICATION EXAMPLE:
EMERGENCY RESPONSE IN THE UNDERGROUND

We demonstrate the use of reconstruction and exploration in an application example that deals with emergency response in a subway system. The example also illuminates how MIND supports exploration of data from real operations.

On November 22, 2000, a unique training operation took place in downtown Stockholm, the capital of Sweden. Some 200 first responders and command staff from the local fire department, county medical services, and county police joined forces with personnel from the urban transport authorities and train operators to practice their response to a subterranean train derailment. Researchers from the Swedish Defence Research Agency participated in the planning and execution of the exercise to support documentation and analysis.

Scenario

The scenario centered on a train derailment in the Stockholm subway system, caused by sabotage. In a tunnel, 150 m from the platform of a downtown subway station, an object on the track caused a train to derail, hit the tunnel wall, and come to an abrupt stop. The impact left 86 people on the scene with various injuries, including 5 fatalities, represented by mannequins. Some passengers left the train and made their way to the platform and street, whereas others remained aboard. The train driver, who had sustained only slight injuries, used the train's radio to notify the traffic control center about the incident. From that point, personnel in the traffic control center initiated emergency procedures according to their standard procedures.

Application of the Methodology

Domain analysis started early in the planning of the exercise. Participatory observation in this phase provided insight into tentative topics and problems. Interviews with subject matter experts from the agencies involved clarified standard procedures and anticipated problems. Experts and researchers jointly decided to concentrate the analysis on the incident command post, where commanders from the fire department, the police, and the medical services coordinate the operation. However, to delimit this function it was also necessary to cover its interaction with the responding teams as well as with the agencies' rear command posts. To measure the effect of the operation, the analysis team decided to represent in the mission history the flow of casualties from the train, through the chain of medical attendance, all the way to the three participating hospitals.

The object models used in this operation mainly represented the type and location of the responding teams. Casualty models included information about the type of injury, treatment, and transportation. Instrumentation reused existing methods for capturing position data using the Global Positioning System, for collecting digital photographs and video, and for recording radio communication. Two problems needed special attention: (a) the monitoring of the casualty flow and (b) the tracking of people indoors and underground. Researchers solved the first problem by using the extras, acting as casualties, for observing their own treatment and transportation. The second problem remained unsolved. Instead of tracking all personnel, observers followed key actors.

During the exercise, which started at 10:00 a.m. and ended at 12:40 p.m., researchers recorded data from 10 communication channels and a large amount of contextual data. They produced the first version of the mission history to support an after-action review at 3:30 p.m. This version included position data, digital photographs, casualty data, and some audio messages. They prepared an extended version of the mission history for the in-depth analysis of the operation in February 2001 by conducting extended link analysis (Thorstensson et al., 2001) on four of the communication channels and providing text annotations to two more channels.

Analysis and Findings

Key personnel from the various agencies and researchers participated in the in-depth analysis. The purpose was partly to give feedback to participants but primarily to form a basis for future development of joint operations. We provide two examples of how exploration and context aided the use of communication analysis in this process.

The opening issue in the analysis was who first received information about the incident and how that person disseminated this information. The radio call from the train driver started at 10:00 a.m. and provided vague information about the train hitting something on the track and possibly derailing. Figure 5.3 shows the screen shot from MIND presenting the situation at 10:09, when the first fire unit was alerted. What caused the delay,

Figure 5.3. Communication timeline and context. The screen shot shows the situation 9 minutes after the incident, when the first fire unit received a call to the scene. At the top of the figure is a map view with an aerial photograph and symbols (boxes with numbers) representing vehicles (left) and a photo view showing police vehicles outside the subway station (right). At the bottom of the figure is a dynamic timeline that provides a graphic representation of communication sequences on multiple networks. This view prompted the question of why, 9 minutes after the incident, there were only police units on the scene.

and why are there police units on the scene? In fact, the timeline in Figure 5.3 shows that the police have been active since approximately 10:03. The first message on the police network revealed that Unit 9770 belonged to the subway branch of the police and therefore could monitor radio traffic on the subway network. They simply overheard the call from the train driver and decided to go to the scene immediately. The fire department received their call through an emergency dispatcher. However, the call from the traffic control center to the emergency dispatch center was delayed approximately 4 minutes while the traffic controller talked to the driver and dispatched traffic supervisors to the scene. This finding led to a modification of the emergency procedures of the traffic control center.

Another issue was the 67 minutes that elapsed before the first patient left the scene for the hospital. (The mission history showed that the first patient left the subway station at 11:07 a.m. and was loaded onto Ambulance B887, which left the incident area at 11:13 and arrived at the hospital at 11:25.) Was there a plausible explanation for the delay? To answer this question, researchers examined how the chain of medical attendance was organized. A critical strategic decision is whether to establish a *casualty collection point* (CCP) or to rush patients to hospitals with only minimum on-scene prioritization and stabilization. The senior medical commander is responsible for this decision, but he or she needs to consult the fire commander regarding a suitable location for a CCP. In either case, the police are responsible for registering the casualties. Table 5.2 summarizes the use of the mission history to explore this situation. In it, items are listed in the order they were consulted. Time points in the table refer to the mission time.

The first three items in Table 5.2 raised the initial question. Item 4 is a photograph that shows police officers establishing a CCP in the station's ticketing area. This picture, displayed in Figure 5.4, indicates that a decision regarding the CCP had been made at 10:14 a.m. Browsing police communication around 10:14 using the Communication Link View revealed Item 5, an audio link at 10:15 that suggests that an officer in Fire Unit 123 was involved in the decision. Eight minutes later, there is a message (Item 6) from the police commander that informs Police Team 1710 that the CCP will be deployed in tents outside the station. Is there a way to explain this discrepancy? Using the Communication Explorer, we can find information relevant to this question.

Figure 5.5 shows an annotated screen shot from the Communication Explorer applied to the police network. The hypothesis driving this exploration is that the confusion about the location of the CCP should be reflected in questions asked by teams of their supervisors. The example demonstrates how the Communication Explorer was used to identify questions from Unit 1710 to the police commander (10:50 a.m.). Repeating the procedure for all subordinate units that are failing only in the sender dimension (indicated by black color), one at a time, reveals all such questions. In Figure 5.5, the only subordinate unit meeting this criterion is Unit 9760. (Unit 70 is the police headquarters.) These steps produce Items 7 and 8. Item 9 results from applying the same technique on the next organizational level by selecting Unit 1050 as the sender and Unit 70 as the receiver. We find that the police commander passed the question from Unit 9760 (Item 8) on to the police headquarters. It is clear that the police commander, at the joint incident command post, and Unit 1710, in the ticketing area, had diverging views on the location and status of the CCP. At 10:30 a.m., this circumstance became apparent to both of them (see Item 7 in Table 5.2).

To understand how this situation occurred, we consult the mission history. Items 10 through 12 explain when the medical and fire–rescue teams arrived. In particular, Item 11 is consistent with Item 5. It is plausible that the first fire officer on the scene (from Unit 123) met the police officers from Unit 1710 in the ticketing area and decided to collect casualties there. The fire commander (102) assumed command at 10:16 a.m.—after this meeting—but should have been briefed about such an arrangement. Item 13 describes how the fire commander ordered Unit 435 to deploy tents in the street to accommodate the CCP. It offers an explanation for the message

TABLE 5.2
Exploration of the Ambiguous Casualty Collection Point

Item	Time (a.m.)	Medium	Source	Description
1	10:00	Audio	Traffic control network	Train driver reports incident to traffic control center.
2	11:07	Digital photo	Medical observer	Ambulance crew brings first patient out from the station.
3	11:13–11:25	Position track	GPS	Ambulance B887 takes the first patient to the hospital.
4	10:14	Digital photo	Police observer	Police officers prepare a CCP in the ticketing area.
5	10:15	Audio	Police network	Officer 1710 reports to the police commander (1050) that the fire officer initially in charge (123) has ordered the CCP to be in the ticketing area.
6	10:23	Audio	Police network	1050 informs 1710 that the CCP is going to be in tents in the street outside the station.
7	10:30	Audio	Police network	1710 requests from 1050 a clarification of the location of the CCP, because medical personnel are going to remain in the ticketing area.
8	10:10	Audio	Police network	One of the first police units on the scene (9760) asks 1050 where the CCP is located.
9	10:11	Audio	Police network	1050 asks police headquarters (70) if they know where the CCP is located.
10	10:10	Position track	GPS	Emergency medical team B880 and ambulance B881 arrive.
11	10:11	Digital photo	Fire observer	First fire units arrive. The officer of Unit 123 assumes command.
12	10:16	Digital photo	Fire observer	The ranking fire commander (102) arrives and assumes command.
13	10:23	Audio	Fire command network	102 orders Fire Unit 435 to deploy tents for the CCP in the street outside the station.
14	10:39	Audio	Fire tunnel network	Fire Unit 193 asks the fire commander (102) where the CCP is located.
15	10:49	Digital photo	Medical observer	Four ambulances idling outside the station with drivers.

Note. GPS = global positioning system; CCP = casualty collection point.

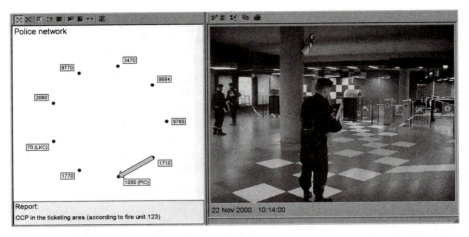

Figure 5.4. Context-driven communication analysis. The screen shot displays the situation at 10:16 a.m. The right view shows a photograph from the ticketing area, where police officers are establishing a casualty collection point. The left view is a communication link view that displays links from the police network. The selected link represents a report to the police commander informing him about the decision to set up a casualty collection point.

in Item 6, because both the fire commander and the police commander were at the joint incident command post. It seems reasonable that the police commander would inform the fire commander about the ambiguity of the CCP shortly after becoming aware of it (see Item 7). Nevertheless, an audio link from an alternate fire network (Item 12) shows that, at 10:39, some fire teams did not have a clear picture of where to bring casualties.

Although sometimes confusing and contradictory, Items 4 through 14 suggest that the operation was going to include a CCP; however, Item 15 indicates that the medical services did not share this view. It shows ambulances idling with drivers ready to pull up to the station entrance to load patients. Unfortunately, there was no evidence in the mission history about who made the decision to keep ambulance crews waiting in the street.

Summary

This example is representative of explorative analysis. A piece of data triggered a question. Another piece provided a clue and a time point. Browsing communication data around that time point revealed additional relevant data. Multiple sources made it possible to corroborate findings and construct a chain of evidence to support conclusions. The Communication Explorer provided structure and insight into large volumes of communication data.

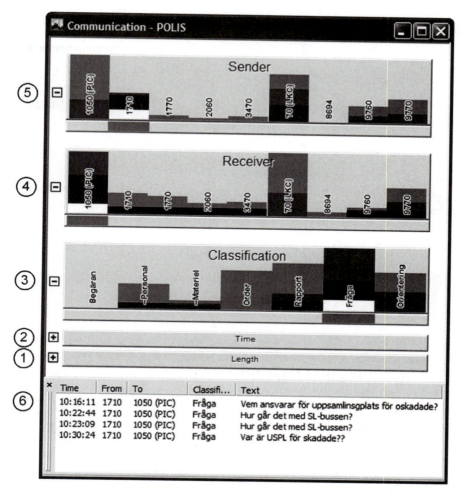

Figure 5.5. Exploring police communication using the Communication Explorer. If one selects all items in the Length (1) and Time (2) dimensions and closes those histograms, then selects the category Question (*Fråga*) in the Classification histogram (3), selects the Police Commander (1050) in the Receiver histogram (4), and selects the first team close to a full hit (1710) in the Sender dimension (5), then the resulting list (6) displays all questions sent from 1710 to 1050. Among those is a question concerning the casualty collection point, asked at 10:30:24 a.m.

Although the analysis could not identify a single plausible cause for the transportation delay, it certainly found problems that influenced the medical care, many of which pertained to the command and control of the operation. The mission history aided this investigation by presenting base facts to direct the search for clues and evidence. The MIND presentation tool facilitated exploration by supporting access and navigation in the mission history.

DISCUSSION

In any domain, successful distributed work requires adequate arrangements for coordination and collaboration between teams and team members. The complexity of distributed tactical operations makes the need for effective command and control especially pressing. In this chapter, we have concentrated on the role of communication in the command and control of multiple teams. Communication offers tangible traces of how key actors have perceived dynamic situations and what decisions they have made. Capturing and analyzing such traces can provide essential input both for systems design and for team training. On the basis of the assumption that exploration and context can greatly facilitate communication analysis, we have demonstrated how our methodology and tools support this task.

Technical and social artifacts shape human activities, which in turn affect the artifacts people create and use (Woods, 1998). Winograd and Flores (1986) viewed *breakdowns*—situations uncovering that something is amiss in the interaction between people and artifacts—as central for design. In our application, the delayed alert from the traffic control center to the emergency dispatch center is one example of a breakdown. Another example is the failure to establish an unambiguous CCP. Breakdowns and the anticipation of breakdowns provide incentives for design and redesign. In a distributed setting, with complex interactions among multiple individuals and teams, it is difficult to understand the nature of a breakdown and its ultimate ramifications. Exploring mission histories from representative operations is one way of identifying and analyzing actual and potential breakdowns. The modified checklist for emergency procedures in the traffic control center is one concrete result from such an analysis. Exploratory findings can also direct future research, for instance, by suggesting new field studies (Fransson & Axelsson, 2001), by providing guidelines for designing prototypes as hypotheses of future use (Albinsson & Fransson, 2002), or by raising issues for laboratory experiments (Albinsson & Zhai, 2003).

In training, reflection on performance is a crucial element for further development (Kolb, 1984; Norman, 1993). Reflection requires a conscious effort from the learner, and it takes time (Lederman, 1992). Accurate feedback on the actions taken is crucial for effective processing, which is typically a problem in dynamic and distributed environments, where the team members may not see the effects of their actions (Hoffman, Crandall, & Shadbolt, 1998). To overcome this problem, the mission history may serve as a cognition-aiding artifact that helps participants keep track of the parallel activities of multiple teams and form a big picture of the course of events. There is always a social dimension in this process. Issues concerning rank, status, and organization may restrict dialogue and impede learning. Exploring a mission history together allows participants from multiple agencies to reconcile their views of the operation, as a basis for improving performance. When the facts about the operation are publicly available, there is typically less confrontation and more focus on solutions. In our example, the fire commander acknowledged that the decision of where to establish the CCP was not clearly communicated. On the other hand, the briefing he received from the first fire officer on the scene did not mention a CCP in the ticketing area. One lesson learned was to improve the procedures for transferring command. In team training, this type of debriefing is commonly referred to as an *after-action review* (Jenvald & Morin, 2004; Morrison & Meliza, 1999).

The key idea in reconstruction and exploration is to construct a multimedia representation of a tactical operation from multiple sources of data and explore this representation in a multimedia presentation tool. Reconstruction is inspired by Woods's (1993) work on behavioral protocols. Exploration adds the dimension of interactive discovery, which makes the data collected available to a wider audience of stakeholders. Using multiple sources is advantageous from an epistemological point of view, as data from one source can corroborate findings based on data from another source. In addition, maintaining multiple levels of representations and keeping them readily accessible—for example, audio data and communication links—makes it possible to check original data to verify conclusions drawn from abstract representations. Moreover, it helps detect problems in the underlying data. Xiao and Vicente (2000) viewed the ability to maintain levels of representation and aggregation as central in their suggested framework for epistemological analysis in empirical studies.

Indeed, the analysis of audio communication is laborious. The explorative approach presented here does not eliminate the need to listen to the recorded audio, because to construct the abstract link representation the analyst still needs to extract the sender, receiver, and main contents from the recorded sequences. There is no need, however, to transcribe the messages. In more advanced communication systems, such as radios using selective calls, or in computerized communication systems, such as electronic mail, data collection and link extraction can be automated to a higher degree. In high-tech environments, means of systematic data collection and feedback can be integrated in the operational command and control systems. However, to leverage this potential the systems must provide standardized data formats and access methods.

We have described reconstruction and exploration as a means of capturing, presenting, and analyzing mission histories from tactical operations that involve numerous distributed teams. We have concentrated on the role of communication in the command and control of such operations and the corresponding need for communication analysis to understand the interplay between people and artifacts. To this end, our approach combines rich representations of context with explorative analysis tools. A key contribution in this respect is the support for reconciling multiple views of a complex, distributed operation to facilitate team training, systems design, and systems validation. We are convinced that these methods and tools are essential for creating the high-tech teams needed in today's safety-critical work environments.

REFERENCES

Albinsson, P.-A., & Fransson, J. (2002). Representing military units using nested convex hulls—Coping with complexity in command and control. In J. Jenvald & S. Palmgren (Eds.), *Proceedings of the 1st Swedish–American Workshop on Modeling and Simulation* (Tech. Rep. No. FOI-R—0597—SE, pp. 25–32). Linköping, Sweden: Swedish Defence Research Agency.

Albinsson, P.-A., & Morin, M. (2002). Visual exploration of communication in command and control. In D. Williams (Ed.), *Proceedings of the Sixth International Conference on Information Visualization* (pp. 141–146). Los Alamitos, CA: IEEE Computer Society.

Albinsson, P.-A., Morin, M., & Fransson, J. (2003). Finding information needs in military command and control systems using exploratory tools for communication analysis. In *Proceedings of the 47th Annual Meeting of the Human Factors and Ergonomics Society* (pp. 1918–1922). Santa Monica, CA: The Human Factors and Ergonomics Society.

Albinsson, P.-A., & Zhai, S. (2003). High precision touch screen interaction. In V. Bellotti, T. Erickson, G. Cockton, & P. Korhonen (Eds.), *Proceedings of the CHI 2003 Conference on Human Factors in Computing Systems* (pp. 105–112). New York: ACM Press.

Baldonado, M. Q., Woodruff, A., & Kuchinsky, A. (2000). Guidelines for using multiple views in information visualization. In S. Levialdi, V. Di Gesù, & L. Tarantino (Eds.), *Proceedings of ACM Advanced Visual Interfaces 2000* (pp. 110–119). New York: ACM Press.

Brehmer, B. (2000). Dynamic decision making in command and control. In C. McCann & R. Pigeau (Eds.), *The human in command: Exploring the modern military experience* (pp. 233–248). New York: Kluwer/Plenum.

Cooke, N. J. (1994). Varieties of knowledge elicitation techniques. *International Journal of Human–Computer Studies, 41*, 801–849.

Fisher, C., & Sanderson, P. (1996). Exploratory sequential data analysis: Exploring continuous observational data. *Interactions, 3*(2), 25–34.

Flin, R. (1996). *Sitting in the hot seat: Leaders and teams for critical incident management.* Chichester, England: Wiley.

Fransson, J., & Axelsson, M. (2001). Computer-supported usability evaluation in field settings based on visualization of user actions and mission history. In M. J. Smith & G. Salvendy (Eds.), *Systems, social and internalization design aspects of human–computer interaction* (Vol. 2, pp. 167–171). Mahwah, NJ: Erlbaum.

Hoffman, R. R., Crandall, B., & Shadbolt, N. (1998). Use of the critical decision method to elicit expert knowledge: A case study in the methodology of cognitive task analysis. *Human Factors, 40*, 254–276.

Jenvald, J., & Morin, M. (2004). Simulation-supported live training for emergency response in hazardous environments. *Simulation & Gaming, 35*, 363–377.

Keithly, D. M., & Ferris, S. P. (1999). *Auftragstaktik*, or directive control, in joint and combined operations. *Parameters, 29*, 118–133.

Kolb, D. A. (1984). *Experiential learning: Experience as a source of learning and development*. Englewood Cliffs, NJ: Prentice Hall.

Lederman, L. C. (1992). Debriefing: Toward a systematic assessment of theory and practice. *Simulation & Gaming, 23*, 145–160.

Morin, M. (2002). *Multimedia representations of distributed tactical operations*. Doctoral dissertation, Linköping University, Linköping, Sweden.

Morin, M., Jenvald, J., & Thorstensson, M. (2000). Computer-supported visualization of rescue operations. *Safety Science, 35*(1–3), 3–27.

Morrison, J. E., & Meliza, L. L. (1999). *Foundations of the after action review process* (Special Report No. 42). Alexandria, VA: U.S. Army Research Institute for the Behavioral and Social Sciences.

Norman, D. A. (1993). *Things that make us smart*. Reading, MA: Addison-Wesley.

North, C., & Shneiderman, B. (2000). Snap-together visualization: Can users construct and operate coordinated visualizations? *International Journal of Human–Computer Studies, 53*, 715–739.

Orfali, R., Harkey, D., & Edwards, J. (1996). *The essential distributed objects survival guide*. New York: Wiley.

Pigeau, R., & McCann, C. (2000). Redefining command and control. In C. McCann & R. Pigeau (Eds.), *The human in command: Exploring the modern military experience* (pp. 163–184). New York: Kluwer/Plenum.

Rasker, P. C., Post, W. M., & Schraagen, J. M. C. (2000). Effects of two types of intra-team feedback on developing a shared mental model in command & control teams. *Ergonomics, 43*, 1167–1189.

Rogalski, J., & Samurçay, R. (1993). Analysing communication in complex distributed decision-making. *Ergonomics, 36*, 1329–1343.

Shattuck, L. G., & Woods, D. D. (2000). Communication of intent in military command and control systems. In C. McCann & R. Pigeau (Eds.), *The human in command: Exploring the modern military experience* (pp. 279–291). New York: Kluwer/Plenum.

Shneiderman, B. (1998). *Designing the user interface: Strategies for effective human–computer interaction* (3rd ed.). Reading, MA: Addison-Wesley.

Spence, R. (2000). *Information visualization*. Harlow, England: Addison-Wesley.

Spence, R., & Tweedie, L. (1998). The Attribute Explorer: Information synthesis via exploration. *Interacting With Computers, 11*, 137–146.

Thorstensson, M., Axelsson, M., Morin, M., & Jenvald, J. (2001). Monitoring and analysis of command-post communication in rescue operations. *Safety Science, 39*(1–2), 51–60.

Winograd, T., & Flores, F. (1986). *Understanding computers and cognition: A new foundation for design*. Norwood, NJ: Ablex.

Woods, D. D. (1988). Coping with complexity: The psychology of human behavior in complex systems. In L. P. Goodstein, H. B. Andersen, & S. E. Olsen (Eds.), *Tasks, errors and mental models* (pp. 128–148). London: Taylor & Francis.

Woods, D. D. (1993). Process-tracing methods for the study of cognition outside of the experimental psychology laboratory. In G. A. Klein, J. Orasanu, R. Calderwood, & C. E. Zsambok (Eds.), *Decision making in action: Models and methods* (pp. 228–251). Norwood, NJ: Ablex.

Woods, D. D. (1998). Designs are hypotheses about how artifacts shape cognition and collaboration. *Ergonomics, 41*, 168–173.

Xiao, Y., & Vicente, K. J. (2000). A framework for epistemological analysis in empirical (laboratory and field) studies. *Human Factors, 42*, 87–101.

6

ENHANCING COMMAND AND CONTROL TEAMWORK IN OPERATION ENDURING FREEDOM

JANEL H. SCHERMERHORN AND RONALD A. MOORE

Military operations require the coordination, cooperation, and collaboration of numerous people and resources. Often, these people and resources are distributed across different locations and represent diverse specialties. Using these distributed, specialized assets to accomplish a mission is a major part of the command and control process. The following example illustrates a typical planning and coordination task faced by a military command and control team:

> The commander of a carrier battle group is ordered to destroy a portion of an enemy air base within a specified time period. His staff needs to determine the appropriate number and type of missiles and planes to use in the attack—routes, fuel, ammunition, weather, and security are just a few of the many factors to consider. This team of specialists must work together to complete the plan within hours.

We are grateful to Gerald Malecki of the Office of Naval Research and Jeffrey G. Morrison of the Space and Naval Warfare Systems Center, San Diego, for their continued support, encouragement, and contributions throughout this effort.

Once the operation is underway, the commander and his team need to maintain situation awareness and remain coordinated with each other to monitor the operation and make adjustments, as needed. Throughout the operation, new information and status need to be reported as soon as available.

Such complex tasks would be impossible without teamwork—and without advanced technology to support rapid information exchange among distributed team members. Yet few command and control systems fully support these requirements. Decision makers frequently report difficulty in maintaining situation awareness and in keeping their teams focused on tasks of high priority. The traditional solution is for the commander and his or her staff to meet for a briefing. This allows the team to gain a common understanding of current events and to learn about new tasks and priorities. This shared understanding, however, occurs only once or twice a day—and even then, the information is often several hours old because of the time required to prepare the brief. Command and control teams need a way to share current information quickly and continuously.

Sharing *relevant* and *usable* information is a key aspect of teamwork in command and control environments. In today's high-tech world, exchanging vast amounts of data and information can be accomplished easily. Sharing useful and usable *knowledge*,[1] however, is not so easily accomplished. Effective command-level decision making requires the understanding of all aspects of a problem and awareness of the implications of every decision made. Command-level support staff must share their information and knowledge with each other and their commander in a form that conveys full understanding of the current situation, discusses implications of relevant issues, and accurately predicts potential outcomes.

The Office of Naval Research sponsored a project known as "Command 21," which focused on improving information and knowledge exchange among command and control teams. New tools, technologies, and concepts of operations have been developed under this project. Specifically, a concept known as *Knowledge Web* (K-Web) was developed whereby users store and access operationally relevant knowledge-based information in real time via the World Wide Web.

It is this focus on operationally relevant, knowledge-based information that makes the K-Web concept different from ordinary Web sites. In a K-Web, information is gathered, fused, filtered, processed, and then translated and presented by experts in one area for use by nonexperts in other areas. In doing so, the experts try to impart the benefit of their knowledge

---

[1] We define *knowledge* as the internally possessed familiarity, awareness, understanding, and expertise one has that is gained through experience or study.

to others for use in a particular situation. For example, in support of a planned assault on an enemy ground position, a weather expert may gather, analyze, and process large amounts of complex meteorological data, such as barometric pressure, humidity, air temperature, and historical atmospheric data, and then present this information in such a way that it is easily understood and used by people who are not experts in weather. Instead of providing the raw meteorological data to nonexperts, the weather expert translates these data into useful, usable information for the reader. Further differentiating a K-Web from an ordinary Web site is that many diverse but operationally related topic areas are often presented in a single hyperlinked K-Web—usually in the larger context of a particular operation or mission. Thus, a K-Web is a highly specialized kind of Web site representing the knowledge and experience of many content authors (each an expert in one or more areas) that is constantly revised and updated with useful, usable, easily understood, and highly relevant information.

Using a human factors approach to system and interface design, the Pacific Science & Engineering Group and the Space and Naval Warfare Systems Center, both located in San Diego, California, developed a number of tools for command-level decision makers and their staffs to facilitate the input, maintenance, and access of K-Web information.

In this chapter, we present the K-Web design and concept of operations, along with initial user feedback from a war game environment. K-Web tools and business rules were then modified on the basis of this feedback and installed on the *USS Carl Vinson*, where K-Web ultimately played an important role in Operation Enduring Freedom (OEF). Although K-Web design was originally based on human factors and team process research, its rapid transition to an operational setting enabled us to learn additional lessons about supporting command and control teams.

KNOWLEDGE WEB DESIGN CONSIDERATIONS

In this section, we examine the different factors we considered in designing the K-Web system. Obviously, information requirements formed the framework for the design, but we also considered interdependency among team members, factors arising in distributed teams, and information exchange in support of decision making. We look at these in detail here.

Information Requirements

We adopted a user-centered design approach for the development of the K-Web. Therefore, we started by meeting with representative users to gain an understanding of what functions and capabilities the system should have. User-centered design can prevent technology underutilization, errors, and excessive development costs while promoting effective performance.

We conducted a cognitive task analysis (CTA) to determine the specific tools and features that military command center personnel require in performing their jobs (Smallman, Oonk, & Moore, 2000). The findings of this analysis were consistent with several recent studies and analyses conducted in other team- and command-level decision-making environments (Bolstad & Endsley, 1999; Klein et al., 1996; Miller & Klein, 1998; Moore & Averett, 1999; Proctor, St. John, Callan, & Holste, 1998). These analyses revealed consistent operational requirements for improved situation awareness and assessment; dynamic synchronous and asynchronous collaboration; and adaptive, real time resource and action management and planning support. Furthermore, we identified a core set of functional requirements for command-level decision making. These requirements included the following:

- shared situation awareness among the team,
- continuously available mission-relevant status information,
- intuitive graphical interface for ease of use,
- consistent formatting across all Web pages,
- tactical focus for displayed information,
- available mission goals and commander's intent,
- distributed communication/collaboration support,
- flexible configuration for individual users and situations,
- ability to "drill down" for more detailed information,
- access to the age and reliability of displayed information, and
- tactical overlays to filter information.

These functional requirements were used as a starting point in the design of information and knowledge product development tools. K-Web concept and tool development was also guided by relevant research in decision support, human–computer interfaces, and team processes.

K-WEB DESIGN AND DEVELOPMENT

Each of the tools that support the creation, maintenance, and use of a K-Web was developed using an iterative design process. Basic design requirements were identified on the basis of a literature review, user input, and prior research. Subject matter experts and fleet representatives reviewed initial design concepts to determine how well they met operational needs. As necessary, designs were revised and reevaluated. By including subject matter experts throughout the design process, user requirements remained the foundation for prototype development. Three basic requirements were used to guide the development and use of the K-Web tool suite:

1. *Products must feature a basic HTML/Web-based format.* Basic HTML is used for knowledge-based products that populate K-Web. This allows products to be created and disseminated using widely accepted standards, as well as accessed with widely used Internet browsers. Furthermore, because the standard point-and-click, drag-and-drop interface associated with basic HTML is becoming widely understood, the amount of training is dramatically reduced.

2. *Tools must provide a simple, easy-to-use interface.* Tools used to create and view content within the K-Web must feature an easily learned and used interface that facilitates rapid production, dissemination, and access of information- and knowledge-based products. Therefore, point-and-click and drag-and-drop functionality is used wherever possible, while unnecessary features and functions are suppressed or removed.

3. *Information products must be easily viewed.* Many information products developed using the K-Web tool suite are viewed in suboptimum conditions (e.g., from a distance or in poor lighting). To enhance viewing, high-contrast colors (dark text on white background) and large fonts are used when possible.

In the following sections, we describe some K-Web tools that were developed to meet user requirements.

SumMaker

One requirement identified during the CTA was the need for tools to support improved situation awareness. One way to improve situation awareness among decision makers is to make mission-relevant information available easily, rapidly, and in the appropriate context. *SumMaker* (Moore & Averett, 2000b) was designed to create Web pages that provide standardized summary information for inclusion in K-Web. The published product of SumMaker—a basic HTML Summary Page—is used by information consumers to acquire and maintain situation awareness.

Information producers with no experience publishing HTML can quickly and easily create mission- or situation-relevant Web content using the SumMaker template (see Figure 6.1). Once published, Summary Pages convey concise status information to the information consumers. The high-level summary is complemented by hyperlinks to more detailed information available within K-Web (see Figure 6.2).

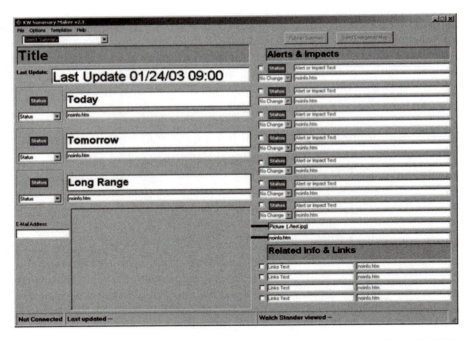

Figure 6.1. Blank SumMaker template for quick and easy production of HTML Summary Pages.

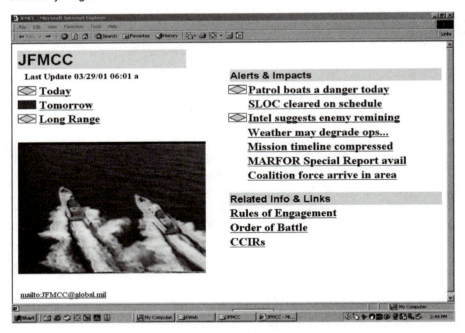

Figure 6.2. Published Summary Page created with SumMaker software. Summary Pages serve as high-level views of underlying K-Web content.

Figure 6.3. TacGraph allows for quick and easy production of cartoon-like maps and images. Each of the standard military symbols links to more detailed information.

TacGraph

Map-based, highly graphical views of tactical data were one of the highest priority information requirements identified in the CTA. *TacGraph* (Bank & Moore, 2000) was designed as an easy-to-use graphical drawing tool for military personnel. Featuring standard military symbols (Military Standard 2525B, U.S. Department of Defense, 1996), TacGraph is used to rapidly summarize tactically relevant images and Web content. TacGraph features imbedded National Imagery and Mapping Agency map data and a number of specialized drawing tools. It produces Web-standard HTML and graphics files. A finished TacGraph product is shown in Figure 6.3. Each of the symbols on the map is an interactive link to information available in the K-Web.

Other K-Web Content

The CTA also yielded the requirement for being able to "drill down" to more detailed information. One of the best features of K-Web is the ability of the producers to use existing information or knowledge products by linking them to SumMaker. The idea is to pull together mission-relevant information that is already being produced (e.g., PowerPoint slides, maps, reports, news clips, etc.) and link it to a Summary Page. The Summary Page provides a processed quick view of the underlying content and an access point to that underlying content.

K-Web Viewer

Other design requirements included access to multiple views of tactical data, mission summaries, alerts/advisories/recommendations, plans and courses of action (COAs), asset/resource management, and collaboration tools. The *K-Web Viewer* (Moore & Averett, 2000a) is a multiscreen Web browser and multiwindow controller that supports navigation and display of information residing in K-Web. The software was designed to run on single- or multidisplay computer systems and affords the display of Web or non-Web content.

K-Web Viewer software is currently in use on very large, wall-sized displays (*Knowledge Walls*) at several locations as well as on smaller, multimonitor desk units (*Knowledge Desks*). A prototype single-user Knowledge Desk running version 2.1.1 of the K-Web Viewer software is shown in Figure 6.4.

Figure 6.4. The Knowledge Desk helps the information consumer to simultaneously browse multiple K-Web content links while also using other systems.

Initial Use of K-Web

The 2000 and 2001 Global War Games, held at the Naval War College in Newport, Rhode Island, afforded invaluable opportunities to observe the prototype K-Web undergoing extensive usage in an operationally realistic setting by the experienced Navy users for whom it was designed.

The staff members of Commander, Carrier Group Three (CCG3) were among the first to use K-Web during the Global 2000 War Game. For them, K-Web provided a means of visualizing mission status for functional areas continuously, eliminating the need for a traditional 8-hour briefing cycle (Oonk, Smallman, & Moore, 2001). Because of its value and ease of use during that exercise, CCG3 requested that K-Web be installed onboard the USS Carl Vinson for use while deployed to the Middle East.

Analyses of K-Web usage at the Global 2000 War Games (Oonk et al., 2001) and continuing feedback from fleet users led to several changes to K-Web tools and business rules.

- Cognitive tools were developed to support attention management and change detection, including tools facilitating navigation to changed pages in the K-Web.
- Tools and improved business processes were developed to support multitiered collaboration, including feedback and guidance for information providers on content access of their pages.
- Display layouts were redesigned to improve text legibility.
- Information integration across functional areas was enabled using graphics.
- Information age and source was added to the Summary Pages.

K-WEB IN OPERATION ENDURING FREEDOM

K-Web prototype tools were installed onboard the USS Carl Vinson in May 2001 for use during their deployment. Commander, Carrier Group Three and Commander, Destroyer Squadron Nine (DESRON9) were both embarked onboard the USS Carl Vinson and used K-Web during their deployment. The USS Carl Vinson battle group arrived in the North Arabian Gulf on September 11, 2001—subsequently, CCG3 became the Composite Warfare Commander (CWC) for military activities associated with OEF. Commander, Carrier Group Three and its staff adopted an enhanced organizational structure for command and control, which was directly supported by K-Web. This combination of enhanced organizational structure and information technology provided CCG3 unique capabilities with regard to the CWC role. Having K-Web onboard allowed the battle group to innovate and explore new ways to use Web-enabled command and control.

Data Collection on K-Web Use

We were able to assess how the K-Web concept and technologies supported users' requirements during OEF using automated collection of performance data as well as postdeployment interviews and surveys.[2] Although both CCG3 and DESRON9 used the K-Web onboard the USS Carl Vinson, they had somewhat different requirements. Each group used K-Web for information dissemination, but their target audiences differed significantly. The staff of CCG3 created information primarily for their own use and for use by other large ships and commands with high bandwidth; in contrast, DESRON9 staff typically created information products for use by smaller ships with lower bandwidth. This enabled us to capture different perspectives and uses of K-Web during the deployment.

K-Web software applications automatically captured and stored several types of quantitative data, resulting in a historical record of Summary Page publication rates, use of specific software features, and structure and content of top-layer Web pages. These data were collected from each of eight functional areas: (a) Air Defense; (b) Command, Control and Communications; (c) CWC; (d) Force Protect; (e) Maritime Operations; (f) Meteorology and Oceanography (MetOc); (g) Rules of Engagement–Judge Advocate General; and (h) Schedules.[3]

No data contained personal identifying information, and automated data collection was conducted with the informed consent of the K-Web users. Users actually *encouraged* automatic data collection because these same data could be used as backup.[4]

Upon returning from deployment, 19 K-Web users were interviewed, mostly individually. All were both producers and consumers of K-Web content, representing seven functional areas: (a) CWC, (b) Intelligence, (c) Rules of Engagement–Judge Advocate General, (d) Logistics, (e) Maritime Operations, MetOc, and (f) Tomahawk Land Attack Missile. Interview questions centered on the use and utility of the K-Web tools, products, business rules, and training materials. Interview data from the CCG3 staff were analyzed separately from the DESRON9 staff data so we could examine differences between the groups.

Additional qualitative data were collected from users in the commands by means of an anonymous online survey addressing the same topics as in the interviews. The online survey enabled individuals who could not be

---

[2] For a complete report on the usage assessment of K-Web onboard the USS Carl Vinson during OEF, see Schermerhorn, Oonk, and Moore (2003).

[3] This list represents only the functional areas for which we were able to access the data, postdeployment.

[4] Several users reported using these saved data to restore lost or corrupted Summary Page information during their deployment.

interviewed, because of time or availability constraints, to provide their feedback.

K-Web Structure

K-Web was organized by functional areas corresponding to the team structure adopted by the CCG3 staff, with the most commonly used areas represented on the top-level overview page of the K-Web. Top-level Summary Pages for all functional areas followed a standard format, each containing three status titles and indicators, one or more alert headlines, and additional links as appropriate (see the sample Summary Page in Figure 6.2). The structure and depth of links below this top layer, however, varied across areas. For example, one area that had a lot of content created entire "sub-webs" of information focusing on specific issues that linked to their top-level Summary Page. This area produced content using software such as SumMaker, Microsoft Word, FrontPage, and manually coded HTML. Another area, primarily supported by DESRON9, had a more elaborate content structure beneath the Summary Page. Because they had multiple functional areas of their own, their Summary Page remained mostly unchanged, serving as a table of contents to the information beneath, which was updated often—sometimes hundreds of times a day.

Business Practices for Sharing Information

Although business rules based on user requirements were suggested by K-Web developers during training, each command adapted rules for use that best served the needs of the task and mission at hand.

Most CCG3 users participated in K-Web training either during the Global 2000 War Games or onboard ship during K-Web installation. Supplementary training documents were also provided for K-Web business rules, SumMaker, TacGraph, and K-Web Viewer (Pacific Science & Engineering Group, 2000a, 2000b, 2000c, 2001). Users reported that learning to use K-Web was quick and easy. Training new users took between 5 and 30 minutes.

Primarily on the basis of their experiences during training, CCG3 K-Web users adopted business rules that they used throughout their deployment. Examples of their business rules include use of a diamond on a Summary Page to indicate new information and use of status colors (green, yellow, red) to indicate the impact of the information on the mission plan. Business rules were consistently applied to top-level Summary Pages. One functional area, however, used diamonds and colors differently on lower level pages. For example, colors corresponded with preset thresholds of supply availability (these indicators were intended for within-area use only). Another common business rule was that K-Web was to be updated continuously and used as a briefing tool, in lieu of the previously standard PowerPoint presentations.

One business rule that was adapted for use by CCG3 staff was the use of temporal-status categories. Originally, these indicators represented epochs (i.e., today, tomorrow, and long range) across functional areas so that the commander could gain situation awareness chronologically. Chronological organization, however, was found to be inappropriate for some areas, so those areas adopted custom categories.

Unlike CCG3 users, most DESRON9 users did not receive training from K-Web developers and were not aware of training materials available online. This resulted in many users not knowing what the diamonds and colors meant. Because most users produced and updated information products only within lower level links and did not work directly with SumMaker, they tended to ignore colors and diamonds if they did not understand them. Over time, business rules did develop in this group, which led to most people using and understanding alerts in the same manner as CCG3 staff.

When asked what training and business rules improvements would either make K-Web easier to use or enhance its functionality, DESRON9 users responded unanimously that training would be the single most important improvement. Having not been trained, users learned through observing others and trial and error. Once they were "up to speed" on how to use K-Web, its value was recognized. Training could have alleviated many problems during their initial use of the tools. Furthermore, DESRON9 users recommended that help functionality be embedded within the software tools.

CCG3 users reported that they needed few improvements to training and business rules. In general, they felt that the business rules they adopted were adequate. It may be that new CCG3 users were so easily trained because they learned within an established K-Web environment (Goldstein, 1993).

On the basis of these different perspectives, we conclude that properly training the command and establishing consistent business rules prior to K-Web installation is most desirable, economical, and effective. Once the majority of people are comfortable with using the basic K-Web concept and tools, newcomers and veterans may further benefit from online assistance (Kozlowski & Salas, 1997).

K-WEB USE AND ACCESS

K-Web content was initially intended as an internal knowledge management tool for the staff and crew onboard the USS Carl Vinson. Although the majority of data transfer did take place onboard ship, others throughout the battle group, and at other commands, such as Commander, Pacific Fleet,

Central Command, and the Pentagon were also accessing the *USS Carl Vinson* K-Web to get updated information on operations in the North Arabian Gulf.[5] The data collected automatically by the K-Web server show that from September 29, 2001, to December 29, 2001, K-Web was accessed by an average of 482 visitors per day, with a range of 340 to 676 daily visitors.[6] All survey respondents indicated that they used K-Web 7 days a week during deployment, with use ranging from 1 hour to 14 hours per day. *Use* in this discussion is characterized as anything from the actual creation of a Summary Page, to the monitoring of K-Web while on watch, to the access of K-Web information.

Information Producer Perspectives

Information producers used SumMaker software to create and update Summary Pages. All CCG3 users stated that despite lacking Web publishing experience, they found SumMaker easy to learn and use. However, users from almost every functional area expressed the need for more flexibility in the SumMaker with regard to the number of characters and fields allotted per section of the template. One user described the potential value of several different SumMaker templates, each with a different focus: graphic, statistical, or text. Because of limited access, most DESRON9 users updated products linked to SumMaker but did not use SumMaker itself.

Color and Diamond Use

Summary Pages included colored status indicators (see Figure 6.5) to indicate the information's severity of impact on the mission plan (with red indicating most severe, yellow indicating less severe, and green indicating little or no impact; in Figures 6.5 and 6.6 gray represents green, white represents yellow, and black represents red). An analysis of automated

---

[5] Other commands that accessed, viewed, or provided links to K-Web (based on unique domain names and Internet provider [IP] addresses accessing K-Web) included the following: *Carl Vinson* Battle Group (BG), 5th Fleet, 7th Fleet, various meteorological and oceanographic (METOC) commands, Central Command (CENTCOM), Collaboration at Sea systems, Commander Pacific Fleet (COMPACFLT), *Peleliu* Amphibious Readiness Group (ARG), *Theodore Roosevelt* BG, Special Operations Command (SOCOM), Naval Forces Central Command (NAVCENT), *USS Blue Ridge*, various Pentagon offices and users, multiservice, *Enterprise* BG, *Essex* ARG, Defense Intelligence Agency (DIA), Commander Pacific Command (PACOM), II Marine Expeditionary Force (MEF), 15 Marine Expeditionary Unit (MEU), and various Air Force commands. Numerous commands are listed by the IP address only.

[6] A single IP address as recorded by the K-Web server might represent an individual person or a router or firewall behind which many individuals might be hidden. Therefore, it is possible that the actual number of persons visiting K-Web is significantly higher. Determining the number of actual visitors per day is extremely difficult and is based on an elaborate formula taking into account unique IP addresses, domains, and discernibly separate visits or sessions. Because of a number of technical considerations, these numbers may not be entirely accurate. They are, however, a reasonable estimate of the number of K-Web visitors.

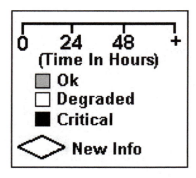

Figure 6.5. Legend for status indicators (colors) and changed information alerts (diamond shape).

SumMaker data shows that most (82%) published status indicators were green (see Figure 6.6). Prominent use of green reflects users' adherence to business rules: They used colors to reflect the impact of information on the mission plan rather than the severity of the situation. Status changes were infrequent.

New or changed information was indicated by diamonds (as seen in Figure 6.2) on a Summary Page (squares indicated no recent change). Across functional areas, a Summary Page displayed an average of 1.47 diamonds. Figure 6.7 illustrates differences in frequency of diamond use between functional areas. Most producers relied on colors and diamonds to alert consumers of new or important information. When information was particularly urgent, they would use the colors and diamonds in addition to other communication methods, such as Microsoft Chat.

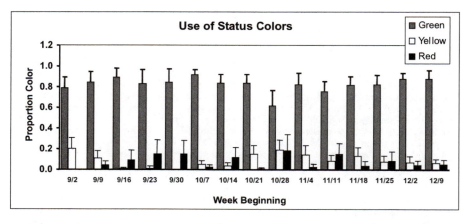

Figure 6.6. The use of status colors on Summary Pages over 15 weeks for eight functional areas.

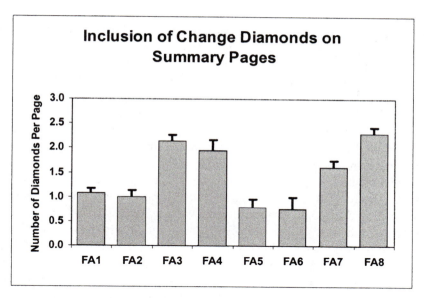

Figure 6.7. The use of diamonds on Summary Pages.

Linking and Cross-Linking

Summary Pages contained an average of 13.61 links to other K-Web content. The most commonly used formats of linked content across all areas were HTML pages, various graphics files, and PowerPoint presentations. HTML pages were created using many different tools, including Microsoft FrontPage, Word, or PowerPoint, and manual HTML coding. The ability to link existing information products is a key capability of K-Web. Once a network of links was established, producers easily updated information in K-Web by updating the linked document rather than by changing the Summary Page.

In addition to being able to link their own information products, several users found cross-linking to pages or to content in other functional areas valuable. One significant problem presented by cross-linking, however, was that there was no easy way for a producer to detect changes in others' cross-linked products. Another problem with cross-linking occurred when the author of the cross-linked content moved or renamed content files, resulting in broken links. Despite these problems, all SumMaker users who responded to the survey rated the practice of cross-linking as either "usually" or "always" helpful when creating K-Web content.

Update Rates

On average, each area published 1.58 Summary Pages a day, although this rate varied considerably over time and across functional areas. It is difficult to interpret this finding, because the underlying content of these Summary Pages was updated far more frequently—sometimes as often as every few minutes. Therefore, K-Web as a whole was extremely dynamic in nature despite the relatively low rate of change to the top-level Summary Pages.

Updating was driven by many factors, including the rate of incoming or changing information, consumers' needs and feedback, and mission requirements. For example, several users reported update rates were influenced by feedback from consumers in distributed locations.

Several users expressed concern regarding the time required to keep K-Web current. Time spent updating pages ranged from 1 hour to several hours a day. Although maintaining K-Web was time consuming from a producer standpoint, all survey respondents and interviewees agreed that posting information to K-Web was less time consuming than previous methods used to update the commander and other personnel. Furthermore, because updating K-Web was more time efficient than creating PowerPoint presentations, users considered K-Web content to be a near real time operational situation awareness tool.

Feedback About Content

When asked what drove the development of specific page content, most users responded that feedback from consumers was a primary consideration. Some information producers reported a significant drop in the number of questions about specific topics once those topics had been addressed in their Web site. Feedback also provided important operational context that enabled producers to frame their contributions, particularly for consumers outside of their functional areas.

Feedback About Access

Users were not concerned to know who had seen their pages. They assumed that the right people had seen it.

Information Consumer Perspectives

Information consumers indicated that the standardized format was useful for quickly and easily locating the mission-related information they needed within K-Web. Furthermore, Summary Page structure and space limitations forced information producers to publish only relevant and needed content. Survey respondents reported that information was usually presented in the format and level of detail that met their needs without further clarification. Also, the pace at which information was updated in K-Web made it a one-stop resource for operational information.

Color and Diamond Use

Users from CCG3 reported that status indicator colors and shapes were helpful for identifying important or changed information. They agreed that keeping track of new information in K-Web was usually easy. Unlike CCG3 users, many DESRON9 users did not find the colors and diamonds useful during the first half of deployment because they were not aware of what they meant. Even after establishing a business rule for their use, they tended to rely more on established methods of alerting, such as telephone, computer-based chat interface (e.g., MS Chat), or face-to-face discussions. Both groups expressed the need for a timestamp associated with colors and diamonds to more easily determine precise information age.

Usefulness of Content

Information consumers considered K-Web a valuable resource. They used it regularly as a resource for the information they needed to do their jobs. Not all information in K-Web was considered useful, though; some users indicated that because it was so easy for information producers to put information into K-Web, they sometimes found irrelevant or incomplete content there.

IMPACTS ON TEAMWORK AND INFORMATION EXCHANGE

PowerPoint is traditionally used to brief senior commanders and their staff one or more times a day. Often, staff and support personnel use a variety of real time and non-real-time resources to prepare the PowerPoint presentations several hours before the commanders are briefed, making the content outdated. Because K-Web is updated continuously as events occur, it features near real time information. During postdeployment interviews, users described how K-Web was used to update senior commanders instead of using lengthy PowerPoint presentations. Because K-Web was continuously updated, commanders had access to current information at all times. As a result, they came to briefing sessions already aware of critical issues, the latest intelligence, and current and unfolding events. This allowed the entire focus of daily meetings to shift from traditional updates and presentations to problem-solving and planning sessions. Interview and survey respondents also agreed that K-Web was useful as a complement to other tactical tools. Using K-Web in this manner, to support problem-solving and planning activities, was consistent with what was observed during CCG3 participation in the Global 2000 War Game.

Although easy access to information was in many ways beneficial, it did not come without consequences. There were concerns regarding who might be looking into K-Web content and how the information might be used. For some users, this influenced decisions on what should have been included in (or excluded from) K-Web. There were no established business rules that addressed this issue; therefore, each producer decided on his or her own what should be included.

One issue that came up repeatedly among interviewees was K-Web access by off-ship users; specifically, smaller ships had a difficult time viewing K-Web content because of their bandwidth limitations. Some users resorted to requesting that information that could not easily be seen in K-Web be shared via electronic mail. This led to the suggestion by some users that there be text-only versions of K-Web available to users with limited bandwidth. Many K-Web producers became aware of this problem during the deployment and began modifying their products to be more bandwidth friendly, by either decreasing the file size of linked files, creating simpler Web pages, or hiding larger attachments behind warnings that long download times would result from clicking on certain links.

Despite bandwidth and connectivity issues, several off-ship groups relied heavily (sometimes exclusively) on the USS Carl Vinson K-Web for mission-related information, which led to problems when the Vinson left the operational area to return home. The issue of passing K-Web and the responsibility for its maintenance off to another ship had not been addressed prior to deployment because the tool was originally intended for internal test and evaluation use only. Many ships and shore facilities that had come to rely on the USS Carl Vinson K-Web as a one-stop shop for OEF-related information were suddenly left without access to this information. Issues related to the use of K-Web as a multiship–multibattle group information space are complicated. There are many potential solutions to address these issues, such as creating K-Webs associated with specific areas of the world or operations instead of tying them to specific battle groups. These solutions, however, have implications as complex as the issues they address. For example, on the one hand, who would be responsible for maintaining a K-Web that didn't belong to a specific entity? On the other hand, having each battle group maintain its own K-Web would likely result in redundant work.

When asked whether it was difficult to integrate K-Web into their organization and business processes, CCG3 staff thought it was an easy, natural transition. Many attributed this to strong direction and support from the admiral regarding the K-Web's purpose and use. DESRON9 staff, however, had a somewhat more difficult time integrating the K-Web concept and tools. Although they also cited support from above as a factor critical to the successful transition of K-Web, the lack of adequate training, as well as some technical problems unrelated to K-Web, made it more challenging to adopt.

Users from both the producer and the consumer groups recognized the great value added by using Knowledge Desks (six-screen workstations). These multiscreen display systems helped them simultaneously monitor multiple K-Web pages, participate in multiple chat rooms, interact with the tactical information systems, and use various other applications.

Like the Knowledge Desks, the large, shared displays onboard the USS Carl Vinson also proved extremely useful—but for different reasons. These large, shared displays served as loci for discussion, collaboration, and problem-solving activities. In the past, large displays served simply as surfaces on which to host noninteractive presentations (e.g., speaker to audience). However, users reported that the combination of an interactive K-Web and the large, touch-sensitive display surface helped them "get into the problem space." Instead of playing the role of passive audience, they could become active participants.

COMPARING THE WAR GAME TO THE WAR

The findings from this real-world evaluation can be compared with those from a previous evaluation of K-Web in the more artificial war game environment of Global 2001 (Oonk, Rogers, Moore, & Morrison, 2002). The convergence of findings strengthens the conclusions from the two evaluations, whereas contrasting results highlight the importance of examining concepts and tools in multiple settings. A brief discussion of the most prominent similarities and contrasting results that emerged from the two evaluations follows.

Similarities

Training

Results of the current evaluation stress the importance of integrated training prior to any implementation of the K-Web concepts and tools. Similarly, one of the most significant findings that emerged from the Global 2001 K-Web evaluation was the importance of training. Because of a number of factors, the K-Web training conducted at Global 2001 was limited and sporadic (relative to the training provided for the Global 2000 War Game and for CCG3 users aboard the USS Carl Vinson), resulting in K-Web being updated less frequently and being populated with less content and consequently not being used significantly as a briefing tool. Although many factors varied across the two exercises, the most notable cause of these observed differences was the amount of training received.

Business Rules

The results of the current evaluation also stress the need for establishing business rules related to tool use and intended audience prior to implementation. Similarly, the need for mechanisms for improved dissemination of K-Web business rules to support optimal use of K-Web by information producers and consumers emerged from Global 2001, where observations and user comments frequently pointed to a lack of consistency and understanding of the K-Web concept and business rules.

Need for Flexible Tools

The evaluation onboard the USS Carl Vinson highlighted that different functional areas have different content organization needs, implying the need for more flexibility in the templates. Comments and observations at Global 2001 also suggested a need for tools that are flexible and customizable to meet the needs of different users.

Differences

Update Rates

The way in which K-Web products were updated was different across the two environments. During Global 2001, information producers updated their Summary Pages relatively frequently (on average, 2.2 times/hour), whereas the current evaluation indicated a lower update rate (on average, 1.58 Summary Pages/day). However, the information producers onboard the USS Carl Vinson updated the links underlying the Summary Pages much more often, up to hundreds of times per day. This difference may imply that, when learning to use K-Web, producers concentrate on updating the content of the high-level summaries. Once the high-level structure is established, producers spend more time fine tuning the underlying content. Note, however, that game time at the global war game was much faster than real time (i.e., events were occurring faster than they normally would), causing information to be updated at a higher rate.

Need for Feedback About Use

Another difference was in the expressed need for feedback from information consumers. Producers at Global 2000 and Global 2001 repeatedly stressed the need to know who was using their information products, as well as how they were being used. Conversely, USS Carl Vinson producers indicated that they did not need to know who had looked at the products they created, and they assumed that the appropriate people had seen it. Again, this need might be related to the limited experience game players had with the K-Web concept and tools. Explicit awareness of consumers' needs and activities was perhaps no longer necessary once K-Web usage and associated informal feedback mechanisms were established.

CONCLUSIONS

The use of K-Web and its related tools and business rules aboard the *USS Carl Vinson* provided a unique opportunity to observe the impact of new, network-centric tools on team performance in an information sharing environment. Many valuable lessons were learned from this experience, and these same lessons are serving as a foundation for the next round of technology development efforts.

K-Web as a New Concept of Operations

The use of K-Web onboard the *USS Carl Vinson* during OEF provided an invaluable opportunity to assess a new way for the military to conduct business: via Web-centric command and control.

Shared Information

K-Web proved to be a valuable tool for the production, dissemination, and access of information during OEF. The staff of CCG3 reported substantial increases in relevant and effective communications among their own teams as well as between teams from different battle group units. This led to dramatic improvements in shared knowledge and, ultimately, to a faster speed of command.

The results of this assessment show that the presence of K-Web onboard the *USS Carl Vinson* changed the way in which individuals and teams interacted. Instead of one-way exchanges, interactions became more participatory and collaborative in nature. The emphasis shifted from passing the information to acting on it. To a large degree, these outcomes resulted from the use of a Web-based information system that enabled many people to simultaneously produce and view a common set of relevant information. Consequently, they were all sharing and acting on a common operational picture.

This leads us to make a strong recommendation for the implementation of a system that can be easily and continuously updated. Although it is also tempting to conclude that greater user access is beneficial, there are consequences that must be considered. Currently, some of the challenges for future iterations of K-Web include access permissions. Although all consumers and producers may need access to some part of K-Web, it may not be appropriate for them to have access to all K-Web content. Beyond what is appropriate, not every user needs access to all K-Web content, and some users may want only a limited view, for example, of content that pertains to a specific subset of tasks and decisions. Because of the inherent nature of a web structure, implementing a limited view or permissions at any node in the information network is a complicated problem.

Multi-Echelon Information Exchange

Originally, K-Web was installed aboard the *USS Carl Vinson* as an in-house information tool. As such, the primary intended consumers were the senior decision makers aboard the ship. However, K-Web's audience eventually expanded to include other battle group units and shore-based command centers. At that point, it became difficult for K-Web information producers to determine the appropriate type of information and level of detail that was desired. As a result, it was not uncommon to see not only extremely specific content on some pages but also high-level situation summaries and command-level information on others. In spite of these problems, K-Web information producers reported that their products were driven by continuous feedback from the consumers. In effect, the information products offered in K-Web, although they varied greatly in content and level of detail, were what their respective consumer audiences wanted to see.

The *USS Carl Vinson* K-Web became a central source of information for participants in OEF. As such, K-Web provided a wealth of information—some of which comprised very large files, such as satellite imagery, resource spreadsheets, battle damage assessment and strike videos, and mission planning summaries. Although CCG3 users considered these products to be useful and necessary, the large file sizes presented problems for some users with more limited bandwidth.

Business Rules and Organizational Support

In the face of the challenge of producing knowledge-based information products for a continuously growing audience, initial K-Web business rules helped structure and normalize team communications in terms of regularity, format, level of detail, and content. This was cited as a strong, positive influence on team communications. K-Web usage logs indicate that the business rules were followed and that users found these business rules useful.

An important benefit of K-Web was the ease of updating it, which was usually as simple as editing an existing linked document (e.g., a Word file) or linking a new document through SumMaker. K-Web logs show that users updated their top-level Summary Pages, on average, several times a day, but users reported that they updated the underlying content far more often, sometimes every few minutes. Although keeping information in K-Web updated was time consuming, users unanimously reported that the end product—a near real time information source for mission-relevant information—was worthwhile. Furthermore, users thought that creating and maintaining a K-Web was preferable to their previous business practices.

Because K-Web represented a fundamental shift in how information was produced, disseminated, and used within the battle group, senior leadership support was critical to its successful adoption. Most users admitted that they would likely not have adopted K-Web as a means of sharing information had their senior commanders not mandated it.

Support from senior leadership, however, was not in itself enough to successfully integrate K-Web; user training was essential. Users who received training on K-Web tools and business rules found it easy to use and adopt; however, those who did not receive this training found it more challenging.

These conclusions about leadership support and the need for training are certainly not groundbreaking but rather serve as a reminder of how to maximize the potential for success when planning an organizational intervention, especially of this magnitude.

Information Organization and Structure

Organizing K-Web content and teams around specific missions or tasks, rather than by traditional departments, proved to be quite valuable. This enabled teams to update their K-Web Summary Pages as frequently, and with as much detail, as needed to communicate current issues and status. K-Web also allowed different functional areas to adapt the content and format to meet their unique needs.

Enhancing Teamwork

The experience with K-Web during OEF and the global war games underlines the significance of user-centered design for decision support and information technology. K-Web was developed to meet the needs articulated by potential users; as a result, it was very well accepted and was found to be useful under demanding operational conditions.

Similarly, the way that K-Web was used provides valuable lessons about what teams need from information technology to be most effective. Information technologies that are intended to enhance teamwork need to provide capabilities for promoting shared situation awareness, adapting to team configurations and tasks, facilitating team interaction, and supporting information needs of other (external) teams.

To establish a foundation for effective teamwork, each member needs to share a consistent understanding of the current situation. Access to a common information space enabled the *USS Carl Vinson* staff to see the same information as soon as it was available. In addition, teamwork was enhanced by common procedures and definitions and by well-understood, standardized formats for information exchange; that is, they had a common understanding of not only the information content but also the communication procedures and format. Also, techniques that prioritized information (status alerts), called attention to changes (diamonds), and built relationships between information from different sources (cross-linking) were especially important for maintaining shared situation awareness in a dynamic information environment.

Adapting to Team Configuration and Tasks

Effective teams have specific and well-defined roles for their members, yet many teams operate in complex, dynamic environments where they must quickly reconfigure themselves and draw on external resources to address new challenges. Under such conditions, information technology must be as flexible and agile as the teams themselves. Systems need to be easily reconfigured to support collaboration among different team members, some of whom may be working from other locations. Beyond team composition, the reporting formats themselves need to be flexible. By allowing modified formats as well as hierarchical and cross-referenced linking, teams can best communicate information in a way that matches the characteristics of the task.

Teams are most effective when the combined resources of their members are directed toward the task facing them. Mechanisms that promote dynamic interaction among the team support this goal. We noted that by focusing teams around specific missions and tasks with input from various departments, team interaction improved. It appeared that the traditional departmental lines of communication were broadened, encouraging greater innovation and agility. Also, we found that group displays and workspace layout created an environment that can promote group interaction. The shared "Knowledge Wall" display with an interactive touch-screen became a focal point for team discussions. Frequent interaction with consumers of the team's products is also vital. This type of feedback helps shape more useful products and facilitates teamwork.

Supporting Information Needs of Other Teams

Perhaps the biggest surprise about the use of K-Web during OEF was the extent to which others outside of CCG3 and DESRON9 used it. Although there was certainly a great deal of interest in monitoring a high-profile operation such as OEF, this external use of the K-Web was more than passive observation. Instead, K-Web served as a vital information node for other teams. Although this is an added benefit of K-Web technology, it does require a different level of data summary and analysis. K-Web information needs to be developed for a clearly defined audience, such as CCG3. When information produced for one team is used by another, whether a peer team (e.g., a III Marine Expeditionary Force) or an organizationally superior team (e.g., U.S. Central Command), it will probably need to be revised or customized. In that way, each team will receive information that is relevant for its missions and tasks.

Finally, special effort should be made with regard to exchanging information with subordinate teams, because they often operate with much more limited bandwidth. The K-Web is an excellent opportunity to include smaller, limited bandwidth groups in the information circle, but only if they are provided with an alternate, low-bandwidth information format. By producing a text-only version or by allowing these users to preselect which pieces of the K-Web to view, the impact on their bandwidth could be significantly reduced.

REFERENCES

Bank, T., & Moore, R. A. (2000). TacGraph: A tactical graphics tool [Computer software]. San Diego, CA: Pacific Science & Engineering Group.

Bolstad, C. A., & Endsley, M. R. (1999). Shared mental models and shared displays: An empirical evaluation of team performance. In *Proceedings of the Human Factors Society 43rd Annual Meeting* (pp. 213–217). Santa Monica, CA: Human Factors and Ergonomics Society.

Goldstein, I. (1993). *Training organizations* (3rd ed.). Pacific Grove, CA: Brooks/ Cole.

Klein, G., Schmitt, J., McCloskey, M., Heaton, J., Klinger, D., & Wolf, S. (1996). *A decision-centered study of the regimental command post.* Fairborn, OH: Klein Associates.

Kozlowski, S. W. J, & Salas, E. (1997). An organizational systems approach for the implementation and transfer of training. In K. J. Ford, S. W. J. Kozlowski, K. Kraiger, E. Salas, & M. Teachout (Eds.), *Improving training effectiveness in work organizations* (pp. 247–290). Mahwah, NJ: Erlbaum.

Miller, T. M., & Klein, G. (1998). *Decision centered design: Cognitive task analysis.* PowerPoint presentation, Klein Associates, Inc., Fairborn, OH.

Moore, R. A., & Averett, M. G. (1999). Identifying and addressing user needs: A preliminary report on the command and control requirements for CJTF staff. In *Proceedings of the 1999 Command and Control Research and Technology Symposium* (pp. 403–420). Newport, RI: Naval War College.

Moore, R. A., & Averett, M. G. (2000a). Knowledge Wall: A K-Web view manager [Computer software]. San Diego, CA: Pacific Science & Engineering Group.

Moore, R. A., & Averett, M. G. (2000b). SumMaker: An easy-to-use web-publishing tool [Computer software]. San Diego, CA: Pacific Science & Engineering Group.

Oonk, H. M., Rogers, J. H., Moore, R. A., & Morrison, J. M. (2002). *Knowledge Web concept and tools: Use, utility and usability during the Global 2001 war game*. San Diego, CA: SPAWAR Systems Center.

Oonk, H. M., Smallman, H. S., & Moore, R. A. (2001). *Usage, utility, and usability of the Knowledge Wall during the Global 2000 War Game*. San Diego, CA: Pacific Science & Engineering Group.

Pacific Science & Engineering Group. (2000a) *Building summary and miscellaneous links pages—Operator instructions for use of the summary maker (SumMaker) software*. PowerPoint presentation, Pacific Science & Engineering Group, San Diego, CA.

Pacific Science & Engineering Group. (2000b). *Knowledge Web Viewers: Knowledge Walls and Knowledge Desks—Operator instructions*. PowerPoint presentation, Pacific Science & Engineering Group, San Diego, CA.

Pacific Science & Engineering Group. (2000c). *Using the tactical graphics drawing tool (TacGraph)—Operator instructions*. PowerPoint presentation, Pacific Science & Engineering Group, San Diego, CA.

Pacific Science & Engineering Group. (2001). *Knowledge Web (KWeb) Business rules recommendations for information producers and consumers*. PowerPoint presentation, Pacific Science & Engineering Group, San Diego, CA.

Proctor, S., St. John, M., Callan, J. R., & Holste, S. (1998). Sharing situation awareness in a Marine Corps command post. In *Proceedings of the Human Factors and Ergonomics Society 42nd Annual Meeting* (p. 1610). Santa Monica, CA: Human Factors Ergonomic Society.

Schermerhorn, J. H., Oonk, H. M., & Moore, R. A. (2003). *Knowledge Web usage during Operation Enduring Freedom*. San Diego, CA: Pacific Science & Engineering Group.

Smallman, H. S., Oonk, H. M., & Moore, R. A. (2000). *Knowledge Wall for the Global 2000 War Game: Design solutions to match JOC user requirements*. San Diego, CA: Pacific Science & Engineering Group.

U.S. Department of Defense. (1996). *Common warfighting symbology* (Report No. Mil-STD-2525B). Washington, DC: Author.

7

OPERATIONAL CONCEPTS, TEAMWORK, AND TECHNOLOGY IN COMMERCIAL NUCLEAR POWER STATIONS

JOHN M. O'HARA AND EMILIE M. ROTH

Nuclear power plant operations are an example of a domain in which performance depends on the coordinated activity of multi-person teams. Nuclear power plant personnel play a vital role in the productive, efficient, and safe generation of electric power. Operators work as a team to monitor and control plant systems to ensure their proper functioning. Test and maintenance personnel help ensure that plant equipment is functioning properly, and they restore components when malfunctions occur. Crew members may perform a task cooperatively from one location, such as the main control room, whereas in other cases a control room operator may have to coordinate tasks with personnel in a remote location. Operators share information and perform their tasks in a coordinated fashion to maintain safe plant operation as well as to restore the plant to a safe state should a process disturbance arise.

As new technology has been introduced into control rooms and throughout nuclear power plants, there has been growing recognition that design of technology needs to consider not only individual performance but also teams. In this chapter, we summarize some of the research that has examined the factors that contribute to effective team performance in power plants and how technology can affect team processes in both positive and unexpected, negative ways. We draw on this experience base to offer principles for using technology to foster effective teamwork. We end the chapter with a discussion of future changes expected in power plant operations and the new design challenges they raise.

TEAMWORK IN NUCLEAR POWER PLANT OPERATIONS

A control room team is made up of a core set of members that is augmented as conditions require. During normal operations, there may be two or three operators responsible for monitoring the status of the plant and taking control actions and a supervising operator directing and coordinating the team. This core team is augmented during other-than-normal plant states when the cognitive or physical workload is higher. For example, during plant startup, additional board operators may be brought in to offload some of the physical tasks. In an emergency, staff with greater technical expertise, such as Shift Technical Advisors, would augment the core team to support situation assessment and response planning.

Team members have clearly defined individual roles and responsibilities. Individual operators are responsible for particular plant processes. For example, there might be a Reactor Operator, who is responsible for managing the reactor, and a Balance of Plant Operator, who is responsible for managing other plant systems, such as steam generators and electrical systems.[1] A unique aspect of power plant operations is that operator performance, particularly under emergency conditions, is highly governed by procedures. When an emergency arises, the supervising operator immediately picks up written operating procedures that dictate the actions to be taken by each crew member and how those actions are to be coordinated.

Although team members have clearly defined roles, they nevertheless fluidly support each other and back each other up (Roth, Mumaw, & Lewis, 1994). This happens in the performance of both physical tasks, when operators will perform actions for each other in overload conditions, and problem-solving and decision-making tasks, when operators will volunteer hypotheses and suggest actions in cognitively complex situations; this support is consistent with observations of high-reliability teams in other domains (Klein,

---

[1]The exact division of responsibilities across operators and how rigidly the roles are defined varies across countries.

Armstrong, Woods, Gokulachandra, & Klein, 2000; Rochlin, La Porte, & Roberts, 1987).

Behaviors that are typically identified as important elements of teamwork apply to power plant operations as well. These include having common and coordinated goals, maintaining shared situation awareness, engaging in open communication, and cooperative planning. Successful teams monitor each other's status, back each other up, actively identify errors, and question improper procedures (Cannon-Bowers & Salas, 1998; Pascual, Mills, & Henderson, 2001a). All of these behaviors have been observed in power plant operator teams (Lang, Roth, Bladh, & Hine, 2002; Montgomery, Gaddy, & Toquam, 1991; Roth et al., 1994; Roth & O'Hara, 2002; Sebok, 2000).

Montgomery et al. (1991) were among the first to explicitly examine teamwork skills in the context of nuclear power plant operations. They identified six dimensions of team interaction skill and developed the Behaviorally Anchored Rating Scale (BARS) for measuring crew performance on those dimensions. The six dimensions are (a) Communication, (b) Openness, (c) Coordination, (d) Team Spirit, (e) Task Focus, and (f) Adaptability.

Roth et al. (1994) examined team performance in cognitively challenging simulated emergencies. Crews that performed well from a technical perspective had higher mean BARS ratings on communication, openness, coordination, and adaptability than crews that were classified as "less good" from a technical perspective. The differences were statistically significant in the case of communication, openness, and coordination. The results pointed to specific crew behaviors that appeared to characterize better teamwork and contribute positively to technical performance of the crews. These included ensuring that all crew members were cognizant of key plant state information and control actions that were taken, providing periodic recaps of current situation assessment and upcoming activities, having all crew members participate in situation assessment and response-planning activities, and adapting reorganizations of team structure to deal with unusual conditions.

Roth et al. (1994) identified three types of cognitively demanding situations in which specific types of crew interaction contributed positively to successful crew performance from a technical perspective:

- cases in which situation assessment required integration of information that was distributed across crew members, for example, a case in which a piece of evidence that was needed to identify the plant fault had been seen by only a single crew member and there was no explicit procedure step that specifically requested that piece of information;

- cases in which crews had to evaluate the appropriateness of a procedural path and decide to take actions not explicitly specified in the procedures; and
- cases in which operators needed to adapt crew distribution of tasks so as to be able to pursue multiple objectives in parallel, specifically, where they had to manage dual requirements to (a) proceed through the procedure to bring the plant to a more stable condition and (b) engage in extraprocedural activities to handle aspects of the situation that were not covered by the procedures.

The results pointed to the importance of a shared understanding of the current operational state, the goals to be achieved, and how the procedures supported (or failed to support) these goals. It also pointed to the importance of openness in teams—a willingness of the supervising operator to seek out and welcome input from all team members as well as a willingness on the part of team members to volunteer hypotheses and suggestions. Openness of teams was shown to be particularly important in cases in which crews had to evaluate the appropriateness of a procedure path, decide whether to take actions not explicitly specified in the procedures, or both. Analysis indicated that openness in crew interaction was important both from the perspective of generating proposed actions to take and from the perspective of evaluating those proposed actions.

Roth et al.'s (1994) study characterized the elements of effective teamwork in a power plant context and provided suggestive evidence that teams that demonstrated better teamwork behavior also had better technical performance. The link between teamwork and technical performance was established more definitely in a recent study conducted by Lang et al. (2002) that demonstrated a statistically significant link between process measures of teamwork and various objective measures of technical performance. As teamwork ratings increased, the tendency to detect target events and correctly perform actions increased. Conversely, the commission of action deviations, particularly operationally important action deviations, decreased.

IMPACT OF TECHNOLOGY ON TEAMWORK

The studies previously reviewed highlight the importance of active team processes in maintaining a shared understanding of the current operational state, the goals to be achieved, the actions being taken by different team members in support of those goals, and the appropriateness of those goals to the situation. In many respects, the open physical layout of a conventional control room inherently supports these types of team processes. Their human–system interfaces (HSIs) are primarily hardwired controls (e.g., switches, knobs, and handles) and displays (e.g., gauges, linear scales, and indicator lights) laid out on a large control board. As a result, operators have a broad field of view, facilitating the observation of team activities. Crew members can often understand much about an individual's activities by observing the individual's position at the control panels. Observers can infer information about the type of control action performed and the affected plant system by observing the action that the operator performs with the control and the location of that control on the main control panel. Furthermore, most interactions between crew members consist of verbal communication that can be heard from across the control room, increasing the likelihood that information will be heard by all team members. These properties of a conventional control room facilitate the maintenance of shared situation awareness of the state of the plant and the goals and activities of other team members.

As conventional control rooms are upgraded with digital technology and cockpit-style control rooms, where operators sit at workstation control consoles, each with multiheaded video monitors, it becomes important to understand the impact these new technologies are likely to have on teamwork. Several recent studies explicitly examined the impact of these changes on individual and team performance and have shown significant impacts (Roth, Lin, Kerch, Kenney, & Sugibayashi, 2001; Roth & O'Hara, 2002; Sebok, 2000; Vicente, Roth, & Mumaw, 2001). Changes in technology can influence the distribution of information across crew positions and communication across crew members (in terms of both frequency and content). Technology has the potential to foster improved team situation awareness and collaborative processes. However, if poorly designed, it has the potential to disrupt team processes. In particular, technology can make it more difficult to maintain awareness of other team members' situation assessments, goals, and actions, making it harder to detect and correct misunderstandings and inappropriate action. In the following section, we review some of this research.

Openness of the Physical Workspace

One of the consequences of control room redesign is that it can affect the physical characteristics of the workspace, which in turn can affect the ability of team members to maintain a shared awareness of the plant state and each other's goals and actions. Hutchins (1995) provided a framework for describing characteristics of the work environment that contribute to teamwork:

- *Horizon of observation* refers to the portion of the team task that can be seen or heard by each individual. It is largely determined by the arrangement of the work environment (e.g., proximity of team members), the openness of interaction, and the openness of tools. By making portions of a job more observable, other team members are able to perform error monitoring and identify situations in which additional assistance may be helpful.
- *Openness of tools* refers to the degree to which an observer is able to infer useful information about the problem at hand through observation of tools used by another individual. For example, performing an alignment of a piping system through the manipulation of pump and valve icons on a graphical mimic display may provide more useful information to an observer than if the same task were performed by means of text commands on a keyboard.
- *Openness of interaction* refers to the degree to which the interactions between team members provide an opportunity for others with relevant information to make contributions. Openness of interaction depends on the nature of communication (e.g., discussing actions or decisions in the presence of others) and the style of interaction (e.g., the degree to which unsolicited input is accepted). Openness of interaction is also influenced by characteristics of the work environment that provide other team members with an opportunity to see and hear the interaction.

The older, more conventional control rooms possess the characteristics of an open environment that foster teamwork, as specified by Hutchins (1995). The displays and controls are available in parallel, dedicated positions. This enables operators to notice changes and rapidly shift their attention to areas of interest. Also, a conventional control board creates an open environment that provides multiple-person teams with a shared view of the plant state and each other's actions. It also allows new people coming into the room to quickly assess plant conditions and understand what the crew is doing. There is a risk that unless explicit attention is placed on design features that foster effective teamwork, the positive features of conventional control rooms may be lost in computer-based control rooms.

In more advanced, computer-based control rooms, crews work at seated workstations rather than large control boards. The extent of software processing of information, such as alarm reduction and management, is much greater than in earlier generation control rooms. Improved instrumentation and signal-validation techniques help ensure that the information is more accurate, precise, and reliable. In addition, data processing techniques and the flexibility of computer-based information presentation enable the presentation of information in ways that are better tailored to personnel tasks and information-processing needs.

The benefits of these advanced HSI technologies have been compelling. The digital technology developed for new plants is now also being used to modernize control rooms of existing plants. The introduction of the digital technology has not proceeded without surprises, however, and the surprises have begun to tell a lot about the relationship between crew, teamwork, and technology.

Potential to Create Closed Workspaces That Isolate Operators

On the basis of a review of a computer-based control room, Stokke, Haugset, Nelson, and Bjorlo (1991) observed that "the work environment and the manner in which the console is laid out tend to isolate the operator, as all information is concentrated in front of him. Therefore, he feels no need to communicate with his colleagues to coordinate the tasks" (Stokke et al., 1991, p. 46). Similarly, Stubler and O'Hara (1996) identified a number of problems with computerized control rooms, including the following:

- *Limiting awareness of other crew members' actions.* Operator actions performed at a computer-based workstation can be less visible and more difficult to interpret than actions performed at a conventional control panel; therefore, the crew's awareness of each other's actions is reduced. Also, because controls can be accessed from many different workstations, it is possible for more than one operator to perform tasks involving the same equipment without being fully aware of the other's specific control actions and intentions.
- *Inhibiting communication.* Expressing ideas through face-to-face interactions using gestures or verbal communication, especially when viewing plant information, can be difficult because of physical separation and isolation.
- *Reducing opportunity for collaboration.* When operators do need to collaborate on tasks, they may have individual views of the plant and may not be looking at the same information (e.g., display page). These different views can be an obstacle to coordinated actions.

Potential to Re-Create Benefits of Open Workspaces

Although there is a potential for new technology to disrupt team processes by converting open workspaces into closed ones, technology can also be used to overcome limitations of closed physical workspaces, facilitating the ability of team members to see each other's activities, understand each other's goals, coordinate more effectively, and catch and recover from errors. An example of the use of technology to improve teamwork in an older plant was provided by O'Hara, Higgins, and Almeida (2001), who studied a conventional control room in which the displays and controls used by operators for the emergency operating procedures were distributed on front and back panels. The physical layout of the panels inhibited teamwork because the board operators were separated from the supervising operator who handled the procedures. The supervisor could not see the operators, and communication was difficult because of the presence of floor-to-ceiling panels between them and the noise created by various sources, including alarms and the HVAC system. Additional teamwork issues involved

- difficulty for the two board operators to communicate;
- poor layout of controls and displays such that HSIs needed by the different board operators were located on the same panels, thus creating potential conflict in HSI access; and
- lack of high-level information about the plant's status for the operators.

The control room layout was determined to contribute significantly to risk. As a consequence, a systematic human factors review was conducted using a methodology specified by O'Hara et al. (1994). The analyses included detailed task analyses for important scenarios and simulations of team activity. Several design improvements were identified with the objective of improving teamwork. These included

- installation of communications equipment at both front and back panels to facilitate communication between the board operators and supervisor and between the board operators themselves;
- modification of the procedures and communication protocol in an effort to improve the reliability of communication, for example, breaking complex, multi-action steps into separate individual steps and establishing a clear and unambiguous communication protocol that repeats key aspect of the steps;
- installation of a video camera at the back panels so that the supervisor could observe the general location of the board operators who were out of the supervisor's view (to help prevent information access or control actions from taking place at the wrong panel through monitoring by the supervising operator);

- slight rearrangement of individual controls and displays to avoid access conflicts;
- improvement of high-level information at the back panels, including installation of a monitor to provide safety parameter status information to board operators working at the back panels and the addition of mimic lines to improve the operator's understanding of the relationship between individual controls and displays and the systems and functions to which they relate; and
- installation of new computer-based monitoring displays at the supervisor's workstation (that provide information about the displays and controls in the back panels, thus allowing the supervisor to follow along as the board operators accessed information and took actions).

The preceding example illustrates how careful deployment of new technology can provide new media for meeting the requirements of an open workspace that fosters effective teamwork. Attempts have been made to design group-view displays that reproduce many of the positive aspects of a conventional control room (Stubler & O'Hara, 1996). One example is a large, wall-mounted group view display designed by Westinghouse as part of their Advanced AP600 control room design (Roth et al., 2001). The group-view display, called the *Wall Panel Information System* (WPIS), is designed to provide operators (as well as new people entering the control room) with a shared understanding of the state of the plant and of the goals of the team and the steps to achieve those goals as reflected in the procedures. The goal is to support coordination of activity as well as enhance the ability to detect and correct errors in the execution of the plan. The WPIS attempts to achieve this by including the following:

- a plant overview area intended to support situation awareness of plant state and changes in plant state;
- an area devoted to information on task state, plans, and procedures; and
- an operator-configurable area where operators can put up situation-specific displays.

The area devoted to task state information is intended to provide the control room staff with a common understanding of the state of currently ongoing tasks. During normal operations, this is achieved by displaying planned and ongoing system tests, maintenance activities, and power change maneuvers. Keeping track of currently ongoing activities is critical to interpreting changes in plant state (e.g., an alarm may come on because of a currently ongoing test) as well as avoiding the potential for team members to inadvertently take actions that interact negatively (Mumaw, Roth, Vicente, & Burns, 2000; Vicente et al., 2004). In emergencies, the task state portion of the WPIS is used to display a high-level overview of the current procedure being followed. It is intended to support the control room crew in maintaining a common understanding of the procedure currently being executed, the goals to be achieved, and the progress being made in working through the procedure. The objective is to support operators in assessing the appropriateness of the procedure to the situation, whether it is achieving the desired goals, and whether a change in plan is required.

Roth et al. (2001) evaluated the ability of the WPIS to support team performance under normal and emergency conditions using a high-fidelity simulation of a compact control room. Roth et al. (2001) collected objective performance measures and subjective evaluations of the elements of the WPIS using experienced power plant operators as test participants. The results supported the value of group-view displays in fostering a shared team awareness of plant state and task state.

Distribution of Information Across Team Members

In addition to altering the physical workspace, the introduction of new digital technology affords the opportunity to alter the information provided and its distribution across team members. This has the potential to dramatically affect team processes. It can reduce the workload associated with gathering and integrating individual pieces of data to form situation assessments, reduce the size of crews required to control the plant, alter communication patterns across team members, or some combination of these. This in turn can affect the quality of team problem solving and decision making.

Potential to Reduce Crew Size

One of the earliest studies examining the impact of new technologies on the performance of power plant teams was conducted by Sebok and her colleagues (Sebok, 2000; Sebok, Hallbert, & Morisseau, 1996). The study was motivated by a desire on the part of utility companies to use advanced technology to reduce the size of teams. Crew size was manipulated. Two types of control rooms were used: (a) a conventional control room and (b) an advanced, fully digital, compact control room. Both were high-fidelity simulators that provided an opportunity to compare individual and team performance. Teamwork behaviors as measured by the BARS rating scale were significantly higher in the compact control room compared with the conventional control room, as were objective measures of performance. There were also impacts of control room technology on situation awareness, although control room technology interacted with crew size. Although larger crews (four persons) had better situation awareness than smaller crews (three persons) in a conventional control room, the reverse turned out to be the case in the compact control room, where smaller crews (two persons) had higher situation awareness scores than did larger crews (four persons), illustrating the importance of mapping overall workplace layout with crew member roles and responsibilities. Overall, the results suggested positive benefits of compact control room technology on both technical performance and teamwork and offered the potential for improved performance with reduced crew size.

Potential to Impact Communication Patterns

Although the Sebok (2000) study highlights potential for positive benefits of new control room technologies, a study conducted by Roth and O'Hara (2002) suggests that there can also be unintended negative side effects on team processes: disrupting communication patterns and the ability to maintain shared situation awareness. This in turn can affect the quality of decision making. Roth and O'Hara's study points to the importance of explicitly supporting shared situation awareness and joint problem solving and decision making through design and training.

Roth and O'Hara (2002) examined the impact of introducing advanced HSIs into a conventional control room, including a computer-based procedure system, an advanced alarm system, and a graphic-based plant information system. It was conducted when the HSIs were in the final phases of implementation and operators were undergoing training on the use of the systems on a high-fidelity, full-scope simulator. Five crews were observed in four simulated emergency scenarios over a 2-day period. The observations provided the opportunity to see how the operators interacted with the new systems and with each other. They also provided the opportunity to observe and document cases that illustrate the kinds of complexities that can arise in accident situations and how the new HSIs affected the ability of the crews to identify and respond to those complications. At the end of the 2 days of observation, the operators were interviewed in crews. Questions probed the perceived impact of the new systems on operator workload, situation awareness, distribution of tasks and responsibility among team members, and communication and coordination among the team members.

The new HSI had a broad effect on the cognitive performance of individual crew members as well as on the functioning of the crew as a team. It affected the scope of responsibility of the different crew members, the communication pattern among crew members, and the situation awareness of the different crew members. In a conventional control room, when there is an emergency that causes the plant to shut down (i.e., a plant trip), the supervising operator reads aloud paper-based emergency procedures that guide the crew step by step through the emergency response. The board operator's job is to read plant parameter values from the board for the shift supervisor and take control actions as directed by the procedures that the shift supervisor reads aloud. The introduction of the new HSIs removed the need for this detailed level of communication. The computer-based procedure provided the supervising operator with the plant parameter data required for him or her to work through the procedures, eliminating the need for the board operators to serve as the "eyes" of the supervising operator. This allowed the supervising operator and board operators to work in more of a parallel fashion. The supervising operator concentrated on working through the procedures. As a parallel, independent check, the board operators concentrated on monitoring the alarms, graphics display, and control board HSIs.

The change in information distribution and communication pattern across team members resulted in improved individual situation awareness but interfered with the team members' ability to maintain awareness of each other's situation assessments and activities. Board operators reported that their understanding of plant state was better but that more cognitive effort was required to maintain awareness of the supervising operator's progress through the procedures. Similarly, supervising operators reported improved situation awareness and greater confidence in the accuracy and speed of their own performance. At the same time, they reported a new element of workload: the need to keep the crew informed of their assessments of the situation and the status and direction of the procedural path as they worked through procedures. Supervising operators reported a need to consciously remember to inform the crew of their status through the procedure and to consciously formulate what to communicate. The new communication requirement is a substantial cognitive task that appeared to improve with training and experience.

One of the main lessons of Roth and O'Hara's (2002) study was that new technology can alter communication patterns, which in turn can affect the cognitive demands associated with maintaining shared situation awareness. The study points to the importance of explicitly supporting shared situation awareness and joint problem solving and decision making through design and training.

Information Source Diversity

One of the benefits of digital technology is that it makes it possible to provide multiple, redundant, and diverse sources of information to support problem solving and decision making. This was illustrated in Roth and

O'Hara's (2002) study. Teams are able to exploit multiple, diverse sources of information to handle diagnostically challenging conditions and catch and correct problems—but only if team members actively communicate to maintain shared awareness of the state of the plant and each other's situation assessments, goals, and actions.

Vulnerability to Information Compartmentalization

With increased computerization, there is a tendency toward greater compartmentalization of information, with different crew members having access to different information sources. This places increased emphasis on the need for crew members to actively share information learned and situation assessments generated. This was illustrated by an instance that arose during Roth and O'Hara's (2002) study in which a significant communication breakdown occurred. The board operators failed to communicate to the supervising operator that a major malfunction had occurred and that they had taken an important action in response that had terminated the malfunction. As a result, the supervising operator remained unaware throughout the scenario that a major malfunction had occurred that the crew had detected and corrected. Given that the malfunction had been corrected, the failure in communication was not a serious problem; nevertheless, the case illustrates the importance of keeping everyone in the crew informed of major malfunctions, actions, and changes in plant state.

In this particular event, a steam line break occurred outside containment. The board operators identified the break early in the scenario, partly because of the alarm system, and they isolated the leak by closing the main steam isolation valves. The supervising operator was not told about the steam generator problem by the board operators and could not find out from the computerized procedure because by the time the computerized procedure reached the step that checked for this condition, the problem had been corrected. As a result, he did not see or hear about the steam line break and was not aware of it throughout the scenario. This example illustrates the importance of good crew communication in ensuring accurate situation awareness on the part of all crew members. No one informed the supervising operator that a steam line break had occurred and had been terminated. This is an important piece of information of which the supervising operator should have been made aware.

This example highlights the need for operators to take an active role in keeping supervisors aware of their actions and of changes in the plant. Operators need to keep the supervising operator informed of plant changes and major actions in conventional control rooms as well. Effective communication on the part of operators becomes even more important in computerized control rooms, where information may be more compartmentalized.

Roth and O'Hara's (2002) study illustrated the power of advanced control rooms to provide multiple, diverse sources of information and the importance of effective team communication in being able to exploit this information diversity. In several diagnostically challenging situations, the computer-based procedures provided misleading information, specified inappropriate action, or both. However, operators were able to detect that the procedures were off track because they were actively monitoring other sources of plant state information (alarms, graphic displays, board indicators) that allowed them to recognize that the actions that the supervising operator directed them to take based on the procedures were inappropriate to the situation and to alert the supervisor of this.

The ability of the operators to recognize that the actions specified were inappropriate depended on an accurate understanding of current plant state, a solid knowledge of the goals and assumptions of the procedures and the consequences of the actions indicated by the procedure, and strong communication between the supervising operator and the board operators that allowed the board operators to keep track of the procedural path that the supervising operator was on.

These cases revealed that, as in the case of paper-based procedures, situations can arise in which computer-based procedures provide misleading information, indicate inappropriate action, or both. The availability of alternative sources of information on a plant's state is critical to enable operators to recognize that they are on a wrong procedural path and take action to redirect the procedural path. Roth and O'Hara's (2002) study highlighted the importance of having multiple, diverse sources of information available to operators in the control room and effective communication among the operators to detect and correct cases in which the team is on the wrong procedural path.

PRINCIPLES FOR USING TECHNOLOGY TO FOSTER EFFECTIVE TEAMWORK

In the previous sections, we summarized research from the commercial nuclear industry on the relationship between teamwork and technology. The studies highlight the potential of new technology to affect the openness of the physical workspace; the range, quality, and diversity of information available; and the distribution of information across team members. These changes can increase the level of knowledge and understanding of individual crew members and enhance joint problem solving and decision making through effective exploitation of multiple, diverse sources of knowledge. At the same time, technology can repartition information across team members. It can increase the compartmentalization of knowledge and eliminate what had previously served as "forcing functions" for communication that naturally fostered shared awareness of the plant state and of each other's situation assessments, goals, and actions. With the introduction of new technology, the need to keep each other informed to ensure a common frame of reference becomes potentially more important but also potentially more difficult. This places an increased premium on communication explicitly targeted at building and maintaining shared team situation awareness. These results highlight the importance of design and training to foster communication, shared situation awareness, and joint decision making.

In this section, we draw on these lessons learned, as well as the more general research base on teamwork and technology, to offer principles for the design of computer-based environments to support teamwork. We think that the principles are generalizable to many domains in which teamwork plays a critical role in system performance and safety.

The field of computer-supported cooperative work (CSCW) was developed to support cooperative work between individuals (Greenberg, 1991; Grief, 1988; Pascual, Mills, & Henderson, 2001b). We refer to displays and other HSI elements explicitly intended to support the cooperative work of teams as *CSCW displays*. The key elements of CSCW functionality include providing the following:

- a workplace layout that supports crew interaction,
- common frames of reference,
- resources that support awareness of the activities of others,
- collaborative workspaces, and
- tools for team interaction with CSCW displays.

The following principles address the design of CSCW displays. These may constitute specific new displays explicitly intended to support teamwork, or they may be implemented as functionality that is integrated into displays already available. (For a more detailed discussion of CSCW, see chap. 10, this volume.)

Principle 1: The overall layout of the workplace, such as a control room, should reflect the overall concept of operations and the role of teamwork in supporting the human role in the system.

The impact of the facility design on teamwork starts with decisions that are made regarding the overall layout of the workplace. Examples include

- whether crew workstations are separate, single-person islands or large, integrated workstations at which multiple crew members work;

- the orientation of separate workstations with regard to each other or the shape of a single, large multiperson workstation;
- the facilities provided for supporting personnel, such as maintenance or engineering personnel who have to coordinate and communicate with the control room crew; and
- the orientation of workstations to other control room resources, such as wall panel displays.

Decisions regarding these types of considerations can result in overall workplace designs that foster or inhibit teamwork.

Principle 2: HSIs should specifically include functionality to support teamwork when the following conditions exist: (a) there is a high need for operators to work together on the same task/problem (e.g., complex diagnoses of system failures) and (b) face-to-face interaction and collaboration is difficult because of the arrangement of the workplace and the demands of concurrent tasks.

CSCW displays can provide a means for operators to perform control actions in a collaborative manner. Two or more operators may access the same schematic view of a plant system from separate workstations to perform a control action, such as a valve lineup, by providing inputs to the display in a coordinated manner. This is analogous to multiple operators performing the control actions on different portions of a hardwired mimic display. Presenting this control activity on a CSCW display also provides the crew with an opportunity to more closely observe control actions and detect errors, if they occur. Collaborative control may also be applicable to control actions performed by personnel in different locations in the plant, such as control room personnel working with personnel at a local control station.

Principle 3: A common frame of reference for overall system status should be provided to support shared group situation awareness.

It is desirable that a common frame-of-reference display be presented as using group-view technology (i.e., as a wall panel or large display visible from anywhere in the control room). The WPIS, as previously discussed, is a good example of a common frame of reference for the crew. In addition to supporting crew monitoring from anywhere in the control room and away from workstations, the overview display can provide a common frame of reference for the entire crew, especially for activities such as shift turnover. O'Hara, Pirus, and Beltracchi (2003) identified the types of information that should be included in such displays.

Principle 4: A crew-member-addressable frame of reference should be provided when users have to collaborate to perform an activity.

Although a common frame-of-reference display such as that identified in Principle 3 provides common high-level information that is permanently in view, it is equally important that the display system support crew-member-addressable frames of reference; that is, crew members should have a workspace in which they can put displays that they wish other crew members to see. Attempting to coordinate activities when looking at different displays can be very difficult. If users need to collaborate on some aspect of a task, they should be able to view the same information, whether locally or remotely. This will enable multiple personnel to work on the same task without leaving their workstation.

Principle 5: A CSCW display should support one crew member's understanding of another's activities. This can be accomplished by providing information for common team activities, such as shift turnover and maintenance activities.

This function can take many forms, including providing information about operators' locations in the display system, locations in ongoing procedures, and actions performed using computer-based controls. It may also serve to orient other personnel in the control room while causing minimal disruption to the operators on duty. For example, during plant upsets the overview display may allow personnel—such as additional technical support, regulatory personnel, and plant managers—to follow the course of the procedures and changes in plant conditions. Overview displays may also be placed in remote facilities, such as the technical support center, for this purpose.

Principle 6: Supervisor workstations should provide the capability to easily monitor the current displays at operator workstations.

This capability can be accomplished by providing small windows on the supervisor's workstation that repeat the displays at other workstations. If such a display is provided, the supervisor could click on any one of the windows to enlarge the view for closer inspection.

Principle 7: When multiple crew members have to work together on the same task, displays should provide a collaborative workspace.

A *collaborative workspace* is a display that is common to all users, one on which an individual user can place information that can be viewed by all other users.

Principle 8: The display should provide tools that enable users to interact with the HSI or the plant. Other crew members should be able to infer useful information about the nature of the task and the specific actions taken by observing the crew member's use of the HSI.

The display should allow personnel to observe a control action, such as the alignment of a fluid processing system. In this case, a mimic display, in which operators manipulate graphical objects, may provide more useful information to an observer than if the same task were performed by means of text commands on a keyboard. This is because the display conveys to the observer physical characteristics of the task, such as the type of valve being operated, and functional characteristics, such as the relationship of the valve to the overall piping system. This provides the observer with a better understanding of what action has been performed and its significance to the plant system.

Principle 9: Crew members should not be permitted to make changes to CSCW displays in ways that would reduce their usefulness to others.

Control of changes in a CSCW display, such as changing variables or their ranges, may lead to misinterpretation or confusion. Use of administrative procedures is one way to control changes that may be confusing or otherwise detract from personnel performance.

Principle 10: When multiple crew members share a single device, such as a pointer or cursor, for interaction with CSCW displays, features should be provided to manage access to the device and indicate current ownership. When multiple crew members operate individual devices for interaction with the group-view display, a coding scheme should be provided so the crew members can readily identify their own devices and identify the users of the other devices.

LOOKING TO THE FUTURE OF TEAMS AND TECHNOLOGY

From the time nuclear plants were first designed to produce electrical power, control rooms have evolved from large workplaces filled with discrete analog HSIs to compact, computer-based workstations. One thing has remained unchanged, however: that nuclear plants are operated by teams and that the technology provided affects the ability of the team to function effectively—that is, the design of the control room can facilitate or hinder teamwork and the communication and crew coordination that is vital to its success.

In the early days, the effects were unplanned. However, research and operational experience have revealed the interplay between technology and teamwork, so that efforts can now focus on designing technology to support teamwork. In this chapter, we have reviewed some of these studies and provided 10 principles for designing HSIs to support teamwork.

The nuclear industry is now looking ahead to the development of new reactor design concepts to meet energy in the decades to come. This has been called the *Generation IV initiative.* The vision for Generation IV plant designs includes ambitious goals of improved productivity, safety, reliability, and economic competitiveness.

To meet these goals, and to take full advantage of digital instrumentation and control and computer technology developments, new and innovative approaches to improving human interaction with the plants from a team perspective are needed. In all likelihood, significant changes in the concept of operations and how teams interact will occur. For example, current plants have a large number of on-site personnel organized into functional groups, including operations, maintenance, engineering, administration, and security. From an operations perspective, a plant is controlled by a crew, including numerous individuals both in the control room and out in the plant. However, shift staffing and training of plant personnel are very costly aspects of plant operations. Generation IV reactor technology will be fundamentally different than current plants and will require new models of how to operate and staff the plant.

Once appropriate models are identified, they become design drivers for levels of automation, incorporation of intelligent agents as part of teams, staffing, qualifications, HSI design, personnel training, and so on. To use one example, consider a decentralized functional groups model. The plant would be staffed with a very small number of on-site personnel. Unlike today's operational environment, the on-site crew is largely made up of technicians who keep an eye on the highly automated operation and occasionally perform a minor operations or maintenance task. This crew has minimal training. Responsibility for all but normal operations is handled by off-site specialists who either come to the plant when needed (e.g., for maintenance) or perform their tasks remotely. For example, a very highly qualified crisis team will assume control (which is possible from a remote location) when a disturbance occurs. Because of the low probability of such an accident, this team is available for many reactor sites. This model would support Generation IV economic goals because of the greatly reduced staffing and training burdens. It would also support safety goals because this highly trained team would be responsible for nothing but handling crises; thus, their level of expertise and ability to use analysis tools would be superior to what could be attained when a single crew has to handle everything (today's model).

Although the notion of a nuclear power plant team is likely to change considerably, the functioning of the team must still be considered an integral aspect of the new designs. The technology for fostering teamwork and interaction between team members (e.g., locally and remotely) and between human team members and technology team members (e.g., intelligent agents) will be a significant element of the HSI. Such an approach will provide the opportunity for full team–technology integration in joint, collaborative human–machine systems.

REFERENCES

Cannon-Bowers, J. A., & Salas, E. (Eds.). (1998). *Making decisions under stress: Implications for individual and team training.* Washington, DC: American Psychological Association.

Greenberg, S. (Ed.). (1991). *Computer-supported cooperative work and groupware.* San Diego, CA: Academic Press.

Grief, I. (1988). *Computer-supported cooperative work: A book of readings.* San Mateo, CA: Morgan Kaufmann.

Hutchins, E. (1995). *Cognition in the wild*. Cambridge, MA: MIT Press.

Klein, G., Armstrong, D., Woods, D., Gokulachandra, M., & Klein, H. (2000). *Cognitive wavelength: The role of common ground in distributed replanning* (Technical Report No. AFRL-HE-WP-TR-2001-0029). Dayton, OH: Wright Patterson Air Force Research Laboratory.

Lang, A. W., Roth, E. M., Bladh, K., & Hine, R. (2002). Using a benchmark-referenced approach for validating a power plant control room: Results of the baseline study. In *Proceedings of the Human Factors and Ergonomics Society 46th Annual Meeting* (pp. 1878–1882). Santa Monica, CA: Human Factors and Ergonomics Society.

Montgomery, J., Gaddy, C., & Toquam, J. (1991). Team interaction skills evaluation criteria for nuclear power plant control room operators. In *Proceedings of the Human Factors Society 35th Annual Meeting* (pp. 918–922). Santa Monica, CA: Human Factors and Ergonomics Society.

Mumaw, R. J., Roth, E. M., Vicente, K. J., & Burns, C. M. (2000). There is more to monitoring a nuclear power plant than meets the eye. *Human Factors, 42*, 36–55.

O'Hara, J., Higgins, J., & Almeida, P. (2001). *Risk implications of the panel arrangement in the José Cabrera Nuclear Power Plant control room: Recommendations for improvements*. Upton, NY: Brookhaven National Laboratory.

O'Hara, J., Higgins, J., Stubler, W., Goodman, C., Eckenrode, R., Bongarra, J., & Galletti, G. (1994). *Human factors engineering program review model* (Report No. NUREG-0711). Washington, DC: U.S. Nuclear Regulatory Commission.

O'Hara, J., Pirus, D., & Beltracchi, L. (2003). *Information display: Considerations for designing modern computer-based display systems* (Report No. EPRI-1002830). Palo Alto, CA: Electric Power Research Institute.

Pascual, R., Mills, M., & Henderson, S. (2001a). Teamworking. In J. Noyes & M. Bransby (Eds.), *People in control: Human factors in control room design* (pp. 69–77). London: Institution of Electrical Engineers.

Pascual, R., Mills, M., & Henderson, S. (2001b). Training and technology for teams. In J. Noyes & M. Bransby (Eds.), *People in control: Human factors in control room design* (pp. 133–150). London: Institution of Electrical Engineers.

Rochlin, G. I., La Porte, T. R., & Roberts, K. H. (1987). The self-designing high reliability organization: Aircraft carrier flight operations at sea. *Naval War College Review, 40*, 76–90.

Roth, E. M., Lin, L., Kerch, S., Kenney, S. J., & Sugibayashi, N. (2001). Designing a first-of-a-kind group view display for team decision making: A case study. In E. Salas & G. Klein (Eds.), *Linking expertise and naturalistic decision making* (pp. 113–135). Mahwah, NJ: Erlbaum.

Roth, E. M., Mumaw, R. J., & Lewis, P. M. (1994). *An empirical investigation of operator performance in cognitively demanding simulated emergencies* (Report No. NUREG/CR-6208). Washington, DC: U.S. Nuclear Regulatory Commission.

Roth, E. M., & O'Hara, J. (2002). *Integrating digital and conventional human system interfaces: Lessons learned from a control room modernization program* (Report No. NUREG/CR-6749). Washington, DC: U.S. Nuclear Regulatory Commission.

Sebok, A. (2000). Team performance in process control: Influences of interface design and staffing levels. *Ergonomics, 41*, 1210–1236.

Sebok, A., Hallbert, B., & Morisseau, D. (1996). Crew performance issues in nuclear power plant process disturbances. In *Proceedings of the 1996 American Nuclear Society International Topical Meeting on Nuclear Plant Instrumentation, Control, and Human–Machine Interface Technologies* (pp. 645–651). La Grange, IL: American Nuclear Society.

Stokke, E., Haugset, K., Nelson, W., & Bjorlo, T. (1991). *Instrumentation and control systems in nuclear power plants*. Halden, Norway: Halden Reactor Project.

Stubler, W. F., & O'Hara, J. M. (1996). *Group-view displays: Functional characteristics and review criteria* (Technical Report No. E2090-T-4-4-12/94). Upton, NY: Brookhaven National Laboratory.

Vicente, K. J., Mumaw, R. J., & Roth, E. M. (2004). Operator monitoring in complex dynamic work environment: A qualitative cognitive model based on field observations. *Theoretical Issues in Ergonomic Science, 5*, 359–384.

Vicente, K. J., Roth, E. M., & Mumaw, R. J. (2001). How do operators monitor a complex, dynamic work domain? The impact of control room technology. *International Journal of Human–Computer Studies, 54*, 831–856.

8

GROUP PERFORMANCE
AND SPACE FLIGHT TEAMS

BARRETT S. CALDWELL

The U.S. space program launched only a single astronaut at a time during the Mercury missions of 1961 to 1963. There has been only one U.S. launch of a pair of astronauts since 1967: The first space shuttle mission carried only two pilot crew members. Thus, multiple crew member performance in space flight has been a continuous element of the National Aeronautics and Space Administration's (NASA's) activities for most of its history, and crews of three or more persons have represented almost all of U.S. activity in space for 35 years. The Russian space program, because of the continuous operations of the Salyut and Mir stations, has even more cumulative experience with the behavior and performance of multi-person missions in space.

Group dynamics and social psychology have been frequently studied areas of intense interest for decades; the applications of psychology to human space flight have been recognized since the initiation of Project Mercury in 1957. However, a tension has continued to exist between external researchers and NASA operational personnel (astronauts, mission control engineers, and spacecraft designers). Very few academic researchers outside of NASA have conducted research on group performance in the space flight environment. Several factors contribute to this lack of collaboration; there are difficulties in communication and understanding between psychologists and engineers. Social psychologists and space systems engineers often approach their subjects with a very different emphasis on quantitative detail and level of analysis. Historically, tensions have also been based on fears that a psychologist would only serve to prevent the astronaut or mission control engineer from being able to do the task on which he or she is focused and for which he or she is trained and relentlessly driven (Connors, Harrison, & Akins, 1985; Harrison, 2001).

Nonetheless, the space flight environment provides in many ways the most purely defined, human-constructed setting for the study of group performance. Because of the dangers and risks involved, as well as the number of unknown factors, developers and managers of space missions want to be as well prepared as possible for contingencies that could endanger crew survival and mission success. As human presence in space has expanded, most participants and observers recognize that an improved understanding of personal, interpersonal, and team performance factors has become a dominant issue affecting the success of future space missions.

TEAM PERFORMANCE CONTEXTS

Academic research of group dynamics and team performance has been a popular aspect of social psychology. Some researchers (McGrath, 1984; Sundstrom, De Meuse, & Futrell, 1990), however, point out that the majority of "group" research fails to consider critical aspects of the essential context of space flight crews. Some potentially relevant literature even involves conflicts on concepts and definitions regarding whether a collection of individuals (or even a pair of individuals) qualifies as a group. (For the purposes of this discussion, I restrict the definition of *group* to three or more persons. This more restrictive definition is at odds with some scholars and in fact excludes a large fraction of "group" research focused on the behavior of dyads. However, only in groups of three or more does one find issues of multiple communication paths, majority–minority interactions, subgroup formation, or distributed information flow.)

Social psychology and sociology perspectives on the study, purpose, or interpretation of group interactions vary widely (McGrath, 1984; Mills, 1967; Sundstrom et al., 1990). In this section I do not attempt a comprehensive examination of multiple theories of groups or assume that the reader will implicitly adopt a particular perspective. Instead, I simply describe a set of criteria that may help to clarify astronaut crews and flight controllers as members of teams, and not simply groups, behaving in a unique social and technological context. (These criteria summarize the perspectives of a number of authors and theoretical constructs; in addition to the authors previously cited, readers are directed to a comprehensive summary, such as Shaw, 1981, for general theoretical descriptions of group dynamics.)

Group Issues

To be considered members of a group, individuals must be aware of, and participate in, interactions that support the ongoing existence and shared goals that define the group's existence. Groups have patterns of membership entrance, socialization to group norms, and expected patterns of behavior, and they develop references to shared experiences and shared membership to distinguish group members from nonmembers.

Task Issues

In addition to the components of group membership, team members have additional elements and characteristics due to their focus on task performance, and not simply group interaction. In other words, teams have to *do* something goal oriented (e.g., win games, construct buildings, or perform surgeries) through a combination of shared understandings and specialized areas of expertise or task activity. The separation of expertise or function indicates that team members play coordinated, not identical, roles in performance and are not strictly interchangeable. Teams studied from this perspective, therefore, require the development of coordinated performance based on relatively consistent cycles of activities that occur repeatedly over a longer time scale.

The majority of social psychology and group dynamics literature does emphasize the interactions occurring in *short-term teams*, with membership created and operating over relatively short time frames (McGrath, 1984). In such environments, the study of emerging patterns of information exchange and task coordination can be of interest (see, e.g., Caldwell & Everhart, 1998). However, with additional time (and, more important, additional repetitions of task experiences), teams develop stable patterns of interaction based on shared experiences and known task roles (Burke, Volpe, Cannon-Bowers, & Salas, 1993; Orasanu & Salas, 1993; Sundstrom et al., 1990). Both mission control and space flight crews are distinguished by very long periods (months or years, with thousands of hours logged) spent training together on dozens to hundreds of presentations of specific task scenarios (Glenn, 1999; Harrison, 2001; Kranz, 2000). As a result, this chapter focuses on the dynamics of long-term team behaviors.

Context Issues

Individuals who perform tasks in a laboratory setting lack several elements of context that are shared by members of functioning teams. Being able to perform tasks that are seen as relevant and important to ongoing team membership, and that are valued by team members, is seen as a crucial factor that influences performance quality, persistence, and perceived stress. Laboratory studies are unable to fully replicate the contextual elements that can strongly affect team behavior norms, stress effects, or resource constraints in extreme and unusual environments (e.g., space, Antarctic research stations, or other remote settings; Harrison, Clearwater, & McKay, 1991). Relatively few studies of team behavior in such environments exist, and rarely are researchers granted (or choose) direct access to conduct participant observation of team performance in such remote settings, despite the richness of findings that are possible in such studies (Valen & Caldwell, 1991).

The concept of the *standing group* (a collection of people with continuing interactions and established reasons for existence) performing *group interaction processes* (performing tasks together, and not simply interacting for the group's own sake) in a *situated context* (in a real environment, with task, time, and resource constraints) is part of a cybernetic–feedback control model of group dynamics common to psychology and sociology (McGrath, 1984; Mills, 1967). This approach is conceptually similar to that of the systems engineer examining the performance of an open feedback control system performing in a dynamic environment (D'Azzo & Houpis, 1966; Dorf & Bishop, 1995; Sage, 1992).

The behavior of the group conducting social interactions and performing tasks in a technology-mediated environment can be described in terms of sociotechnical systems theory (Pasmore, 1988; Trist, 1981). Although prior attempts at unified theories and quantitative descriptions of complex systems (Forrester, 1968) have fallen into some disfavor, modern computational capabilities and greater understanding of mathematical descriptions of system dynamics and complexity are resulting in new attempts to provide such quantitative integration (Wolfram, 2001). As I discuss in the following section, the success of such attempts will depend on the ability of researchers to describe similar aspects of the world under study using similar tools, descriptions, and techniques.

This combination of theoretical approaches, spanning engineering, behavioral, and social science, can be seen in some senses as a difficult coordination exercise across multiple disciplines. In fact, this coordination can also be seen as a strength of an integrative approach to the study of group performance in a complex engineering environment. Some researchers in the field of human performance and human factors engineering present this combination of *human, activity,* and *context* as essential components of the design, evaluation, and improvement of human interactions with information and communications technology (Bailey, 1996). The study of both human–machine interaction and technology-mediated human–human communications involve how humans acquire, process, respond to, and share information in a technological environment.

Traditional approaches to the group dynamics of extended space flight derive from the communications and social psychology literature (see Connors et al., 1985). The systems engineering approach is one favored by NASA engineers and operations managers (Kranz, 2000; Swanson, 1999). As a result of personal training and desire for compatibility with other aerospace systems engineering applications, the perspective of this chapter emphasizes a combination of classical group dynamics, social information processing, and adaptive feedback control approaches to group-level information flow, knowledge sharing, and task coordination in the space flight context.

GROUP INFORMATION AND PERFORMANCE

If groups can be seen as adaptive, cybernetic systems responding in a dynamic environment, the immediate question to be raised by a systems engineer is "What is the critical process for connecting parts of the system?" A social psychologist or sociologist would ask, "What function maintains group coordination, shared experience and purpose, and overall performance?" In both cases, the primary answer is "information flow." A flow variable, in the engineering sense, describes mathematically how energy or material travels from one part of a system to another. Thus, a system flow description explains "what is connected to what" and how well those connections link components across the system and over time. One of the primary tasks of groups and teams is to share appropriate information, within time and resource constraints for effective processing, to coordinate understanding and synchronize performance (Orasanu & Salas, 1993; Swezey & Salas, 1992).

Much research in social and group information processing is based on the information theory work of Shannon and Weaver (1949). However, it is critical to point out that the primary focus of that theory emphasizes the effective transmission of data to represent a particular message. This transmission process can be seen as part of a hierarchy of information flow processes:

- *data transmission* (exchanging signals with possible meaning without loss of relevant signals),
- *data into information* (interpreting data signals within a task context for effective operations),

- *information into knowledge* (processing information into usable and accessible reference experience), and
- *knowledge into expertise* (recognition and awareness of relevant stores of knowledge to achieve strategic and goal-related performance).

Both team members and the technologies they use must be able to effectively communicate and coordinate this range of flows and coordination efforts. Because teams are also attempting to perform cycles of activities within time constraints, it is important to recognize that information flow must be achieved effectively within those time constraints.

Shared information in the team environment supports coordination and synchronization of shared mental models or other forms of coordinated information (see, e.g., Rouse, Cannon-Bowers, & Salas, 1992; Swezey & Salas, 1992). However, there are considerable problems in fostering the sharing of information, including issues of recognizing when information is not currently shared and whether all members have processed and considered information as being relevant or have been able to communicate the importance of the information within the social constraints of the task environment (Stasser & Titus, 1987). The field of cockpit resource management is based on recognition that effective sharing of information must be trained, and the consequences of poor knowledge synchronization can be fatal (Foushee & Helmreich, 1988).

Interviews with flight controllers and astronauts indicate the critical sensitivity to time in space operations. The nature of the space flight environment, and the culture of NASA, dictate that decisions must be made that retain flexibility of later options and that information and tasks that support increasing the time available for problem resolution are highly valued. This criterion not only defines relative weighting of available information but also helps people understand tolerance for delays in obtaining relevant information for effective decision making or stable task performance. Delay tolerance is not just a factor of absolute clock time but is modified by situational context and task factors related to expected cycles of activity. One can consider four classes of tolerance conditions: (a) asynchronous, non-time-critical communications; (b) procedural operations in which criticality is recognized only by violations of expected time patterns; (c) synchronous, increasingly time-critical communications; and (d) time urgent, limited-alternative conditions in which quick responses based on limited information are required. To understand how these conditions affect group-level coordination and task performance, flight controllers and astronauts were asked to qualitatively describe how information transmission or availability delays regarding vehicle information affected task-related decision making and action.

Controller responses paralleled other, more quantitative research that has applied feedback control analysis to the acceptance of information transmission delay (Caldwell, 1992, 1994, 1997). The process of energy, information, or material flow and feedback in a wide range of physical systems are analyzed using the mathematical tools of engineering control theory (Dorf & Bishop, 1995). The fundamental feedback control model most often studied is the second-order model:

$$M\, A''(t) + 2c\, A'(t) + b^2 A(t) = 0,$$

where M, b, and c represent engineering parameters related to inertia and damping (affecting the sensitivity of the system to inputs over time) and A is the primary measure of system performance. Research has applied this model to human manual control and cognitive–motor processes with time delays (Jagacinski & Flach, 2003; Smith & Smith, 1987), using the rationale that "the linear second-order system may be the most common and most intuitive of physical systems" (Bahill, 1981, cited in Jagacinski & Flach, 2003, p. 46). A quantitative model of this type applied to group-level information exchange has been a goal of human performance modeling and human–computer interaction design for some time (Jagacinski & Flach, 2003; Nickerson, 1995).

With these approaches as a baseline, the classes of behavior of the second-order model were the starting point for interview questions for flight controllers assessing time delay and its effects on mission control–crew information exchange and performance (see Figure 8.1). In this formulation, t is replaced by Δt (elapsed time delay, measured in absolute seconds or normalized event cycles), M is related to controller expertise (not evaluated in this study), and A is the controller's acceptance of incoming information delayed by Δt after it was requested. The parameters b and c relate to the benefit of availability of timely ("fresh") information and the cost of sampling and acquiring that information.

According to interview results, *asynchronous communications* (Class 1) correspond to a condition in which freshness decays slowly over a significant period of time (e.g., in electronic mail or scheduled tasks to be completed in the future). *Synchronous communications* (Class 3) correspond to conditions in which freshness decays more rapidly (with real time interaction expectations and task constraints, e.g., checking on current status). *Procedural information* (Class 2) represents a special case where increasing M (expertise) and b (freshness) are not relevant—which best describes routine procedure following. *Reaction time responses* (Class 4) require immediate response much more strongly affected by freshness and expertise than cost, as would be true in time-critical reaction time behaviors. Thus, the impact of time, as well as the coordination of information within temporal and other resource

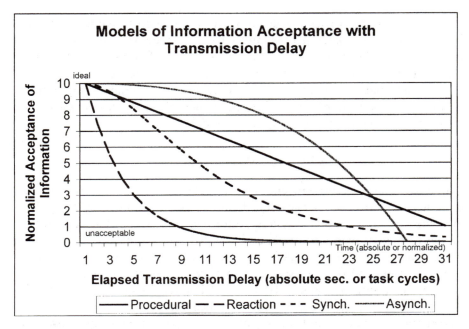

Figure 8.1. Models of information acceptance with transmission delays for mission control flight controllers.

constraints, play critical roles for training, functional allocation, and development of shared expertise among space flight teams.

TRAINING AND ALLOCATION OF FUNCTION

In all group-level task-performing environments, the issue of the development of expertise becomes a major emphasis of attention. For space flight teams, selection and training take on a special significance, in part because of the highly visible, risky, and unusual task setting.

During the early days of space flight, a great deal of effort and attention was focused on the process of astronaut selection (Connors et al., 1985; Swanson, 1999). Because the behaviors of the human body under conditions of acceleration, microgravity, and radiation associated with space travel were unknown, extremely stringent physiological criteria for selection were developed. There was a corresponding attempt to develop stringent psychological criteria, but without an understanding of the human experience of space, developing such criteria was problematic at best. In addition, the criteria for selecting a solo astronaut for Mercury would necessarily be different than selecting a member of a seven-person crew for the space shuttle, because of the issues of team and task compatibility and the greater range of functional demands on members of the crew.

The process of astronaut selection has evolved in several steps over the history of the space program. Astronaut (and flight controller) selection is strongly (and increasingly) affected by group-level social and cultural factors (as is any other socialization to an elite group) that is not readily reduced to purely technical criteria (Atkinson & Shafritz, 1985; Harrison, 2001; Kranz, 2000). Assignment to a particular team is also based on compatibility, coordination, and appropriate distribution of task and domain expertise across members of the team. As the duration of the space mission increases, these factors become increasingly important (Harrison, 2001; Lucid, 1998). Note that these processes occur only as the number of functioning teams increases so that selection and assignment are to *which* flight crew, not *whether* a potential crew member is assigned at all. (Obviously, five pilots cannot be assigned to a single crew, but if there are five pilots available and five distinct missions, it is reasonable to assign a pilot to a crew that has the most compatible commander and mission specialists and best expertise match to the mission requirements.)

Once selection and assignment are made, the process of training is highly intense and occurs over an extended period (Glenn, 1999; Lucid, 1998). (Astronauts are often selected several years in advance, and assigned over 1 year in advance, for a particular mission. Controllers require approximately 3 years of training to move into a lead controller position assigned to a particular mission and shift.) The primary mode of training in the space flight environment is task and context simulation. Because operational experience is rare (the record for most missions for a single astronaut is seven, and space shuttle controllers are constrained by the number of missions per year at six or fewer), the facilities of the mission control center (MCC) also operate as a high-fidelity training and simulation testbed.

The use of mission control flight control rooms for both simulation and actual flight operations represents the ultimate expression of the concept of a "microworld" for development and analysis of decision making in dynamic environments (Brehmer, 1992; Brehmer & Allard, 1991). A *microworld* is a computer-based simulation that allows supervisory controllers to perform realistic tasks in a controlled, repeatable environment to gain required operational expertise other than during live system performance. Most microworlds are simplified versions of real supervisory control tasks, providing partial exposure to the dynamics of the engineering system being controlled. The microworld therefore provides opportunities for overtraining and for exploration of behaviors and system performance in an environment that will not lead to actual danger or damage to controllers, engineered systems, or other personnel.

However, the MCC is the actual facility for space mission operations, and the three flight control facilities can all be shifted from live operations to simulation status in a matter of hours. Complex simulations based on real mission data can be fed to the MCC computer systems by a separate system controller (known as the *simulation supervisor*), resulting in computer-generated data, displays, and MCC operational behavior that are functionally identical to those of a live mission. Although simulation scenarios are not constructed according to a strict experimental paradigm of the type most familiar to experimental psychologists, in all other facets these scenarios are prime examples of the computer-generated microworld design (Brehmer & Dörner, 1993). The only difference, according to discussions with flight controllers, is that live missions are usually, and pleasantly, less stressfully challenging than simulations (Kranz, 2000).

Information flow and team performance in the MCC environment is based on a function allocation matrix of flow types and coordination processes. There are two distinct areas of team training and coordination requiring information sharing and support, as defined by Cooke and colleagues (Cooke et al., 2000; Cooke, Kiekle, & Helm, 2001):

- *taskwork*, or technical content domain knowledge exchanged to support achievement of task goals, and
- *teamwork*, or social interaction process expertise to manage task coordination, shared understandings, and knowledge synchronization.

In very complex team environments, in which information technology systems must be used to support multiple channels or types of information flow (e.g., voice channels, vehicle telemetry, and spacecraft command sequences), a third type of information support is required (Caldwell, 1999, 2002): *pathwork*, or technical domain knowledge to identify, maintain, and troubleshoot available, active, and relevant communication channels to support flows of information, including taskwork and teamwork flows.

MCC controller consoles reflect this division of taskwork, teamwork, and pathwork emphases, distinguishing content focus from process focus (Patterson, Watts-Perotti, & Woods, 1999). In addition, some controllers focus on *sensemaking* (transformations from data to information) of specific data streams within specific engineering subsystems (e.g., propulsion, trajectory calculations, or electrical systems). Other controllers (e.g., the flight director, who coordinates the performance of the other controllers) are more responsible for coordinating across subsystems to support coordinated activity and knowledge synchronization (transformations from information to knowledge). This function allocation process is also discussed in the following section.

MULTITEAM PERFORMANCE: MISSION CONTROL CENTER–CREW INTERACTIONS

A long-standing concern in the sociology of group interactions and group performance is the negotiation of in-group ("we") and out-group ("they") dynamics. The astronaut selection and training process is intense; the historic perception of the astronaut is rarified; the working environment of the astronaut in space is unique and dangerous. It is therefore to be expected that some form of tension would be associated with multiple team performance incorporating groups of astronauts and other associated professionals involved in the ongoing operational management of space missions (Kanas & Caldwell, 2000). During the mission training and actual mission phases, the primary source of interaction for astronauts regarding vehicle status, system performance, and mission achievement is with flight controller teams.

From a purely technical perspective, astronauts and flight controllers must coordinate activity to maintain the effective functioning of an extremely complex engineering system. Traditionally, between 18 and 24 primary flight controllers (*front room* controllers) are supported by dozens of additional technical personnel (*back room* support) in the system management, control, troubleshooting, and performance enhancement of the space vehicle. During the early years of the NASA space program, almost all space vehicle functions had to be controlled from the ground, describing an engineering command and control system known as *supervisory control* (Sheridan, 1992). With the increasing complexity of the space vehicle, the expanding range of mission activities, and the enhancements in computing power and miniaturization, the roles and responsibilities of the flight controllers have changed with respect to members of the astronaut crew.

From a group dynamics perspective, flight controllers represent another elite set of trained professionals engaged in the complex and demanding world of space flight: In the eyes of many in the public, they are the true practitioners of "rocket science." Whereas admission to the astronaut corps would be considered the ultimate validation of skill and capability for a 1960s test pilot, participation in a space flight mission as a member of the flight controller team would be a similar validation for the aerospace systems engineer (Kranz, 2000). The training and flight qualification process for a flight controller may, in some elements, rival that of the astronaut: It is estimated that, between 2000 and 2002, only approximately 30% of those who begin the 3-year training process of moving to the front room will succeed in their efforts. For the most part, however, the flight controller role has been less visible than that of the astronaut and subject to less scrutiny, public image management, and official publicity (Harrison, 2001; Kranz, 2000).

Of course, the attempt to create a stigmatizing in-group–out-group competition between flight controllers and astronauts is both technically problematic and socially counterproductive. Both groups represent the epitome of U.S. technological capability and expertise, and human space flight without the shared and mutually integrated performance of both groups is impossible. However, the distinctions of task context, physical environment, and information availability and use between flight controllers and astronaut crews makes the study of controller–crew communications an invaluable component of understanding group performance in the space flight environment.

Because of the professional status of the astronauts, and the distribution of expertise and information among members of the flight controller team, the concept of supervisory control is not strictly applicable to the controller–crew setting. The leader of the flight controller team, the flight director, is responsible for coordinating and utilizing the expertise of the various flight controllers, who are in turn responsible for various technical domains and coordinating the activity of more specialized back room support personnel—all in real time. The complexity of the space flight setting; the distributed nature of information, expertise, and engineering system components; and the severe time constraints and consequences associated with MCC operations create a unique style of coordination described as *distributed supervisory coordination* (Caldwell, 2000).

A special flight controller is known as the *capsule communicator* (CAPCOM, derived from original references to the Mercury astronaut orbital vehicles as "capsules") and is responsible for communications with astronaut crew members on board the space vehicle. CAPCOM holds a unique place in several respects: The CAPCOM console position in the MCC is always next to that of the flight director, showing its critical importance to flight controller coordination. CAPCOM is also always another astronaut, thus attempting to bridge the controller–crew differences in group membership and task role and providing a unique indication that astronauts are a distinct and autonomous group rather than simply distant or subordinate members of the flight controller team (Kranz, 2000). During task performance, CAPCOM is the only flight controller authorized to speak directly with members of the crew—not even the flight director speaks directly with the crew, except via CAPCOM. (Select others, most notably flight surgeons, have authorization during nontask periods to engage in "private conferences.")

Communications between CAPCOM and the crew use specialized radio frequency channels, known as *air-to-ground* or *space-to-ground*, with a distinctive "beep" preceding them. (This "beep" is an artifact of the information technology designs of the early 1960s. Although one could remove it using digital filtering, the "beep" remains as a critical cue indicating that a crew communication event is taking place.) These and all other flight controller communications take place through a proprietary technology known as the *Digital Voice Intercommunications System* (DVIS), which allows a controller to listen to multiple communication channels (with their associated voice traffic) simultaneously, to support the needs of managing the spacecraft.

DVIS must support communications between flight controllers and the astronaut crew, between front room and back room support controllers, and between controllers with distinct technical domain areas of expertise. In addition, the mission control facility itself consists of a number of individual computer displays that each controller uses for his or her own specialty, as well as shared displays for coordinated controller awareness of vehicle status and mission activity. Thus, the DVIS and other information technology systems supporting information flow within mission control, and between mission control and the spacecraft, represent a separate engineering system (focused on data exchange, information flow, knowledge sharing, and expertise coordination) that operates in parallel with, and in support of, the space flight engineering system of the vehicle. Flight controllers must use these information and communication systems to develop and enhance their understanding of vehicle activity and to synchronize understanding and task performance with members of the onboard crew, resulting in a unique form of distributed supervisory coordination represented by combinations of taskwork, teamwork, and pathwork (see Figures 8.2 and 8.3).

Mission Control Center research conducted by my research group has examined patterns of voice intercom channel use in MCC operations, including controller–crew interactions, during mission simulations (Caldwell, 2003; Wang & Caldwell, 2003). The primary MCC voice channel for controller coordination (the "flight" loop) and controller–space crew coordination channel are the highest priority, and most used, channels (with duty cycles of approximately 15%–35% of possible time in use). However, their use levels and patterns change significantly with the phase of space flight operations. Very familiar and often-simulated activities (primarily, launch and entry–landing operations) have well-defined protocols that result in short, crisp communications (known to the communications engineer as *bursty* patterns of communication) during highly time constrained activities.

Although on-orbit activity may also have time constraints, the relative lack of established procedures results in more communication channel activity (and cognitive workload) associated with less routine, procedure-validated tasks. In addition, on-orbit operations (particularly those on the International Space Station) allow crew members to have greater distances between them, requiring more use of technology-mediated communications and increased information flow in voice rather than direct observation or nonverbal communication (e.g., hand signals).

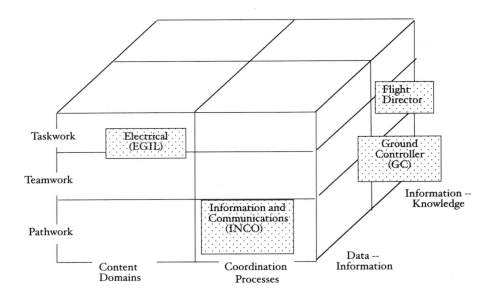

Figure 8.2. Levels of information flow and task coordination in controller–crew operations.

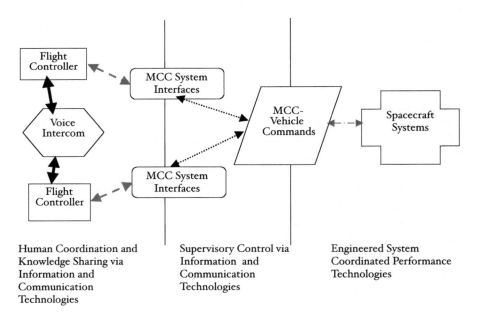

Figure 8.3. Information flow requirements and relevant paths for mission control–vehicle coordination.

Thus, there are four critical task context factors affecting controller–crew communications activity across the range of space flight operations:

- *urgency* (limits of time available for performance, with demands for rapid, easily communicated, and quickly processed information flow);
- *distribution/distance* (physical or task function separations requiring additional information coordination not available through shared displays or understandings of local activity, or unmediated sharing of information, e.g., nonverbal gestures or physical exchanges of material);
- *content volume* (amount and type of information flow required, including and influenced by availability of local references rather than explicit processing of new information through the voice channel); and
- *relevant experience* (expertise and standardization of task patterns based on repeated exposures to similar operational contexts, with available and tested/validated references to past experience with similar tasks).

These four factors are identical to those that have been shown to have significant effects on patterns of information technology use, and user tolerance for degraded system performance, in a range of studies including office-based task settings (Caldwell & Paradkar, 1995; Caldwell, Uang, & Taha, 1995). Past communication research literature highlighted issues of information richness and social presence in information technology use (Daft & Lengel, 1986; Lea, 1991). Long training patterns (including multiple flight segment simulations before crew launch) help to increase shared experience and social presence among crew and flight controllers, as well as developing operational experience bases to help increase the efficiency of communication reference acts. Available channel bandwidth remains limited in the mission control environment, approximating network flow and data exchange capabilities of leading-edge computer networks circa 1990. Satellite communications protocols and requirements for validation of software commands before task execution represent barriers to rapid increases in net data exchange capabilities over the near term.

Increasing recognition of, and matching communication activity to support, the context factors previously described will remain a robust area of research and operational emphasis during the next 5 to 15 years. (Communications engineering research designed to provide increases of 1–4 orders of magnitude in data throughput, eventually achieving gigabit-per-second bandwidth, continues to progress but is not likely to relieve communications bottlenecks during space station construction and initial operation.) The multinational, multilanguage training of space station crews has highlighted tremendous cultural differences in worldviews and values, not only in terms of general belief systems but also in approaches to mission operations (Burrough, 1998; Lucid, 1998). Aspects of the nature (and scarcity) of time, technology versus human roles in assuring system performance, ranges of acceptable risk and prioritization of actions, and the importance of procedure versus creativity in task performance are all issues affecting crew coordination, information flow, and task performance in the space station environment.

ISSUES AND CONTEXTS FOR FUTURE SPACE CREWS

Experience, expectation, and perspectives for the performance of future space crews have changed substantially during the relatively brief period of 1997–2004. Following the shuttle–Mir program, the construction and continuous habitation of the International Space Station have greatly expanded awareness of capabilities and challenges of international astronaut crews to spend extended periods in space interacting with multiple flight controller teams. Interactions between ground-based mission control personnel and on-board space flight crews have been an ongoing challenge for future space flight evolution. Both the U.S. and Russian experiences in space have highlighted a move toward increasing crew autonomy and greater availability of information, decision latitude, and global planning flexibility resident in on-board systems (Kranz, 2000).

The differences in Russian Mir and U.S. shuttle experiences in the 1980s and 1990s do indicate the effects of, and current attitudes toward, discrete missions as distinct from continuous operations in moving toward this view of crew autonomy (Burrough, 1998; Harrison, 2001; Launius, 2004; Lucid, 1998). James Oberg's (2002) analysis of China's launch of its own human space crews brings in another independent model of space flight planning and mission operations.

The nature of the Chinese planning structure indicates a strong reliance on central control and coordination of research, development, crew activity, and mission management. Initial Chinese space missions are likely to combine this central planning and control emphasis with a discrete set of missions. Advanced technology design and system implementation efforts are required for function allocation of supervisory automation, information presentation, and bandwidth requirements for transmitting graphical and multimodal data streams from ground to a crew of 3 to 8 (rather than a mission control center of 20 front-room personnel). Such efforts are tremendously affected by assumptions of a U.S., Russian, Chinese, or some combination of perspectives on the design of mission control–crew interactions and the expectations of an emerging culture of spacefarers (Harrison, 2001; Oberg & Oberg, 1985).

Administrative and management difficulties within NASA, however, have seriously undermined the general culture and credibility of projections of future space activity (Launius, 2004; Moon, Mars, and Beyond, 2004). A presentation in *Wired* magazine demonstrated the differences in timelines between NASA planning documents of the period 1967–1996 and actual historical and current activity (di Justo, 2002). According to prior planning documents, extended mission stays on the moon, multiple human explorations of Mars, and outposts of anywhere from 10 to 50 people in low earth orbit were envisioned—all by early 2003.

Even before the loss of the space shuttle *Columbia* in February 2003, there were significant concerns about the ability of NASA to cost-effectively complete space station construction because of repeated cost overruns (Launius, 2004; Space Studies Board, National Research Council, 1997). Thus, a critical separation was already growing between the sense of competence and accomplishment of flight crews and controllers (representing the positive aspects of the NASA culture) and the loss of trust associated with fiscal and program management of NASA's bureaucracy. Pressure from these concerns also led to conflicts of cultural orientation and priorities for crews, and especially flight controllers, causing substantial role and goal conflicts (Columbia Accident Investigation Board, 2003).

Multiteam coordination and exchange of technical information in a timely, accurate, and unbiased manner has been highlighted as a serious breakdown affecting risk assessment and mediation during both the *Challenger* and the *Columbia* shuttle accidents (Columbia Accident Investigation Board, 2003; Launius, 2004). Improved communication and event management during all phases of space operations are at the core of the President's commission recommendation for a significant reorganization and evolution of the NASA structure and operational culture (Moon, Mars, and Beyond, 2004).

The technical challenges of supporting a space crew for durations ranging from 100 to 1,000 days (characteristic of space station operations through Mars explorations) are multiplied by issues of evolving controller and crew cultures and unique experiences changing on time scales much faster than the overall bureaucratic organization. Mission experience with the space station indicates that as elapsed crew time on board increases, the actual configuration, operation, and performance requirements for the space vehicle and crew members increasingly deviate from original designs. In addition, local experience and events (which may not be relevant or significant individually but aggregate over time) eventually accumulate to significant distinctions between ground-based understandings, expectations, or tolerances of crew or system behavior and those of the on-board crew.

Simple issues such as current location of objects, time required to access or stow equipment, or accuracy of current procedures have been identified as elements of concern for improving ground–crew coordination (J. Blume, personal communication, 2002; confidential astronaut and controller interviews, 1998–2001).

Continuous space operations do not have the distinct knowledge synchronization and version control capabilities of discrete missions (see Garrett, 2002); therefore, the challenges of maintaining appropriate knowledge and expertise coordination between ground-based flight controllers and onboard flight crews will certainly increase. By definition, group norms, identity, and shared understandings derive from these experiences. Therefore, crews that share information resources and references on extended duration missions will continue to experience greater needs for, and pressures to maintain, group culture and autonomy distinct from any ground-based planning or mission management entity. In addition, flight controllers will continue to experience substantial tensions between experiential bonding and operational responsibility to the flight crew and continued exposure to/ pressure from the larger (and less flexible) space flight organization.

The development and maintenance of effective, productive, and reduced-risk space flight operations depends on a critical sensitivity to and enhancement of the group dynamics and team–task coordination of both the controllers and the flight crews and the larger spacefaring organization that supports ground control and onboard crew members. Of course, selection and performance of the crew in space is essential to mission success; however, an organizational culture that allows for effective flow and synchronization of the team, task, and information path integration of the crew on the ground is clearly a required emphasis for future space operations.

REFERENCES

Atkinson, J. D., Jr., & Shafritz, J. M. (1985). *The real stuff: A history of NASA's astronaut recruitment program.* New York: Praeger.

Bailey, R. W. (1996). *Human performance engineering: Designing high quality professional user interfaces for computer products, applications, and systems* (3rd ed.). Upper Saddle River, NJ: Prentice Hall.

Brehmer, B. (1992). Dynamic decision making: Human control of complex systems. *Acta Psychologica, 81,* 211–241.

Brehmer, B., & Allard, R. (1991). Dynamic decision making: The effects of task complexity and feedback delay. In J. Rasmussen, B. Brehmer, & J. Leplat (Eds.), *Distributed decision making: Cognitive models for cooperative work* (pp. 319–347). London: Wiley.

Brehmer, B., & Dörner, D. (1993). Experiments with computer-simulated microworlds. *Computers in Human Behavior, 9,* 171–184.

Burke, C. S., Volpe, C., Cannon-Bowers, J. A., & Salas, E. (1993, March). *So what is teamwork anyway? A synthesis of the team process literature.* Paper presented at the 39th annual meeting of the Southeastern Psychological Association, Atlanta, GA.

Burrough, B. (1998). *Dragonfly: NASA and the crisis aboard Mir.* New York: Harper-Collins.

Caldwell, B. S. (1992). Group isolation and performance factors in human–environment systems. *AIAA Space Programs and Technologies Conference* (Report No. AIAA 92-1530). Huntsville, AL: American Institute of Aeronautics and Astronautics.

Caldwell, B. S. (1994). Coordination and synchronization of skilled performance in groups conducting space-based tasks. In C. A. Ntuen, E. H. Park, & J. H. Kim (Eds.), *Proceedings of the 1994 Human Interaction With Complex Systems Symposium* (pp. 126–132). Greensboro: North Carolina A&T State University.

Caldwell, B. S. (1997). Feedback control principles applied to long-term information technology use in organizations. In P. Seppala, T. Luopajarvi, C.-H. Nygard, & M. Matilla (Eds.), *Proceedings of the 13th Triennial Congress of the International Ergonomics Association* (pp. 567–569). Helsinki: Finnish Institute of Occupational Health.

Caldwell, B. S. (1999). Team performance in complex systems. In H.-J. Bullinger & J. Ziegler (Eds.), *Human–computer interaction: Communication, cooperation, and application design, Proceedings of HCI International '99, the 8th International Conference on Human–Computer Interaction* (Vol. 2, pp. 412–416). Mahwah, NJ: Erlbaum.

Caldwell, B. S. (2000). Information and communication technology needs for distributed communication and coordination during expedition-class space flight. *Aviation, Space, and Environmental Medicine, 71*(Suppl. 9), A6–A10.

Caldwell, B. S. (2002). Developing tools to support knowledge synchronization in distributed supervisory coordination. In H. Luczak, A. E. Çakir, & G. Çakir (Eds.), *Proceedings of the 6th International Scientific Conference on Work with Display Units: WWDU 2002—World Wide Work* (pp. 554–556). Berlin, Germany: ERGONOMIC.

Caldwell, B. S. (2003). *Distributed supervisory coordination with multiple operators and remote systems.* In IEEE International Conference on Systems, Man and Cybernetics (pp. 442–447). Washington, DC: IEEE.

Caldwell, B. S., & Everhart, N. C. (1998). Information flow and development of coordination in distributed supervisory control teams. *International Journal of Human–Computer Interaction, 10,* 51–70.

Caldwell, B. S., & Paradkar, P. (1995). Factors affecting user tolerance for voice mail message transmission delays. *International Journal of Human–Computer Interaction, 7,* 235–248.

Caldwell, B. S., Uang, S.-T., & Taha, L. H. (1995). Appropriateness of communications media use in organizations: Situation requirements and media characteristics. *Behaviour and Information Technology, 14,* 199–207.

Columbia Accident Investigation Board. (2003). *Columbia Accident Investigation Board report* (Vol. 1). Washington, DC: Author/NASA.

Connors, M. M., Harrison, A. A., & Akins, F. R. (1985). *Living aloft: Human requirements for extended spaceflight.* Washington, DC: NASA Scientific and Technical Information Branch.

Cooke, N. J., Cannon-Bowers, J. A., Kiekel, P. A., Rivera, K., Stout, R. J., & Salas, E. (2000). Improving teams' interpositional knowledge through cross training. In *Proceedings of the IEA 2000/HFES 2000 Congress* (pp. 2-390–2-393). Santa Monica, CA: Human Factors and Ergonomics Society.

Cooke, N. J., Kiekel, P. A., & Helm, E. E. (2001). Comparing and validating measures of team knowledge. In *Proceedings of the Human Factors and Ergonomics Society 45th Annual Meeting* (pp. 361–365). Santa Monica, CA: Human Factors and Ergonomics Society.

Daft, R. L., & Lengel, R. H. (1986). Organizational information requirements, media richness and structural design. *Management Science, 32,* 554–571.

D'Azzo, J. J., & Houpis, C. H. (1966). *Feedback control systems analysis and synthesis* (2nd ed.). New York: McGraw-Hill.

di Justo, P. (2002, December). The eagle has floundered. *Wired,* p. 054.

Dorf, R. C., & Bishop, R. H. (1995). *Modern control systems* (7th ed.). Reading, MA: Addison-Wesley.

Forrester, J. W. (1968). *Principles of systems* (2nd preliminary ed.). Cambridge, MA: MIT Press.

Foushee, H. C., & Helmreich, R. L. (1988). Group interaction and flight crew performance. In E. L. Wiener & D. C. Nagel (Eds.), *Human factors in aviation* (pp. 189–227). San Diego, CA: Academic Press.

Garrett, S. K. (2002). *Operational knowledge development and utilization: A study of process and usability.* Unpublished master's thesis, Purdue University.

Glenn, J. (with Taylor, N.). (1999). *John Glenn: A memoir.* New York: Bantam.

Harrison, A. A. (2001). *Spacefaring: The human dimension.* Berkeley: University of California Press.

Harrison, A. A., Clearwater, Y. A., & McKay, C. P. (Eds.). (1991). *From Antarctica to outer space: Life in isolation and confinement.* New York: Springer-Verlag.

Jagacinski, R. J., & Flach, J. M. (2003). *Control theory for humans: Quantitative approaches to modeling performance.* Mahwah, NJ: Erlbaum.

Kanas, N., & Caldwell, B. S. (2000). Personal, interpersonal, and group dynamic issues. *Aviation, Space, and Environmental Medicine, 71*(Suppl. 9), A26–A28.

Kranz, G. (2000). *Failure is not an option.* New York: Simon & Schuster.

Launius, R. D. (2004). *Frontiers of space exploration* (2nd ed.). Wesport, CT: Greenwood Press.

Lea, M. (1991). Rationalist assumptions in cross-media comparisons of computer-mediated communication. *Behaviour and Information Technology, 10*, 153–172.

Lucid, S. W. (1998, May). Six months on Mir. *Scientific American, 278*, 46–55.

McGrath, J. E. (1984). *Groups: Interaction and performance.* Englewood Cliffs, NJ: Prentice Hall.

Mills, T. M. (1967). *The sociology of small groups.* Englewood Cliffs, NJ: Prentice Hall.

Moon, Mars, and Beyond. (2004). *Report of the President's Commission on Implementation of United States Space Exploration Policy: A journey to inspire, innovate, and discover.* Washington, DC: Author.

Nickerson, R. S. (Ed.). (1995). *Emerging needs and opportunities for human factors research.* Washington, DC: National Academy Press.

Oberg, J. E. (2002, October 9). *The next space race?* Presentation given at Purdue University, West Lafayette, IN.

Oberg, J. E., & Oberg, A. R. (1985). *Pioneering space: Living on the next frontier.* New York: McGraw-Hill.

Orasanu, J., & Salas, E. (1993). Team decision making in complex environments. In G. Klein, J. Orasanu, R. Calderwood, & C. E. Zsambok (Eds.), *Decision making in action: Models and methods* (pp. 327–345). Norwood, NJ: Ablex.

Pasmore, W. A. (1988). *Designing effective organizations: The sociotechnical systems perspective.* New York: Wiley.

Patterson, E. S., Watts-Perotti, J., & Woods, D. D. (1999). Voice loops as coordination aids in space shuttle mission control. *Computer Supported Cooperative Work, 8*, 353–371.

Rouse, W. B., Cannon-Bowers, J. A., & Salas, E. (1992). The role of mental models in team performance in complex systems. *IEEE Transactions on Systems, Man, and Cybernetics, 22*, 1296–1308.

Sage, A. P. (1992). *Systems engineering.* New York: Wiley.

Shannon, C. E., & Weaver, W. (1949). *The mathematical theory of communication.* Urbana: University of Illinois Press.

Shaw, M. E. (1981). *Group dynamics: The psychology of small group behavior* (3rd ed.). New York: McGraw-Hill.

Sheridan, T. B. (1992). *Telerobotics, automation, and human supervisory control.* Cambridge, MA: MIT Press.

Smith, T. J., & Smith, K. U. (1987). Feedback-control mechanisms of human behavior. In G. Salvendy (Ed.), *Handbook of human factors* (pp. 251–293). New York: Wiley.

Space Studies Board, National Research Council. (1997). *The human exploration of space.* Washington, DC: National Academy Press.

Stasser, G., & Titus, W. (1987). Effects of information load and percentage of shared information on the dissemination of unshared information during group discussion. *Journal of Personality and Social Psychology, 53*, 81–93.

Sundstrom, E., De Meuse, K. P., & Futrell, D. (1990). Work teams: Applications and effectiveness. *American Psychologist, 45,* 120–133.

Swanson, G. E. (Ed.). (1999). *"Before this decade is out . . .": Personal reflections on the Apollo program.* Washington, DC: NASA History Office.

Swezey, R. W., & Salas, E. (Eds.). (1992). *Teams: Their training and performance.* Norwood, NJ: Ablex.

Trist, E. (1981). *The evolution of socio-technical systems* (Occasional Paper No. 2). Toronto, Ontario, Canada: Ontario Quality of Working Life Centre.

Valen, R. J., & Caldwell, B. S. (1991). National Park Service areas as analogues for Antarctic and space environments. In A. Harrison, Y. Clearwater, & C. McKay (Eds.), *From Antarctica to outer space: Life in isolation and confinement* (pp. 115–121). New York: Springer-Verlag.

Wang, E., & Caldwell, B. S. (2003). Human information flow and communication pattern in NASA mission control center. In *Proceedings of the 47th Annual Meeting of the Human Factors and Ergonomic Society* (pp. 11–15). Santa Monica, CA: Human Factors and Ergonomics Society.

Wolfram, S. (2001). *A new kind of science.* Champaign, IL: Wolfram Media.

III

THE FUTURE
OF TEAMWORK:
TECHNOLOGY AS A
TEAM MEMBER

Any state-of-the-art book on high-tech teams would fall short of its goals if it did not conclude with a look into the future and speculate about the things to come. With the joint evolution of teams and technology, we are beginning to look at technology as more than just a tool that supports team performance. As shown in Part II, the introduction of technology into a team environment can fundamentally change the way in which team members interact with one another. However, even the nature of teams and their makeup are affected by technology, and the future will bring new and exciting opportunities in this respect, as the chapters in this part show.

Part III begins with a detailed overview of the emerging phenomenon of virtual teams. It then takes the reader one step further by suggesting that different technologies can be used to support the newly emerging, previously unseen types of teams. Finally, in the last chapters, the traditional notions that teams of humans simply interact with technology are expanded by suggesting that technology itself may be an integral part of the team. For example, one may ask whether technology can act as a team member. The final two chapters both suggest that it can—and, in some cases, actually already does. Consequently, contemporary teams may no longer be easily classified as "teams" under the traditional definitions. As technology constantly evolves, we must keep in mind that our approach to defining critical concepts and to conducting research on team performance must consequently also evolve.

9

VIRTUAL TEAMS: CREATING CONTEXT FOR DISTRIBUTED TEAMWORK

HEATHER A. PRIEST, KEVIN C. STAGL, CAMERON KLEIN, AND EDUARDO SALAS

In a global community, competitive organizations must navigate complex, chaotic contexts. In fact, modern operational environments are most characterized by increasingly sophisticated challenges encountered when organizations attempt to capitalize on emerging domestic and global opportunities. For example, Amazon.com, Inc.'s, recent purchase of Joyo.com, China's largest online retailer of books, music, DVDs, and videos, presents a host of challenges to coordinating across time zones. Addressing these challenges requires innovative solutions, which for many organizations increasingly takes the form of team-based systems and cutting-edge technology. The use of teams and technology can, in turn, lead to unprecedented amounts of available information and performance capability. The accumulated information can be mined, and an organization's capability applied, to seize new domestic and transcontinental opportunities. Thus, the entire process can be described as a recursive cycle of progress.

The complexities illustrated by the recursive cycle of progress have served to ensure the ubiquity of teams within organizations. Furthermore, changes spurred by the ongoing technological revolution are nowhere more prevalent than as witnessed in the movement away from hierarchical structures to the use of multiteam systems (Mathieu, Marks, & Zaccaro, 2002). In fact, the results of a poll suggest that 80% of employees belong to at least one team (Fiore, Salas, & Cannon-Bowers, 2001). Furthermore, 68% of Fortune 1000 companies report using self-managed teams (Boiney, 2001). These estimates will certainly increase in the future because the coordination of "activities of individuals in large organizations is like building a sand castle using single grains of sand" (West, Borrill, & Unsworth, 1998, p. 6).

As teams become a preferred performance arrangement, there has been a simultaneous increase in the scientific investigation of team processes, performance, and effectiveness (Salas, Stagl, Burke, & Goodwin, in press). To date, most of the emphasis has been directed at colocated teams because, until recently, the interdependencies inherent to teamwork required teammates to be physically colocated in space and time (i.e., space–time). However, recent advances in computing have created the platforms, media, and architecture to facilitate teamwork across temporal or geographic locations (Bell & Kozlowski, 2002). These changes have had profound implications, resulting in a *distributed coordination space* where teamwork and team performance can occur almost anytime or anyplace (Fiore, Salas, Cuevas, & Bowers, 2003).

A number of organizational pioneers have already begun to capitalize on distributed team performance arrangements to cope with the increased complexity of today's operating environments. For example, GTECH reported improvements in the manageability of their manufacturing process and an annual savings of approximately $3 million as a result of using telework and distributed teams (Gaspar, 2001). AGI reported higher levels of flexibility and competitiveness as a result of implementing a virtual organizational design (Leimester, Weigle, & Krcmar, 2001). Similarly, Verifone has enjoyed considerable success as a result of company officials' decision to integrate virtual teams into its marketing and manufacturing functions (Pape, 1997). Moreover, Hewlett-Packard, Whirlpool, Johnson & Johnson, IBM, and Ford—all large, public corporations—currently are benefiting from virtual teamwork (Arnison & Miller, 2002).

As witnessed by the preceding examples, the ongoing shift to distributive team structures can be successful when properly orchestrated. However, the process of fostering virtual teamwork is currently more of an art than a science and, as such, many important questions remain to be answered. Therefore, in this chapter we present five areas of focus that address aspects of virtual teamwork. We begin by briefly describing our perspective of what defines a distributive performance arrangement and a virtual team. We follow this discussion by addressing several virtual team challenges (e.g., team opacity, distributed communication) and some solutions to facilitating adaptation and optimal performance. Next, we make an effort to reconcile these challenges by advancing a set of techniques (e.g., shared leadership systems, virtual environments [VEs]) for overcoming the process losses resulting from distribution. In the fourth section, we summarize, in the form of a set of guidelines for fostering effective virtual teamwork, the research and practice supporting these strategies. Finally, we discuss the implications of our research, along with future issues and challenges for virtual teams.

DISTRIBUTED PERFORMANCE ARRANGEMENTS AND VIRTUAL TEAMS

There is a building wave of research investigating effective teamwork and team performance (e.g., Marks, Mathieu, & Zaccaro, 2001; Salas, Stagl, & Burke, 2004; Sundstrom, McIntyre, Halfhill, & Richards, 2000). Although teamwork has been studied extensively, it remains to be established what differences, if any, exist between colocated coordinated action and distributed teamwork (Zaccaro & Ardison, 2003). Therefore, in this section we describe the nature of distributed performance arrangements and virtual teams in an effort to better understand these phenomena.

Distributed Performance Arrangements

As organizations become increasingly dependent on teams to operate successfully, the globalization process poses a unique challenge: How do organizations that are distributed globally use a system (i.e., teams) that is traditionally colocated? Like organizations themselves, teams have been forced to change with the times (Salas, Priest, Stagl, Sims, & Burke, in press). Distributed performance arrangements allow teams to operate across space–time. As few as a single team member, or as many members as the entire team, may be physically located in different offices, time zones, or even countries.

In the simplest sense, distribution is a performance arrangement that affects how the team members send, receive, interpret, and encode information. The "space between" thus has a profound impact on how team members think, act, and feel. For example, distribution influences the nature of team members' mental models and the cues on which functional experts can call during naturalistic decision making. Moreover, distributed performance arrangements can be traced to issues with conflict and shared identity (Mortensen & Hinds, 2001), workload or team opacity (Fiore et al., 2001), and team leadership (Bell & Kozlowski, 2002).

Virtual Teams

Virtual teams are not constrained by typical size limitations, have distributed functional expertise, and interact a majority of the time via computer-mediated communication. However, virtual teams are not in the strictest sense a unique type of team per se (e.g., management teams can be either colocated or distributed teams) but, rather, a type of team member configuration that facilitates the achievement of system and societal goals.

Because of their distributed nature, virtual teams must rely on some form of technology, ranging from primitive (e.g., telephone) to advanced (e.g., virtual reality). Thus, virtual teams are dispersed in space–time and use some form of technology to cross their divide. Beyond these basic parameters, there is considerable variability in defining what is meant by *virtual teams*. In fact, virtual teams have been defined in multiple but similar ways and are all but indistinguishable from *distributed teams*, the term typically used in current team literature.

Although there is a great deal of overlap between the definitions of *virtual* and *distributed*, we feel there remain important differences between these concepts. We defer to the prevailing practice of using interchangeably the labels *distributive teams* and *virtual teams*. However, as noted elsewhere (see Sundstrom et al., 2000; Zaccaro & Bader, 2003), and by us, albeit from a more technologically grounded perspective, there are differences between virtual and distributed teamwork that should be systematically investigated (see The Future of Virtual Teams in Distributed Environments, in this chapter).

Despite this definitional ambiguity, distinctions have been made concerning the characteristics of virtual teams (Bell & Kozlowski, 2002). In addition to the mode of communication used by virtual teams (e.g., asynchronous, synchronous), it has been suggested that four other characteristics also serve as differentiators: (a) temporal distribution, (b) boundary spanning, (c) life cycle, and (d) member roles (see Figure 9.1).

Temporal distribution refers to whether a team operates in the same locale or is distributed across space–time. In other words, teams can operate in the same place at different times (e.g., shift workers at a manufacturing plant), or at the same time in different places (e.g., air traffic control for the National Aeronautics and Space Administration at Houston, Texas, and Cape Canaveral, Florida). Virtual teams also have boundaries besides space–time that can be crossed. Virtual team members have the capability to span organizational, functional, and cultural boundaries (i.e., boundary spanning). Furthermore, virtual teams' life cycles are often discrete, although there is a great deal of variability. Thus, virtual teams are often created as temporary collaborations to fix a particular problem, and upon solution they disband. Even if a team has a longer life cycle, team membership is typically

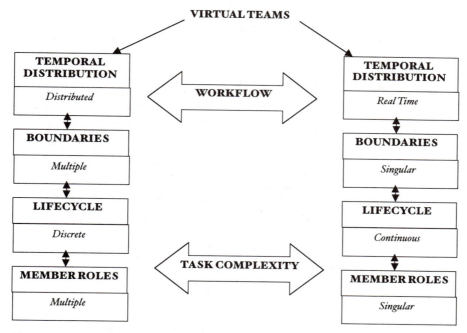

Figure 9.1. Characteristics that determine different types of virtual teams.

highly dynamic, with members frequently leaving and being replaced. Virtual team members also have more flexible and dynamic roles because they are not confined by rigid organizational responses.

Each of the four previously mentioned characteristics (i.e., temporal distribution, boundary spanning, life cycle, member roles) are determined in part by task complexity and workflow, which varies from team to team. Therefore, team members can be temporally distributed or operate in real time, boundaries can be singular or multiple, life cycles can be discrete or continuous, and member roles can be singular or multiple. Where a team falls along these four characteristics should not be considered in isolation but rather as a unique pattern that collectively determines the nature of the virtual team and, by consequence, its challenges.

Virtual teams have a number of benefits that can enhance public and private sector organizations (see Table 9.1). These benefits have contributed to an ever-increasing number of incumbents performing in locations that are separated from their supervisors, subordinates, and fellow team members. In fact, Bruck (2000) reported that some companies estimate that as much as 45% of their workforce are not colocated with management. Remarkably, Bruck's research concluded that much of the witnessed distribution was not due to conscious planning but likely resulted from the circumstances of

TABLE 9.1
Benefits of Virtual Teams

Area of benefit	Virtual teams
Time	• Allow flexible hours so employees can spend more time with their families • Result in employees who are more satisfied with their family and personal lives than before virtual teamwork • Save time and money in the daily transportation between home and work • Can operate around the clock and allow team members to work anytime, anywhere
Process improvement	• Disperse improved processes across organizations
Performance advantages	• Allow organizations to hire the best people for the job, regardless of location • Make collaboration across organizational boundaries possible • Allow flexible work hours and job design
Money	• Reduce restrictions on working hours • Require less parking space and office space • Reduce heating and electricity costs • Save money used for travel so team members can meet face to face • Allow team members to be less inhibited • Are less time intensive in the long run because of less socializing and more work

modern industry and global work, further emphasizing the need to study such an industry-fueled phenomenon. In the section that follows, we address some of the challenges that are faced by all virtual teams, irrespective of their particular characteristics.

CHALLENGES OF VIRTUAL TEAMWORK

The anecdotal evidence previously reported, which suggests that organizations are naturally evolving toward distributive structures, strengthens our conviction that the trend toward virtual teamwork will accelerate as operating environments become increasingly fluid. If the spread of virtual teams and distributed performance arrangements is all but inevitable, it is important to develop a deeper understanding of the challenges confronting this ongoing movement. The team literature already provides a variety of examples of knowledge/skills/attitudes and teamwork processes that may be adversely affected when teams use computer-mediated communication. For example, researchers have noted that distribution is detrimental to decision making (McLeod, 1992), social motivation (Cuevas, Fiore, Salas, & Bowers,

2004), cohesiveness (Straus, 1997), status equalization (Weisband, Schneider, & Connolly, 1995), and normative behavior (Siegel, Dubrovsky, Kiesler, & McGuire, 1986). Research also suggests that team development may be more complex in virtual teams (Driskell, Radtke, & Salas, 2003). In the remainder of this section, we provide a multilevel perspective (i.e., individual, team, organizational) of the primary challenges to fostering virtual team effectiveness. Building on this understanding, we advance a set of suggestions that are grounded in relevant literature that may alleviate some of these challenges.

Individual: Social Isolation

Despite the increased availability of communication technologies to support virtual workers, distribution often results in less frequent communication and social isolation (Belanger, Watson-Manheim, & Jordan, 2002). This is consistent with research proposing that the actual distance of team member separation is of secondary concern to the impact of computer-mediated communication on team processes (Bell & Kozlowski, 2002). The isolation resulting from separation and decreased interaction is a key factor limiting the adoption of distributed work. This is because many employees derive satisfaction from their interactions with their coworkers, "both in the act of socializing and through the social support they receive" (Ellison, 1999, p. 344). Furthermore, when employees are not colocated, social and task support may break down, causing people to identify less with the organization (Stohl, 1995). Proximity has been linked to informal channels of communication (e.g., the "water cooler") and is vital for disseminating information about organizational norms, socializing new employees, and encouraging collaboration and sharing of information (National Research Council, 1994). To the extent that distributed team members feel socially isolated from their coworkers, supervisors, and subordinates, the quality of both their work and family lives will suffer.

Research suggests that distributed team members experience lower levels of work–family conflict and commute time while concomitantly enjoying higher levels of personal control, job satisfaction, and productivity (Belanger et al., 2002). Hence, the much coveted goal of simultaneously improving employee satisfaction and productivity seems to be offered via distributed arrangements. Unfortunately, distribution can result in social isolation.

One solution already advanced in the current body of research suggests that increasing media richness, and thereby the number of cues available to team members, may be an important mechanism for reducing social isolation. Moreover, increasing media richness may help foster a social presence. *Social presence* is the degree to which technology facilitates a personal connection with others (Duarte & Tennant-Snyder, 1999). Interactions with high social presence are described as more lively, social, warm, and intimate than those with little social presence. Synchronous communications, such as face-to-face (FTF) meetings and audio- and videoconferences, result in more social presence than asynchronous communications such as electronic mail (e-mail) and voicemail. Synchronous communication facilitates social presence primarily because it enables the spontaneous, back-and-forth exchanges associated with normal conversation.

Although we acknowledge that a great deal of social presence and information richness is not always desirable, it seems reasonable that VEs are uniquely positioned to provide a level of cue richness normally restricted to FTF meetings, as well as the rendering and simulation of three-dimensional objects, avatars, and agents. In turn, digital avatars and agents can provide trusted companions to team members when navigating corporate archives, engaging in distributed self-directed training, or querying the organization about routine processes.

A second strategy for reducing social isolation is by building *communities of practice*, which have been defined as "naturally occurring informal groups in the workplace that come together, develop, evolve, and disperse according to the rhythm and energy of their participants" (Rossett & Sheldon, 2001, p. 217). These informal groups evolve over time and foster interpersonal exchanges about interests, hobbies, and skills. If a distributed team member can connect with a community of practice in his or her immediate vicinity, the ongoing interpersonal exchanges characterizing this activity may help offset the social decrements that occur because of distribution.

Team Opacity

As discussed throughout this chapter, teams separated by space–time have additional demands placed on them during distributed interaction. Interaction in distributed environments often leads to artificial and ambiguous experiences, in part based on a shortage of, or change in, the cues available to team members. Fiore and colleagues (2003) coined the term *team opacity* to describe the debilitating effects of distribution inherent to being virtual. Team opacity has been discussed as a special form of workload resulting from teams that are not colocated. *Team opacity* is defined as "the experience whereby distribution decreases awareness of team member actions and may thus alter their interaction" (Fiore et al., 2003, p. 5).

Cue deprivation can increase the workload of team members because they must adjust routine strategies to seek out additional cues. The absence of cues, typically present when teams are colocated, taxes the working memory of team members and prevents much of the scaffolding often used to reduce memory load in colocated teams (Fiore et al., 2003). Also, the lack of or change in cues affects interaction when teams are relegated to computer-mediated communication because of the loss of nonverbal cues such as facial expressions, nods, and gestures (Driskell et al., 2003).

Research suggests that information flow and information format can significantly influence team opacity (Fiore et al., 2003). Specifically, team opacity can be curtailed in part by increasing the synchrony and richness of available information (e.g., flow, format). These additional cues influence if, how, and when distributed team members enact knowledge/skills/ attitudes, thereby reducing opacity and increasing performance effectiveness. Appropriate communication channels and information formats should be implemented to strengthen the relationship between cognition and team behavior and lessen the workload (i.e., team opacity) of team members.

Individual, Team, and Organizational

Communication

Another important issue for distributed teams is their communication process. Because virtual members are not colocated in space–time, they do not receive as many cues as traditional teams. Thus, it is not surprising that some distributed teams have been found to be less effective than teams that are colocated, thanks in large part to poorer communication (Allaire, 1998). Therefore, it is vital that distributed teams have communication mechanisms that are sufficient, appropriate, and evolved enough to convey messages clearly and effectively. We believe the technological tools teams use influence the types of communication in which they can engage.

Clark and Brennan (1996) discussed factors that determine the nature of communication in distributed and FTF teams. They asserted that there are eight aspects of FTF and distributed settings that determine the nature of communication within a team: (a) copresence (i.e., team members share the same physical space), (b) visibility (i.e., team members can see each other), (c) audibility (i.e., team members can hear each other), (d) contemporability (i.e., team members receive communication at the approximate time it is sent), (e) simultaneity (i.e., team members can communicate simultaneously), (f) sequentiality (i.e., team members must communicate in sequence), (g) reviewability (i.e., team members can review each other's messages, similar to chat rooms), and (h) revisability (i.e., team members can revise each other's messages). These eight characteristics of communication can be linked to the types of communication available for colocated and distributed teams. This research underscores the point that the extent to which team members can communicate effectively has an influence on how well they perform.

The growth in communication technology has led to greater frequency of communication between coworkers or team members who are geographically and temporally distributed. One examination of this phenomenon was undertaken by Venkatesh and Johnson (2002), who examined different approaches and tools for implementing teleworkers and virtual teams. Their research indicates that early distributed teams were forced to communicate and archive through asynchronous communication applications such as electronic bulletin boards and then e-mail, which provided one-on-one communication. These asynchronous communication devices are valuable tools for distributed teams, especially to leave quick virtual notes.

Today, communication technology has evolved to include synchronous communication applications such as teleconferencing and videoconferencing. Synchronous communication offers more cues and is a closer approximation of FTF communication than asynchronous communication, thereby decreasing many of the negative effects of distribution. Therefore, synchronous communication tools should improve virtual team adaptation and performance. This line of thinking is consistent with past research that suggests communication is critical for team processes (Driskell et al., 2003; Fletcher & Major, 2003). The substantive relationships of interest are illustrated in Table 9.2. In essence, Fletcher and Major found that certain means of communication can improve or damage processes between team members.

Trust

Trust is a key influence on the overall performance and viability of distributed teams. We define *trust* as a psychological state comprising the intention to accept vulnerability based on positive expectations of the interactions with, or behaviors of, another (Rousseau, Sitkin, Burt, & Camerer, 1998). Trust supports interrelationships, functional interactions, communication, coordination, and cooperation between team members. Without sufficient trust, team members will expend time and energy protecting, checking, and inspecting each other's work as opposed to collaborating in facilitation of process gains (Cooper & Sawaf, 1996).

Jones and George (1998) found that, in addition to mediating cooperation and teamwork, trust also fosters a willingness to disseminate information more freely among team members. Trust has also been found to increase coordinated teamwork behaviors and reduce individual-based goals (Dirks, 1999). Furthermore, recent evidence indicates that although trust may influence interactions in virtual settings (e.g., Lewicki & Bunker, 1996; Mayer, Davis, & Schoorman, 1995; Meyerson, Weick, & Kramer, 1996), it may also simultaneously be more difficult to foster in these settings (e.g., Cramton, 2001; Jarvenpaa & Leidner, 1999).

One way to overcome this issue may be in the formation of trust based on expectations in distributed teams. The term *swift trust* has been coined in reference to the formation of trust that occurs between interdependent

TABLE 9.2
Communication Characteristics of Colocated and Distributed Environments and Team Process Variables

Communication characteristics	Team process[a]	Environments				
		Face to face	Real time audio/ video	Audio only	Real time electronic mail	Electronic mail
Copresence	Backup behavior Monitoring Intrateam feedback Nonverbal communication	X				
Visibility	Backup behavior Monitoring Intrateam feedback Nonverbal communication	X	X			
Audibility	Backup behavior Monitoring Intrateam feedback	X	X	X		
Contemporality	Backup behavior Monitoring Intrateam feedback Nonverbal communication	X	X	X	X	
Simultaneity	Backup behavior Monitoring Intrateam feedback Nonverbal communication	X	X	X	X	
Sequentiality	Backup behavior Monitoring Intrateam feedback Nonverbal communication	X	X	X	X	
Reviewability	Backup behavior Monitoring Intrateam feedback				X	X
Revisability	Backup behavior Monitoring Intrateam feedback				X	X

[a]Based on results from Fletcher and Major (2003).

individuals whose communication is limited to computer-mediated exchanges and is based on the expectations of the trustworthiness of other team members (Meyerson et al., 1996). Swift trust, also referred to as *conditional trust*, is based only on the impressions, expectations, and individual reputations of team members. Approaches are available for fostering swift trust, such as clearly defining roles to align expectations, creating accountability systems, and measuring both processes and outcomes.

In this section we have described some of the more widely discussed challenges of virtual teams. If these individual, team, and organizational challenges are addressed directly, they can be headed off before they debilitate team members, virtual teams, and multiteam systems and thereby damage the organization. Thus, key stakeholders must be diligent in implementing and maintaining virtual teams by providing them with the tools and resources to be successful.

STRATEGIES FOR NAVIGATING DISTRIBUTIVE CHALLENGES

In addition to the communication tools and swift trust promotion discussed earlier as possible solutions to the challenges inherent in distributed work, we believe broader interventions can also be used to improve the probability of success in virtual teams. On the basis of what we know about traditional teams and what we have learned to date about the vulnerabilities of virtual teams, certain approaches can be applied during team training and the implementation of teams in distributed environments to lessen the negative effects of distribution.

We begin this three-part section with a discussion of team competencies, processes, and emergent states that should be targeted in training. In the last two sections, we directly address interventions that are critical to the implementation and maintenance of virtual teams in organizations. The competencies (e.g., metacognition), emergent states (e.g., shared mental models), and interventions (e.g., VEs) we review in the following section are believed to be of particular importance to promoting distributed teamwork. In the second and third parts of this section, we outline specific strategies (e.g., training, VEs) that can be called on to promote target competencies and emergent states.

Target Appropriate Competencies and Emergent States

Individual and Team Cognitions

Researchers are increasingly incorporating constructs and theories from cognitive psychology to understand effective team performance in colocated settings (e.g., Cohen, Freeman, & Wolf, 1996; Lord & Emrich, 2001). The growing interest in the cognitive underpinnings of teamwork is in part driven by the premise that higher order cognitions, such as individual and team metacognition, are critical to promoting adaptive and effective performance. In fact, research results suggest that leader metacognition predicts adaptive team performance (Marsh, Kiechel-Koles, Boyce, & Zaccaro, 2001). With the potential for leadership ambiguity and the need for distributed cognition in virtual teams, the effect of cognition at the individual and team levels in distributed teamwork may be even more important than in traditional settings.

Metacognition. *Metacognition* has been defined in terms of its executive roles as "both an awareness of and ability to regulate one's own cognitive processes" (Banks, Bader, Fleming, Zaccaro, & Barber, 2001, p. 10). Metacognition serves to control the application of cognitive skills and abilities, such as information processing, inductive reasoning, and deductive reasoning. It should be understood, however, that metacognition and self-regulation are distinct cognitive processes operating at different levels of goal specificity but operating in concert.

Self-regulation, like metacognition, is believed to influence team performance and processes (Driskell et al., 2003). Specifically, *self-regulation* refers to the active process whereby individuals set performance standards, monitor progress, seek and evaluate feedback, detect discrepancies in their performance, and take actions to reduce discrepancies. "This perspective rejects the view of task performers as passive recipients of information, but instead views effective team members as actively trying to make use of information from the task and the social environment to guide and improve performance" (Driskell et al., 2003, p. 25).

Metacognition and self-regulation are particularly important in virtual teams, where team members must be proactive and diligent in their pursuit of effective teamwork. Distributed team members must be aware of their use of cognitive resources when faced with team opacity in order to effectively communicate and coordinate with their distributed teammates. Also, distributed teams are often self-managed and therefore must be especially effective at self-regulating during task, team, contextual, and adaptive performance.

Transactive memory. *Transactive memory* can be defined as a mechanism for transforming individual-level information into team knowledge or "a group's shared understanding of who knows what" (Griffith & Neale, 2001, p. 381). As might be expected, transactive memory can be vital to team performance, especially in dynamic or complex environments where team members need a great deal of interaction to overcome the problems associated with distribution. In other words, team members, especially under pressure, need to know which team member can do which job or to whom they can turn for help in a given situation (Austin, 2003). We assert that knowing who can do what, and when, is critical to dynamically reallocating functions and, ultimately, to facilitating adaptive team performance.

With regard to virtual teams, there are a number of hurdles to sharing and encoding knowledge to foster a reliable transactive memory system. For example, team members must be willing to share with one another the knowledge they bring with them. Mutual respect, interpersonal trust, and the extent to which members identify with their teammates have all been found to influence the likelihood that teams will develop transactive memory (Moreland, 1999). However, virtual teams have difficulties developing the social identity necessary to establish the levels of trust and interpersonal relationships requisite to fostering transactive memory systems.

Communication is also vital to establishing transactive memory in virtual teams (Yoo & Kanawattanachai, 2001). When teams are not FTF, team members must communicate what they know to each other explicitly. Implicit information passed from member to member based on everyday interaction around the office is limited in distributed settings. Also, because virtual teams' life cycles are often discrete, team members may not have the time to learn requisite information about their fellow teammates. Therefore, for virtual teams to develop shared knowledge structures, it is acutely necessary to spell out the information that all team members need to know. In sum, developing trust and interpersonal relationships as soon as possible into the team's life cycle, establishing a social identity for team members within the context of the virtual team, and encouraging open and frequent communication among team members are all ways to improve transactive memory in virtual teams.

Shared mental models. The loss of both overt and covert cues (e.g., social status, reactionary facial gestures) in distributed environments amplifies the need for teams to develop shared mental models. Shared mental models influence the cues team members perceive in their operating environments and how recognized cues are reacted on (Senge, 1990). A given shared mental model can relate to equipment, tasks, team members, team interactions, and problems/situations. In essence, team members operating from a shared mental model have a common conceptual framework that enables them to perceive, interpret, and respond to dynamic environments in a synchronized, adaptive fashion (Schlechter, Zaccaro, & Burke, 1998).

The driving philosophy behind this cognitively laden approach to understanding teamwork assumes that synchronicity can be achieved when team members develop clusters of shared, accurate, and instantiated knowledge structures and activate those structures in working memory (i.e., shared mental models). This line of reasoning is supported by accumulating research (Cannon-Bowers & Salas, 1998; Cooke, Salas, Cannon-Bowers, & Stout, 2000; Ensley & Pearce, 2001). In fact, numerous studies have shown that shared mental models facilitate coordinated team action (Burke & Zaccaro, 2000; Marks, Sabella, Burke, & Zaccaro, 2002; Mathieu, Heffner, Goodwin, Salas, & Cannon-Bowers, 2000).

From the preceding discussion one can intuit that shared mental models will significantly benefit team members who operate at a distance. Unfortunately, however, distributed teams may have more difficulty with the initial formation of accurate shared mental models because their dispersion reduces the opportunity for FTF contact. However, we suspect that the additional cues afforded by synthetic environments will offset the process losses that result from distribution. As such, virtual cues may help teams form and maintain mental models and thus ensure process gains in distributed performance arrangements.

A second strategy for promoting shared mental models is to bring distributed team members together initially to meet one on one before they perform their tasks virtually. An initial FTF meeting can help teams form shared mental models and thereby improve coordination and interpersonal relationships. Once accurate shared mental models are formed, distributed teams should perform in a more efficient manner because they will be better able to perceive and interpret cues through a common perceptual lens.

Organizational: Shared Leadership Systems

As operational environments become increasingly complex, there is mounting pressure on teams and their members to be adaptive (Klein & Pierce, 2001; Kozlowski, 1998). In response to this challenge, research is underway to examine the role of shared cognition in facilitating shared leadership and team adaptability (Burke, Fiore, & Salas, 2002; Burke, Stagl, Salas, & Kendall, 2005). The need for adaptability can be cued by events that are internal or external to the team and can be reactively or proactively orchestrated. Although adaptive team performance can occur because of the efforts of a single empowered team member, or by means of the coordinated action of the collective, it is often the team leader who initially picks up on, interprets, and initiates an adaptive response. This process will increasingly need to be pushed to lower echelons and empowered team members, especially in distributed teams where leadership is often shared.

Effective team leaders engage in a sense-making and sense-giving process (Weick, 1996). This continual exchange between a team leader and the team's environment, and between a team leader and his or her team, contributes to the development and maintenance of shared mental models (Burke & Zaccaro, 2000). Furthermore, sense-giving facilitates adaptive performance by means of the creation and maintenance of team coherence (Burke, Salas, Stagl, & Fowlkes, 2002). Although sense-making and sense-giving have seldom been generalized to the domain of distributed teamwork, today it is not uncommon to find that expert team members are empowered, enabled, and sharing leadership functions and roles. Shared leadership systems reduce the complexity of the process whereby events are recognized, meaning is ascribed, and an adaptive response is cued, because this type of intervention provides every team member with the autonomy to recognize the need for and enact appropriate innovations and modifications.

In order for team members to flourish in shared leadership systems, as well as become effective leaders within VEs, organizations must create and provide the systems, tools, protocols, and training to ensure their success. In essence, organizations should seek to implement a system of systems that allows team members to regulate their own performance (Kozlowski, 1998). An empowering leadership system helps create distributed minds. The key is to link the minds together, not to superimpose the minds of the leaders on those of the workers (Fisher & Fisher, 1998).

Developing Distributed Team Members

Training

The process of developing distributive team members is founded on the same three pillars that support all comprehensive developmental initiatives: (a) formal training, (b) operational assignments, and (c) self-development. The emphasis herein, however, is toward formal training activities. In this section, we highlight scenario-based training (SBT), also known as *event-based training*, an instructional strategy that can be delivered by means of simulation technologies. Coupling SBT with high- or low-fidelity simulation creates a learning environment that is powerful enough to facilitate the development of core teamwork competencies and flexible enough to be deliverable in distributed team environments. In what follows, we emphasize the use of SBT for developing virtual team member meta-cognition.

SBT is an instructional strategy that presents trainees with an integrated set of trigger events that are based on training objectives. The presented events are tightly scripted to provide trainees with repeated opportunities to practice and receive developmental feedback while immersed in a fluid context (Cannon-Bowers, Burns, Salas, & Pruitt, 1998). Furthermore, advanced forms of SBT can be designed to incorporate a structured measurement system known as TARGETS (i.e., Targeted Acceptable Responses to Generated EvenTS). The TARGETS system is engineered to facilitate a trainer's efforts to recognize and capture multiple manifestations of targeted competencies (Dwyer, Fowlkes, Oser, Salas, & Lane, 1997).

SBT simulations create a *microworld* that increases psychological fidelity, experimental realism, mundane realism, risk taking, and trainee experimentation (Senge, 1990). Microworlds encourage virtual team members to invoke strategies and plans that would be deemed too risky for actual performance environments because they are characterized by a sense of psychological safety (Edmondson, 1999, 2002). Virtual team members who participate in the simulated experience benefit by developing more accurate cognitive maps or mental models of the key tasks, equipment, and problems likely to be encountered during performance.

Intertwining SBT with simulation technologies provides an instructional strategy and medium for developing virtual team member metacognition. This approach assumes that "metacognition is somewhat malleable and can be influenced, at least for some individuals" (Schmidt & Ford, 2001, p. 25). Specifically, team member metacognitive skills can be developed in an adaptive learning environment that incorporates advanced organizers, promotes trainee control, presents mastery goals, and encourages trainees to adopt a learning goal orientation. It has also been suggested that training design characteristics such as difficulty, sequencing, complexity, and variability influence the depth and speed of knowledge acquisition (Kozlowski, 1998).

Additional research is needed to examine the role of different forms of interpretative feedback during training for promoting metacognition and create the potential for scenario-based designs with embedded error events that trigger metacognition and foster self-regulation (Kozlowski, 1998). Similarly, researchers have investigated incorporating embedded prompts to trigger metacognitive monitoring and control during Web-based training (Toney & Ford, 2001). The results from this research initiative suggest that embedded prompts are successful in promoting both metacognitive monitoring and metacognitive control.

Virtual Environments

As organizations turn to team-based structures as a preferred performance arrangement, there has been increasing attention directed at the benefits of distributed performance arrangements. As noted throughout this chapter, however, distributed teams are wrought with taskwork and teamwork challenges.

Some authors (see Venkatesh & Johnson, 2002) propose that the next step must be taken to ensure the full utilization of teleworkers, distributed teams, and their work environments. This next step is the combination of synchronous communication applications and virtual reality technology, which currently can be seen in amusement parks and arcades. Aspects of virtual reality serve as visual and auditory tools and create the possibility of a common virtual meeting place for team members (e.g., a "virtual office").

Like Venkatesh and Johnson (2002), we suggest that many of the challenges can be overcome by creating VEs within which distributed team members can perform. Specifically, we suspect that the use of VEs will promote the development of shared mental models, trust, and coordination. This is because VEs allow team members to have an alternative common workplace, receive more and richer cues, and meet "face to face" in a virtual space. By virtually colocating teams, organizations can provide better leadership, enrich sense-giving messages, and reduce social isolation.

However, media richness and increased cues are not always the solution. Although the technology driving high-fidelity simulation is truly impressive, there are many low-fidelity, low-cost simulators that are equally effective. In fact, Marks's (2000) findings suggest that the physical fidelity of the simulator is not nearly as important as the psychological fidelity that results from its use. As a rule of thumb, the complexity replicated by a simulator should approximate the psychological complexity experienced by a team in its natural operational environment. Thus, low-cost simulators are available as an affordable alternative for researchers or businesses that would like to capitalize on the benefits of simulation (Jentsch & Bowers, 1998; Koonce & Bramble, 1998).

As discussed earlier, the degree of media richness of communication modalities determines the amount of cues received by team members. This can have a significant effect on aspects we labeled as challenges for virtual teams (e.g., team opacity). Richer cues can lead to improvements in team processes because, with improving technology, FTF interaction can be simulated. However, little is known to date about the effects of virtual reality technology on team process. This is because the majority of research investigating how virtual simulation technologies (see Draper, Viirre, Furness, & Gawron, 2001; Waller, 2000) have targeted the individual has been more concerned with the technology than with teams.

Although there is a paucity of team research in this area, more companies than ever are implementing simulation technology into their operations, and the military has long used VE simulations for soldiers. For example, practitioners have relied on a virtual office to provide a meeting place for distributed teams (Helms & Raiszadeh, 1997). On the basis of what is currently known about VEs from literature on individuals, there are a number of factors that can enhance team member experiences and, perhaps, make team members feel like they are FTF. In the remainder of this section, we continue this line of thinking by addressing the benefits of VEs.

One way to overcome the challenges of distributed teams is to establish a VE that creates a sense of involvement, immersion, and presence. The virtual aspect of teams (i.e., the technology that allows team members to see and hear each other) may be seen as an enabling tool for distributed teams to carry out their work. Involvement and immersion can best be described as psychological states that contribute to the experience of presence (Witmer & Singer, 1998). Specifically, *involvement* results from the user's focus of attention and energy on a coherent set of stimuli or related set of activities (Witmer & Singer). *Immersion* is defined by numerous studies as the feeling of "being there," getting caught up in an environment, and a feeling of being enveloped by the environment (Jacobson, 2002; Lombard & Ditton, 1997; Psotka, 1995). Ultimately, a VE that produces higher levels of involvement and immersion will lead to higher levels of presence for the user.

Previous literature describes the concept of presence as a subjective experience. Presence extends the feeling of immersion to describe the experience and feeling of a user actually being in an alternative environment (e.g., a VE) than the one in which they are actually physically located. *Presence* can be thought of as a feeling of "getting lost or wrapped up in the representations; of being involved, absorbed, engaged, or engrossed in or by them" (Jacobson, 2002, p. 2). Simply stated, a user who interacts with a VE may become involved and feel immersed within his or her virtual surroundings. The result of this increased level of involvement is that users actually feel like they are in the VE and that they can affect, and be affected by, it.

Increased involvement, immersion, and presence can contribute to increased cues and social context that, as discussed in previous sections, may help virtual teams overcome some of their difficulties. For a deeper understanding of the various aspects that contribute to involvement, immersion, and presence, please see Table 9.3 for empirical findings revolving around these issues.

GUIDELINES FOR VIRTUAL TEAMWORK

On the basis of the information in the virtual teamwork literature to date, certain trends can be identified. We have distilled and synthesized these trends to advance a set of guidelines for practitioners and researchers who manage and interact with virtual teams. Although one could argue that different guidelines should be applied to different types of teams, the following 17 points are intended as a general advice to help promote effective performance when teams are not colocated:

1. Provide clear, engaging directions and specific individual goals for virtual team members to enhance self-regulation, metacognition, and shared mental models.
2. Create structure, standard operating procedures, rules, protocols, and guidelines to promote habitual routines.
3. Distribute leadership functions to the team, moving away from hierarchical organization.

TABLE 9.3
Empirical Findings Identifying Factors That Contribute to Presence (Witmer & Singer, 1998)

Source	Findings
Barfield & Hendrix (1995)	Update rate (i.e., the frequency in frames per second at which computer-generated images change in response to user actions or to other dynamic aspects of the situation) affects performance in virtual environments.
Barfield & Weghorst (1993)	On a presence survey, "being there" questions were correlated with comfort, presentation quality, and location information; "inclusion" questions were correlated with general comfort, ease of interaction, ease of movement, and the ability to introspect; and "presence" questions were correlated with enjoyment, orientation, and presentation quality.
Hoffman, Prothero, Wells, & Groen (1998)	Presence in chess players was higher when chess pieces were arranged in meaningful patterns.
Prothero & Hoffman (1995)	Using an eye mask to limit the field of view near the eye reduces the amount of presence reported.
Witmer & Singer (1998)	Control (which affects immersion), selective attention, perceptual fidelity, naturalness of the interaction, and how closely the interactions mimic real world experiences affect how much presence is reported.

4. Support both synchronous and asynchronous interaction.
5. Select appropriate virtual work tasks that are not so complex that they are better suited for FTF teams.
6. Supply team members with information that may not be available through the VE (e.g., team member availability).
7. Provide enhanced distributed activity using project management software, structured workflow, and decision support systems to teams using virtual technology.
8. Create opportunities for all team members to participate in group discussions to maintain relationships among team members.
9. Provide metacognitive training to promote efficiency in distributed teams.
10. Hold initial FTF meetings to promote shared mental models and the formation of interpersonal relationships.
11. Use scenario-based training to help distributed teams develop team processes vital for success.

12. Provide tools to help team members adapt to changing circumstances.
13. Select team tasks that are appropriate for virtual teamwork.
14. Provide team building and collaboration training.
15. Create project deadlines that agree with the team development model.
16. Share critical information among team members.
17. Allow personal communication and informal social time, if only virtually, to foster improved interpersonal relations.

THE FUTURE OF VIRTUAL TEAMS IN DISTRIBUTED ENVIRONMENTS

There has been an explosion of interest in distributed teams and virtual teamwork. These investigatory streams have predictably taken multiple directions in their explorations. Therefore, it is not surprising to find that there has been a marked rise in the number of definitions and operationalizations of related team constructs, with mounting conceptual ambiguity spilling over into team research. In fact, on reviewing the last century of team research, Sundstrom et al. (2000) stated there is "a huge variety of operational definitions" (p. 52). This is especially troublesome in light of the fact that the behavioral sciences have had a history of difficulty with encoding, accessing, and storing accumulated knowledge (Campbell, 1990). Thus, we argue for common ground across virtual team constructs.

Distributed or virtual teamwork is becoming increasingly vital to organizations in wide-ranging industries. Although researchers have been quick to recognize the challenge of distributed teams, there is still a great deal to be resolved. A common, overarching delineation of terms and concepts is a good first step. For example, research often labels collectives as virtual teams when in fact they may be better identified as distributed teams engaging in some level of virtual teamwork. The virtual aspect of a team's performance environment does not constitute a type of team per se but rather describes a medium through which distributed teams accomplish their goals.

All of the avenues of research discussed herein contribute to the understanding of distributed and virtual teamwork. Furthermore, a strong argument can be made that divergent approaches to investigating teams are essential for innovation as well as for triangulation of constructs in a nomological network of lawful relations. However, researchers must take care to systematically collect, integrate, and synchronize this diverse set of findings or, as the pace of research accelerates, the investigation of teams risks fragmentation.

CONCLUSION

We undertook this investigation of virtual teamwork to provide readers with a view of where globalization and technological innovation have taken teams in the 21st century. The goal of this chapter was to leave readers better informed about the state of current research and industry practices regarding virtual teams. More important, however, we must also realize how much there is to be learned about the complexity of teams that are virtually connected. The benefits (e.g., more time, less money, better workers) bring about challenges (e.g., social isolation) that have not yet been fully resolved. Emerging technologies (e.g., virtual reality) offer hope in compensating for process losses (e.g., as caused by rigid shared mental models). Moreover, training has long been a vital ingredient to effective and efficient performance. There are already guidelines to assist professionals in implementing virtual teams, but many more need to be articulated. Empirical evidence of the effects of distribution on teams will need to be accumulated to ensure that virtual teams deliver on their potential. The final lesson here is that although we have come a long way and gained a great deal of insight, there is more yet to learn.

REFERENCES

Allaire, P. (1998). Lessons in teamwork. In D. C. Hambrick, D. A. Nadler, & M. L. Tushman (Eds.), *Navigating change: How CEOs, top teams, and boards steer transformation* (pp. 119–120). Boston: Harvard Business School Press.

Arnison, L., & Miller, P. (2002). Virtual teams: A virtue for the conventional team. *Journal of Workplace Learning, 14,* 166–173.

Austin, J. R. (2003). Transactive memory in organizational groups: The effects of content, consensus, specialization, and accuracy on group performance. *Journal of Applied Psychology, 5,* 866–878.

Banks, D., Bader, P., Fleming, P., Zaccaro, S., & Barber, H. (2001, April). Leader adaptability: The role of work experiences and leader attributes. In S. J. Zaccaro (Chair), *Leadership and team adaptation: Examining the attributes and training strategies that promote effective performance in dynamic environments.* Symposium conducted at the 16th annual conference of the Society for Industrial and Organizational Psychology, San Diego, CA.

Barfield, W., & Hendrix, C. (1995). The effect of update rate on the sense of presence within virtual environments. *Virtual Reality: Research, Development, and Application, I(1),* 3–15.

Barfield, W., & Weghorst, S. (1993). The sense of presence within virtual environments: A conceptual framework. In G. Salvendy & M. J. Smith (Eds.), *Proceed-*

ings of the fifth international conference on human–computer interaction: Vol. 2, (pp. 699–704). Amsterdam: Elsevier.

Belanger, F., Watson-Manheim, M. B., & Jordan, D. H. (2002). Aligning IS research and practice: An agenda for virtual work. *Information Resources Management Journal, 15,* 48–70.

Bell, B. S., & Kozlowski, S. W. J. (2002). A typology of virtual teams: Implications for effective leadership. *Group & Organization Management, 27,* 14–49.

Boiney, L. G. (2001). *Gender impacts virtual work teams: Men want clear objectives while women value communication.* Retrieved March 13, 2003, from http://gbr. pepperdine.edu

Bruck, B. (2000). *How companies work: Creating virtual teams that work.* Retrieved January 23, 2003, from http://www.caucus.com/whitepapers.html

Burke, C. S., Fiore, S. M., & Salas, E. (2002). The role of shared cognition in enabling shared leadership and team adaptability. In C. L. Pearce & J. A. Conger (Eds.), *Shared leadership: Reframing the hows and whys of leadership* (pp. 103–122). Thousand Oaks, CA: Sage.

Burke, C. S., Salas, E., Stagl, K. C., & Fowlkes, J. E. (2002, April). Leading multinational teams. In J. C. Ziegert & K. J. Klein (Cochairs), *Team leadership: Current theoretical and research perspectives.* Symposium conducted at the 17th annual conference of the Society for Industrial and Organizational Psychology, Toronto, Ontario, Canada.

Burke, C. S., Stagl, K. C., Salas, E., & Kendall, D. L. (2005). *Understanding team adaptation: A conceptual analysis and model.* Manuscript submitted for publication.

Burke, C. S., & Zaccaro, S. J. (2000, April). Leadership effects on team adaptability: Implications on team and leader training. In S. W. J. Kozlowski (Chair), *Developing complex adaptive skills: Individual and team level training strategies.* Symposium conducted at the 15th annual conference of the Society for Industrial and Organizational Psychology, New Orleans, LA.

Campbell, J. P. (1990). The role of theory in industrial and organizational psychology. In M. D. Dunnette & L. M. Hough (Eds.), *Handbook of industrial and organizational psychology* (Vol. 1, pp. 39–74). Palo Alto, CA: Consulting Psychologists Press.

Cannon-Bowers, J. A., Burns, J., Salas, E., & Pruitt, J. (1998). Advance technology in scenario-based training. In J. A. Cannon-Bowers & E. Salas (Eds.), *Making decisions under stress: Implications for individual and team training* (pp. 365–374). Washington, DC: American Psychological Association.

Cannon-Bowers, J. A., & Salas, E. (1998). Individual and team decision making under stress: Theoretical underpinnings. In J. A. Cannon-Bowers & E. Salas (Eds.), *Making decisions under stress: Implications for individual and team training* (pp. 17–38). Washington, DC: American Psychological Association.

Clark, H. H., & Brennan, S. E. (1996). Grounding in communication. In L. B. Resnick, J. M. Levine, & S. D. Teasley (Eds.), *Perspectives on socially shared cognition* (pp. 127–149). Washington, DC: American Psychological Association.

Cohen, M. S., Freeman, J. T., & Wolf, S. (1996). Metacognition in time-stressed decision making: Recognizing, critiquing, and correcting. *Human Factors, 38*, 206–219.

Cooke, N. J., Salas, E., Cannon-Bowers, J. A., & Stout, R. J. (2000). Measuring team knowledge. *Human Factors, 42*, 151–173.

Cooper, R. K., & Sawaf, A. (1996). *Executive EQ: Emotional intelligence and leadership in organizations*. New York: Perigree Books.

Cramton, C. D. (2001). The mutual knowledge problem and its consequences for dispersed collaboration. *Organization Science, 12*, 346–371.

Cuevas, H. M., Fiore, S. M., Salas, E., & Bowers, C. A. (2004). Virtual teams as sociotechnical systems. In S. H. Godar & S. P. Ferris (Eds.), *Virtual and collaborative teams: Process, technologies, and practice* (pp. 1–19). Hershey, PA: Idea Group.

Dirks, K. T. (1999). The effects of interpersonal trust on work group performance. *Journal of Applied Psychology, 84*, 445–455.

Draper, M. H., Viirre, E. S., Furness, T. A., & Gawron, V. J. (2001). Effects of image scale and system time delay on simulator sickness within head-coupled virtual environments. *Human Factors, 43*, 129–146.

Driskell, J. E., Radtke, P. H., & Salas, E. (2003). Virtual teams: Effects of technological mediation on team performance. *Group Dynamics: Theory, Research and Practice, 7*, 29–33.

Duarte, D. L., & Tennant-Snyder, N. (1999). *Mastering virtual teams: Strategies, tools, and techniques that succeed*. San Francisco: Jossey-Bass.

Dwyer, D. J., Fowlkes, J. E., Oser, R. L., Salas, E., & Lane, N. E. (1997). Team performance measurement in distributed environments: The TARGET's methodology. In M. T. Brannick, E. Salas, & C. Prince (Eds.), *Assessment and management of team performance: Theory, research, and applications* (pp. 137–154). Mahwah, NJ: Erlbaum.

Edmondson, A. C. (1999). Psychological safety and learning behavior in work teams. *Administrative Science Quarterly, 44*, 350–383.

Edmondson, A. C. (2002, April). *Leading for learning: How team leaders promote speaking up and learning in interdisciplinary action teams*. Symposium presented at the 17th annual conference of the Society for Industrial and Organizational Psychology, Toronto, Ontario, Canada.

Ellison, N. B. (1999). Social impacts: New perspectives on telework. *Social Science Computer Review, 17*, 338–356.

Ensley, M. D., & Pearce, C. L. (2001). Shared cognition in top management teams: Implications for new venture performance. *Journal of Organizational Behavior, 22*, 145–160.

Fiore, S. M., Salas, E., Cuevas, H. M., & Bowers, C. A. (2003). Distributed coordination space: Toward a theory of distributed team performance. *Theoretical Issues in Ergonomic Science, 4(3–4)*, 340–363.

Fiore, S. M., Salas, E., & Cannon-Bowers, J. A. (2001). Group dynamics and shared mental model development. In M. London (Ed.), *How people evaluate others in organizations* (pp. 309–336). Mahwah, NJ: Erlbaum.

Fisher, K., & Fisher, M. D. (1998). *The distributed mind: Achieving high performance through the collective intelligence of knowledge work teams.* Washington, DC: American Medical Association.

Fletcher, T. D., & Major, D. A. (2003, April). The effects of communication modality on teamwork processes. In T. M. Nielson (Chair), *Virtual teams: Exploring new frontiers in research and practice.* Symposium conducted at the 18th annual conference of the Society for Industrial and Organizational Psychology, Orlando, FL.

Gaspar, S. (2001). Virtual teams, real benefits. *Network World.* Retrieved December 22, 2002, from www.nwfusion.com/careers/2001/0924man.html

Griffith, T. L., & Neale, M. A. (2001). Information processing in traditional, hybrid, and virtual teams: From nascent knowledge to transactive memory. In R. Sutton & B. Staw (Eds.), *Research in organizational behavior* (Vol. 23, pp. 379–421). Stamford, CT: JAI Press.

Helms, M. M., & Raiszadeh, F. M. E. (1997). Virtual offices: Understanding and managing what you cannot see. *Work Study: A Journal of Productivity Science, 51,* 240–247.

Hoffman, H. G., Prothero, J., Wells, M., & Groen, J. (1998). Virtual chess: The role of meaning in the sensation of presence. *International Journal of Human–Computer Interaction, 10,* 251–263.

Jacobson, D. (2002). On theorizing presence. *Journal of Virtual Environments, 6.* Retrieved September 11, 2002, http://www.brandeis.edu/pubs/jove/html

Jarvenpaa, S. L., & Leidner, D. E. (1999). Communication and trust in global virtual teams. *Organization Science, 10,* 791–815.

Jentsch, F., & Bowers, C. A. (1998). Evidence for the validity of PC-based simulations in studying aircrew coordination. *International Journal of Aviation Psychology, 8,* 261–276.

Jones, G. R., & George, J. M. (1998). The experience and evolution of trust: Implications for cooperation and teamwork. *Academy of Management Review, 23,* 531–546.

Klein, G., & Pierce, L. (2001). *Adaptive teams* (Draft Report, Purchase Order H438556[A] for Link Simulation and Training Division/Army Prime Contract No. DAAD17-00-A-5002). Fairborn, OH: Klein Associates.

Koonce, J. M., & Bramble, W. J. (1998). Personal computer-based flight training devices. *International Journal of Aviation Psychology, 8,* 277–292.

Kozlowski, S. W. J. (1998). Training and developing adaptive teams: Theory, principles, and research. In J. A. Cannon-Bowers & E. Salas (Eds.), *Making decisions under stress: Implications for individual and team training* (pp. 115–153). Washington, DC: American Psychological Association.

Leimester, J. M., Weigle, J., & Krcmar, H. (2001). The efficiency of virtual organizations: The case of AGI. *Electronic Journal of Organizational Virtualness, 3,* 12–43. Retrieved March 3, 2005, from http://www.ve-forum.org

Lewicki, R. J., & Bunker, B. B. (1996). Developing and maintaining trust in work relationships. In R. M. Kramer & T. R. Tyler (Eds.), *Trust in organizations: Frontiers of theory and research* (pp. 114–139). Thousand Oaks, CA: Sage.

Lombard, M., & Ditton, T. (1997). At the heart of it all: The concept of presence. *Journal of Computer-Mediated Communication, 3.* Retrieved September 1, 2002, from http://www.ascusc.org/jcmc/vol3/issue2/lombard.html

Lord, R., & Emrich, C. G. (2001). Thinking outside the box by looking inside the box: Extending the cognitive revolution in leadership research. *Leadership Quarterly, 11,* 551–579.

Marks, M. A. (2000). A critical analysis of computer simulations for conducting team research. *Small Group Research, 31,* 653–675.

Marks, M. A., Mathieu, J. E., & Zaccaro, S. J. (2001). A temporally based framework and taxonomy of team process. *Academy of Management Review, 26,* 356–376.

Marks, M. A., Sabella, M. J., Burke, C. S., & Zaccaro, S. J. (2002). The impact of cross-training on team effectiveness. *Journal of Applied Psychology, 87,* 3–13.

Marsh, S. M., Kiechel-Koles, K. L., Boyce, L. A., & Zaccaro, S. J. (2001, April). *Leader emergence and functional leadership: The role of leader traits and information provisions in adaptive situations.* Paper presented at the 16th annual conference of the Society for Industrial and Organizational Psychology, San Diego, CA.

Mathieu, J. E., Heffner, T. S., Goodwin, G. F., Salas, E., & Cannon-Bowers, J. A. (2000). The influence of shared mental models on team process and performance. *Journal of Applied Psychology, 85,* 273–283.

Mathieu, J. E., Marks, M. A., & Zaccaro, S. J. (2002). Multi-team systems. In N. Anderson, D. S. Ones, & C. Viswesvaran (Eds.), *Handbook of industrial, work and organizational psychology: Volume 2. Organizational psychology* (pp. 289–313). London: Sage.

Mayer, R. C., Davis, J. H., & Schoorman, D. (1995). An integrative model of organizational trust. *Academy of Management Review, 20(3),* 709–734.

McLeod, P. L. (1992). An assessment of the experimental literature on electronic support of group work: Results of a meta-analysis. *Human–Computer Interaction, 7,* 257–280.

Meyerson, D., Weick, K. E., & Kramer, R. M. (1996). Swift trust and temporary groups. In R. M. Kramer & T. R. Tyler (Eds.), *Trust in organizations: Frontiers of theory and research* (pp. 166–195). Thousand Oaks, CA: Sage.

Moreland, R. L. (1999). Transactive memory: Learning who knows what in work groups and organizations. In L. L. Thompson, J. M. Levine, & D. Messick (Eds.), *Shared cognition in organizations: The management of knowledge* (pp. 3–31). Mahwah, NJ: Erlbaum.

Mortensen, M., & Hinds, P. J. (2001). Conflict and shared identity in geographically distributed work teams. *International Journal of Conflict Management, 12,* 212–238.

National Research Council. (1994). *Research recommendations to facilitate distributed work.* Washington, DC: National Academy Press.

Pape, W. R. (1997). Group Insurance. *Inc., 19,* 29–31.

Prothero, J. D., & Hoffman, H. D. (1995). *Widening the field-of-view increases the sense of presence within immersive virtual environments.* (Tech. Rep. No. R-95-4). Seattle: University of Washington, Human Interface Technology Laboratory.

Psotka, J. (1995). Immersive training systems: Virtual reality and education and training. *Instructional Science, 23,* 405–423.

Rossett, A., & Sheldon, K. (2001). *Beyond the podium: Delivering training and performance to a digital world.* San Francisco: Jossey-Bass.

Rousseau, D. M., Sitkin, S. B., Burt, R. S., & Camerer, C. (1998). Not so different after all: A cross-discipline view of trust. *Academy of Management Review, 23,* 393–404.

Salas, E., Priest, H. A., Stagl, K. C., Sims, D. E., & Burke, C. S. (in press). Work teams in organizations: A historical reflection and lessons learned. In L. Koppes (Ed.), *The science and practice of industrial–organizational psychology: The first hundred years.* Mahwah, NJ: Erlbaum.

Salas, E., Stagl, K. C., & Burke, C. S. (2004). 25 years of team effectiveness in organizations: Research themes and emerging needs. In C. L. Cooper & I. T. Robertson (Eds.), *International review of industrial and organizational psychology* (pp. 47–91). New York: Wiley.

Salas, E., Stagl, K. C., Burke, C. S., & Goodwin, G. F. (in press). Fostering team effectiveness in organizations: Toward an integrative theoretical framework of team performance. In W. Spaulding & J. Flowers (Eds.), *Modeling complex systems: Motivation, cognition and social processes.* Lincoln: University of Nebraska Press.

Schlechter, T. R., Zaccaro, S. L., & Burke, C. S. (1998, May). *Toward an understanding of the shared mental models associated with proficient team performance.* Paper presented at the meeting of the American Psychological Society, Washington, DC.

Schmidt, A. M., & Ford, J. K. (2001, April). *Promoting active learning through metacognitive instruction.* Paper presented at the 16th annual conference of the Society for Industrial and Organizational Psychology, San Diego, CA.

Senge, P. M. (1990). *The fifth discipline: The art and practice of the learning organization.* New York: Doubleday.

Siegel, J., Dubrovsky, V., Kiesler, S., & McGuire, T. W. (1986). Group processes in computer-mediated communication. *Organizational Behavior and Human Decision Processes, 37,* 157–187.

Stohl, C. (1995). *Organizational communication: Connectedness in action.* Modesto, CA: Sage.

Straus, S. G. (1997). Technology, group process, and group outcomes: Testing the connections in computer-mediated and face-to-face groups. *Human–Computer Interaction, 12,* 227–266.

Sundstrom, E., McIntyre, M., Halfhill, T., & Richards, H. (2000). Work groups: From the Hawthorne studies to work teams of the 1990s and beyond. *Group Dynamics, 4*, 44–67.

Toney, R., & Ford, J. K. (2001, April). *Leveraging the capabilities of Web-based instruction to foster active learning*. Paper presented at the 16th annual conference of the Society of Industrial and Organizational Psychology, San Diego, CA.

Venkatesh, V., & Johnson, P. (2002). Telecommuting technology implementations: A within- and between-subjects longitudinal field study. *Personnel Psychology, 55*, 661–687.

Waller, D. (2000). Individual differences in spatial learning from computer-simulated environments. *Journal of Experimental Psychology: Applied, 6*, 307–321.

Weick, K. E. (1996). Drop your tools: An allegory for organizational studies. *Administrative Science Quarterly, 41*, 301–313.

Weisband, S. P., Schneider, S. K., & Connolly, T. (1995). Computer-mediated communication and social information: Status salience and status differences. *Academy of Management Journal, 38*, 1124–1151.

West, M. A., Borrill, C. S., & Unsworth, K. L. (1998). Team effectiveness in organizations. In C. L. Cooper & I. T. Robertson (Eds.), *International review of industrial organizational psychology* (pp. 1–48). Chichester, England: Wiley.

Witmer, B. G., & Singer, M. J. (1998). Measuring presence in virtual environments: A presence questionnaire. *Presence, 7*, 225–240.

Yoo, Y., & Kanawattanachai, P. (2001). Development of transactive memory systems and collective mind in virtual teams. *International Journal of Organizational Analysis, 9*, 187–208.

Zaccaro, S. J., & Ardison, S. (2003, April). *Leader development for virtual teams*. Symposium conduced at the 18th annual conference of the Society for Industrial Organizational Psychology, Orlando, FL.

Zaccaro, S. J., & Bader, P. (2003). E-leadership and the challenges of leading e-teams: Minimizing the bad and maximizing the good. *Organizational Dynamics, 31*, 377–387.

10

UNDERSTANDING AND DEVELOPING VIRTUAL COMPUTER-SUPPORTED COOPERATIVE WORK TEAMS

LORI FOSTER THOMPSON AND MICHAEL D. COOVERT

High-tech teams have a lot to offer, and organizational gains are most likely to occur when technology facilitates the types of interactions that allow team members to share information and capitalize on each other's knowledge and skills. *Computer-supported cooperative work* (CSCW) is an area that examines how people use computer and communication technologies to work together, often from remote locations (J. S. Olson & Olson, 1999; Spector, 2003). It is the study of how team members interact with new technology and how they interact with each other while sharing technology. In this chapter we explore the concept of CSCW, describe the issues confronted by virtual teams of distributed knowledge workers, and offer ideas for developing effective CSCW teams.

Several issues are covered in this chapter. We first provide an overview of CSCW, stressing the interdisciplinary aspects of the field from both the researcher's and the practitioner's perspective. We also highlight three dimensions on which CSCW and groupware vary. After this, we discuss the characteristics and benefits of virtual teamwork. Characteristics of virtual teams include being distributed in geographic location and time, and the benefits of this type of distribution to the workers and organization include, among others, enhanced performance by means of reduction in stress, fewer distractions, and greater networks for expertise. Of course, not every aspect of virtual teamwork is positive; we include a section dealing with three of the primary challenges of virtual teams: (a) communication quality, (b) lack of awareness of others, and (c) ineffective interpersonal relationships. The next major section of the chapter deals with developing effective CSCW teams. The literature points to several strategies that can be used; these include providing sufficient time for the virtual teams to deal with the problem at hand, providing for initial kick-off meetings, allowing channels for instant communication (e.g., electronic chat or instant messaging), sufficient training of team members, and dealing with leadership issues in the virtual context. The chapter ends with some concluding remarks about the direction of modern-day CSCW teams.

OVERVIEW OF COMPUTER-SUPPORTED COOPERATIVE WORK

The overall objective of CSCW involves a greater understanding of the requirements for, the development of, and the effects of innovative and natural technologies during cooperative work (Greenberg & Neuwirth, 1998). Because of its potential influence on productivity and the quality of work life, CSCW has captured the interest of consultants, managers, vendors of collaborative technologies, and workers in general. From a scientific standpoint, CSCW has also attracted a great deal of multidisciplinary attention because of its broad focus and impact on many aspects of personal, professional, organizational, and societal well-being. The CSCW literature, which is a rich and eclectic body of knowledge reflecting a range of methods and theories, has benefited from work within the fields of anthropology, business, cognition, computer science (especially research concerned with networks, messaging services, and distributed systems), ergonomics, human–computer interaction, human factors, information technology, management, office automation, organizational design, psychology, sociology, and others (Scrivener & Clark, 1994; Spurr, Layzell, Jennison, & Richards, 1994; Wilson, 1991). The methods of sociology and anthropology have often guided CSCW research, which tends to rely on qualitative, ethnographic, and field observations rather heavily (J. S. Olson & Olson, 1999). Psychology has not necessarily played a dominant role in the development of the field, despite its emphasis on human behavior and mental processes (Finholt & Teasley, 1998). Critics have called for more participation from the field of psychology and a greater reliance on experimental and quasi-experimental methodologies to increase the internal validity of the conclusions drawn from CSCW research and perhaps improve our ability to explain and predict interactions between people, teams, and technology (Finholt & Teasley, 1998; J. S. Olson & Olson, 1999). Clearly, there is a great deal of room to develop and expand the already-impressive body of CSCW knowledge that has surfaced during the past 20 years.

CSCW researchers and practitioners commonly agree that effective computer-supported collaboration requires tools that enable and facilitate natural team interactions. Although computer technology was historically designed for individual work, the past 20 years have seen the emergence of *groupware*, specialized computer aids (hardware, software, and services) designed to support collaboration (Johansen, 1988). Many different types of groupware have been built to serve a wide variety of functions. In general, however, CSCW and associated groupware can be classified along just a few dimensions (J. S. Olson & Olson, 1999). First, groupware varies according to the location (colocated vs. distributed collaboration) of the interaction it was designed to aid (J. S. Olson & Olson, 1999). Groupware devised to facilitate colocated interactions includes, for example, group decision support and electronic meeting room systems, which typically allow teams to meet in a room of networked computers with screens arranged so that members can see their teammates without seeing their partners' screens. Group decision support systems commonly structure the team process, and a public screen resides at the front of the room to display input from team members who use keyboards to enter ideas, respond to ideas, and comment on the thoughts of others, often anonymously (Burdett, 2000). Unlike electronic meeting rooms, some kinds of groupware are built to support dispersed members who are geographically separated from one another. Videoconferencing, which uses cameras, microphones, computers, and monitors to allow remote teammates to see and hear each other during meetings, is an example. Still other groupware technology facilitates both colocated and distributed teamwork. For instance, people use electronic mail (e-mail) to interact with colleagues working across the hall as well as those located across the country.

Second, groupware varies according to the timing of the supported interaction (asynchronous vs. real time collaboration; J. S. Olson & Olson, 1999). Electronic bulletin boards and voicemail are examples of groupware that facilitates asynchronous cooperation. Conversely, real time collaboration is supported by technology such as chat rooms, which allow team members working at the same time to type to each other in an each-to-all fashion.

Third and finally, groupware differs in terms of the function the technology itself supports (conversations vs. object sharing; J. S. Olson & Olson, 1999). Although some CSCW technologies are designed to support discussions (e.g., video-mail that allows people to transfer videotaped messages directly to their colleagues' personal computers or cellular phones; Whitney, 2001), others are built for the purpose of sharing objects such as drawings or documents. Object sharing can occur, for instance, via a communal folder or directory that allows more than one person to open, modify, and close electronic spreadsheets residing on an internal organizational Web site or intranet accessible to the entire team.

In short, there are several fundamentally different forms of groupware and CSCW, and the effects of technology on team functioning clearly depend on the type of computer-supported collaboration under investigation. Extensive bodies of work have been devoted to the understanding and improvement of teamwork within various CSCW environments (real time, face to face conversations; real time, remote object sharing; asynchronous, distributed object sharing; etc.). A thorough review of each domain could fill volumes and is well beyond the scope of this chapter. We therefore narrow our focus to what is becoming one of the most common types of CSCW in the contemporary work world: distributed, virtual teams. In the following sections we highlight some of the issues such teams confront and suggest ways for improving this type of computer-supported collaboration.

CHARACTERISTICS AND BENEFITS OF VIRTUAL TEAMWORK

Distributed and virtual teamwork go hand in hand. Distributed teams are collections of colleagues who attempt to engage in coordinated work from remote sites via "virtual" computer network connections (Ramesh & Andrews, 1999; Salas, Burke, & Samman, 2001). Reliance on distributed, virtual teams is considered one of the top workplace trends underway; in fact, some studies have indicated that offsite personnel will eventually comprise as much as two thirds of an organization's workforce (Kemske, 1998). Even firms that may not look virtual at the surface are increasingly relying on virtual teams for selected processes and activities (DeSanctis & Monge, 1999). According to Townsend, DeMarie, and Hendrickson (1998), *virtual teams* are collections of geographically or organizationally dispersed coworkers who use a combination of telecommunications and information technologies to accomplish an organizational task; infrequently meet in a face-to-face environment; may be set up as temporary structures, existing only to accomplish a specific task, or may be relatively permanent structures that are used to address ongoing issues, such as strategic planning; and often have fluid membership that evolves according to changing task requirements.

Virtual teams can consist of individuals who each reside at a separate location, but they are often made up of clusters or subteams of people at the same location. At times, they include membership spanning cultural or professional boundaries, and they may have a limited history as a team (Cramton, 2002; Salas et al., 2001). To complete their work, modern-day virtual teams must converse and share documents within the constraints of the imperfect groupware technologies that are accessible to them. They are often confined to everyday technologies such as e-mail, voicemail, and perhaps videoconferencing equipment; many lack access to the more novel groupware described in the CSCW literature, much of which is still in the prototype stage of development (Wiesenfeld, Raghuram, & Garud, 1998). Finally, today's virtual teams typically have the option of collaborating asynchronously or in real time and may avail themselves of both forms of interaction during the course of their teamwork.

The movement from traditional to virtual teamwork has enabled some indisputable benefits, which are many and well documented. Teams that collaborate asynchronously from remote locations enjoy, for example, conveniences that free them from time and space restrictions: Members can contribute when they want, from the location of they prefer, thereby reducing the need to synchronize schedules (Thompson & Coovert, 2003). Encouraging distributed, virtual teamwork minimizes travel costs (airfare, hotels, etc.) required to bring teams together, and allowing personnel to work from home saves money otherwise spent housing permanent employees (office space, electricity, etc.). From the worker's perspective, commuting expenses (financial costs, psychological stressors, and time sacrifices) are greatly reduced, as are other costs that occur when people are away from their families and communities (Nardi & Whittaker, 2002). Distributed teamwork also decreases time wasted with on-site, low-productivity meetings. It minimizes unwelcome interruptions from coworkers while increasing privacy and generally giving workers more control over their schedules and their lives (Kraut, Fussell, Brennan, & Siegel, 2002; Nardi & Whittaker, 2002; J. S. Olson, Teasley, Covi, & Olson, 2002). The physical absence of others during virtual teamwork can even enhance the performance of difficult tasks by reducing the stress, distractions, lack of privacy, and evaluation apprehensions that sometimes plague colocated teams (Kiesler & Cummings, 2002).

By eliminating time and space constraints, virtual team arrangements can increase an organization's skills, network of expertise, and demographic diversity (Kraut et al., 2002). Freedom from travel and relocation costs allows organizations to easily draw from a global pool of talent rather than limiting team membership to particular geographic areas. Employers can capitalize on distributed resources and recruit personnel with specialized expertise and access to services, goods, or customers unique to particular geographic regions (Mortensen & Hinds, 2002). Such diversity can serve a team and an organization well. In fact, research has shown that by increasing the diversity and novelty of team membership, virtual CSCW increases the degree to which teammates are salient to one another. Heightened salience subsequently improves *boundary agreement* (the degree to which members agree on who is and is not on the team), and increased boundary agreement benefits teams by improving awareness of and access to expertise within the team while enhancing performance (Mortensen & Hinds, 2002).

Other virtual team benefits stem from the reliance on electronic communication technologies themselves. Computer-mediated communication allows people to include many teammates in discussions and plans while encouraging input, even from relatively low-status individuals (Kiesler & Cummings, 2002; Sproull & Kiesler, 1991). Freedom from turn-taking norms and the potential for multiple, concurrent threads can result in an environment conducive to participation. In fact, research has shown that more people contribute in chat rooms than in face-to-face conversations (McDaniel, Olson, & Magee, 1996). Researchers have therefore argued that computer-mediated interaction is more egalitarian than face-to-face communication (Bordia, 1997), with computer-mediated teams participating more evenly, feeling less inhibited, and sensing less pressure to conform to team norms under certain conditions (Adrianson & Hjelmquist, 1991; Daly, 1993; Dubrovsky, Kiesler, & Sethna, 1991; Hiltz, Johnson, & Turoff, 1986; Kiesler, Siegel, & McGuire, 1984; Kiesler & Sproull, 1992; McGuire, Kiesler, & Siegel, 1987; Siegel, Dubrovsky, Kiesler, & McGuire, 1986; Smilowitz, Compton, & Flint, 1988; Straus, 1996; Thompson & Coovert, 2003; Weisband, 1992). According to the Social Identity model of Deindividuation Effects (i.e., the SIDE model), computer-mediated teams are particularly apt to disregard social norms when they feel individuated, or sensitive to their individual identities and those of their teammates (Postmes, Spears, & Lea, 1998, 1999). Mortensen and Hinds (2002) argued that the explicit identification of interaction partners typically found during virtual teamwork (e.g., selecting names from an address book prior to sending a message) makes team membership quite salient. Thus, the freedom from social norms, which serves as an advantage for groups prone to dysfunctional customs (Thompson & Coovert, 2002), seems particularly likely during virtual collaboration due to the salience and individuation of teammates.

It is worth noting that the use of text-based computer-mediated communication, such as e-mail, is also advantageous because it allows teams to maintain a record of communication. Having such records can support the memory of teammates and benefit long-term collaborations (Kraut et al., 2002; J. S. Olson & Olson, 1999). Overall, the movement from personal to interpersonal computing increases the amount of information available to a team while amplifying the speed and power with which members acquire, process, and share their individual and collective efforts (McGrath & Hollingshead, 1994). For these and other reasons, the trend toward virtual CSCW is not likely to reverse itself anytime soon.

CHALLENGES OF VIRTUAL TEAMWORK

Despite its benefits, virtual teamwork is far from costless. Some have asserted that modern-day groupware falls short in supporting tightly coupled, interdependent teamwork (G. M. Olson & Olson, 2000; J. S. Olson et al., 2002), and others contend that the people extolling the virtues of boundary-less, anytime–anywhere CSCW have vastly overstated the advantages of this type of interaction while overlooking the subtler and less understood sacrifices associated with virtual collaboration (Schwarz, Nardi, & Whittaker, 1999). In general, virtual teams are susceptible to a variety of pitfalls that can impede effective team processes and outcomes. In the following sections we emphasize three of the particularly serious challenges faced by virtual teams: (a) communication difficulties (in terms of the quality and quantity of exchanges), (b) a lack of awareness of teammates' endeavors, and (c) a failure to develop effective interpersonal relationships.

Communication Quality and Quantity

It is generally believed that clear, concise communication strategies are critical to the success of teams working in complex environments (e.g., Salas et al., 2001). Unfortunately, many of the challenges faced by distributed CSCW teams stem from inefficient and ineffective communication, which occurs when correspondence is unclear and infrequent. To the extent that virtual teams lack the chance for face-to-face interaction, they lack access to the easiest and most direct route to cooperation and coordination (Kiesler & Cummings, 2002). Consider the use of a text-based medium, such as e-mail, as a conversation tool. From the perspective of the sender, typing is usually more difficult than speaking, and from the recipient's viewpoint verbal messages are processed more slowly during computer-mediated communication than they are in speech (Walther, 2002). Feedback is hindered by the absence of adequate backchannels, which are listener responses, uttered during a teammate's speech, to signal understanding, agreement, and so on (e.g., "uh-huh," head nods, and furrowed brows; J. S. Olson & Olson, 1999). Moreover, both senders and recipients lack access to visual and other nonverbal and paraverbal cues, such as facial expressions, vocal intonations, timing, gaze, and pointing (J. S. Olson & Olson, 1999). Verbal substitutes to replace these cues during computer-mediated communication (e.g., complex syntax and *emoticons*, graphic representations of facial expressions that people can embed in their e-mail messages) require a great deal of effort and are generally regarded as low-quality, time-consuming substitutes for paraverbal and nonverbal cues (Kraut et al., 2002; McGrath & Hollingshead, 1994; Walther & D'Addario, 2001).

When computer-mediated discussion ideas remain undeveloped because of the effort and limitations involved in this form of communication, a team member's true or intended meaning may be unclear to online teammates (Valacich & Schwenk, 1995). In addition, with e-mail and other text-based communication media, mix-ups arise because multiple conversational threads emerge in the absence of turn taking, input is lost in the volume, and it is difficult to reinstate context when this occurs (Kraut et al., 2002; J. S. Olson & Olson, 1999). After examining 1,649 pieces of e-mail generated by 13 intact teams, Cramton (2001) concluded that communication across distance and via technology is an extraordinarily leaky process: "People worked from different information far more often than they realized . . . Confusion and conflict was promulgated . . . by different interpretations of the same information" (p. 364).

Miscommunication during computer-mediated communication is exacerbated by the fact that virtual teams have trouble recognizing when mix-ups have occurred:

> In a distributed environment, even under the best conditions, there are often delays in communication due to the technology used. Therefore, not only is it easy to misinterpret communication, but the feedback on that misinterpretation or updating of information may not be immediate. (Salas et al., 2001, p. 319)

Communication faults tend to snowball, and the more quickly a misunderstanding is repaired, the less costly it will be (Clark & Brennan, 1991). Consequently, miscommunications during computer-mediated communication are not only more frequent but also more costly, in part because distributed groups are slower to identify and correct misunderstandings (Armstrong & Cole, 2002; Kraut et al., 2002). Despite these difficulties, virtual workers increasingly rely on electronic, text-based media such as e-mail to communicate with their peers, accomplish their work, and link themselves to the overall organization (Walther, 2002; Wiesenfeld et al., 1998).

Of course, virtual teams are not always confined to text-based communication, yet even the voice media alternatives generally fail to reproduce the richness of face-to-face interaction. Audioconferencing permits the transmission of certain backchannels; however, teams engaged in audioconferences still have trouble interpreting the meaning of silence and tend to experience disruptions in turn taking and feedback because of the loss of visual cues to guide conversational flow and assess understanding and attention (J. S. Olson & Olson, 1999). Finholt, Sproull, and Kiesler (2002) reported that although using the telephone rather than asynchronous text-based communication can increase the social presence experienced by dyads, social presence degrades rapidly when more than two people join the conversation.

Although some researchers have predicted that extensive use of video technologies may mitigate the negative effects of reduced face-to-face communication during virtual teamwork (Mortensen & Hinds, 2002), the literature suggests that even videoconferencing does not solve all of the problems associated with remote collaboration. Video plus audio may not provide a big advantage over audio alone for small, established, distributed teams using shared editors to support real-time design work (J. S. Olson & Olson, 1999). J. S. Olson, Olson, and Meader (1995) indicated that members of video–audio groups generate output that is only marginally superior to that produced by audio-only groups. Compared with remote audio-only teammates, speakers using video-mediated communication do spend less time requesting verbal feedback; however, this efficiency advantage is canceled out by the fact that video-mediated collaborators say significantly more to achieve the same level of task success as their audio-only counterparts (Anderson et al., 1997).

Anderson et al. (1997) demonstrated that low-bandwidth video-mediated communication can seriously harm task outcomes and communication flow, and even high-bandwidth video-mediated communication does not deliver all of the advantages afforded by face-to-face interaction. Research on newly formed teams has shown that impressions of video-mediated interaction partners are less positive than impressions of face-to-face partners (Storck & Sproull, 1995). Perhaps this is why some people maintain that teleconferencing works best when people already know each other (Nardi & Whittaker, 2002; Short, Williams, & Christie, 1976). Teams with a history of working together can use videoconferencing as a tool for maintaining momentum established prior to the introduction of the technology (Johansen, 1984). They may not be as susceptible to impression formation problems and other pitfalls experienced by newly formed teams collaborating in a video-mediated environment.

There are many possible reasons why videoconferencing technologies fail to enable rich communication exchanges. For instance, low-bandwidth desktop videoconferencing systems produce a delay in the transmission of audio, which can upset turn taking. Other systems produce an incongruity between sound and picture. This problem can cause team members to misinterpret backchannels, such as when an image shows a speaker pointing to one work object while discussing another. The result is increased confusion, effort, and time requirements (J. S. Olson & Olson, 1999). According to Nardi and Whittaker (2002), "technologies such as videoconferencing, which attempt to replicate the face-to-face experience, may fail because they provide neither the high-fidelity interactivity of face-to-face nor the social benefits of sharing a common physical space" (p. 107).

In sum, a reliance on text-based computer-mediated communication and even richer media, including audio components, video components, or both, can lead to exchanges that are more laborious and ambiguous than face-to-face interaction. Delayed, sparse, and inaccurate feedback can bring about arduous and time-consuming communication that requires several iterations for clarification (Weisband, 2002). The frustrations associated with this type of collaboration can lead to some rather unfortunate consequences, including a reduction in the overall quantity of communication. Research has shown that distance decreases the frequency of communication not only among potential work partners but also among collaborators already working together (Kraut, Egido, & Galegher, 1990; Kraut et al., 2002). It reduces daily contact, lowers the odds of chance encounters (e.g., water cooler conversations), reduces the inclination to initiate conversation, and lessens the frequency of informal conversations (Kiesler & Cummings, 2002). Some have suggested that communication frequency drops as distance increases and reaches its asymptote after about 30 meters (Kraut et al., 1990; J. S. Olson et al., 2002). Others have complained that although distributed CSCW teams have adequate tools for scheduling meetings and writing reports, they have little technology to support bumping into a colleague in the coffee room (Fish, Kraut, & Chalfonte, 1990). Indeed, the adage "out of sight, out of mind" may ring true for virtual teams, who even tend to send more e-mail to colocated teammates than to teammates on other continents (Armstrong & Cole, 2002).

It is worth noting that the solution to problems involving infrequent encounters is not as simple as activating video links among interaction partners. Research has shown that people operating in face-to-face settings are more likely to interact than are those working in virtual environments with constant visual and auditory connections (Fish et al., 1990). This finding is perhaps due to challenges stemming from low-resolution video images and asymmetries between what people on opposing ends of the video link can see and hear (Kraut et al., 2002). Thus, although unambiguous, frequent, spontaneous, and informal conversations are not impossible during virtual teamwork, they are more difficult and less likely. This challenge has important implications during virtual CSCW. As Kiesler and Cummings (2002) pointed out, casual encounters not only increase the ease and pleasure of communication but also permit unplanned and multipurpose work interactions, which serve a team well in the long run.

Shared Awareness

According to Salas et al. (2001), *shared situation awareness*, which enables team members to maintain a common picture of the problem at hand, is vital to effective team functioning. It allows members to monitor each other's progress, develop shared mental models, anticipate teammates' strengths and failings, coordinate actions implicitly, and engage in compensatory and backup behaviors (Kiesler & Cummings, 2002; Salas et al., 2001). Recent research has documented the importance of awareness during virtual CSCW (Weisband, 2002).

Shared awareness and a related construct, *mutual knowledge*, are relatively difficult to achieve during distributed collaboration. Cramton (2001) proposed that the failure to maintain mutual knowledge is a fundamental, overarching problem fueled by the text-based, online, communication channels often used during virtual teamwork. Mutual knowledge occurs when team members possess not only the same information but also an awareness that they share the knowledge in common. It is achieved through several mechanisms, including direct knowledge (information gained through first-hand experience with individuals) and interactional dynamics (information acquired through collaborative discussions; Krauss & Fussell, 1990).

Virtual teams cannot physically see each other work. They therefore lack direct knowledge, which is gained through common experiences in particular settings and first-hand observations of teammates' habits, situations, and environments (Cramton, 2001; Krauss & Fussell, 1990). During distributed CSCW, it is difficult and often impossible to passively monitor activities and pick up relevant information in the absence of explicit communication (Kraut et al., 2002; Weisband, 2002). Consequently, remote collaborators must operate in the absence of visual cues indicating that a teammate is absent, busy, stressed, experiencing technical difficulties, in trouble, dealing with unusual or unexpected circumstances, and so forth. Virtual teamwork also precludes constant and easy access to shared artifacts, such as whiteboards and flip charts, which help make projects and progress on projects visible. Without direct knowledge, distributed teammates who are unable to see each other's work evolve tend to develop very different pictures of the environment in which the team is operating (Salas et al., 2001). They lack a shared interpretative context.

Effective communication is especially critical when direct knowledge is infeasible. During teamwork, each communication episode provides the potential for people to learn something new about their partners, monitor the state of both individual and team progress, and gain a common understanding of the situation at hand (Kraut et al., 2002). Effective interactional dynamics enable teams to fill the gaps in each member's spotty understanding, attain a shared awareness of relevant situational constraints, and develop a full picture of the collective environment in which the team is functioning. Unfortunately, the ineffective and infrequent communication habits that characterize virtual teamwork only exacerbate the awareness problem. Although distributed teams can theoretically share situational cues through interactional dynamics, in practice they do not do so effectively because of the problems (decreased communication quality and quantity) discussed earlier.

Few situational cues and inadequate communication can cause people to feel disoriented and without context, making it difficult to quickly diagnose situations prompting unexpected events and requiring team members to explicitly envision what events might have caused unforeseen circumstances to occur. This state of affairs not only creates the potential for cognitive overload by expending attentional resources that would normally remain available for other aspects of the team's work (Salas et al., 2001; Weisband, 2002); it also breeds confusion. Following an analysis of virtual project teams, Cramton (2001) concluded that a lack of mutual knowledge muddled the collaborative process considerably. Virtual collaborators (a) failed to communicate and retain contextual information; (b) unevenly distributed information that should have gone to the whole team simultaneously; (c) had trouble communicating and understanding the salience of information, such as a question or a request; (d) differed in the speed with which they were willing or able to access information; and (e) had trouble interpreting the meaning of silence.

To summarize, insufficient communication can lead remote collaborators to operate from individual, unshared contexts and then base their interpretations of each other's behaviors on unique sets of assumptions (Armstrong & Cole, 2002). This problem can lead to an incomplete understanding of the overall project, including its history, current status, and future directions. Without shared awareness, collaborators lack not only task knowledge but also team knowledge. They have trouble developing detailed and accurate mental models regarding collaborators' attributes and capabilities (knowledge, skills, motivation, availability, individual progress, etc.), and they are unable to develop a common understanding of the team's coordination requirements, which, if established, help teams assign tasks, appropriately and function smoothly (Cramton, 2001; Kraut et al., 2002; Salas et al., 2001). "If members of the . . . team do not have a common idea of what the current situation is, and who has done what, the potential for redundancy, as well as non-action (things slipping through the crack) is tremendous" (Salas et al., 2001, p. 316).

Interpersonal Issues

Cohesion, trust, and other interpersonal factors have been deemed critical for team effectiveness (Paris, Salas, & Cannon-Bowers, 2000). As Kiesler and Cummings (2002) asserted, successful teamwork depends on the coordination of individual efforts and the cohesiveness of the group. Because of their importance, interpersonal and attitudinal variables such as these have attracted a great deal of attention among CSCW researchers and practitioners. Overall, the literature suggests that the various challenges encountered during virtual teamwork have the potential to prompt relationship conflict and undermine trust, cooperative behavior, commitment to the team, cohesion, and satisfaction.

A lack of visibility can prevent virtual teams from establishing and maintaining trusting and cooperative relationships. The establishment of trust is typically based on social interaction and performance patterns, yet trust can be hard to develop when teammates cannot see each other's actions and body language (Salas et al., 2001). Meanwhile, cooperative behavior is impeded by weak social linkages and a lack of commitment, which stems from insufficient opportunity for informal, spontaneous, or face-to-face interaction (Nardi & Whittaker, 2002). More than 100 studies have shown the powerful effects that face-to-face discussions can have on cooperative choices in social dilemmas (Kiesler & Cummings, 2002). These effects presumably arise from the obligations people feel when they make face-to-face social contracts, and they are also thought to result from the increased group identity caused by face-to-face interaction (Kiesler & Cummings, 2002). Thus, the absence of face time can impair virtual team cooperation.

To some extent, virtual team environments may also disrupt interpersonal relationship development by prompting misattribution. By decreasing cohesion and the salience of situational variables, distributed CSCW arrangements can lead to an increased susceptibility to the *fundamental attribution error*. Research has shown that when there are no obvious external factors to excuse or explain problems and failures, members of unsuccessful teams generally seek to deny personal responsibility for the team's performance, particularly when they lack cohesion, as is often the case during virtual collaboration (Brawley, Carron, & Widmeyer, 1987; Norvell & Forsyth, 1984). Without a shared awareness of the context in which the team is operating, virtual team members are especially inclined to blame collaborators for unavoidable problems stemming from situational constraints (Cramton, 2002). For instance, a virtual collaborator dealing with unfulfilled communication exchanges is apt to negatively attribute e-mail nonresponse to the teammate ("that person is lazy or unreliable") rather than the situation (a technology failure at the teammate's home site prevented the mail from going through) (Cramton, 2001; Kraut et al., 2002). Years of research demonstrate that the consequences of misattributions can be dire. Negative attributional patterns affect feelings of satisfaction and the willingness to cooperate, among other things (Cramton, 2002; McDonald, 1995; Wang, 1994). It seems that virtual teams, whose social and work ties are already underdeveloped because of infrequent spontaneous communication events (Kiesler & Cummings, 2002), are particularly vulnerable to the negative effects of misattributions. This problem may explain some of their interpersonal difficulties.

Virtual teams with clusters of people at the same site tend to form subgroups based on location (Cramton, 2002). Such teams are particularly susceptible to social categorization biases; the development of an us-versus-them mentality; and the formation of out-groups that get excluded, psychologically and literally, especially when core members are colocated and others are dispersed. Social categorization processes and the establishment of out-groups lead people to view other teammates as deficient, thereby reducing satisfaction, cohesiveness, communication, and cooperation while increasing turnover and conflict (Williams & O'Reilly, 1998). To make matters worse, virtual teams are slow to recognize, express, and address the types of conflict that are promptly nipped in the bud during colocated collaboration. Virtual conflict therefore tends to fester, encouraging members to e-mail planned, carefully prepared objections to problems, which are rarely resolved quickly and thoroughly (Armstrong & Cole, 2002). Forgetting that there is a person reading the message at the other end can even lead to "flaming," asocial emotive messages that are upsetting, offensive, and conflict laden (J. S. Olson & Olson, 1999). This type of conflict can be particularly disruptive during distributed CSCW because virtual teams are already prone to pitfalls, such as weak commitment to the team, which may make it exceedingly difficult to recover from interpersonal quarrels (Mannix, Griffith, & Neale, 2002). Although the literature suggests that task conflict can be healthy, relationship conflict (personality clashes, animosity, and annoyance between individuals) tends to be quite detrimental. It can adversely affect member satisfaction, performance, and the likelihood of future collaboration (Jehn, 1995; Jehn & Mannix, 2001; Mannix et al., 2002).

There are many barriers that distributed CSCW teams must overcome if they are to function effectively. Although we have highlighted only a few (infrequent and ineffective communication, lack of shared awareness, interpersonal difficulties) at the exclusion of others (e.g., the decreased opportunity for informal cross-training acquired by watching teammates work), it should be clear that the conveniences of virtual collaboration are accompanied by some noteworthy costs. Acknowledging that many of the same troubles can also afflict colocated teams, we concur with Salas et al.'s (2001) assertion that these challenges become more pronounced and difficult within virtual teams. The results of a recent case study describing virtual software product development teams (with some members at common sites and others distributed) concisely sum up a variety of the problems faced by virtual teams. According to the researchers investigating these teams,

> Communications were often fragmented, with gaps and misunderstandings among distant group members. There was confusion in telephone conferences, with people on different pages of documents. Group members failed to return telephone calls or respond to inquiries from distant members. Key group members at remote sites were left off e-mail dis-

tribution lists. Distant members were not informed of key decisions or information. Misunderstandings developed on the basis of different assumptions about the tasks and assignments. Messages were interpreted differently in different places, sometimes fueling ongoing conflicts among office sites. (Armstrong & Cole, 2002, pp. 168–169)

Although it is widely believed that virtual teams are particularly susceptible to the types of problems described in the preceding excerpt, the source of these problems is not always clear. Groupware technologies differ on a number of specifics, and even small variations can significantly affect team processes. As J. S. Olson and Olson (1999) pointed out, many groupware systems have never been evaluated, some have been evaluated only by their designers, and others have been evaluated only through case studies that lacked comparison groups. Whereas some CSCW research has experimentally isolated the effects of the more common technologies, such as e-mail, many works (field research, ethnographic studies) have examined virtual collaboration in relatively naturalistic settings with the goal of describing the characteristics and consequences of CSCW. In short, the effects of team composition, distribution, inexperience, and technologies often go hand in hand during CSCW research. In all likelihood, some of the costs of virtual teamwork are the result of dispersion; others stem from the use of technology; some arise from inexperience with the team; and still others are a consequence of the cultural, professional, and organizational heterogeneity that tends to characterize distributed CSCW. At present, it is not always possible to attribute the challenges faced by virtual teams to a single causal variable. Moreover, the nature and maturity of virtual teams; the strength of their trust, culture, and efficacy; the kind of work in which they engage; the degree to which they anticipate a future together; and the features of the groupware all influence how people behave and may moderate the team's susceptibility to the pitfalls described earlier (Mannix et al., 2002; J. S. Olson & Olson, 1999).

DEVELOPING EFFECTIVE CSCW TEAMS

It is clear that we are only beginning to understand the problems encountered by distributed CSCW teams, and we need to clarify their sources and moderators so that workers and organizations can better account for the hidden costs of virtual teamwork and take steps to lessen the difficulties faced by CSCW teams. Developing rules for effectively applying CSCW to teams in the absence of this clarification is premature, although guiding principles are sorely needed. Devoid of such prescriptions, the literature has begun to offer ideas for minimizing the problems faced by virtual teams. The practical value of many of these strategies is admittedly limited. Some lack specificity, by stating, for instance, that virtual teams need to increase cohesiveness to function more smoothly—without outlining the steps that should be executed to accomplish this goal. Other suggestions lack immediate utility because of a focus on either futuristic technologies or sophisticated computing environments not generally available to most teams (e.g., virtual teams should interact in an immersive, virtual reality environment). Fortunately, the literature also presents a variety of workable strategies for teams operating within the constraints of currently accessible technologies. In the following sections, we highlight a few of the more feasible ideas for developing effective CSCW teams in today's work world.

Give Them Time

Perhaps the most straightforward technique for supporting and facilitating virtual teamwork is to ensure ample time allotments. Computer-mediated communication slows team discussion and decision-making processes considerably. According to some estimates, computer-mediated groups take four to five times longer than face-to-face groups, without producing more messages (Dubrovsky et al., 1991; Walther, 2002; Weisband, 1992). Not only do most people type more slowly than they talk, but it takes time for virtual teams to adapt to the media through which they must collaborate, regardless of whether it is text-based. Virtual teams with tight deadlines are thus particularly vulnerable to the negative effects of media novelty and time pressure.

Although the effect of computer-mediated communication on discussion time is widely known, the consequences of time pressure and media novelty are less obvious. Virtual teams given ample time tend to focus their initial efforts on talking about and adjusting to their communication media (Walther, 2002). Electronic team discussions then shift from mechanics toward interpersonal matters as members gain experience with the medium (Lebie, Rhoades, & McGrath, 1996). Time pressure may prevent virtual teams from working up to this important phase. Coupled with media novelty, insufficient time can hinder collaboration by suppressing affective discussion content (as rational conversation gives way to rushed consensus), resulting in strained relational dynamics, frustration, and poor performance (Walther, 2002).

The literature suggests that many of the negative effects of computer-mediated communication, which are partially a function of temporal pressure and inexperience, diminish over time. For instance, longitudinal research by Hollingshead, McGrath, and O'Connor (1993) demonstrated that computer-mediated team performance improves over time and eventually parallels that of face-to-face teams. One can therefore conclude that giving virtual teams time to adjust to computer-mediated communication and to coalesce as a group can facilitate collaboration. "When time is plentiful, people adapt to their systems and each other, reach decisions and finish tasks, build impressions, and manage positive interpersonal relations" (Walther, 2002, p. 251).

Kick-Off Meetings

A 1998 study by Rocco demonstrated a rather fascinating phenomenon with implications for virtual teamwork. Teams were asked to play a game in which members, who repeatedly decided what to invest in a common pool, could benefit either by defecting (with potential individual benefit at a cost to teammates) or by cooperating (everyone got the same benefit). Members met three times throughout the game; half of the groups met face to face, and the other half used a nonanonymous e-mail list to converse. Those who met via e-mail defected most often, whereas those who met in the face-to-face environment were more cooperative. More important, people who met face to face prior to the game eventually cooperated even when they were restricted to e-mail communication during the game. This finding indicates what many authors have repeatedly asserted: Virtual teamwork works best after initial face-to-face contact (Armstrong & Cole, 2002). Face-to-face "kick-off" meetings can give virtual teams the opportunity to review collaborative goals while encouraging the informal social contact that facilitates mutual understanding and trust (Armstrong & Cole, 2002). Face time provides a means for building the social integration of a dispersed team (Cramton, 2002). A shared social identity, in turn, focuses teams on a common set of values and increases awareness of teammates' perspectives, interpersonal styles, and skills (Mannix et al., 2002).

Recent work has indicated that chat rooms can be a viable alternative for teams lacking the resources to hold initial face-to-face meetings. Zheng, Bos, Olson, and Olson (2001) found that people who did not meet face to face but rather engaged in a text chat to "get to know each other" before engaging in teamwork demonstrated more trust than those who did not hold such meetings. Zheng, Veinott, Bos, Olson, and Olson's (2002) work led to similar conclusions, indicating that using text-based chat to get acquainted is nearly as good as meeting face to face. Walther, Slovacek, and Tidwell's (2001) research suggests that when time is short and members are unacquainted, even a simple photograph can enhance social attraction and affection. Work by Zheng et al. (2002) also demonstrated that a photo is better than nothing when a team is attempting to promote trust, because visual identification emphasizes collaborators' humanity and implies accountability (one can be visually recognized by their teammates in the future). In contrast, a static presentation of personal information (e.g., a biography sheet listing the kinds of social information that are normally discussed during initial meetings) prior to collaboration does not improve trust among virtual CSCW teams (Zheng et al., 2002).

Chat Rooms and Instant Messaging

Building "awareness moments" into virtual collaboration can slow the degradation of communication zones and facilitate team functioning (Nardi & Whittaker, 2002). Whereas real-time video links that are always on and always running may feel a bit intrusive, distributed teams may be able to add new levels of presence and awareness by maintaining real-time connections through chat rooms and instant messaging (Walther, 2002). Virtual chat rooms typically permit each-to-all communication, and instant messaging requires the user to create a dyadic chat window with another. Distributed teammates can use these media to exchange brief questions, relay just-in-time answers and tidbits, and initiate availability awareness by negotiating the timing of future communications (e.g., asking when someone will be available for a telephone call; Walther, 2002). People can open and close chat rooms and instant-messaging services as they wish. Although an open connection does not ensure availability (members may be away from the computer, or too busy to respond), it can signal that a teammate is nearby, working, and potentially available for interaction. By keeping chat and instant-messaging connections open, teams create a virtual environment similar to a shared physical office, where conversations can be advanced at any time (Nardi, Whittaker, & Bradner, 2000; Walther, 2002).

The norms of e-mail do not necessarily apply to the use of chat and instant-messaging media. Whereas e-mail often requires a reply, and not necessarily a prompt one, members need not always feel obligated to respond to instant messages they missed. Sending a note via chat or instant message is relatively informal and akin to sticking one's head in someone's office doorway to ask a quick question if time allows. Kraut et al. (2002) pointed out several key differences between chat and e-mail correspondence: "The relatively quick exchanges in chatrooms and instant messaging systems make feedback and repair much easier. The potential for rapid interaction has led to a style of communication more like spoken conversation, with short installments and frequent responses" (p. 152).

Research has shown that users perceive instant messaging to be less intrusive than a telephone call and more likely to prompt a quick reply than e-mail (Nardi et al., 2000). People who use instant-messaging systems tend to experience a strong sense of others and feel positive about knowing who is around even if they do not want to communicate directly (Nardi et al., 2000). Nardi and Whittaker (2002) suggested that instant messaging can aid in developing a sense of social connection and awareness. Also important, it may also increase daily contact and stimulate the types of impromptu, water cooler conversations that nurture understanding and trust. The use of chat rooms may also permit "overhearing," which promotes communication and learning during collaboration.

Training

Any team, virtual or not, can benefit from training, but organizations may need to pay special attention to the education and development of distributed CSCW teams. For starters, virtual teams need to be trained on the groupware tools that are available to them. Even the best groupware will do no good if teams fail to use it because of a lack of familiarity with the technology. Consider the collaborative authoring of documents, which can involve many paper drafts and a great deal of time entering edits. Technology attached to word processing programs can ease this process by allowing people to cross out words, attach voice and text commentary to sections of a manuscript, date- and time-stamp various edits, and so forth (J. S. Olson & Olson, 1999). Such features are useful only when all team members understand how to use them. When some or all members are not aware of available tools, or do not know how to use them, teams quickly develop norms of ignoring potentially beneficial groupware. In many cases, technological skills even affect virtual team members' ability and motivation to provide and request information to support group awareness (e.g., regarding availability and progress on projects; Weisband, 2002). Groupware training clearly is of paramount importance.

Training should also encourage open conversations about the difficulties of computer-mediated communication while educating teams on the potential consequences of these challenges and teaching them strategies for overcoming potential pitfalls (Armstrong & Cole, 2002; Cramton, 2002). For instance, virtual teammates should be coached to get to know each other. Research has shown that frequent communication at the outset and early maintenance of social awareness predict virtual team performance (Weisband, 2002). Gathering and sharing personal information at the outset to learn each other's habits, schedules, and so on, pays off in the long run, especially as important deadlines approach (Weisband, 2002).

Next, training should emphasize that virtual teams, which need information about what others are doing, should strive to create and reinforce awareness of others and their work. CSCW teams should be coached to exchange (offer and seek out) situational information (Cramton, 2002; Weisband, 2002). As Salas et al. (2001) pointed out, situation updates can help virtual teams manage meaning. Teams should be told to explicate goals and progress, request information from teammates, alert others regarding their own activities, and explain themselves and their contexts (Weisband, 2002). They should be forewarned that virtual teams, who must give and adjust to text-based social and task feedback, may need to explain themselves and their contexts more fully than they would during face-to-face collaboration (Walther, 2002).

Virtual teams should be taught that

> the need to communicate continuously is essential for sharing information and knowledge of group and individual activities related to the task, informing about work progress (Rasker, Post, & Schraagen, 2000), and anticipating others' needs or actions to achieve successful outcomes (Sheppard & Sherman, 1998). (Weisband, 2002, p. 311)

Moreover, they should be sensitized to the need to integrate smaller, distant groups, especially when connected via telephone, because such groups commonly get forgotten during audioconferences. The need to discuss "hallway conversation" during videoconferencing can also be emphasized during training (Armstrong & Cole, 2002).

Distributed CSCW teams should be forewarned of the difficulties regarding cohesion, and they should be coached to search for strategies to enhance unity. For example, because eating and drinking together are one of the most fundamental ways in which people get connected (Nardi & Whittaker, 2002), food and beverage can be incorporated into team meetings. Virtual teams studied by Armstrong and Cole (2002) were known to celebrate project milestones together by sharing food during videoconferences, with U.S. members sending video images of coffee and bagels (9:00 a.m. their time) to their Italian teammates, who sent images of champagne and cookies (3:00 p.m. their time). Considering the amount of informal interaction that tends to occur over food, such tactics may help enhance a team's social awareness and cohesion. Other multicultural virtual teams have worked to develop cohesion via shared humor and jokes, such as kicking off synchronous meetings by requiring a member to sing a song in his or her native tongue (Armstrong & Cole, 2002).

Virtual teams' vulnerability to the fundamental attribution error may also justify a particular emphasis on perspective taking during training. Research has shown that training designed to enhance positive attributional styles can effectively modify employees' attributional patterns while enhancing team satisfaction and performance (Wang, 1994). Cross-training can also help teammates better understand each other's roles, responsibilities, and viewpoints (Salas et al., 2001). In addition, swapping places while videoconferencing may prove useful. Armstrong and Cole (2002) recently described how one member of a virtual team regularly invited teammates to his site on some pretext so they would end up sitting on his end of the videoconference. This tactic may not only improve communication (e.g., the traveling member may go home and inform those typically on her end of the line to talk more slowly for the sake of clarity) but also encourage people to take situational factors into account, thereby reducing the rate at which they jump to dispositional conclusions when unanticipated events occur.

Leadership

Leaders of virtual teams certainly can play critical roles in implementing the preceding strategies, which can be introduced during training and then initiated, modeled, and reinforced by the leader. Recent research supports the notion that a leader's behavior may substantially affect virtual team performance. After studying 15 distributed CSCW teams working on a month-long project, Weisband (2002) concluded that teams with leaders who initiated pressure to complete the project on time performed better than those without such leaders. Likewise, teams having leaders who pursued "other-awareness" by assessing what members were doing performed the best. (Early initiations of pressure and other-awareness were more effective than later attempts.) Meanwhile, team members in nonleadership roles who initiated pressure and pursued other awareness were not able to boost performance (Weisband, 2002).

To some degree, virtual teams need the same kinds of direction required by their colocated counterparts (e.g., rewards should be linked to team rather than individual performance); however, distributed CSCW teams may need even more leadership at the time of formation than do conventional teams (Mannix et al., 2002). Virtual managers must use integrating practices that promote understanding and liking (e.g., enforcing equality, creating shared goals, promoting frequent contact and social ties, and supporting mutual knowledge) to increase cohesion (Armstrong & Cole, 2002). Distributed teams also require a leader who provides a clear and engaging direction, sets distinct objectives and role assignments, exhibits consideration, and initiates structure (Mannix et al., 2002; Weisband, 2002). According to CSCW researchers, monitoring and providing structure are even more important for virtual leaders than for people managing colocated teams (Mannix et al., 2002). Several authors have suggested that CSCW leaders should diligently monitor group communication practices (Armstrong & Cole, 2002; Cramton, 2002); however, some have warned that electronic managerial monitoring can backfire by increasing workers' stress levels, impairing their physical health, and discouraging people from using potentially beneficial groupware (Markus, 1983; J. S. Olson & Olson, 1999). Face-to-face monitoring may be a viable alternative, as indicated by Armstrong and Peter (2002), who suggested that trust can be maximized when team leaders visit remote members, talk with them while they are working, and allow time to gauge members' private concerns and problems.

Virtual teams will benefit from leaders who encourage frequent and highly structured communication (Armstrong & Cole, 2002). Colocated teams have been known to deal with communication difficulties by initiating *closed-loop communication*, in which "communication is initiated by the sender, the intended recipient acknowledges receipt of the message, and the sender follows up to ensure that the message was interpreted as intended" (Salas et al., 2001, p. 314). Leaders who encourage closed-loop communication during periods of low workload may help virtual teams maintain shared cognition and achieve success (Salas et al., 2001).

Leaders' attempts to structure teamwork should also focus on helping teams develop conventions for sharing groupware and then modeling the desired use of technology (Armstrong & Cole, 2002). Conventions for sharing technology (e.g., activating a track-changes feature prior to editing a shared document) are especially important when groupware is flexible and the team lacks a shared history. Conventions minimize process losses and allow new members to adapt to electronic work. Despite the importance of conventions, case studies have shown that in the absence of strong leadership, virtual teams can have a difficult time enforcing agreed-on rules of groupware usage (Mark, 2002). Commitment to a convention requires a team to cross an acceptance threshold, where a critical mass of members agrees to adhere to particular rules and procedures (Finnemore & Sikkink, 1998; Mark, 2002). Team leaders can structure teamwork not only by helping to form groupware usage conventions but also by persuading members to follow conventions until an acceptance threshold is reached (Mark, 2002).

In 2002, Kiesler and Cummings argued that highly controlled *structured management* approaches (e.g., task decomposition dividing teamwork into manageable chunks and standardized administration procedures) may be a necessary remedy when virtual teams lack cohesion. Structuring work in this manner essentially allows members to operate autonomously and then hand over work according to a standard procedure (Kiesler & Cummings, 2002). Salas et al. (2001) suggested that leaders should build some overlap into members' functions to promote the cognitive capabilities needed for backup behavior. Meanwhile, Nardi and Whittaker (2002) cautioned that too much structure can be dangerous: "The workers who will be most compromised in the rush to virtuality will be midlevel employees in medium to large organizations who cannot access organizational resources or reorganize themselves" (p. 107). To some degree, virtual team leadership appears to be something of a balancing act. Leaders must monitor communication without invading members' privacy, and they must structure teamwork while still allowing the flexibility to reorganize as necessary.

CONCLUSION

Although years of research have indicated that traditional teams face significant challenges in their own right, the literature suggests that these difficulties pale in comparison to those currently confronted by virtual teams (Mannix et al., 2002). The preceding strategies may help distributed CSCW teams overcome some of the barriers they face. To date, however, these ideas remain largely untested and therefore warrant careful consideration and empirical attention.

Some of these strategies are inelegant and even temporary solutions to problems that would be better solved by improved technology. Fortunately, the individuals designing CSCW tools are diligently working to create such solutions, and it is perhaps only a matter of time before new innovations cause many of the pitfalls described in this chapter to disappear. A large share of the CSCW literature is devoted to descriptions of exciting new ideas for improving virtual collaboration. For example, *ambient media*, which allow a person working alone in an office to sense activity in other parts of the team, are being developed to combat social distance and lack of awareness. Ambient media communicate digitally mediated senses of activity and presence at the periphery of human awareness (Coovert & Thompson, 2001). This type of technology could use a series of moving spotlights on a worker's office wall, for instance, to represent the amount of traffic on a team's intranet. When many people are moving about the common space, the lights could shift quickly, and slowly moving lights could indicate little activity (Berggren, Montán, Nord, & Östergren, 2000; Coovert & Thompson, 2002).

It is regrettable that modern-day CSCW teams do not generally have access to ambient media and other such innovations; instead, they are confined to contemporary groupware technologies, which fuel many of the problems discussed in this chapter by ignoring the interconnected features that distinguish groups from teams. Teams need "teamware" that allows coworkers to develop and maintain shared goals, shared understanding, relationships, and the coordination of cognitive and physical activities (Coovert & Thompson, 2001). The long-term aim of CSCW is to develop teamware that aids passive awareness of the team, task, and environment in which a person is operating without invading privacy and overwhelming people with too much information (Kraut et al., 2002). While working toward this goal, researchers and practitioners must strive to better understand the characteristics and consequences of virtual collaboration, as it evolves, so that increasingly effective technologies, interventions, and strategies can be developed to improve the effectiveness of CSCW in the days to come.

REFERENCES

Adrianson, L., & Hjelmquist, E. (1991). Group processes in face-to-face and computer-mediated communication. *Behaviour & Information Technology, 10,* 281–296.

Anderson, A. H., O'Malley, C., Doherty-Sneddon, G., Langton, S., Newlands, A., Mullin, J., et al. (1997). The impact of VMC on collaborative problem solving: An analysis of task performance, communicative process, and user satisfaction. In K. E. Finn, A. J. Sellen, & S. B. Wilbur (Eds.), *Video-mediated communication* (pp. 133–155). Mahwah, NJ: Erlbaum.

Armstrong, D. J., & Cole, P. (2002). Managing distances and differences in geographically distributed work groups. In P. Hinds & S. Kiesler (Eds.), *Distributed work* (pp. 167–186). Cambridge, MA: MIT Press.

Armstrong, D. J., & Peter, E. B. (2002). Addendum: Virtual proximity, real teams. In P. Hinds & S. Kiesler (Eds.), *Distributed work* (pp. 187–189). Cambridge, MA: MIT Press.

Berggren, M., Montán, S., Nord, H., & Östergren, M. (2000). *Smart spaces.* Retrieved March 12, 2001, from http://www.docs.uu.se/~cmb/smart-spaces.pdf

Bordia, P. (1997). Face-to-face versus computer-mediated communication: A synthesis of the experimental literature. *Journal of Business Communication, 34,* 99–120.

Brawley, L. R., Carron, A. V., & Widmeyer, W. N. (1987). Assessing the cohesion of teams: Validity of the Group Environment Questionnaire. *Journal of Sport Psychology, 9,* 275–294.

Burdett, J. (2000). Changing channels: Using the electronic meeting system to increase equity in decision making. *Information Technology, Learning, and Performance Journal, 18*(2), 3–12.

Clark, H. H., & Brennan, S. E. (1991). Grounding in communication. In L. B. Resnick, J. M. Levine, & S. D. Teasley (Eds.), *Perspectives on socially shared cognition* (pp. 127–149). Washington, DC: American Psychological Association.

Coovert, M. D., & Thompson, L. F. (2001). *Computer supported cooperative work: Issues and implications for workers, organizations, and human resource management.* Thousand Oaks, CA: Sage.

Coovert, M. D., & Thompson, L. F. (2002). Technology and workplace health. In J. C. Quick & L. E. Tetrick (Eds.), *Handbook of occupational health psychology* (pp. 221–241). Washington, DC: American Psychological Association.

Cramton, C. D. (2001). The mutual knowledge problem and its consequences for dispersed collaboration. *Organization Science, 12,* 346–371.

Cramton, C. D. (2002). Attribution in distributed work groups. In P. Hinds & S. Kiesler (Eds.), *Distributed work* (pp. 191–212). Cambridge, MA: MIT Press.

Daly, B. L. (1993). The influence of face-to-face versus computer-mediated communication channels on collective induction. *Accounting, Management, and Information Technologies, 3,* 1–22.

DeSanctis, G., & Monge, P. (1999). Introduction to the special issue: Communication processes for virtual organizations. *Organizational Science, 10*, 693–703.

Dubrovsky, V. J., Kiesler, S., & Sethna, B. N. (1991). The equalization phenomenon: Status effects in computer-mediated and face-to-face decision-making groups. *Human–Computer Interaction, 6*, 119–146.

Finholt, T. A., Sproull, L., & Kiesler, S. (2002). Outsiders on the inside: Sharing know-how across space and time. In P. Hinds & S. Kiesler (Eds.), *Distributed work* (pp. 357–380). Cambridge, MA: MIT Press.

Finholt, T. A., & Teasley, S. D. (1998). The need for psychology in research on computer-supported cooperative work. *Social Science Computer Review, 16*, 40–52.

Finnemore, M., & Sikkink, K. (1998). International norm dynamics and political change. *International Organization, 52*, 887–917.

Fish, R. S., Kraut, R. E., & Chalfonte, B. L. (1990). The VideoWindow system in informal communications. In *Proceedings of the ACM Conference on Computer Supported Cooperative Work (CSCW '90)* (pp. 1–11). New York: ACM Press.

Greenberg, S., & Neuwirth, C. (1998). From the papers co-chairs. In *Proceedings of the ACM Conference on Computer Supported Cooperative Work (CSCW '98)* (p. v). New York: ACM Press.

Hiltz, S. R., Johnson, K., & Turoff, M. (1986). Experiments in group decision making: Communication process and outcome in face-to-face versus computerized conferences. *Human Communication Research, 13*, 225–252.

Hollingshead, A. B., McGrath, J. E., & O'Connor, K. M. (1993). Group task performance and communication technology: A longitudinal study of computer-mediated versus face-to-face work groups. *Small Group Research, 24*, 307–333.

Jehn, K. A. (1995). A multimethod examination of the benefits and detriments of intragroup conflict. *Administrative Science Quarterly, 40*, 256–282.

Jehn, K. A., & Mannix, E. A. (2001). The dynamic nature of conflict: A longitudinal study of intragroup conflict and group performance. *Academy of Management Journal, 44*, 238–251.

Johansen, R. (1984). *Teleconferencing and beyond: Communications in the office of the future.* New York: McGraw-Hill.

Johansen, R. (1988). *Groupware: Computer support for business teams.* New York: Free Press.

Kemske, F. (1998). HR 2008: A forecast based on our exclusive study. *Workforce, 77*, 46–60.

Kiesler, S., & Cummings, J. N. (2002). What do we know about proximity and distance in work groups? A legacy of research. In P. Hinds & S. Kiesler (Eds.), *Distributed work* (pp. 57–80). Cambridge, MA: MIT Press.

Kiesler, S., Siegel, J., & McGuire, T. W. (1984). Social psychological aspects of computer-mediated communication. *American Psychologist, 39*, 1123–1134.

Kiesler, S., & Sproull, L. (1992). Group decision making and communication technology. *Organizational Behavior and Human Decision Processes, 52,* 96–123.

Krauss, R. M., & Fussell, S. R. (1990). Mutual knowledge and communicative effectiveness. In J. Galegher, R. E. Kraut, & C. Egido (Eds.), *Intellectual teamwork: Social and technological foundations of cooperative work* (pp. 111–145). Hillsdale, NJ: Erlbaum.

Kraut, R. E., Egido, C., & Galegher, J. (1990). Patterns of contact and communication in scientific research collaboration. In J. Galegher, R. E. Kraut, & C. Egido (Eds.), *Intellectual teamwork: Social and technological foundations of cooperative work* (pp. 149–171). Hillsdale, NJ: Erlbaum.

Kraut, R. E., Fussell, S. R., Brennan, S. E., & Siegel, J. (2002). Understanding effects of proximity on collaboration: Implications for technologies to support remote collaborative work. In P. Hinds & S. Kiesler (Eds.), *Distributed work* (pp. 137–162). Cambridge, MA: MIT Press.

Lebie, L., Rhoades, J. A., & McGrath, J. E. (1996). Interaction process in computer-mediated and face-to-face groups. *Computer Supported Cooperative Work, 4,* 127–152.

Mannix, E. A., Griffith, T., & Neale, M. A. (2002). The phenomenology of conflict in distributed work teams. In P. Hinds & S. Kiesler (Eds.), *Distributed work* (pp. 213–233). Cambridge, MA: MIT Press.

Mark, G. (2002). Conventions for coordinating electronic distributed work: A longitudinal study of groupware use. In P. Hinds & S. Kiesler (Eds.), *Distributed work* (pp. 259–282). Cambridge, MA: MIT Press.

Markus, M. L. (1983). *Systems in organization: Bugs and features.* San Jose, CA: Pitman.

McDaniel, S. E., Olson, G. M., & Magee, J. C. (1996). Identifying and analyzing multiple threads in computer-mediated and face-to-face conversations. In *Proceedings of the ACM Conference on Computer Supported Cooperative Work (CSCW '96)* (pp. 39–47). New York: ACM Press.

McDonald, D. M. (1995). Fixing blame in *n*-person attributions: A social identity model for attributional processes in newly formed cross-functional groups. In M. J. Martinko (Ed.), *Attribution theory: An organizational perspective* (pp. 273–288). Delray Beach, FL: St. Lucie Press.

McGrath, J. E., & Hollingshead, A. B. (1994). *Groups interacting with technology: Ideas, evidence, issues, and an agenda.* Thousand Oaks, CA: Sage.

McGuire, T., Kiesler, S., & Siegel, J. (1987). Group and computer-mediated discussion effects in risk decision making. *Journal of Personality and Social Psychology, 52,* 917–930.

Mortensen, M., & Hinds, P. (2002). Fuzzy teams: Boundary disagreement in distributed and collocated teams. In P. Hinds & S. Kiesler (Eds.), *Distributed work* (pp. 283–308). Cambridge, MA: MIT Press.

Nardi, B. A., & Whittaker, S. (2002). The place of face-to-face communication in distributed work. In P. Hinds & S. Kiesler (Eds.), *Distributed work* (pp. 83–110). Cambridge, MA: MIT Press.

Nardi, B. A., Whittaker, S., & Bradner, E. (2000). Interaction and outeraction: Instant messaging in action. In *Proceedings of the ACM Conference on Computer Supported Cooperative Work (CSCW '00)* (pp. 79–88). New York: ACM Press.

Norvell, N., & Forsyth, D. R. (1984). The impact of inhibiting or facilitating causal factors on group members' reactions after success and failure. *Social Psychology Quarterly, 47*, 293–297.

Olson, G. M., & Olson, J. S. (2000). Distance matters. *Human–Computer Interaction 15*, 139–178.

Olson, J. S., & Olson, G. M. (1999). Computer supported cooperative work. In F. T. Durso, R. S. Nickerson, R. W. Schvaneveldt, S. T. Dumais, D. S. Lindsay, & M. T. H. Chi (Eds.), *Handbook of applied cognition* (pp. 409–442). New York: Wiley.

Olson, J. S., Olson, G. M., & Meader, D. K. (1995). What mix of video and audio is useful for small groups doing remote real-time work? In *Proceedings of the ACM Conference on Human Factors in Computer Systems (CHI '95)* (pp. 362–368). New York: ACM Press/Addison-Wesley.

Olson, J. S., Teasley, S., Covi, L., & Olson, G. (2002). The (currently) unique advantages of collocated work. In P. Hinds & S. Kiesler (Eds.), *Distributed work* (pp. 113–135). Cambridge, MA: MIT Press.

Paris, C. R., Salas, E., & Cannon-Bowers, J. A. (2000). Teamwork in multi-person systems: A review and analysis. *Ergonomics, 43*, 1052–1075.

Postmes, T., Spears, R., & Lea, M. (1998). Breaching or building social boundaries: SIDE-effects of computer-mediated communication. *Communication Research, 25*, 689–715.

Postmes, T., Spears, R., & Lea, M. (1999). Social identity, normative content and "deindividuation" in computer-mediated groups. In N. Ellemers, R. Spears, & B. Doosje (Eds.), *Social identity* (pp. 164–183). Malden, MA: Blackwell.

Ramesh, R., & Andrews, D. H. (1999). Distributed mission training: Teams, virtual reality, and real-time networking. *Communications of the ACM, 42*(9), 65–67.

Rasker, P. C., Post, W. M., & Schraagen, J. M. C. (2000). Effects of two types of intra-team feedback on developing a shared mental model in command & control teams. *Ergonomics, 43*, 1167–1189.

Rocco, E. (1998). Trust breaks down in electronic contexts but can be repaired by some initial face-to-face contact. In *Proceedings of the ACM Conference on Human Factors in Computing Systems (CHI '98)* (pp. 496–502). New York: ACM Press/Addison-Wesley.

Salas, E., Burke, C. S., & Samman, S. N. (2001). Understanding command and control teams operating in complex environments. *Information Knowledge Systems Management, 2*, 311–323.

Schwarz, H., Nardi, B. A., & Whittaker, S. (1999). *The hidden work in virtual work.* Retrieved December 15, 2002, from http://www.mngt.waikato.ac.nz/ejrot/cmsconference/documents/Technology/Schwarz.pdf

Scrivener, S. A. R., & Clark, S. (1994). Introducing computer-supported cooperative work. In S. A. R. Scrivener (Ed.), *Computer-supported cooperative work* (pp. 19–38). Brookfield, VT: Ashgate.

Sheppard, B. H., & Sherman, D. M. (1998). The grammars of trust: A model and general implications. *Academy of Management Review, 23,* 422–437.

Short, J., Williams, E., & Christie, B. (1976). *The social psychology of telecommunications.* New York: Wiley.

Siegel, J., Dubrovsky, V., Kiesler, S., & McGuire, T. W. (1986). Group processes in computer-mediated communication. *Organizational Behavior and Human Decision Processes, 37,* 157–187.

Smilowitz, M., Compton, D. C., & Flint, L. (1988). The effects of computer mediated communication on an individual's judgment: A study based on the methods of Asch's social influence experiment. *Computers in Human Behavior, 4,* 311–321.

Spector, P. E. (2003). *Industrial and organizational psychology: Research and practice* (3rd ed.). New York: Wiley.

Sproull, L., & Kiesler, S. (1991). *Connections: New ways of working in the networked organization.* Cambridge, MA: MIT Press.

Spurr, K., Layzell, P., Jennison, L., & Richards, N. (1994). *Computer support for co-operative work.* West Sussex, England: Wiley.

Storck, J., & Sproull, L. (1995). Through a glass darkly: What do people learn in videoconferences? *Human Communication Research, 22,* 197–219.

Straus, S. G. (1996). Getting a clue: The effects of communication media and information distribution on participation and performance in computer-mediated and face-to-face groups. *Small Group Research, 27,* 115–142.

Thompson, L. F., & Coovert, M. D. (2002). Stepping up to the challenge: A critical examination of face-to-face and computer-mediated team decision making. *Group Dynamics: Theory, Research, and Practice, 6,* 52–64.

Thompson, L. F., & Coovert, M. D. (2003). Teamwork online: The effects of computer conferencing on perceived confusion, satisfaction, and post-discussion accuracy. *Group Dynamics: Theory, Research, and Practice, 7,* 135–151.

Townsend, A. M., DeMarie, S. M., & Hendrickson, A. R. (1998). Virtual teams: Technology and the workplace of the future. *Academy of Management Executive, 12*(3), 17–29.

Valacich, J. S., & Schwenk, C. (1995). Devil's advocacy and dialectical inquiry effects on face-to-face and computer-mediated group decision making. *Organizational Behavior and Human Decision Processes, 63,* 158–173.

Walther, J. B. (2002). Time effects in computer-mediated groups: Past, present, and future. In P. Hinds & S. Kiesler (Eds.), *Distributed work* (pp. 235–257). Cambridge, MA: MIT Press.

Walther, J. B., & D'Addario, K. P. (2001). The impacts of emoticons on message interpretation in computer-mediated communication. *Social Science Computer Review, 19,* 324–347.

Walther, J. B., Slovacek, C. L., & Tidwell, L. C. (2001). Is a picture worth a thousand words? Photographic images in long-term and short-term computer-mediated communication. *Communication Research, 28,* 105–134.

Wang, Z. (1994). Group attributional training as an effective approach to human resource development under team work systems. *Ergonomics, 37,* 1137–1144.

Weisband, S. P. (1992). Group discussion and first advocacy effects in computer-mediated and face-to-face decision making groups. *Organizational Behavior and Human Decision Processes, 53,* 352–380.

Weisband, S. P. (2002). Maintaining awareness in distributed team collaboration: Implications for leadership and performance. In P. Hinds & S. Kiesler (Eds.), *Distributed work* (pp. 311–333). Cambridge, MA: MIT Press.

Whitney, D. (2001). Video and more coming soon to a cell near you. *Electronic Media, 20(33),* 19.

Wiesenfeld, B. M., Raghuram, S., & Garud, R. (1998). Communication patterns as determinants of organizational identification in a virtual organization. *Journal of Computer-Mediated Communication, 3(4).*

Williams, K. Y., & O'Reilly, C. A. III (1998). Demography and diversity in organizations: A review of 40 years of research. In B. M. Staw & L. L. Cummings (Eds.), *Research in organizational behavior: An annual series of analytical essays and critical reviews* (Vol. 20, pp. 77–140). Greenwich, CT: JAI Press.

Wilson, P. (1991). *Computer supported cooperative work.* Oxford, England: Intellect.

Zheng, J., Bos, N., Olson, J. S., & Olson, G. M. (2001). Trust without touch: Jumpstart trust with social chat. In *Proceedings of the ACM Conference on Human Factors in Computer Systems (CHI '01)* (pp. 293–294). New York: ACM Press.

Zheng, J., Veinott, E., Bos, N., Olson, J. S., & Olson, G. M. (2002). Trust without touch: Jumpstarting long-distance trust with initial social activities. In *Proceedings of the ACM Conference on Human Factors in Computer Systems (CHI '02)* (pp. 141–146). New York: ACM Press.

11

AUTOMATED SYSTEMS IN THE COCKPIT: IS THE AUTOPILOT, "GEORGE," A TEAM MEMBER?

RAEGAN M. HOEFT, JANEEN A. KOCHAN, AND FLORIAN JENTSCH

In the earliest days, air transports were operated by a single pilot because the airplanes in the 1920s were small and rudimentary. As the size and the sophistication of equipment increased, a copilot was added to help the captain in controlling the airplane and monitoring the systems, thereby improving safety. The 1930s brought about four-engine transports, the artificial horizon, and the first autopilot prototypes. As flights became longer and cockpits acquired more equipment, a flight engineer was added to the crew. Soon thereafter, multiple engineers, navigators, radio operators, and stewards were also necessary to accomplish all of the tasks facing the team on a typical flight or mission.

By the 1950s, the size of the human team began to shrink as navigators and radio operators were replaced with new, more reliable ground-based communication and navigation equipment. At first, the main thrust for the rapid development and implementation of automation revolved around human performance limitations as aircraft flew higher, faster, and for longer periods of time. Early research studies on pilot stress and fatigue (e.g., McFarland, 1953) were often presented as evidence for the advantages of having and using automated functions. The 1960s found aircraft owners, operators, and the military looking to the plethora of automated options for improved safety and reliability and even more so for the cost savings associated with fewer human operators and more efficient operation of the equipment. Today's commercial, military, and corporate-use transport category airplanes are typically flown by a host of automated components, programmed and controlled by a relatively small complement of human crew members, usually one or two. As the hunt for a means of safer and cheaper air travel continued, so did the recurring theme of eliminating the human from the cockpit team altogether (Billings, 1997; McFarland, 1946).

VIEWS ON AUTOMATION

Automation has been defined in numerous ways, often depending on the context of the discussion. For the purposes of this chapter, we have adopted a definition of automation put forth by Parasuraman and Riley (1997): a machine agent or agents carrying out tasks (or partial tasks) once allocated to the human. The competing views on the use, misuse, and extent to which automated functions would participate in or control the flying and navigating duties of aircraft emerged as early as the 1940s. McFarland (1946) argued that "the weight of evidence tends to favor the use of automatic pilots on air transports in the interests of safety, comfort, and flight efficiency" (p. 393), whereas opponents felt pilots would not remain alert and that their manual flying skills might deteriorate if mechanized flight was used to a great degree. First-generation autopilots, such as the Sperry A-12 gyropilot, were originally developed to improve aircraft stability to help minimize passenger airsickness. The rudimentary engineering and unreliable controllability resulted in early and strong skepticism from the pilots. Even when consulted by the designers as to the type of control these early-automated units should provide, the pilots preferred "loose" control, because it more closely resembled their own operation of the aircraft, even though "tight" control would have been better for human comfort and navigation accuracy. While improvements in electronics and flight control component technology created the opportunity for designers to automate and integrate other functions heretofore assigned to the human pilot into newer autopilot and autoflight systems, the struggle for dominant control by the human continued.

The aircraft operating team of the 1980s primarily consisted of at least three human team members: (a) a captain, (b) a first officer, and (c) a flight engineer. In a continued effort to improve safety and efficiency through reduced pilot workload and reduce costs via precise navigation and aircraft system operation, more sophisticated automated systems were engineered into new aircraft designs and added to existing ones. Now, with often only one or two human crew members in the cockpit interacting with any number of automated components, the question arose as to whether automation could be considered an additional crew member of sorts.

In recent years, researchers have assumed that the necessary coordinated actions on the part of the humans and the automation do constitute a team, taking the automation into consideration as another team member (Billings, 1997; Malin, 2000). For example, Sarter, Woods, and Billings (1997, p. 1931) and Christoffersen and Woods (2002, p. 3) stated that the addition of automated systems to assist or coordinate with a human operator is at least in some ways "like adding a new team member." In addition, Emerson, Reising, Taylor, and Reinecke (1989, as cited in Morgan, Herschler, Wiener, & Salas, 1993) actually referred to automated systems as "electronic crewmembers." In fact, pilots have anthropomorphized automated systems as early as World War II, naming their autopilots "George."

The purpose of this chapter is to gain a better understanding of the "team" composed of human crew members and automated systems that are in control of today's modern aircraft. We begin by reviewing the definition of *teams* to see whether it is reasonable to include automated systems as additional team members. Then we use a team process model to analyze how an automated team member would interact with human team members. On the basis of evidence from team research and automation research, and using the *team effectiveness model* (TEM; Tannenbaum, Beard, & Salas, 1992), we consider whether the automated systems in cockpits can truly be considered additional crew members. Furthermore, if automated systems are really members of the team, do they exhibit the same qualities as human team members? Finally, we extract lessons learned from automation in the aviation industry to make suggestions for other industries in which automated systems are currently in use or on the verge of being implemented into team environments.

TEAMS

As stated in the introduction of this book, the generally accepted definition of a *team* includes two key elements: (a) interdependence of the team members and (b) a common purpose or goal (cf. Salas, Dickenson, Converse, & Tannenbaum, 1992). Team research has, in the past, focused on teams of humans; however, this definition can easily apply to teams composed of both human team members and automated team members. In general, *automation* refers to computers or automated systems that have taken over certain tasks typically performed by humans in the past. Although this definition is fairly simplistic, it should be noted there are many different types of automated systems as well as many levels of automation (Parasuraman, Sheridan, & Wickens, 2000). The degree to which an automated system might be considered a team member might be influenced by these levels and types; however, in this chapter we consider the previously mentioned broad definition of automation that encompasses these subclasses.

To determine whether computers could be teammates, Nass, Fogg, and Moon (1996) studied human–computer communication by manipulating the identity of the computer and interdependence of the tasks. Their results showed that interdependence was vital to convincing participants they were part of a team composed of themselves and a computer, although identity had no effects on perceptions of a team. In addition, the participants who recognized their role in a team with a computer exhibited the same types of attitudes and behaviors as are normal when working with human teammates. Specifically, participants in the interdependent condition perceived information given by the computer to be of higher quality, perceived themselves to be more similar to the computer, and perceived the computer to be friendlier than did participants in the noninterdependent condition.

Nass et al.'s (1996) study demonstrated how a team could be created with one person and one computer simply by requiring reciprocal interdependence, that is, that the two communicate by taking information from each other, processing that information, inputting new information, and continuing the process until a decision is reached. There are a variety of types of interdependencies that may play a role in the perception of a team. For example, Tesluk, Mathieu, Zaccaro, and Marks (1997) used the term *intensive work situations* as the type of interdependence representative of teams continuously facing novel situations that require problem diagnosis and problem solving. The cockpit, one of the most complex environments, requires these multifaceted types of interdependence between crew members and automated systems, providing compelling evidence of the existence of one integrated team. Given that the characteristics of automated systems and crew members within a cockpit are representative of those within a team, it is necessary to determine whether the processes involving the automated team member are comparable to team processes within all-human teams.

TEAM EFFECTIVENESS MODEL

The TEM (Tannenbaum et al., 1992) is a model that describes the variables thought to influence team performance (see Figure 11.1). The model consists of inputs (individual characteristics, team characteristics, work structure, and task characteristics), throughputs (team processes and team interventions), and outputs (team changes, team performance, and

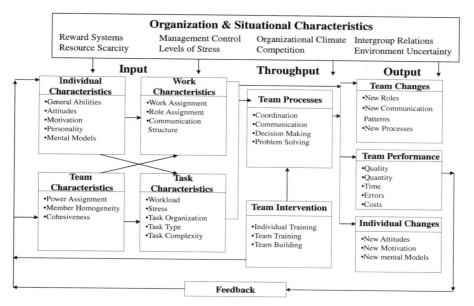

Figure 11.1. The team effectiveness model. From "Team Building and Its Influence on Team Effectiveness: An Examination of Conceptual and Empirical Developments," by S. I. Tannenbaum, R. L. Beard, and E. Salas, 1992, in K. Kelley (Ed.), *Issues, Theory, and Research in Industrial/Organizational Psychology* (p. 121), Amsterdam: Elsevier Science. Copyright 1992 by Elsevier Science. Reprinted with permission.

individual changes). Individual characteristics are distinct qualities that each team member brings to the team, that is, general abilities, attitudes, mental models, and personality factors. Team characteristics are factors that define team composition, specifically, member homogeneity, power distribution, and cohesiveness. Task characteristics are those variables specifically related to the team's task, for example, workload, stress, task type, and task complexity. The final input variable, work characteristics, includes aspects associated with carrying out the task, in particular, communication structure and role and work assignments.

Each of the previously mentioned input factors plays a crucial role in how team members will work together to accomplish the given task. The actual procedure used to reach the ultimate goal of the team lies in the throughput section of the model. Included in the throughput section are team processes that involve coordination, communication, decision making, and problem solving. The efficiency of these team processes will ultimately determine whether the task will be completed successfully. The TEM suggests that if there are deficiencies in the team processing, team interventions, such as individual and team training, as well as team building, may be used to positively influence the input variables, which should in turn promote more effective team processes.

The output factors of the model describe the results of a team performing a particular task. Team performance aspects include quality, quantity, time, errors, and costs. Team changes are team characteristics that have been altered because of the experiences of the team during task completion, including new roles, new communication patterns, and new processes. Similarly, individual changes are individual characteristics that have been modified on the basis of the experiences of individual team members (new attitudes, mental models, and motivations). The model also contains a feedback loop in which these output variables are suggested to affect the input variables for future tasks. Finally, the model contains organization and situational characteristics (reward systems, resource scarcity, management control, levels of stress, organizational climate, competition, intergroup relations, and environment uncertainty) that affect all aspects of the model.

The TEM has been used to describe teams composed of solely human team members. Bowers, Oser, Salas, and Cannon-Bowers (1996) used the model to discuss the impact of automated systems on team performance; however, they too considered a human team with the automation as an outside resource. In the following sections, we use the TEM to analyze the performance of a team comprising human and automated team members and describe the potential unique challenges faced by such a team. In addition, this analysis will provide a comprehensive look at the extent of the positive and negative characteristics of an automated team member.

Individual Characteristics

As mentioned earlier, individual characteristics are facets of team members that are brought with them into the team environment. Individual characteristics for an automated system are, in many respects, quite different from those that human team members bring to the group. For instance, attitudes are not a component of an automated system. Automated systems do not have biases in their judgment or decisions based on opinion or annoyance with another team member. In contrast, human team members do come in with attitudes toward their job, their teammates, and their assigned tasks, as well as the automated systems with which they are forced to interact (Sheridan, 2002). Although these attitudes generally remain stable over time, they may also change with experience. However, because the automated systems do not have varying attitudes, they always remain stable on this particular individual characteristic. This may or may not be a benefit, because although these traits are stable, they are not necessarily apparent or understood by the human team members.

A second individual characteristic of interest when discussing auto-mated team members is the mental models of the task at hand as viewed by each team member. Automated teammates have mental models of their functions as preprogrammed by the designer and in essence are a reflection of the designer's mental model. These mental models will not be influenced by experience, mistakes, or practice, and thus can be altered only by repro-gramming. In contrast, humans may arrive at a setting with a poor mental model of how things work and, through experience, their mental models have the opportunity be modified or altered. However, the remodeling of the humans' mental models may not always result in improvement, as there is always the potential to update a model that is based on faulty designs, poor information, or negative experience (Norman, 1988). For the entire team to work together to accomplish its goals, the human team members must have a true picture of the automated team members, the tasks of both the humans and the automation, and the team itself (Cannon-Bowers, Salas, & Converse, 1993).

Another important individual characteristic is trust. The research on trust in automation has found mixed results. Humans vary in the degree to which they trust automation, and this is affected strongly by how reliable they believe the system to be (Moray, Inagaki, & Itoh, 2000). In fact, Sheridan (1980) suggested that there are seven characteristics of human trust in automated systems: (a) reliability, (b) competence, (c) familiarity, (d) understandability, (e) explication of intent, (f) usefulness, and (g) depen-dency. In addition, studies have found that human trust in automated systems actually interacts with the person's own self-confidence (Lee & Moray, 1994). For instance, Amalberti (1999) pointed out that a pilot is more likely to believe that he or she does not understand the situation rather than blame the automation for making a mistake. Thus, the interaction of a human team member with an automated team member is affected by a multitude of factors. It is interesting to note that pilots are explicitly taught to be wary of automated systems, to double-check and verify all actions and responses, and to continually monitor all automated activities.

Indeed, human team members have at times had reason to doubt the information and decisions the automation was providing. An Air New Zealand Boeing 767, with 165 passengers and 11 crew on board, commenced a go-around after descending to an altitude of about 400 ft (122 m) above the ground, more than 6 miles (9.65 km) short of the runway. An exhaustive investigation revealed that the ground-based Instrument Landing System (ILS) was transmitting invalid guidance information, while cockpit glide path and localizer indications were normal and no malfunctions or equip-ment failure alerts were presented to the flight crew. The automated team members accepted erroneous information as valid because preprogrammed parameters were not exceeded, and thus they continued to lead the crew and passengers into harm's way. Only peripheral cues from lights on a mountainside, combined with the flight crew's unspecified uneasiness about the approach, resulted in what may have been a lifesaving decision by the human crew members: to initiate a go-around and climb to safety. In this case, the automated team member trusts that it was given the correct information from the human team members and the other automated systems involved in the task. Although the automated teammate often has a double-checking capability (i.e., "Are you sure those are the correct coordinates?"), the final decision for verifying correct data falls into the hands of a human team member.

The dichotomy in trust between human and automated team members is most pronounced when new automated systems are first introduced to the fleet. For example, numerous false terrain warnings from first-generation Ground Proximity Warning Systems led to mistrust, and eventually pilots failed to heed the warnings and the required ground avoidance maneuvers. Unfortunately, in many cases the warnings were true, and an abundance of fatal accidents resulted because of the human mistrust of the automated systems information (Mejdal, McCauley, & Beringer, 2001). More recently, conflicting information from human air traffic controllers and the automated Traffic Alert and Collision Avoidance Systems in two aircraft regarding an impending midair collision resulted in disaster (National Transportation Safety Board, 2002). A Boeing 757 collided with a Tupolov TU154, even though both aircraft Traffic Alert and Collision Avoidance Systems indications gave correct indications for evasive maneuvers. Instructions from air traffic control, contrary to the automated instructions, were followed, resulting in 71 fatalities.

Team Characteristics

Team characteristics are those factors that describe the team as a whole. The first relevant team characteristic is *member homogeneity*. The literature is replete with studies comparing homogeneous and heterogeneous teams (cf. the meta-analysis by Bowers, Pharmer, & Salas, 2000). There appear to be some advantages and disadvantages to both types of teams. For example, Watson, Johnson, and Zgourides (2002) found that culturally heterogeneous teams initially fall behind culturally homogeneous teams in overall team performance; however, that gap lessens throughout the life cycle of the team, and culturally heterogeneous teams ultimately outperform culturally homogeneous teams. It is reasonable to assume that a team composed of human and automated teammates will always be heterogeneous. In contrast to an all-human group, in which variables such as culture, religion, ethnicity, and gender contribute to heterogeneity, the automated team members are unique in their capabilities, such as problem solving, decision making, communication mode, and personality characteristics. Consequently, it is unclear how much of the research on team composition can be extrapolated to these human–automated heterogeneous teams. Helmreich, Chidester, Foushee, Gregorich, and Wilhelm (1995) stated that automated teammates should be treated in the same manner as humans, suggesting the two types of teams are comparable. However, there is still a need for specific research on the unique advantages and disadvantages of human–automated teams.

Power distribution is also an important team characteristic. It has been argued that the introduction of automation into a team setting affects the power distribution of the human team members (Wiener, 1989). Traditional human–human interactions in the cockpit are likely to be disrupted by the presence and attentional needs of the automation. The monitoring of the automation also serves to blur the pilot flying and pilot monitoring duties. The "flying pilot's" primary duty is to monitor the automation, but what does the monitoring pilot ("non-flying pilot") keep track of: the flying pilot or the automation? This idea is important because it is relevant not only to teams that have automated resources but also to teams composed of human and automated team members. Yet the power distribution facet of teams does not solely apply to the human team members. In fact, automated systems can take on both leadership and subordinate roles, depending on the task at hand. Automated team members can assume leadership positions, often with the blessing of the human team members. Automated team members may also relinquish the leadership role to the human team members, or they may bypass human team members altogether and hand over power to other automated team members. Conversely, there are some automated systems over which human team members have no direct control or override capability. Thus, there are distinct power distribution issues for human–automated teams revolving around the lack of clarification in roles, boundaries, and authority for both the human and automated teammates.

Task Characteristics

Task characteristics relate to specific aspects of the task at hand and how the team is affected by those aspects. The main task characteristic that is significant in the human–automated team environment is workload. The introduction of automated systems into the cockpit has had a profound impact on the amount of workload experienced by crew members (Guide, Wise, Abbott, & Ryan, 1993; James, McClumpha, Green, Wilson, & Belyavin, 1991; Wiener, 1989). The exact nature of this impact is difficult to pinpoint, as it appears that the perceived workload is greatly influenced by individual differences. Overall, the automated systems contribute to reduced workload in certain regimens of flight, although instances of increased workload often occur during takeoff and landing or other critical phases of flight. Automated team members vary the order of task accomplishment on the basis of conditions, mode selections, and so on (e.g., depending on descent mode selected, the aircraft automation may slow down, and then descend, or it may descend and then slow down). Human team members vary tremendously in their abilities to cope with workload and to alter their strategies accordingly. Some may be extremely efficient at prioritizing and delegating tasks, whereas others may not be so capable of workload management. Thus, although *perceived* workload strongly influences the performance of a human team member (Wickens & Hollands, 2000), the automated team member remains relatively stable and only reacts to *true* changes in workload demands.

Work Characteristics

The most important work characteristic in the analysis of human–automation teams is that of *communication structure*. Communication between computers and humans is much different from that between humans and humans. Whereas humans can have face-to-face conversations, including nonverbal cues, automated teammates give and receive information in specific formats through a host of display units. Sarter et al. (1997) noted that this failure to use the knowledge of human–human communication skills to automated system designs is fundamental to problems with modern automated systems. In addition, because of the lack of nonverbal cues—and, consequently, contextual cues—it has been argued that a computer's reliance on only syntax and semantics lies at the heart of misunderstandings between humans and automation (Suchman, 1990). The manner in which one interacts with the automated teammate, which may clearly provide cues about the current state of a situation, might be observed and understood by other human team members but will have no effect on the automated team member (Segal, 1989). Automated teammates are programmed to provide certain types of information and ask for certain types of information, and that is all they can receive. Thus, human teammates must know both how to acquire the information they need and how to format the information for the automated teammate. The formalities structured into communicating with automated team members may impose restrictions that can interfere with the spontaneous, free-flowing nature of human–human communication.

Team Processes

As mentioned previously, all of the input factors interact with one another to influence team processes. It is during the processing stage that the team members work together to accomplish their goals; thus, interdependency is key. However, Boys and Palko (1988) suggested that the integration of automation could drastically modify human team member roles and interactions within the cockpit. Numerous studies have delved into the effects of automated systems on team processes (e.g., Bowers, Deaton, Oser, Prince, & Kolb, 1993; Morgan et al., 1993). Again, these studies focus specifically on the human–human communication and the potential disruptions taking place when in the presence of an automated system.

Coordination is a key element to goal attainment for any team. It is essential that the human team members can manage their own tasks in conjunction with the tasks of the automated team members, and vice versa. As we mentioned at the beginning of this chapter, interdependence between team members is the essence of the team itself, and thus coordination among team members is crucial. One challenge to effective coordination stems from the humans' feeling of being left out of the loop regarding the status of the aircraft. Often it is difficult for the human team member to "see" or understand the automated teammates' intentions and actions, most notably when the feedback provided is subtle or opaque (Sarter et al., 1997). If the human team members do not understand what the automated team members are doing, and why they are doing it, it is extremely difficult for them to coordinate their actions with the automated team members and, consequently, with each other. It is at this point that feedback is extremely important: The automated team members must be capable of providing feedback tailored to the given situation. Feedback is one of the communication avenues through which the automated team member can coordinate with the team.

Decision making is also a key part of the team process. Making informed decisions in the cockpit requires the coordinated efforts of the human and automated team members; nonetheless, these team members have vastly different methods of integrating information to make those decisions. In an ideal situation, humans should make decisions by gathering all available information, identifying and considering potential alternatives, assessing the relative risk of those alternatives, and making an unbiased decision as to the best alternative on the basis of facts. Yet this is certainly not the case, as human decision making is often far from accurate. Instead of rational, unbiased decisions, humans use their own biases from past experiences, as well as heuristics, or shortcuts, to guide them toward an appropriate decision (e.g., Tversky & Kahneman, 1974). One particular problem that is relevant to human–automated teams is *automation bias* (Mosier, 2002), the process by which human team members treat information from automated team members as fact and do not seek out additional information to confirm or deny the validity of that information. Even when multiple human team members are available to cross check and double check information, automation biases can still lead to errors associated with placing too much trust in the automated team member's information (Mosier, Skitka, Dunbar, & McDonnell, 2001).

These shortcomings of human decision making should not overpower the fact that humans are adaptive and flexible and have the ability to interpret new and unexpected events. Automated teammates, although they are extremely efficient at following algorithms and other preprogrammed models, do not have the capabilities to adapt to novel situations. They also do not have the wherewithal to know that information input by the human team members or other automated team members is inaccurate. So, although human team members can double-check information provided by automated team members, but sometimes do not, automated team members do not have the same privilege. Thus, it is important for human team members to double check not only the information they input for the automated team members but also the information given back to them, at the same time being fully aware that the automated team members are extremely efficient at following the logic preprogrammed into them *only in familiar situations*.

AUTOMATED TEAM MEMBERS

For years, the idea that automated systems in the cockpit were team members has been hinted at; however, no one had officially included automated team members as part of the team. As we have shown, automated systems and humans are forced to communicate and coordinate with one another to accomplish their goals, and hence they do fall under the generally accepted definition of a team. With technology becoming increasingly more advanced and accessible, these types of teams will become more prevalent. We argue that these automated systems are team members and should be treated accordingly. That is not to say that they are ideal team members; however, humans are not necessarily ideal team members either. As highlighted in Table 11.1 and Table 11.2, automated team members also exhibit qualities representative of both good and bad teammates.

CONCLUSION

Now that we have acknowledged automated team members, we must begin to respect the uniqueness of teams composed of human and automated team members and start treating these teams accordingly. For instance, our analysis of a human–automated team using the TEM showed that the automated team member does not fit into all of the dimensions explicitly created for human team members. Thus, to better describe this type of team, future research needs to focus on creating appropriate models of

TABLE 11.1

Input Variables and Corresponding Characteristics of Automated Team Members

Input variables →	Good characteristics →	Bad characteristics
Individual characteristics		
General abilities	Unlimited capacity	Inflexible in novel situations
Attitudes	Stable, unaffected by environment	Opaque to human teammates
Motivation	Stable due to lack of motivation	
Personality	Stable as programmed	Opaque to other teammates
Mental models	Reflect designer's mental model (only if designer's model is accurate)	Cannot alter mental model
Team characteristics		
Power distribution	Unbiased actions	Lack of clarification of roles
Member homogeneity[a]		
Cohesiveness[a]		
Task characteristics		
Workload	Only affected by true workload, no detrimental effects of underload	Can become overloaded
Stress	Not affected by stressors–distractions	
Task organization	Consistent as programmed	Inflexible in novel situations
Task type	Flexible for preprogrammed events	Inflexible in novel situations
Task complexity	No performance decrement due to complexity alone	Inflexible in novel situations
Work characteristics		
Work assignment	Does not complain	Inflexible in novel situations
Role assignment	Maintains assigned role	Role ambiguity
Communication structure	Multimodal	Rigid and routine

Note. Each row is composed of an input variable and its corresponding characteristics.

[a]Areas in need of research.

TABLE 11.2
Throughput and Output Variables and Corresponding Characteristics of Automated Team Members

Variables →	Good characteristics →	Bad characteristics
Throughput		
Team processes		
Coordination	Plays well with others	May be opaque to other teammates
Communication	Clear and concise as programmed	Rigid and routine
Decision making	Unbiased, consistent as programmed	Inflexible in novel situations
Problem solving	Unbiased, consistent as programmed	Inflexible in novel situations
Output		
Team changes		
New roles	Only through reprogramming	Only through reprogramming
New communications	Only through reprogramming	Only through reprogramming
New processes	Only through reprogramming	Only through reprogramming
Team performance		
Quality	Enhanced in most situations	
Quantity	Enhanced	
Time	More efficient	
Errors	Fewer in most situations	
Costs	Lower in most situations	
Individual changes		
New attitudes	Only through reprogramming	Only through reprogramming
New motivation	Only through reprogramming	Only through reprogramming
New mental models	Only through reprogramming	Only through reprogramming

Note. Each row is composed of a throughput or output variable and its corresponding characteristics.

team performance for human–automated teams. Team research has enabled researchers to better understand the processes that affect team performance, yet no one has attempted to create team performance models of human–automated teams. Until then, our only choice is to use what is already in existence, specifically, models of team performance that may not take into account automated team members. Furthermore, modern training programs for integrated human–automated teams will need to consider all combinations and permutations of the possible composition of the new high-tech team. The ultimate goal for the trainer is to develop an effective team, where "George" is most likely a major player.

REFERENCES

Amalberti, R. R. (1999). Automation in aviation: A human factors perspective. In D. J. Garland, J. A. Wise, & V. D. Hopkin (Eds.), *Handbook of aviation human factors* (pp. 173–192). Mahwah, NJ: Erlbaum.

Billings, C. E. (1997). *Aviation automation: The search for a human-centered approach.* Mahwah, NJ: Erlbaum.

Bowers, C. A., Deaton, J., Oser, R., Prince, C., & Kolb, M. (1993). The impact of automation on crew communication and performance. In R. S. Jensen & D. Meumlister (Eds.), *Proceedings of the Seventh International Symposium on Aviation Psychology* (pp. 758–761). Columbus: The Ohio State University.

Bowers, C. A., Oser, R. L., Salas, E., & Cannon-Bowers, J. A. (1996). Team performance in automated systems. In R. Parasuraman & M. Mouloua (Eds.), *Automation and human performance: Theory and applications. Human factors in transportation* (pp. 243–263). Mahwah, NJ: Erlbaum.

Bowers, C. A., Pharmer, J. A., & Salas, E. (2000). When member homogeneity is needed in work teams: A meta-analysis. *Small Group Research, 31,* 305–327.

Boys, R., & Palko, K. (1988). Automation and dynamic allocation: Engineering issues and approaches. In *Proceedings of the IEEE Conference National Aerospace and Electronics Conference* (pp. 850–855). Retrieved June 6, 2004, from http://ieeexplore.ieee.org/iel2/748/5021/00195105.pdf?arnumber=195105

Cannon-Bowers, J. A., Salas, E., & Converse, S. (1993). Shared mental models in team decision making. In J. C. Castellan (Ed.), *Individual and group decision making* (pp. 221–246). Hillsdale, NJ: Erlbaum.

Christoffersen, K., & Woods, D. D. (2002). How to make automated systems team players. In E. Salas (Ed.), *Advances in human performance and cognitive engineering research: Automation* (Vol. 2, pp. 1–12). Amsterdam: Elsevier Science.

Guide, P. C., Wise, J. A., Abbott, D. W., & Ryan, L. J. (1993). The opinions of pilots flying automated corporate aircraft with regard to their perceived workload. In R. S. Jensen & D. Meumlister (Eds.), *Proceedings of the Seventh International Symposium on Aviation Psychology* (pp. 849–853). Columbus: The Ohio State University.

Helmreich, R. L., Chidester, T. R., Foushee, H. C., Gregorich, S., & Wilhelm, J. A. (1995). How effective is cockpit resource management training? *Flight Safety Digest*, 9, 1–7.

James, M., McClumpha, A., Green, R., Wilson, P., & Belyavin, A. (1991). Pilot attitudes to flight deck automation. In R. S. Jensen & D. Meumlister (Eds.), *Proceedings of the Seventh International Symposium on Aviation Psychology* (pp. 192–197). Columbus: The Ohio State University.

Lee, J. D., & Moray, N. (1994). Trust, self-confidence, and operators' adaptation to automation. *International Journal of Human–Computer Studies*, 40, 153–184.

Malin, J. T. (2000). Preparing for the unexpected: Making remote autonomous agents capable of interdependent teamwork. In *Proceedings of the International Ergonomics Association/Human Factors and Ergonomics Society 2000 Congress* (pp. 254–257). Santa Monica, CA: Human Factors and Ergonomics Society.

McFarland, R. A. (1946). *Human factors in air transport design*. New York: McGraw-Hill.

McFarland, R. A. (1953). *Human factors in air transportation: Occupational health and safety*. New York: McGraw-Hill.

Mejdal, S., McCauley, M. E., & Beringer, D. B. (2001). *Human factors design guidelines for multifunction displays* (NTIS No. DOT/FAA/AM-01/17). Oklahoma City, OK: Federal Aviation Administration.

Moray, N., Inagaki, T., & Itoh, M. (2000). Adaptive automation, trust, and self-confidence in fault management of time-critical tasks. *Journal of Experimental Psychology: Applied*, 6, 44–58.

Morgan, B. B., Jr., Herschler, D. A., Wiener, E. L., & Salas, E. (1993). Implications of automation technology for aircrew performance and coordination. In W. B. Rouse (Ed.), *Human/technology interaction with complex systems* (Vol. 6, pp. 105–136). Greenwich, CT: JAI Press.

Mosier, K. L. (2002). Automation and cognition: Maintaining coherence in the electronic cockpit. In E. Salas (Ed.), *Advances in human performance and cognitive engineering research: Automation* (Vol. 2, pp. 93–121). Amsterdam: Elsevier Science.

Mosier, K. L., Skitka, L. J., Dunbar, M., & McDonnell, L. (2001). Air crews and automation bias: The advantages of teamwork? *International Journal of Aviation Psychology*, 11, 1–14.

Nass, C., Fogg, B. J., & Moon, Y. (1996). Can computers be teammates? *International Journal of Human–Computer Studies*, 45, 669–678.

National Transportation Safety Board. (2002). *Aviation accident report: DHL Airlines, Boeing 757-23F, Uberlingen, Germany, July 01, 2002.* (NTSB/DCA02RA047A). Washington, DC: Author.

Norman, D. A. (1988). *The psychology of everyday things*. New York: Basic Books.

Parasuraman, R., & Riley, V. (1997). Humans and automation: Use, misuse, disuse, abuse. *Human Factors*, 39, 230–253.

Parasuraman, R., Sheridan, T. B., & Wickens, C. D. (2000). A model for types and levels of human interaction with automation. *IEEE Transactions on Systems, Man, and Cybernetics—Part A: Systems and Humans, 30*, 286–297.

Salas, E., Dickenson, T., Converse, S., & Tannenbaum, S. (1992). Towards an understanding of team performance and training. In R. W. Swezey & E. Salas (Eds.), *Teams: Their training and performance* (pp. 3–29). Norwood, NJ: Ablex.

Sarter, N. B., Woods, D. D., & Billings, C. E. (1997). Automation surprises. In G. Salvendy (Ed.), *Handbook of human factors and ergonomics* (2nd ed., pp. 1926–1943). New York: Wiley.

Segal, L. (1989). Differences in cockpit communication. In R. Jensen (Ed.), *Proceedings of the Fifth International Symposium on Aviation Psychology* (pp. 576–581). Columbus: The Ohio State University.

Sheridan, T. B. (1980). Computer control and human alienation. *Technology Review, 10*, 61–73.

Sheridan, T. B. (2002). *Humans and automation: System design and research issues.* Santa Monica, CA: Wiley.

Suchman, L. A. (1990). What is human–machine interaction? In W. W. Zachary, S. P. Parasuraman, & J. B. Black (Eds.), *Cognition, computing, and cooperation* (pp. 25–48). Norwood, NJ: Ablex.

Tannenbaum, S. I., Beard, R. L., & Salas, E. (1992). Team building and its influence on team effectiveness: An examination of conceptual and empirical developments. In K. Kelley (Ed.), *Issues, theory, and research in industrial/organizational psychology* (pp. 117–153). Amsterdam: Elsevier Science.

Tesluk, P., Mathieu, J. E., Zaccaro, S. J., & Marks, M. (1997). Task and aggregation issues in the analysis and assessment of team performance. In M. T. Brannick, C. Prince, & E. Salas (Eds.), *Team performance assessment and measurement* (pp. 197–224). Mahwah, NJ: Erlbaum.

Tversky, A., & Kahneman, D. (1974, September 26). Judgment under uncertainty: Heuristics and biases. *Science, 185*, 1124–1131.

Watson, W. E., Johnson, L., & Zgourides, G. D. (2002). The influence of ethnic diversity on leadership, group process, and performance: An examination of learning teams. *International Journal of Intercultural Relations, 26*, 1–16.

Wickens, C. D., & Hollands, J. G. (2000). *Engineering psychology and human performance.* Upper Saddle River, NJ: Prentice Hall.

Wiener, E. L. (1989). *Human factors of advanced technology ("glass cockpit") transport aircraft.* (NASA–Ames Contractor Report No. 177528). Moffett Field, CA: NASA–Ames Research Center.

12

TRAINING TEAMWORK WITH SYNTHETIC TEAMS

JARED FREEMAN, CRAIG HAIMSON, FREDERICK J. DIEDRICH, AND MICHAEL PALEY

Training teamwork does not necessarily require teams, at least not human teams. Providing trainees with teammates that are synthetic entities can dramatically reduce the logistical complexity of teamwork training and the attendant costs. It can make teamwork training accessible on demand. This may increase the frequency with which individuals engage in teamwork training and, by increasing time on task (or time in team), boost individual proficiency in teamwork skills and improve the performance of teams of trained individuals. In this chapter, we describe the development of a teamwork skills training platform for Airborne Warning and Control System (AWACS) Air Weapons Officers (AWOs; formerly called *Weapons*

We thank Michael Young and Lt. Matthew Eaton of the Air Force Research Laboratory, and John Tangney and Robert Sorkin of the Air Force Office of Scientific Research, for their support of this work and for their assistance. We gratefully acknowledge the assistance of our colleagues at BBN Technologies (Bruce Roberts, David Diller, and Stephen Deutsch). In addition, we thank the many members of the Air Force who participated in the research reported here. This material is based on work supported by the Air Force Research Laboratory under Contract F33615-01-C-0008 and the Air Force Office of Scientific Research under Contract F49620-01-C-0009. The opinions expressed here are the authors' and do not necessarily reflect the views of the Air Force or the Department of Defense.

Directors; see Appendix 12.1). The work involved a detailed analysis of team training needs and principled design of instruction and software agents that support individual training in communication, information exchange, and supporting behavior.

For newly minted AWOs, there are few opportunities for practice and training, whether in live flight or on full up mission simulators. This scarcity of opportunity is driven, on occasion, by the logistics of real-world operations (e.g., the recent conflict in Iraq engaged almost all AWACS aircraft in operations, leaving few for training flights). More frequently, training is limited by the cost and availability of the few exercise platforms (simulator or aircraft) and the requirements for full crews. Thus, teamwork training that is accessible on demand is of potentially high value in this domain. Delivered on a laptop, the AWO Training System that we describe here is a highly accessible solution to training fragile yet mission-critical teamwork skills.

THE DOMAIN

The central function of AWOs aboard Air Force AWACS command and control aircraft is to enhance the situation awareness of the fighter pilots with whom they are teamed through efficient and effective verbal communication. AWOs monitor air engagements as the action unfolds on a radar display. Because the AWACS sensors cover a larger range than do pilots' sensors, AWOs can provide their teammates with information on the locations, formations, movement (maneuvers), and identities of other aircraft in the monitored airspace long before these can be detected by the pilots' own limited sensors. Moreover, once pilots are at a close enough range to monitor approaching aircraft in their own scopes, their ability to do so is compromised by their need to focus on the many other duties that they are required to perform in the cockpit. Thus, the AWO continues to relay communications that enhance awareness of the ongoing situation to the pilots as is needed throughout the course of the engagement, with the goal of providing critical information in as complete, accurate, and timely a manner as possible.

The verbal communication that transpires between AWOs and pilots is highly formalized; communications generally follow a standardized template (the vocabulary and syntax are precise). The goal of such formalized communication is to facilitate information transfer in a manner that is concise and mutually understandable. For instance, one type of communication that AWOs provide is a *"picture call,"* which alerts the pilots to the number of enemy aircraft, their formation, their location relative to a landmark (the

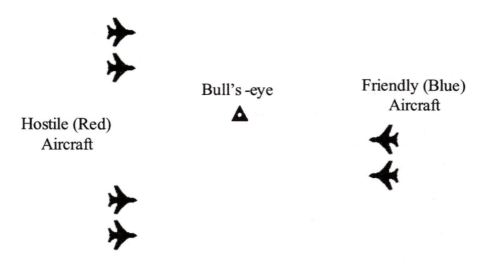

Figure 12.1. Example of hostile (Red) aircraft formation that an Air Weapons Officer might report to friendly (Blue) pilots in the form of the picture call.

bull's-eye), and their classification (e.g., hostile). An example of a typical encounter is shown in Figure 12.1.

Although the standardization of communication formats greatly facilitates the exchange of information between AWOs and pilots, this alone does not ensure effective communication; excellent teamwork skills—particularly *monitoring* the complex communications stream for errors of commission and omission and providing *backup* in the form of additional communications to compensate for those errors—are critical for success. AWOs and pilots engage in a dialogue through which they verify that each understands the full intent of the other's communications. In addition, AWOs monitor and correct pilot-to-pilot communications that contain incomplete or incorrect information. It is critical that they remain sensitive to the workloads with which pilots must contend throughout different phases of the engagement, increasing or decreasing the frequency with which they issue communications in accordance with the level of action facing the pilots (e.g., a skilled AWO knows to refrain from interrupting pilots in the midst of an air battle). Thus, learning to be an AWO involves far more than simply memorizing a language for describing configurations of symbols on a radarscope—AWOs must learn to use this language to build and maintain group situational awareness through coordination with their teammates, providing such information as the situation demands through timely, accurate, and efficient communication.

TRAINING NEEDS ANALYSIS

To develop the AWO Training System, we first conducted a training needs analysis to focus design of measures, tutoring capabilities, and training scenarios on particularly important and troublesome applications of the teamwork skills. The training needs analysis consisted of administration of a survey concerning AWO errors and an open-ended interview concerning these failures. Participants in the training needs assessment were eight active duty instructors at the Air Force schoolhouse for introductory AWACS training, Tyndall Air Force Base (AFB); two active duty instructors at the center for advanced AWACS training and operations, Tinker AFB; and one consulting former AWACS instructor. We framed our analysis in terms of the Team Dimensional Training (TDT) framework developed by Smith-Jentsch and colleagues (Smith-Jentsch, Johnston, & Payne, 1998) for an experimental program of training now integrated into Navy exercises. Team Dimensional Training is composed of four constructs:

- communication: the method of delivery of information;
- information exchange: the transfer of information and content of those transfers;
- supporting behavior: backup behavior that helps teammates to accomplish tasks; and
- initiative/leadership: guiding team members and prioritizing information needs.

These validated constructs are, in turn, composed of subconstructs. For the current work, we used a subset of TDT subconstructs and developed several new subconstructs to represent classes of errors that were critical in this domain (see Table 12.1). We populated this framework with 45 examples of teamwork failure that are documented in the research literature concerning airborne command and control operations (Brobst & Brown, 1998; Elliott, Dalrymple, & Neville, 1997; Fahey, Rowe, Dunlap, & DeBoom, 1997; Gualtieri, Bergondy, Oser, & Fowlkes, 1998; Thordsen, McCloskey, Heaton, & Serfaty, 1998) and interviews with researchers in the field (Maureen Bergondy, of the Naval Air Systems Command (NAVAIR), Orlando, Florida; Jennifer Fowlkes, of CHI Systems, Orlando, Florida; and Michael Paley, PhD, of Aptima, Inc., Washington, DC). We refined the communications construct by defining subconstructs concerning terminology and syntax and by recognizing the importance of timing of communications within the communications cadence (or cycle), as well as the notion of communications priority. Our deconstruction of information exchange highlights the contrast between monitoring information, requesting information, and transmitting it. Examples of these errors are presented in Table 12.1.

TABLE 12.1
Extension of the Team Dimensional Training (TDT) Framework and Examples of Air Weapons Officer Teamwork Errors

TDT construct	TDT subconstruct	Definition	Example of teamwork error
Communication	Brevity	Make brief (efficient) communications	Fails to be concise during communication jamming or high workload
Communication	Clarity	Speak clearly (diction)	Fails to articulate numbers (15 vs. 50) clearly
Communication	Complete report	Make complete reports	Fails to provide all required and useful information in "picture call"
Communication	Inflection[a]	Use of vocal inflection	Fails to speak commandingly when necessary
Communication	Priority[a]	Adhere to communications cadence or priority	Fails to adhere to communications cadence for routine communication
Communication	Syntax[b]	Use correct syntax	Fails to use correct syntax in a "picture call"
Communication	Terms[b]	Use correct terms and codes	Labels hostile groups incorrectly
Information exchange	Monitor[b]	Monitor all useful sources of information	Fails to monitor pilot "commit calls"
Information exchange	Request[b]	Request information or clarification as needed	Fails to request information from aircraft under control
Information exchange	Right network[a]	Use correct communication network	Monitors wrong channels
Information exchange	Right person[b]	Pass information to appropriate persons	Fails to notify package commander that an element is off schedule
Information exchange	Tell	Provide situation updates	Fails to be timely with tactical information
Lead/Initiate	Direct	Provide guidance and direction to team members	Fails to recommend commit in accordance with commit criteria
Support	Backup	Provide or request backup	Fails to support novice pilots with extra information
Support	Correct errors	Correct all errors	Fails to state corrections

[a]A new subconstruct. [b]A modified subconstruct.

TABLE 12.2
Mean Ratings of Errors Per Subconstruct, in Rank Order of Criticality

Team dimensional training (TDT) construct	TDT subconstruct	M	SD
Information exchange	Tell	2.34	0.73
Information exchange	Request	2.33	0.61
Information exchange	Monitor	2.29	0.69
Information exchange	Right person	2.25	0.71
Communication	Terms	2.22	0.71
Lead/initiate	Direct	2.18	0.64
Communication	Priority	2.10	0.64
Communication	Inflection	1.95	0.76
Communication	Brevity	1.90	0.57
Communication	Syntax	1.83	0.50
Support	Backup	1.81	0.63

Participants independently rated the operational priority (or criticality) of 45 putative teamwork errors on a 3-point rating scale (3 = *high criticality*, 1 = *low criticality*). Nine participants rated at least 44 of the 45 errors. One rated 40 errors. The remaining participant rated only 9 errors, but these few ratings were not outliers relative to values given by other participants. All ratings were used in analysis. Accordingly, mean ratings over informants and errors were computed for each TDT construct (see Table 12.2).

Information exchange and leadership were the leading concerns of instructors in the domain of teamwork. Instructors highlighted errors pertaining to requesting information, monitoring communications, and initiating standard communications and more forceful directive communications. Issues of communication were close behind, particularly the two top communication errors: (a) mislabeling (misnaming) hostiles or (b) misusing the labels of hostiles. Having obtained this profile of AWO training needs, we set about developing an instructional design capable of addressing them.

TRAINING METHODS ANALYSIS

A small number of intelligent tutoring systems have been created specifically to develop teamwork skills (e.g., Eliot & Wolf, 1995; Miller, Yin, Volz, Ioerger, & Yen, 2000; Rickel & Johnson, 1999), but the literature offers scant empirical or theoretical guidance concerning coaching during scenarios that simulate high-stakes, time-critical missions. To better understand how to develop coaching that is sensitive to constraints on time and attention in military exercises, we conducted interviews with nine AWO instructors at Tyndall AFB. These interviews provided several key insights into military instructional practices.

- *When to coach.* Several instructors indicated that they coach only in real time when the student can attend to the coaching, that is, when radio communications and other activity are at a lull. Instructors were more likely to coach immediately on time-critical problems, especially when the training scenario provided the student with later opportunities to exercise the same skill (coaching at the only or last practice opportunity may as well be conducted during debrief, they claimed, and potentially wastes the chance to coach a skill that students are about to practice again in the current scenario). Finally, instructors noted that they interrupt training to coach only students who demonstrated very low levels of competency, because interrupting students at higher proficiency levels denies the instructor the opportunity to judge whether the student can correct errors.
- *How to coach.* The instructors provided reports of coaching techniques they use in briefs, practice, or debriefs. These techniques fell into several categories: getting student attention, modeling skills for students, querying trainees, encouraging critical thinking, and choosing techniques appropriate to the student's level of expertise. Several instructors noted that coaching methods must vary with student expertise and drew specific implications: (a) provide more structure to less expert trainees; (b) provide more feedback to less expert trainees; (c) flag errors by pointing them out to less expert trainees, and by asking more expert trainees to identify their own errors; and (d) be more directive with (less expert) trainees who are slow to respond to requests from pilots.
- *How to debrief.* Instructors noted that they had only recently begun standardizing their approach to instruction. All instructors conducted mission reviews, in which they stepped through scenarios with an individual student (often displaying video of the student's display). Although methods varied across these informants, most adhered to a general debriefing agenda: review training objectives; continue with self-assessment, provide an objective performance assessment, review mission; and conclude with a summary of lessons learned and articulation of a learning plan for how to approach the next phase of instruction.

In addition to these interviews, we also had the opportunity to observe several live flight training sessions and subsequent debriefs at both Tyndall AFB and Tinker AFB. During training sessions, we found that coaching interactions were mainly compensatory in character, consisting either of actions to draw student attention to the cue to execute a task by pointing or querying the student, directions to perform that task, or execution of the task (e.g., writing down frequencies, making console actions, or making communications) by the instructor. These actions were used most with a struggling AWO; the instructor offered only indirect support to a highly proficient Senior Director trainee, such as offering directions for refining procedures after (not before) the proficient trainee solved the current problem. As expected, almost all feedback was provided during lulls in the action. During debriefs, we observed a much wider range of instructional strategies. The most frequently observed instructional interaction was the trainer's statement of a rule. Other interactions involved querying students to inquire about the conditions or rationale for a recent action, test knowledge of protocols and terms, or request that students critique their own performance in detail. It was more common to review events in chronological order than by training objective, although this may be partially a product of using technology that supports serial replay of mission events.

We recorded 128 specific observations of instructional events during these sessions, 101 of which were made in debriefs (the low number of observations recorded during training exercises reflects, in part, the rarity with which instructors interrupt trainees, as well as the difficulty of observing and interpreting these interactions in the intensive environment of live flight). These events were classified in accordance with the categorization scheme described in Table 12.3.

These analyses have value in several respects. The observational study suggested a categorization scheme for coaching interactions (e.g., state a rule, direct the student). This scheme helped us to specify the functionality of an automated coach and the rules that implement the functionality. In addition, the frequency data and qualitative notes gave us some guidance concerning the emphasis that instructors place on each coaching behavior and thus helped us to prioritize implementation of each behavior in software.

INSTRUCTIONAL DESIGN OF COACHED PRACTICE

On the basis of our analyses of training needs and methods, we designed our simulation-based training system to instruct student AWOs in two phases: (a) coached practice and (b) debriefing. Practice takes place using a simplified radar scope (see Figure 12.2), a readout of aircraft flight parameters (bearing, range, and altitude), and a microphone with headset. Students

TABLE 12.3
Definition and Frequency of Instructional Events

Category	Definition	Frequency
State rule	Direction (often posterror) concerning future cases in general (as distinct from direction concerning the current case)	41
Compliment	Compliment student on performance	17
Criticize	Flag or critique erroneous performance	16
Summarize mission	Walk-through of mission execution	16
Direct	Specific directions or orders concerning tasks to be performed	7
Draw attention	Focus student attention on an object or issue	7
Query	Query (not concerning syntax or term use)	6
Test protocol	Query focused on syntax or terminology (as distinct from a query on other topics)	5
Monitor attention	Use of trainee cursor to determine locus of attention	4
Perform action	Instructor performs action on behalf of student	4
Summarize lessons	Outline of lessons learned	3
Plan learning	Focus student on upcoming flights or classes	2

control four friendly (Blue) aircraft in a series of brief (~2–4 minutes) scenarios in which they encounter four or six enemy (Red) aircraft, which enter a no-fly zone and assume one of a few standard formations. The AWOs are instructed to direct the Blue pilots through the phases of a Defensive Counter Air situation - Combat Air Patrol (CAP)-Detect, Target-Sort, and Engage phases of a Defensive Counter Air situation, during which they identify the presence of oncoming Red aircraft, report the directions in which the aircraft maneuver and the formations they assume, and monitor Blue pilots as they assign targeting responsibilities and engage the Red forces.

Five synthetic agents support the student during practice and communicate with him or her. Four of these represent friendly pilots and their aircraft, who respond to enemy actions using tactical information they glean from the AWO's verbal communications and a computational model of the radar picture available from the fighter cockpit. In some scenarios, these agents are programmed to err in ways that test the AWO's ability to monitor pilot communications. The remaining synthetic entity is a coach that monitors and critiques communications between the AWO and Blue pilots, given the tactical situation.

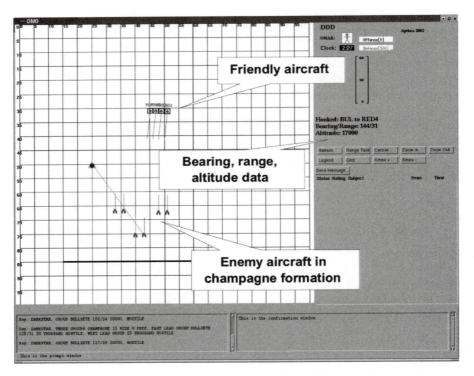

Figure 12.2. The practice environment. DDD = Distributed Dynamic Decision Making.

The coach contains a model of the expected behaviors of the student AWO in response to scenario events. This model enables the tutor to assess student performance using several measures:

- *Timeliness measures* assess the mere occurrence of a communication within a window of opportunity, as well as the latency of a communication.
- *Completeness measures* document the inclusion and omission of available, important information from a communication.
- *Content* or *semantic measures* address the use of accurate data values (e.g., the correct range and bearing) and labels (e.g., "*group*").
- *Priority measures* assess the necessity of each student communication given the system's expectations.
- *Brevity measures* assess the duration of a communication by considering the proportion of words to silences within a communication.
- *Syntax measures* address the student's adherence to certain syntactic formulations mandated by doctrine or convention.

Taken together, these measures address three of the four validated categories of teamwork skills developed by Smith-Jentsch et al. (1998): (a) complete, correct, and timely *information exchange*; (b) brief, syntactically correct, and prioritized *communications*; and (c) *supporting behavior* in the form of monitoring. We do not directly assess (d) *leadership*, the fourth construct, although it is a constant focus of the training scenarios because AWOs are instructed to communicate in a directive manner when appropriate (i.e., to instruct pilots to take certain actions).

The tutor model selectively gives verbal feedback to the student in real time in response to failures on the measures mentioned earlier (e.g., "That comm. was not concise"). It does so using strategies concerning *when to coach* and *how to coach*. The tutor issues feedback when

- the feedback can be delivered before the current context changes (e.g., from the detection phase of an intercept to targeting phase) and
- the feedback pertains to the error of the highest priority in the current queue of student errors.

The tutor's knowledge of *how* to coach consists of several strategies:

- warn the student that he or she erred (e.g., "Your comm. was not concise");
- direct the student to issue a type of communication (e.g., "Give a picture call now");
- model a communication for the student (e.g., "Say this now: . . ."); and
- state a rule, consisting of recent cues and the appropriate response (e.g., "When the enemy completes his maneuver, make a picture call").

Not all coaching actions are appropriate for all errors. For example, prioritization errors, once committed, cannot be remedied by issuing the communication again. Most syntactic errors are not deemed important enough by the operational community to warrant interrupting practice with coaching. Consequently, the tutor does not coach either of these in real time. However, it responds to the remaining errors with feedback selected by simple algorithms (e.g., rotation among coaching options) or heuristics (e.g., issuing direction before modeling) from among two or three appropriate types of coaching (see Figure 12.3).

The AWO Training System logs all data concerning communications, student behaviors, expert expectations, assessments, and coaching activity for use in debriefs or After Action Reviews (AARs). The system's debriefing interface features a brief description of training objectives for the scenario; a sortable, filterable list of automatically generated communications

Error / Coaching	Direct	Model	Warn	Rule
Timeliness	▓	▓	▓	
Completeness		█	▓	▓
Content/Semantics	▓		▓	▓
Priority	█	█		▓
Brevity	█	█	▓	▓
Style/Syntax	█	█	█	

Currently coached	▓
To coach in future	
Can't/Won't coach	█

Figure 12.3. Coaching responses to student errors.

transcripts; an assessment of each communication on the six types of errors previously cited; a snapshot of the scenario during a selected communication; and feedback in the form of guidance, an expert model of the communication, or both.

SYSTEM DESIGN

In designing the AWO Training System, we exploited several existing technologies (see Figure 12.4): a low-to-medium fidelity simulation of the AWACS console (Distributed Dynamic Decision-Making [DDD]), an intelligent agent development environment (Operator Model ARchitecture in

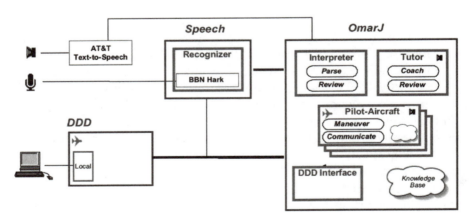

Figure 12.4. The architecture of the Air Weapons Officer Training System. BBN = BBN Technologies; DDD = Distributed Dynamic Decision Making; OmarJ = Operator Model ARchitecture in Java.

Java; Deutsch, 2002 [OmarJ]), and a speech recognition system (Hark™, by BBN Technologies). The system is implemented on a laptop computer to provide anytime, anywhere training for individuals in airborne command and control communications teamwork. We describe each of these components in this section.

The DDD environment is a distributed real time simulation environment that supports synthetic team tasks. The version of the DDD specialized for AWACS captures the real-world environment to the extent that it enables the student AWO to see movement of Red (enemy) and Blue (friendly) forces and to get information on the range, bearing, and altitude of aircraft using a mouse-based tool. Movements of the Red forces are controlled by scripted scenarios implemented on the DDD. These scripted Red maneuvers are standard training content and pose a challenge to most of the student AWOs who have used the system.

The agents (the Blue pilots and the tutor) were developed using OmarJ, which is an implementation of D-OMAR (Deutsch, 1998; Deutsch & Adams, 1995). The DDD and OmarJ communicate using the FIPA ACL (Foundation for Intelligent Physical Agents, 2001) over TCP/IP. OmarJ is a programming environment that provides tools for creating both systems of software agents and models of human behavior. It consists of a procedural language, ScoreJ, for defining human and agent behaviors, a discrete time simulation environment in which to embed human and agent models, a variety of external communication protocols for interacting with distributed heterogeneous systems, an event recording mechanism, and a time management component. Behaviors are defined in ScoreJ as the product of a set of procedures that initiate agent actions, interpret patterns of sensory input, and channel responses in a manner consistent with agent goals. Within a single agent, several procedures may run concurrently at any given moment, some representing components of attended processing and others methods of automatic processing.

As previously noted, speech communication is a key element of the AWO's task. Hence, the system incorporates the BBN Technologies Hark™ recognizer (BBN Technologies, 2001) to allow the student AWO to issue calls just as he or she would do on an AWACS mission. This recognizer is speaker independent—it does not require training for each individual voice—and uses a grammar of expected utterances to deliver high recognition accuracy. In brief, this means that an utterance is compared with a set of expected utterances to find the closest match, rather than trying to compare it with all possible utterances in the English language. This substantially simplifies the recognition problem. Fortunately, AWO communications are relatively well defined and constrained in their form and content to improve human-to-human recognition. This makes grammar-based recognizers such as the BBN Technologies Hark™ recognizer particularly well suited for understanding AWO communication. The output of the recognizer includes timings for individual words and silences, which contribute to an assessment of the AWO's performance by enabling the detection of slow or choppy speech. The grammar necessarily includes some common syntactic errors (omissions, substitutions, additions) to accommodate the range of student AWO calls.

Finally, communication from the pilot to the AWO is simulated using the AT&T Labs Natural Voices™ text-to-speech engine (AT&T, 2002). The same text-to-speech engine simulates communications among the synthetic pilots. This gives the student AWO practice monitoring a pilot's understanding of the situation.

The system architecture is organized as a collection of distributed agents: The DDD, BBN Technologies Hark™ speech recognizer, speech interpreter, Blue aircraft, and the tutor. The Blue aircraft, the speech interpreter, and the tutor are written in OmarJ; they compose a single node in the architecture. The Hark™ recognizer is embedded in an OmarJ agent that exists as a separate node in the architecture. A shared agent communication language (FIPA ACL) and ontology allow other processes—in this case, the DDD and the low-level speech recognizer—to participate in the simulation. The DDD manages user interactions with the training system. As previously noted, it also simulates the Red aircraft, which are controlled by a script, and broadcasts their movements to the OmarJ node. Agent-controlled Blue aircraft similarly transmit their movements to the DDD to be incorporated in the display presented to the AWO.

BEHAVIORAL REPRESENTATIONS OF PILOT AND TUTOR AGENTS

Both Blue aircraft and the tutor are coded within OmarJ as agents with internal decision-making processes and behaviors. Each Blue aircraft is modeled as a single agent that maintains its own knowledge base, in which is represented whatever the agent currently perceives and believes about the airspace. The contents of the knowledge base are provided by visual and radar inputs as well as by communications from the AWO and fellow pilots. This communication is mediated by the speech interpreter agent, which translates calls into a formal representation that can be interpreted by the agents. Agents, in turn, communicate with the AWO using the text-to-speech facility. Blue pilot agent behaviors were modeled loosely on F-15 Fighter procedures and tactics to produce typical responses to various situations. Pilot agents are capable of high-level maneuvers such as formation flying, pursuits, intercepts, and Combat Air Patrols. Pilot agents react and respond to information provided by the AWO as well as request information from an AWO when the circumstances warrant it.

Many of the characteristics and behaviors of the pilot model can be tailored such that individual Blue pilots respond uniquely to different situations in the simulation. Pilot models can have differing latencies for processing and responding to various situations, such as time to sort the picture or target a group. The pilot agents are designed to exhibit variance in sensory capabilities and speed of perceptual processing. Style of communication can also vary stochastically within pilots such that in one instance the pilot may omit information he or she includes in a later communication under similar circumstances. (In the experiments reported herein, variance within pilots was minimized to create more uniform runs of each scenario between participants.)

Furthermore, the probability of making various perceptual processing and decision-making errors can be manipulated across pilots. This enables us to create a suite of individual pilots, each with differing levels of expertise and operating styles, to test the skills of student AWOs, and in particular to test the student's ability to monitor the accuracy of pilot communications. In the experiment we report here, pilot agents could commit several classes of errors that require assistance from the AWO:

- *Fail to commit.* Once the Red aircraft pass a "commit" line (e.g., the edge of a no-fly zone), either the pilots or the AWO should make a "commit" call, which is a directive call to intercept a group of aircraft. The AWO's job is to "recommend commit" if the pilots fail to commit at the correct time.
- *Mislabel.* During targeting of hostile aircraft, the Blue pilots may fail to label (name) the group they are targeting and only provide coordinates (e.g., they may say "Targeting group" rather than "Targeting lead group"). The job of the AWO in this circumstance is to provide the group label to enhance situational awareness.
- *Cross-lock.* During targeting of hostile aircraft, the Blue pilots may each target the same group of Red aircraft (based on spoken coordinates) although they "think" they are targeting separate groups of Red aircraft (based on spoken group names; e.g., "south group" or "lead group"). The job of the AWO is to correct this targeting so that no hostile aircraft accidentally remains untargeted.

In contrast, the tutor model consists of a variety of task behaviors written as OmarJ procedures and as rules in a production system. OmarJ procedures activate under several conditions: proactively, to address the tutor's current agenda; in reaction to events or their absence; or in response to the activation of rules in the inference engine. Ongoing tasks determine their own execution times. They run to completion unless they are preempted by another competing procedure with greater priority or they lose a resource required by the task. Information about the current state of the simulation is continuously integrated into the tutor's knowledge base. In addition, the tutor is aided in its operation by knowledge of the scenario conveyed in the Red aircraft script, which includes hints to the tutor about the high-level goals and actions of the Red aircraft. The tutor also "listens in" on Blue pilot communications. However, the tutor itself is not scripted; it responds to whatever the AWO chooses to say and to events unfolding in the simulated airspace. In particular, the tutor is able to anticipate when calls are warranted and, just as important, unwarranted; conciseness and judicious use of airtime are highly prized in airborne command and control. In sum, the tutor is capable of taking all of the measures described in the section titled "Instructional Design of Coached Practice," using these assessments and other logic to deliver feedback in real time and to drive AARs.

SYSTEM EVALUATION STUDY

We conducted a system evaluation study at Tinker AFB to demonstrate the utility of the AWO Training System to officers in operational AWACS forces.

Method

A total of 32 individuals (29 men and 3 women) volunteered to participate in the study. Participants were student AWOs who had been in training for an average of 1.43 years ($SD = 0.36$); almost all had taken part in live training exercises.

All participants ran through two initial scenarios without online tutoring or AAR functions enabled. Half of the AWOs then completed an additional four scenarios without online tutoring or the AAR. (These participants are referred to as the *late tutor group*). The remaining AWOs ran through these four scenarios with both online tutoring and access to the AAR at the end of each scenario. (These participants are referred to as the *early tutor group*). Finally, all participants ran through an additional six scenarios during which online tutoring and AAR access were provided. Study sessions lasted for approximately 1.5 hours.

Overall, this study design allowed us to observe both tutored and non-tutored student performance at various points throughout the course of system use. The first and last two scenarios were identical to allow for exact comparisons between initial and final periods of system usage. In addition, scenarios presented during the middle of the session were generally of comparable difficulty to those presented at the beginning and end of the session (i.e., Red aircraft assumed the same formations, pilots made the same types of errors, etc.).

Results

We evaluated user performance with respect to several different measures, including total number of communications made during the scenario; specific communication errors, such as lack of brevity or timeliness; overall scenario performance aggregated across the six error types (timeliness, completeness, content, priority, brevity, and syntax); and monitoring of Blue force pilots. The last measure reflected the number of instances in which students either successfully detected and corrected pilot errors ("hits") or failed to do so ("misses"). Specifically, the monitoring score was computed as (hits − misses) ÷ (hits + misses).

On all measures, we obtained evidence of significant performance improvements across scenarios for both groups. For example, as shown in Figure 12.5, the frequency with which the AWOs corrected Blue force pilot errors increased by almost 40% from the first to the last two scenarios, $F(1, 31) = 15.8$, $p < .001$. It is important that this increase in correction behavior did not coincide with a significant increase in errors of commission (i.e., false alarming to nonexistent Blue pilot errors), suggesting that the increase in responses to pilot errors reflected an increase in monitoring

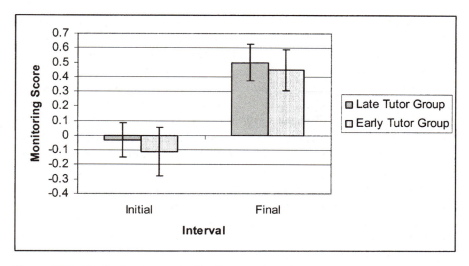

Figure 12.5. Monitoring scores for the first two (Initial) and last two (Final) scenarios.

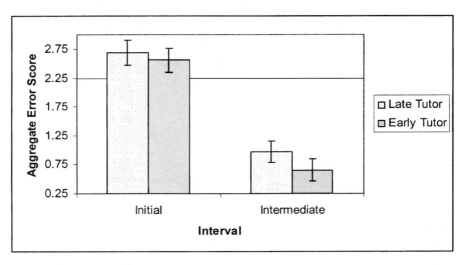

Figure 12.6. Aggregate error scores for the first two (Initial) and middle two (Intermediate) scenarios.

rather than simply an increase in the frequency with which participants issued correction communications (without regard to whether the pilots required them). There were no significant differences between monitoring scores for the early and late tutor groups, even during those scenarios in which the early tutor group received tutoring and the late tutor group did not; most other measures failed to yield between-group differences as well.

Nevertheless, we did find some differences between aggregate error scores for the two tutoring groups. Figure 12.6 displays scores for the initial two scenarios and the first two scenarios during which both groups had the benefit of online tutoring and access to the AAR (Scenarios 7 and 8). Although an overall practice effect is clear within both groups, the reduction in errors was greater for participants in the early tutor group (a 73% reduction) than for those in the late tutor group (a 63% reduction), $t(30) = 1.68$, $p = .052$. This effect, although modest in size, suggests that the early tutor group benefited from more extensive training with the tutor and AAR. Unfortunately, the study design did not permit the effects of online tutoring and those of the AAR to be isolated from one another. However, it is important to note that both reflect the same set of performance assessments generated online by the tutor agent. Whether such feedback is more effectively used online or offline is a question for future research. Ultimately, it is likely that format in which tutoring is delivered most effectively varies with scenario content and error type.

DISCUSSION

Collectively, these data indicate that approximately 50 minutes of training using the AWO Training System improved a participant's ability to deliver the right information, in the right form, at the right time, without promoting delivery of unnecessary information. In addition, the results suggest that monitoring of pilot errors reliably improved. That we obtained significant practice effects across various measures of performance is perhaps not surprising; however, the benefits of this practice alone have the potential to translate into significant improvement in on-the-job performance.

Overall, the specific feedback provided by the online tutor and AAR appeared to provide only modest benefits over practice alone in these scenarios. However, this may simply reflect the fact that within the confines of this study, participants in the early tutor group received only four more trials with the tutor and AAR than did participants in the late group. Given the limited scope of these scenarios, this small difference in tutor presence may not have fully differentiated the conditions. Consequently, that we obtained any differences at all between early and late tutor groups is an encouraging first step toward establishing the efficacy of the instructional interventions. Ultimately, a true test of the system's efficacy can come only through an evaluation of actual job performance for AWOs whose training program either did or did not include extensive practice with the AWO trainer system. Additional system development will be required prior to assessing the transfer of practice effects to the job.

Beyond performance changes, one of our primary goals in running this study was to obtain feedback on the system concept and its implementation from the class of domain specialists who would also likely be future users, that is, student AWOs. We were delighted that the system received strong endorsements from nearly every student AWO who participated in this study. When asked to rate overall satisfaction with the system on a scale of 1 (*low*) to 7 (*high*), none of the participants gave ratings below the midpoint of the scale (4). The modal response was 5, with a mean of 5.47 ($SD = 0.95$). Almost all participants said they would use the system as a training tool if it were available ($M = 6.59$, $SD = 0.76$, mode = 7.00) and that they would strongly recommend its use to others ($M = 6.57$, $SD = 0.77$, mode = 7.00). Respondents saw a use for such a stand-alone practice tool at various stages of AWO training. Among the elements of the system that received praise, the ability to practice monitoring pilot communications for errors and the ability to review a record of past performance (the AAR replays communications, displays snapshots, etc.) were highlighted by many participants. Although some participants complained that the tutor agent lacked flexibility in its evaluation of user inputs, and others saw a need for more complex and varied scenarios, many indicated that they would be content to use the system even in its current stage of development. We were fortunate to receive a large number of insightful suggestions from participants concerning various aspects of the system, ranging from comments about the nature of system buttonology to suggestions for ways to increase the complexity, variety, and realism of scenarios. Such input will serve as a basis for future system development.

CONCLUSION

At the beginning of this chapter, we asserted that training teamwork does not necessarily require human teams. Interpreted broadly, the claim is ludicrous. Human teammates are far more nuanced in their interactions and unpredictable than current synthetic entities. People must train together to appreciate these qualities, compensate for them, and leverage them, as situations allow. Teamwork training that addresses these qualities cannot currently be accomplished exclusively through practice with synthetic entities.

However, unpredictability and nuance are not always desirable training teamwork skills; neither is the presence of a full human team always practical or affordable. Under some circumstances, synthetic teammates may be sufficient for training, or even preferable to humans. For example, synthetic teammates can be programmed to generate on demand the behaviors that are required to meet specific training objectives. Moreover, simulated teammates can repeat the same behaviors time and time again, ensuring the focused drill and practice that cannot be achieved reliably in training with human teammates.

The transferability of practice with synthetic teams to on-the-job settings with human teammates remains an important issue. However, it is an empirical issue whether the lack of realism in interactions with synthetic teammates substantially reduces the training benefits. Advances in behavioral modeling indicate that the realism of synthetic entities may increase in the near future.

We propose—and we believe we have demonstrated—that training teamwork skills using synthetic entities is a practical strategy, provided that the training objectives are well chosen, the instructional design is appropriate, the technology is up to the job, and the product is appealing to its audience. We have gone to some lengths in designing the AWO Training System to satisfy these conditions. Observation, interviews, and surveys were used to identify teamwork training needs of high priority to the AWACS community as well as the instructional practices of that community. Technology was carefully mated to the training challenge;

we focused on tactical knowledge and communication skills that present problems to AWOs but that advanced agent and speech technologies can master. Finally, the product was designed to appeal to AWOs by making standardized training in dry protocols engaging, informative, and accessible. These qualities encourage lots of deliberate practice (Ericsson, Anders, & Charness, 1994), and this, ultimately, is the foundation of expertise.

As a final thought, we note that the development of teams of agents for training purposes foreshadows the probable emergence of human–agent teams in future real world operational settings. Creating systems that promote and train effective interactions between human and agent teammates renders important lessons concerning these new forms of human–machine collaboration.

APPENDIX 12.1

Terms

Airborne Warning And Control System (AWACS): Radar system mounted on Air Force E3 aircraft that supports surveillance and command and control functions.

Air Weapons Officer (AWO): AWACS operator who monitors air engagements on a radar display and communicates information on locations, formations, movement, and identities of other aircraft in monitored airspace to fight pilots.

Situation Awareness: Knowledge and understanding of operational environment at a given time, including expectations for change and potential impact on operational goals.

REFERENCES

AT&T. (2002). *AT&T Natural Voices*. Retrieved September 8, 2004, from http://www.naturalvoices.att.com/

BBN Technologies. (2001). *BBN Hark Recognizer*. Retrieved September 8, 2004, from http://www.bbn.com/speech/bbnhark.html

Brobst, W. D., & Brown, A. C. (1998). *Analysis of E-2C aircrew mission skills* (Tech. Rep. No. CRM 98-26). Alexandria, VA: Center for Naval Analysis.

Deutsch, S. E. (1998). Interdisciplinary foundations for multiple-task human performance modeling in OMAR. In M. A. Gernsbacher & S. J. Derry (Eds.), *Proceedings of the Twentieth Annual Meeting of the Cognitive Science Society* (pp. 303–308). Mahwah, NJ: Erlbaum.

Deutsch, S. E., Diller, D., Anderson, K., Benyo, B., Date, S., & Pattison-Gordon, E. (2002). *OmarJ: The new Java implementation of D-OMAR* (BBN Tech. Rep. No. 8344). Cambridge, MA: BBN Technologies.

Deutsch, S. E., & Adams, M. J. (1995). The operator model architecture and its psychological framework. In *Proceedings of the 6th IFAC Symposium on Man–Machine Systems* (pp. 41–46) Laxenburg, Austria: IFAC.

Eliot, C., & Wolf, B. P. (1995). An adaptive student centered curriculum for an intelligent training system. *User Modeling and User-Adapted Instruction, 5,* 67–86.

Elliott, L. R., Dalrymple, M. A., & Neville, K. (1997, September). *Assessing performance of AWACS command and control teams.* Paper presented at the 1997 Human Factors Conference, Albuquerque, NM.

Ericsson, K., Anders, A., & Charness, N. (1994). Expert performance: Its structure and acquisition. *American Psychologist, 49,* 725–747.

Fahey, R. P., Rowe, A., Dunlap, K., & DeBoom, D. (1997). *Synthetic task design (1): Preliminary cognitive task analysis of AWACS weapons director teams* (Tech. Rep. No. AFRL-HE-AZ-TR-2000-0159). Brooks Air Force Base, TX: Armstrong Laboratory.

Foundation for Intelligent Physical Agents. (2001). *FIPA agent communication language message structure specification.* Retrieved December 3, 2003, from http://www.fipa.org/specs/fipa00061

Gualtieri, J. W., Bergondy, M., Oser, R. L., & Fowlkes, J. E. (1998). Simulation use for training large tactical teams. In *Proceedings of the American Institute of Aeronautics and Astronautics* (pp. 458–467). Reston, VA: American Institute of Aeronautics and Astronautics.

Miller, M., Yin, J., Volz, R. A., Ioerger, T. R., & Yen, J. (2000). Training teams with collaborative agents. In *Proceedings of the Fifth International Conference on Intelligent Tutoring Systems* (ITS-2000) (pp. 63–72).

Rickel, J., & Johnson, W. L. (1999). Virtual humans for team training in virtual reality. In *Proceedings of the Ninth World Conference on AI in Education* (pp. 578–585). Amsterdam, the Netherlands: IOS Press.

Smith-Jentsch, K. A., Johnston, J. H., & Payne, S. C. (1998). Measuring team-related expertise in complex environments. In J. Cannon-Bowers & E. Salas (Eds.), *Making decisions under stress: Implications for individual and team training* (pp. 61–87). Washington, DC: American Psychological Association.

Thordsen, M., McCloskey, M. J., Heaton, J. K., & Serfaty, D. (1998). *Decision-centered development of a mission rehearsal System.* Technical report prepared by Klein Associates and Aptima for the Naval Air Warfare Center/Training Systems Division, Orlando, FL.

CREATING HIGH-TECH TEAMS: A CONCLUSION

RAEGAN M. HOEFT, FLORIAN JENTSCH, AND CLINT BOWERS

As noted in chapter 9, authored by Priest et al., technology is not the future; it is the present. With respect to teams, the chapters in this book certainly support this statement. Already, technology has fully invaded our lives; in the last half-century, in particular, it has fundamentally changed the way that people interact with one another. The organization of this book thus highlights three general ways that technology has changed teams and teamwork: (a) technology can be designed to support teamwork, (b) technology can actually affect the environment in which team members interact with one another, and (c) technology can permeate a team to become an integral part of that team; in essence, technology can become another team member.

Although this book thus captures the current state of the art, it is likely that technology will continue to evolve in such a way that teams will be affected in the same three ways: Complex teams composed of automated agents and humans will use technology to support their behavior in complex, highly technological environments. So, the essential questions become, first, what do we really know now? And second, how can we take that information to prepare for these teams of the future?

HIGH TECHNOLOGY TO SUPPORT TEAMWORK

Technologies, such as groupware or group decision-making support systems, have yielded some promising results with regard to promoting effective teamwork and communication. However, in chapter 1, Driskell and Salas concluded that not enough human factors have been included in the design process to exploit the opportunities that exist to support teamwork. Specifically, they have described how early groupware was actually technology designed for single users that was then modified for groups. Thus, as far as groupware is concerned, developers were essentially searching for users rather than developing products to address existing issues and problems. This is certainly not an uncommon occurrence in technological development, but, as Driskell and Salas pointed out, it often does not address the problems of teamwork that behavioral and cognitive sciences are seeking to answer.

Moreover, in chapter 2, van der Kleij and Schraagen discussed how much of the existing groupware or support systems are still in the prototype stages, which further supports Driskell and Salas's contention that this technology has not lived up to its full potential. The same can be said for other innovative technologies, such as data visualization (described in chap. 3, by Schatz et al.), that are now being applied to the team domain to enhance communication and decision making. Again, teams have adapted to the available technology, and only when things do not work as advertised or imagined do decision makers typically begin to involve behavioral and cognitive sciences to study how technology can adapt to teams.

HIGH-TECH TEAMS IN ACTION

The chapters in Part II of this book amply illustrate that there are many high-technology contexts in which teams must currently operate, yet there is still some disconnect between the science and the practice. As Fiore et al. pointed out in chapter 4, we must be wary about throwing a team into a unique environment and expecting the same resultant performance. It is hoped that, with a push toward user-centered design, these types of supportive technology will greatly enhance team communication and coordination, even though we have not yet reached the point where their true potential is realized and exploited today.

The second two chapters in Part II discuss the development of two types of software used to aid teams in complex command and control environments. Specifically, in chapter 5, Morin and Albinsson discussed a tool designed for reconstruction and exploration of large amounts of data. In essence, they described a data visualization tool (similar to those described in chap. 3) that allows for the quick extraction of critical patterns from large amounts of communications data. Furthermore, in chapter 6, Schermer-horn and Moore discussed the development and evaluation of a tool for improving information exchange between team members. These authors demonstrated that by incorporating the support tool, they were able to provide more up-to-date information to teams, allowing the teams to act on it more quickly. These chapters thus provide two examples of the benefits of taking supportive technology and implementing it into a complex environ-ment to enhance team performance. With the likelihood of more complex environments emerging in years to come, it will be even more important that this union between teams and supportive technologies is not overlooked.

The final chapters in Part II describe two technology-laden environ-ments in which teams are forced to function effectively for safety purposes: (a) in nuclear power stations (chap. 7, by O'Hara and Roth) and (b) in space flight (chap. 8, by Caldwell). Especially with the evolving future of power and energy, as well as the world's continued interest in space explora-tion, these are two environments that will experience rapid changes and new challenges in the years to come. These chapters also highlight two essential factors that influence teamwork: (a) the physical layout of the room in which a team operates (e.g., the control room of a power station) and (b) the selection and assignment of team members (which is so crucial in space operations). It is clear that these two factors are important. However, modern communications technology has fundamentally changed the need for team members to be colocated in the same physical space; instead, there exists a "virtual space" in which more and more teams operate. Further-more, the selection of team members from a large pool of eager and highly qualified applicants is not always possible. Thus, we must also ask, are these the same factors that will affect future teams in complex environments as well?

THE FUTURE OF TEAMWORK: TECHNOLOGY AS A TEAM MEMBER

An answer to the preceding question can be attempted by a look at the chapters in Part III. This part is perhaps the one in which the most exciting changes that have occurred in teamwork are described. In fact, teams are actually changing right before our eyes. Virtual teams are becoming more and more the norm, while fewer and fewer traditional teams exist. As Priest et al. pointed out in chapter 9, teams face unique challenges, including team opacity, isolation, and trust issues due to their distributed nature. Moreover, Priest et al. noted that the field has grown so rapidly that it is now struggling with the problem of too many operational definitions. Instead, these authors suggested that a first step toward understanding virtual teams might be to standardize the terms that are used to describe the teams and the factors associated with these teams. Lack of standardization of constructs and terms is certainly also not a new problem, and behavioral and cognitive scientists are among the most frequent culprits. This notwithstanding, however, we need to come up with a nomenclature and with definitions that not only make sense to experts but also can be shared with and imparted to nonscientists who form the members of many of today's virtual teams.

Continuing the theme of supporting technology, Thompson and Coovert reported in chapter 10 that virtual teams could benefit greatly from advanced forms of groupware, such as tools for computer-supported cooperative work. Yet, reflecting the findings and opinions in chapters 1 and 2, many current virtual teams must by necessity rely on the groupware that is currently available. Thus, virtual teams are another area in which improved and efficient supporting technology could greatly enhance team communication and coordination. As the authors of both chapters 9 and 10 conclude, then, this new focus on virtual teams shows that we have much more to learn about these amalgams of teams and technology.

The final two chapters in Part III investigated the question of whether technology—specifically, automation—can and should be regarded as an additional team member in certain situations. In chapter 11, Hoeft et al. argued that the automation in modern airplanes can be considered a team member because of the interdependence requirements between the crew members and the automation. While acknowledging a team of human and automated team members, however, the authors also showed that the unique composition of two pilots and an automated flight management system does not lend itself completely to a current model of team performance, specifically, the team effectiveness model. Instead, team science will have to be adjusted in its models to account for the differences between an automated and a human team member.

Similarly, in chapter 12, Freeman et al. further expounded on the idea of human–automated teams, noting the "probable emergence of human–agent teams in future real world operational settings" and focusing on the benefits of using synthetic teammates for training purposes. The authors suggested that there are situations in which using synthetic teammates would actually be more beneficial than training with other human trainees. Thus, although these human–automated teams are already in existence, we have yet to determine exactly how different these teams are from all-human teams and to create models of human performance and training that adapt to these differences.

NOW WHAT?

As mentioned in the Introduction, no one was prepared for the emergence of teams and teamwork. The interest in teamwork that was spawned by high-profile accidents prompted society to study how teamwork "works" and "works best." Similarly, at the conclusion of this book, we ponder what unforeseen events will occur to again change the way we view and compensate for teams and the technological advances that will affect them. Teamwork with automated team members, if not a reality today, will be one in a few years. Many organizations are developing and fielding semi-autonomous and autonomous, more or less "intelligent" agents, be they robots, computer agents, or decision support systems. As the final chapters of this book attest, still little is known about how mixed teams of humans and intelligent agents should interact. In fact, the interaction between teams of humans and teams of intelligent agents is one of the hot topics for many organizations, especially the military. So far, technology is fielded even while the research is just beginning, and rules and procedures are often made up "on the fly." So far, no serious incidents or accidents have been reported, but, as more and more robots are fielded, this may unfortunately just be a matter of time. Furthermore, even without a disastrous news story, teams will continue to change shape and become something more than what is described in this book. Thus, we must also honestly ask, Will this book be outdated even before the reader reaches this conclusion?

We believe it will not be, as there are many themes of teamwork that will always be of prominent importance. One of these themes, which pervades this book, is training. Almost every single chapter mentions the need for new and better training that will take into account advances in technology. Are there general measures that can be taken to prepare for the unknown advances? We can begin to acknowledge the existence of human–automated teams and develop training strategies that embrace this new idea. We can also continue to combat the challenges of virtual teams by taking the necessary steps to ensure that there is still cohesion within these types of distributed teams. We can attempt to take what we know about specific complex domains and generalize those findings to similar complex domains. Perhaps most important, we can make sure that we are as prepared as possible by acknowledging now that we expect these changes in technology and their resultant changes in teamwork. Therefore, the far-off visions for teamwork of today may become the realities of the not-so-distant future.

AUTHOR INDEX

Numbers in italics refer to listings in reference sections.

Abbott, D. W., 251, *257*
Abowd, G., 43, *48*
Abrami, P. C., 28, *32*
Adams, M. J., 273, *282*
Adler, A., 45, *48*
Adrianson, L., 218, *236*
Affisco, J. F., 46, 47, *50*
Aggleton, J. P., 82, *84*
Albinsson, P.-A., 94, 99, 108, *110*
Allaire, P., 193, *206*
Allard, R., 169, *178*
Almeida, P., 146, *158*
Amalberti, R. R., *257*, 249
Anders, A., 281, *282*
Anderson, A. H., 221, *236*
Anderson, J. R., 27, 28, 29, *30*
Andrews, D. H., 216, *239*
Aquino, K., 36, *49*
Ardison, S., 187, *212*
Armstrong, D., 140–141, *158*
Armstrong, D. J., 220, 222, 224, 226–
    227, 229, 231, 232, 233, 234,
    236
Arnison, L., 186, *206*
Atkins, F. R., 162, 165, 168, *180*
Atkinson, J. D., Jr., 169, *178*
AT&T, 274, *281*
Austin, J. R., 197, *206*
Averett, M. G., 116, 117, 119, 120, 121,
    137
Axelsson, M., 94, 108, *111, 112*

Baddeley, A., 82, *84*
Bader, P., 187, 188, 197, *206, 212*
Bailey, R. W., 165, *178*
Baker, D. P., 15, *30*, 62, *67*
Baldonado, M. Q., 98, *110*
Bales, R. F., 22, *30*
Ball, P., 53, *65*
Baltes, B. B., 43, *48*
Bank, T., 119, *137*
Banks, D., 197, *206*
Barber, H., 197, *206*

Barfield, W., 204, *206*
Bartel, C. A., 17, 18, *32*
Bastianutti, L., 38, *48*
Bauer, C. C., 43, *48*
Baumeister, R. F., 23, *33*
BBN Technologies, 273, *281*
Beacker, R. M., 42, *48*
Beale, C., 75, *84*
Beale, R., 43, *48*
Beard, R. L., 245, 246, 247, *259*
Belanger, F., 191, *207*
Bell, B. S., 186, 191, *207*
Bellotti, V., 45, *48*
Beltracchi, L., 154, *158*
Belyavin, A., 251, *258*
Benbasat, I., 39, 47, 48, 53, *66*
Berggren, M., 235, *236*
Bergondy, M., 264, *282*
Beringer, D. B., 250, *258*
Bettman, J. R., 36, *50*
Billings, C. E., 244, 245, 252, 253, *257*,
    259
Bishop, R. H., 164, 167, *180*
Bjorlo, T., 145, *159*
Bladh, K., 141, *158*
Blickensderfer, E., 61, *65*
Boiney, L. G., 186, *207*
Bolstad, C. A., 116, *137*
Bordeleau, P., 28, *33*
Bordia, P., 218, *236*
Borgman, C. L., 61, *65*
Borrill, C. S., 186, *212*
Bos, N., 20, *30*, 229, 230, *241*
Bostrom, R. P., 39, 40, *48*
Bovair, S., 61, *66*
Bowers, C. A., 61, 62, 65, 72, 84, 190,
    202, 208, 209, 248, 250, 253,
    257
Boyce, L. A., 197, *210*
Boys, R., 253, *257*
Bradner, E., 230, *239*
Bramble, W. J., 202, *209*
Bransford, J. D., 77, *85*
Brawley, L. R., 225, *236*

Brehmer, B., 92, *110*, 169, 170, *178*, *179*
Brennan, L. L., 24, *30*
Brennan, S. E., 17, *30*, 193, 207, 220, *236*
Broadbent, D. E., 25, *30*
Brobst, W. D., 264, *281*
Brodlie, K., 63, *64*, *65*
Brown, A. C., 264, *281*
Brubaker, B., 75, *85*
Bruck, B., 189, *207*
Buckland, B. K., 45, *50*
Bunker, B. B., 194, *210*
Burdett, J., 215, *236*
Burdick, M. D., 36, *49*
Burgess, P. W., 77, *84*
Burke, C. S., 163, *179*, 186, 187, 198, 199, *210*, *211*
Burns, C. M., 148, *158*
Burns, J., 200, *207*
Burrough, B., 176, *179*
Burt, R. S., 194, *211*
Buschke, H., 75, *85*
Buxton, W. A. S., 42, *48*

Caldwell, B. S., 163, 164, 167, 170, 171, 172, 173, 175, *179*, *180*, *182*
Callan, J. R., 116, *138*
Camerer, C., 194, *211*
Campbell, J. P., 205, *207*
Cannon-Bowers, J. A., 17, *30*, *33*, 39, 50, 59, 61, 62, 65, 66, 67, 82, 86, 87, *141*, *157*, 163, 166, *179*, *181*, 198, 199, 200, *207*, *208*, *210*, 224, *239*, 248, 249, *257*
Canon, L. K., 25, *33*
Card, S. K., 54, *65*
Carey, J. M., 60, *65*
Carron, A. V., 225, *236*
Chaffin, R., 76, *85*
Chalfonte, B. L., 222, *237*
Charness, N., 281, *282*
Chen, C., 51, *65*
Chidambaram, L., 39, 40, *48*
Chidester, T. R., 251, *258*
Christie, B., 20, *34*, 221, *240*
Christoffersen, K., 245, *257*
Claffy, K., 52, 53, *66*
Clark, H. H., 17, *30*, 193, *207*, 220, *236*
Clark, S., 204, *240*
Clearwater, Y. A., 164, *180*

Cohen, M. S., 197, *208*
Cole, P., 220, 222, 224, 226–227, 229, 231, 232, 234, *236*
Columbia Accident Investigation Board, 177, *180*
Compton, D. C., 218, *240*
Connolly, T., 191, *212*
Connors, M. M., 162, 165, 168, *180*
Converse, S., 245, 249, *257*, *259*
Conway, M. A., 82, *84*
Cooke, N. J., 89, *110*, 170, *180*, 198, *208*
Cooper, R. K., 194, *208*
Cooper, W. H., 38, *48*
Coovert, M. D., 18, 20, *34*, 217, 218, 235, *236*, *240*
Copper, C., 18, *33*
Covi, L., 217, *239*
Cramton, C. D., 17, 20, *30*, 194, *208*, 216, 220, 223, 225, 226, 229, 231, 232, 233, *236*
Crandall, B., 108, *111*
Cuevas, H. M., 62, *65*, 72, *84*, 190, *208*
Cummings, J. N., 219, 222, 223, 224, 225, 234, *237*

D'Addario, K. P., 219, *240*
Daft, R. L., 20, *30*, 44, *48*, 175, *180*
Dalrymple, M. A., 264, *282*
Daly, R. L., 218, *236*
d'Apollonia, S., 28, *32*
Davis, J. H., 194, *210*
D'Azzo, J. J., 164, *180*
Deaton, J., 253, *257*
DeBoom, D., 264, *282*
DeMarie, S. M., 72, *87*, 216, *240*
Dennis, A. R., 40, 42, 47, *48*
DeSanctis, G., 21, *31*, 216, *237*
Deutsch, S. E., 273, *281*, *282*
Devine, D. J., 21, *30*
Dickenson, T., 245, *259*
Dickson, G. W., 21, *31*
Dickson, M. W., 43, *48*
Diehl, M., 37, *48*
di Justo, P., 177, *180*
Dirks, K. T., 194, *208*
Ditton, T., 203, *210*
Dix, P., 45, *48*
Domik, G., 58, *66*

Dorf, R. C., 164, 167, *180*
Dörner, D., 170, *179*
Dougherty, M. R. P., 76, *85*
Dourish, P., 45, *48*
Downs, R., 25, *34*
Draper, M. H., 202, *208*
Driskell, J. E., 18, 20, 21, 24, 25, 26, *31,
    32, 33,* 191, *208*
Duarte, D. L., 192, *208*
Dubrovsky, V. J., 24, *31,* 191, *211,* 218,
    228, 237, *240*
Dunbar, M., 36, *49,* 253, 254, *258*
Dunlap, K., 264, *282*
Dwyer, D. J., 200, *208*

Easterbrook, J. A., 25, *31*
Edmondson, A. C., 201, *209*
Edwards, J., 97, *111*
Egido, C., 222, *237*
Einstein, G. O., 76, *84, 85*
Eliot, C., 266, *282*
Elliott, L. R., 264, *282*
Ellis, A. P. J., 16, 28, *31, 33*
Ellis, J. A., 76, 80, *84, 85*
Ellison, N. B., *191, 209*
Emrich, C. G., 197, *210*
Endsley, M. R., 75, *85,* 116, *137*
Ensley, M. D., 198, *208*
Ericsson, K., 281, *282*
Everhart, N. C., 163, *179*

Fahey, R. P., 264, *282*
Fallows, D., 12, *31*
Fenner, B., 52, 53, *66*
Ferris, S. P., 93, *111*
Finholt, T. A., 214, 215, 220, *237*
Finlay, J., 39, 43, *48*
Finnemore, M., 234, *237*
Fiore, S. M., 59, 62, 65, *66,* 71, 72, 75,
    78, 79, 82, *82, 84, 85, 86,* 187,
    190, 192, 193, 199, *207, 208,
    209*
Fish, R. S., 222, *237*
Fisher, C., 89, *110*
Fisher, K., 200, *209*
Fisher, M. D., 200, *209*
Flach, J. M., *167, 180*
Fleishman, E. A., 15, 18, *31*
Fleming, P., 197, *206*

Fletcher, T. D., 194, *209*
Flin, R., 91, *110*
Flint, L., 218, *240*
Flores, F., 108, *112*
Fogg, B. J., 246, *258*
Ford, J. K., 201, *211, 212*
Forrester, J. W., 164, *180*
Forsyth, D. R., 22, *31,* 225, *239*
Foundation for Intelligent Physical
    Agents, 273, *282*
Foushee, H. C., 166, *180,* 251, *258*
Fowlkes, J. E., 18, *34,* 199, 200, *207,
    208,* 264, *282*
Franks, J. J., 77, *85*
Fransson, J., 99, 108, *110, 111*
Freeman, J. T., 197, *208*
Friendly, M., 52, 64, *66*
Furness, T. A., 202, *208*
Fussell, S. R., 217, 220, 223, *238*

Galegher, J., 222, *237*
Gall, M. B., 75, *85*
Gallupe, R. B., 21, *31,* 38, *48, 49*
Garland, D. J., 76, *85*
Garrett, S. K., 178, *180*
Gaspar, S., 186, *209*
Gawron, V. J., 202, *208*
George, J. M., 194, *209*
Gergle, D., 20, *30*
Giffin, K., 58, *66*
Gist, M. E., 28, *31*
Glenn, J., 163, 169, *180*
Glisky, E. L., 77, *85*
Godar, S. H., 72, *87*
Gokulachandra, M., 140–141, *158*
Goldberg, C. B., 36, *49*
Goldstein, I., 124, *137*
Goodwin, G. F., 17, *33,* 186, 199, *210,
    211*
Graf, P., 77, *85*
Green, R., 251, *258*
Greenberg, S., 42, *48,* 153, *157,* 214, *237*
Greeno, J. G., *30*
Gregorich, S., 251, *258*
Grief, I., 153, *157*
Griffith, T. L., 197, *209*
Grisé, M.-L., 43, *48*
Groen, J., 204, *209*
Gronlund, S. D., 76, *85*
Grudin, J., 12, *13, 31,* 42, *48*

Gualtieri, J. W., 264, *282*
Guide, P. C., 251, *257*
Gunawardena, C. N., 27, *31*
Gutkauf, B., 58, 66
Guyon, M. J., 77, 86

Hackman, J. R., 17, *32*
Halfhill, T., 187, 188, *205*, *212*
Hallbert, B., 148, *159*
Hamming, R. W., *51*, 66
Hammond, J., 55, 60, 63, 66
Hancock, T. W., 77, *85*
Hare, A. P., 22, *32*
Hare, J. R., 27, *32*
Harkey, D., 97, *111*
Harrison, A. A., 162, 163, 164, 165, 168,
   169, 171, 176, 177, *180*
Hartley, J. R., 27, *31*
Harvey, C. M., 55, 60, 63, 66, 72, *85*
Haugset, K., 145, *159*
Hayslip, B., 25, *34*
Heaton, J. K., 116, *137*, 264, *282*
Heers, S., 36, *49*
Heffner, T. S., 17, *33*, 199, *210*
Helm, E. E., 170, *180*
Helmreich, R. L., 166, *180*, 251, *258*
Helms, M. M., 202, *209*
Henderson, A., 45, *48*
Henderson, S., 141, 153, *158*
Hendrickson, A. R., 72, 87, 216, *240*
Hendrix, C., 204, *206*
Herik, K. W. van den, 38, *49*
Hermann, D. J., 75, 78, 79, 80, 83, *85*
Herold, D. M., 21, *31*
Herschler, D. A., 245, 253, *258*
Hicks, J. L., 77, *85*
Higgins, J., 146, *158*
Hiltz, S. R., 218, 237
Hinds, P. J., 187, *210*, 217, 221, *237*
Hine, R., 141, *158*
Hirokawa, R. Y., 18, *32*
Hjelmquist, E., 218, *236*
Hoffman, E., 52, 53, 66
Hoffman, H. D., 204, *211*
Hoffman, H. G., 204, *209*
Hoffman, R. R., 108, *111*
Hogan, R., 21, *31*
Hogarth, R. M., 36, *49*
Hollands, J. G., 252, *259*
Hollenbeck, J. R., 16, 28, *31*, *33*

Hollingshead, A. B., 22, *32*, 45, *49*, 218,
   228, *237*, *238*
Holste, S., 116, *138*
Houghton, S. M., 36, *49*
Houpis, C. H., 164, *180*
Hutchins, E., 143, 144, *158*

Ilgen, D. R., 16, 28, *31*, *33*
Ingaki, T., 249, *258*
Inspectie Brandweerzorg en Rampenbes-
   trihding, 35, *49*
Ioerger, T. R., 266, *282*
Isenberg, D. J., 25, *32*
Itoh, M., 249, *258*

Jacobson, D., *203*, *209*
Jagacinski, R. J., *167*, *180*
James, M., 251, *258*
Janick, G. A., 17, 18, *32*
Jarvenpaa, S. L., 194, *209*
Jehn, K. A., 226, *237*
Jennison, L., 214, *240*
Jentsch, F., 202, *209*
Jenvald, J., 94, 96, 109, *111*, *112*
Johansen, R., 215, 222, *237*
Johnson, C., 37, *50*
Johnson, E. J., 36, *50*
Johnson, K., 218, 237
Johnson, L., 250, *259*
Johnson, P., 194, 201, *212*
Johnson, W. L., 266, *282*
Johnston, J. H., 25, 26, *31*, *32*, 266, *282*
Jones, D. G., 75, *85*
Jones, G. R., 194, *209*
Jordan, D. H., 191, *207*

Kacmar, C. J., 60, 65
Kahneman, D., 36, *49*, 253, *259*
Kanas, N., 171, *180*
Kanawattanachai, P., 198, *212*
Kanki, B. G., 18, 32
Keithly, D. M., 93, *111*
Kelly, J. R., 21, 25, *32*, *33*
Kemske, F., 216, *237*
Kendall, D. L., 199, *207*
Kiechel-Koles, K. L., 197, *210*
Kiekel, P. A., 170, *180*
Kieras, D. E., 61, 66

Kiesler, S., 24, *31*, 191, *211*, 217, 218,
219, 220, 222, 223, 224, 225,
228, 234, *237*, *238*, *240*
Kleij, R. van der, 36, 39, 43, 45, 48, *50*
Klein, G., 58, 66, 116, *137*, 140–141,
158, 199, *209*
Kleinman, D. L., 72, *85*
Kline, T. J. B., 12, 13–14, 20, *32*
Klinger, D., 116, *137*
Kolb, D. A., 108, *111*
Kolb, M., 253, *257*
Koonce, J. M., 202, *209*
Koubek, R. J., 55, 60, 63, 66, 72, *85*
Kozlowski, J. M., 199, 200, 201, *209*
Kozlowski, S. W. J., 123, *137*, 186, 191,
207
Kraemer, K. L., 19, 22, *32*
Kramer, R. M., 194, *210*
Kranz, G., 163, 165, 169, 171, 176, *180*
Krauss, R. M., 223, *238*
Kraut, R. E., 222, 237, *237*
Krcmar, H., 186, *210*
Kuchinsky, A., 98, *110*
Kumar, N., 53, 66
Kvavilashvili, L., 76, 84, *85*

LaGanke, J. S., 43, *48*
Lane, S. E., 200, *209*
Lang, A. W., 141, 142, *158*
La Porte, T. R., 141, *158*
Launius, R. D., 176, 177, *180*
Layzell, P., 214, *240*
Lea, M., 175, *181*, 218, *239*
Lebie, L., 228, *238*
Lederman, L. C., 108, *111*
Lee, J. D., 249, *258*
Leidner, D. E., 194, *209*
Leimester, J. M., 186, *210*
Lengel, R. H., 20, 30, 44, *48*, 175, *180*
Levine, J. M., 18, *33*
Lewicki, R. J., 194, *210*
Liang, D., 82, 85, 86
Lim, J., 47, *48*
Lim, L. H., 39, *48*
Locke, E. A., 37, *49*
Lombard, M., 203, *210*
Lord, R., 197, *210*
Lou, Y., 28, *32*
Lucas, D., 74, *85*
Lucid, S. W., 169, 176, *181*

Mackinlay, J., 54, 65
Magee, J. C., 218, *238*
Major, D. A., 194, *209*
Malin, J. T., 245, *258*
Malone, M. P., 25, *34*
Mannix, E. A., 226, 227, 229, 233, 235,
237, *238*
Mark, G., 234, *238*
Marks, M. A., 17, 18, *33*, 186, 210, 246,
259
Markus, M. L., 233, *238*
Marsh, R. L., 77, *85*
Marsh, S. M., 197, *210*
Mathews, K. E., 25, *33*
Mathieu, J. E., 17, *33*, 186, 187, 199,
210, 246, *259*
Mayer, R. C., 194, *210*
Mayer, R. E., 61, 66
McCann, C., 92, 93, *111*
McCauley, M. E., 250, *258*
McCloskey, M. J., 116, *137*, 264, *282*
McClumpha, A., 251, *258*
McDaniel, M. A., 76, 77, 84, *85*
McDaniel, S. E., 218, *238*
McDonald, D. M., 225, *238*
McDonnell, L., 36, 49, 253, 254, *258*
McFarland, R. A., 243, 244, *258*
McGrath, J. E., 12, 13–14, 14, 20, 21, 22,
25, *32*, *33*, *34*, 45, 45, 47, 49,
162, 163, 164, *181*, 218, 219,
228, *237*, *238*
McGuire, T. W., 191, *211*, 218, *237*,
238, *240*
McIntyre, M., 187, 188, *205*, *212*
McIntyre, R. M., 15, 17, 18, *33*
McIssac, M. S., 27, *31*
McKay, C. P., 164, *180*
McKersie, R. B., 25, *34*
McLeod, P. L., 190, *210*
Meader, D. K., 221, *239*
Meier, B., 77, *85*
Mejdal, S., 250, *258*
Meliza, L. L., 109, *111*
Meyerson, D., 194, 196, *210*
Milanovich, D. M., 18, *33*, 61, 67
Miller, M., 266, *282*
Miller, P., 186, *206*
Miller, T. M., 116, *137*
Mills, M., 141, 153, *158*
Mills, T. M., 162, 164, *181*
Monge, P., 216, *237*

Montán, S., 235, *236*
Montgomery, J., *141*, *158*
Moon, H., 16, 28, *31*, *33*
Moon, Mars, and Beyond, 177, *181*
Moon, Y., 246, *258*
Moore, R. A., 116, 117, 119, 120, 121, 131, *137*
Moray, N., 245, 249, *258*
Moreland, R. L., 18, *33*, 82, *85*, 198, *210*
Morgan, B. B., Jr., 245, 253, *258*
Morin, M., 90, 94, 96, 97, 99, 109, *110*, *111*, *112*
Morisseau, D., 148, *159*
Morley, I. E., 43, *49*
Morris, C. D., 77, *85*
Morris, C. G., 17, *32*
Morris, N. M., 60, *60*, *67*
Morrison, J. E., 109, *111*
Morrison, J. M., 131, *138*
Mortensen, M., 187, *210*, 217, 221, *237*
Mosier, K. L., 36, *49*, 253, 254, *258*
Mueller, J. K., 76, *85*
Mullen, B., 18, 23, *33*, 37, *50*
Mumaw, R. J., 140, 143, 148, *158*, *159*
Munzner, T., 52, 53, *66*
Myaskovsky, L., 82, *85*

Nardi, B. A., 217, 219, *221*, 225, 230, 232, 234, *238*, *239*
Nass, C., 246, *258*
National Research Council, 191, *211*
National Transportation Safety Board, 250, *258*
Neale, M. A., *197*, *209*
Nelson, W., 145, *159*
Neuwirth, C., 214, *237*
Neville, K., 264, *282*
Nickerson, R. S., 167, *181*
Nord, H., 235, *236*
Norman, D. A., 108, *111*, 249, *258*
North, C., 98, *111*
Norvell, N., 225, *239*
Nunamaker, J. F., 23, *34*, 39, 42, 44, *50*
Nyquist, Patton, E., 58, *66*

Oberg, A. R., 177, *181*
Oberg, J. E., 176, 177, *181*
O'Connor, K. M., 22, *32*, 45, *49*, 228, *237*

O'Hara, J., 141–142, 143, 146, 149, 150, 151, 152, *158*, *159*
Ohrt, D. D., 76, *85*
Olmstead, B., 24, *31*
Olson, G. M., 20, *30*, 45, *50*, 213, 214, 215, 217, 218, 219, 220, 221, 226, 227, 229, 231, 233, 238, *239*, *241*
Olson, J. S., 20, *30*, 45, *50*, 213, 214, 215, 217, 218, 219, 220, 221, 226, 227, 229, 231, 233, *239*, *241*
Oonk, H. M., 116, 121, 131, *138*
Orasanu, J., 163, 165, *181*
O'Reilly, C. A., 226, *241*
Orfali, R., 97, *111*
Oser, R. L., 200, *208*, 248, 253, 257, *264*, *282*
Östergren, M., 235, *236*

Paashuis, R. M., 43, 45, 46, *48*
Pacific Northwest National Laboratory, 54, 55, *66*
Pacific Science & Engineering Group, 123, *138*
Palko, K., 253, *257*
Pamin, T. A., 25, *34*
Pape, W. R., 186, *211*
Paradkar, P., 175, *179*
Parasuraman, R., 244, 246, *258*, *259*
Parente, R., 78, 79, 83, *85*
Paris, C. R., 39, *50*, 224, *239*
Pascual, R., 141, 153, *158*
Passmore, W. A., 164, *181*
Patterson, E. S., 170, *181*
Patton, B. R., 58, *66*
Payne, J. W., 36, *50*
Payne, S. C., 266, *282*
Pearce, C. L., 198, *209*
Peter, E. B., 233, *236*
Pharmer, J. A., 250, *257*
Phillips, D., 76, *85*
Pierce, L., 199, *209*
Pigeau, R., 92, 93, *111*
Pinsonneault, A., 28, *32*
Pirus, D., 154, *158*
Poole M. S., 21, *33*
Porter, C., 16, 28, 31, *33*
Post, W. M., 89, *111*, 232, *239*
Postmes, T., 218, *239*

Priest, H. A., 187, *211*
Prince, C., 253, *257*
Proctor, S., 116, *138*
Prothero, J. D., 204, *209*, *211*
Pruitt, J., 200, *207*
Psotka, J., 203, *211*

Quaintance, M. K., 15, 18, *31*
Qureshi, S., 45, *50*

Radtke, P. H., 20, *31*, 191, *208*
Ragoonaden, K., 28, *33*
Raiszadeh, F. M. E., 202, *209*
Ramesh, R., 216, *239*
Rasker, P. C., 39, *50*, 61, *67*, 89, *111*, 232, *239*
Reason, J., 74, *85*
Reder, L. M., 27, 29, *30*
Remington, R., 76, *87*
Rhoades, J. A., 228, *238*
Richards, H., 187, 188, *205*, *212*
Richards. N., 214, *240*
Rickel, J., 266, *282*
Riley, V., 244, *258*
Roberts, K. H., 141, *158*
Rocco, E., 229, *239*
Rochlin, G. I., 141, *158*
Rogalski, J., 93, *111*
Rogers, J. H., 131, *138*
Rosenblatt, B., 36, *49*
Rossett, A., *192*, *211*
Ross-Munroe, K., 76, *87*
Roth, E. M., 141, 142, 143, 145, 147, 148, 150, 151, 152, 154, *158*, *159*
Rouse, W. B., 60, *60*, *67*, 166, *181*
Rousseau, D. M., 194, *211*
Routhieaux, B. C., 77, *86*
Rowe, A., 264, *282*
Rubenstein, A. H., 24, *30*
Rubin, S. R., 77, *86*
Rundensteiner, E. A., 52, *67*
Ryan, L. J., 251, *257*

Sabella, M. J., 199, *210*
Sage, A. P., 164, *181*
Salas, E., 8, 15, 17, 18, 20, 21, 23, 25, 26, *30*, *31*, *32*, *33*, *34*, 37, 39,

50, 59, 61, 62, 65, 66, 67, 71, 72, 82, *84*, 86, 87, 123, *137*, 141, *157*, 163, 165, 166, *170*, *181*, *182*, 186, 187, 190, 191, 198, 199, 200, *207*, *208*, *210*, *211*, 216, 219, 220, 222, 224, 225, 226, 231, *232*, *234*, *239*, 245, 246, 247, 248, 249, 250, 253, *257*, *258*, *259*
Samburthy, V., 21, *33*
Samurçay, R., 93, *111*
Sanderson, P., 89, *110*
Sarter, N. B., 245, 252, 253, *259*
Sawaf, A., 194, *208*
Schermerhorn, J. H., 122n, *138*
Schlechter, T. R., 198, *211*
Schlumberger Information Solutions, 56, 67
Schmidt, A. M., 201, *211*
Schmitt, J., 116, *137*
Schneider, S. K., 191, *212*
Schooler, J. W., 75, *85*
Schoorman, D., 194, *210*
Schraagen, J. M. C., 36, 43, 45, 48, 61, 67, 89, *111*, 232, *239*
Schwartz, H., 219, *239*
Schwenk, C., 220, *240*
Scrivener, S. A. R., 204, *240*
Sebok, A., 141, 148, 149, *159*
Segal, L., 252, *259*
Sehulster, J. R., 75, *86*
Senge, P. M., 198, 200, *211*
Serfaty, D., 72, *85*, 264, *282*
Sethna, B. N., 24, *31*, 218, 228, *237*
Shadbolt, N., 108, *111*
Shafritz, J. M., 169, *178*
Shallice, T., 77, *84*
Shannon, C. E., 165, *181*
Shattuck, L. G., 92, 93, *111*
Shaw, M. E., 20, 21, *34*, 37, *50*, 163, *181*
Sheets, V., 75, *85*
Sheldon, K., *192*, *211*
Sheppard, B. H., *232*, *240*
Sheridan, T. B., 171, *181*, 246, 248, 249, *259*
Sherman, D. M., *232*, *240*
Sherman M. P., 43, *48*
Sherrod, D. R., 25, *34*
Shirani A. I., 46, 47, *50*
Shneiderman, B., 98, *111*
Short, J., 20, *34*, 221, *240*

Siegel, J., 191, *211*, 217, 218, *218*, 220, *237*, *238*, *240*
Sikkink, K., 234, 237
Simon, H. A., 27, 29, 30
Simon, M., 36, *49*
Sims, D. E., 187, *211*
Singer, M. J., 202, 203, *212*
Sitkin, S. B., 194, *211*
Skitka, L. J., 36, *49*, 253, 254, 258
Slovacek, C. L., 229, *241*
Slovic, P., 36, *49*
Smallman, H. S., 116, 121, *138*
Smilowitz, M., 218, *240*
Smith, G. M., 18, 32
Smith, K. U., 167, *181*
Smith, T. J., 167, *181*
Smith-Jentsch, K. A., 62, *67*, 266, *282*
Space Studies Board, National Research Council, 177, *181*
Spears, R., 218, *239*
Spector, P. E., 213, *240*
Spence, R., 99, *112*
Sproull, L., 217, 218, 220, 237, *238*, *240*
Spurr, K., 214, *240*
St. John, M., 116, *138*
Stagl, K. C., 186, 187, 199, *207*, *211*
Stasser, G., 18, *34*, 166, *181*
Stein, E. S., 76, *85*
Steiner, I. D., 20, 21, 23, *34*, 37, *50*
Stoh, C., 191, *211*
Stokke, E., 145, *159*
Stone, M., 76, *87*
Stout, R. J., 18, *18*, 33, *34*, 61, *67*, 76, 82, 86, *87*, 198, *208*
Straus, S. G., 20, 21, *34*, 191, *211*
Stroebe, W., 37, *48*
Stubler, W. F., 145, 147, *159*
Suchman, L. A., 252, *259*
Sundstrom, E., 162, 163, *182*, 187, 188, 205, *212*
Swanson, G. E., 165, 168, *182*
Swezey, R. W., 165, 166, *182*

Tafti, M. H. A., 46, 47, *50*
Taha, L. H., 175, *180*
Tannenbaum, S. O., 245, 246, 247, *259*
Teasley, S. D., 214, 215, 217, *237*, *239*
Tennant-Snyder, N., 192, *208*
Tesluk, P., 246, *259*
Thies, S., 58, 66

Thompson, L. F., 18, 20, *34*, 217, 218, 235, *236*, *240*
Thordsen, M., 264, *282*
Thorstensson, M., 94, 96, *111*, *112*
Tidwell, L. C., 229, *241*
Tio, A., 75, *85*
Titus, W., 18, *34*, 166, *181*
Toney, R., 201, *212*
Townsend, A. M., 72, 87, 216, *240*
Trist, E., 164, *182*
Tukey, J. W., 54, *67*
Turoff, M., 218, 237
Tversky, A., 36, *49*, 253, *259*
Tweedie, L., 99, *112*

Uang, S.-T., 175, *180*
Unsworth, K. L., 186, *212*
U.S. Department of Defense, 119, *138*

Valacich, S., 220, *240*
Valen, R. J., 164, *182*
Van Ryssen, S., 72, *87*
Veincott, E., 229, 230, *241*
Venkatesh, V., 194, 201, *212*
Vicente, K. J., 109, *112*
Viire, E. S., 202, *208*
Vincente, K. J., 143, 148, *158*, *159*
Vogel, D., 45, *50*
Vogel, D. R., 23, *34*
Volpe, C. E., 17, 30, 163, *179*
Volz, R. A., 266, *282*

Wainer, H., 57, *67*
Waller, D., 202, *212*
Walther, J. B., 219, 220, 228, 229, 230, *240*
Walton, R. E., 25, *34*
Wang, E., 173, *182*
Wang, Z., 225, 232, *241*
Ward, M. O., 52, *67*
Watson, W. E., 250, *259*
Watson-Manheim, M. B., 191, *207*
Watts-Perotti, J., 170, *181*
Weaver, W., 165, *181*
Weghorst, S., 204, 206
Weick, K. E., 194, 199, *210*, *212*
Weigle, J., 186, *210*
Weingart, L. R., 17, *34*

Weisband, S. P., 191, *212*, 222, 223, 224, 228, 231, *232, 233, 241*
Wellens, A. R., 72, 87
Wells, M., 204, 209
West, B. J., 16, 28, *31, 33*
West, M. A., 186, *212*
West, R., 76, 87
Whiteside, D., 75, 85
Whitney, D., 215, *241*
Whittaker, S., 217, 219, *221*, 225, 230, *232, 234, 238, 239*
Wickens, C. D., 246, 252, 259
Widemeyer, W. N., 225, 236
Wiener, E. L., 245, 251, 253, 258, 259
Wiesenfeld, B. M., 217, *220, 241*
Wilhelm, J. A., 251, 258
Williams, E., 20, *34*, 221, 240
Williams, K. Y., 226, *241*
Wilson, P., 214, *241*, 251, 258
Winograd, T., 108, *112*
Wise, J. A., 54, 67, 251, 257
Witmer, B. G., 202, 203, *212*
Wixom, B. H., 40, 41, 47, 48
Wolf, B. P., 266, *282*
Wolf, S., 116, *137*, 197, 208
Wolfram, S., 164, *182*

Woodruff, A., 98, *110*
Woods, D. D., 89, 91, 92, 93, 108, 109, *111, 112*, 140–141, *158*, 170, *181*, 245, 252, 253, *257, 259*
Wright, Z., 20, *30*
Wynne, B. E., 39, 40, 48

Xiao, Y., 109, *112*

Yang, J., 52, 67
Yen, J., 266, *282*
Yin, J., 266, *282*
Yoder, C., 75, 85
Yoo, Y., 198, *212*
Yukl, G. A., 25, *34*

Zaccaro, S. J., 15, 17, *31, 33*, 186, 187, 188, 197, 198, 199, 206, *207*, *210, 211, 212*, 246, *259*
Zgourides, G. D., 250, *259*
Zhai, S., 108, *110*
Zheng, J., 229, 230, *241*
Zigurs, I., 45, *50*

SUBJECT INDEX

Actors, in distributed tactical operation, 94

Adaptability, as teamwork dimension, 16–17

After action review (AAR [debriefing]), 109
  in Air Weapons Officer training system, 271–272

Airborne Warning and Control System (AWACS) Air Weapons Officer (AWO). *See* Air Weapons Office (AWO) training; Air Weapons Officer (AWO)

Air transport teams, history of, 243–244

Air Weapons Officer (AWO), function of, 262

Air Weapons Officer (AWO)–pilot communications, 262–263

Air Weapons Officer (AWO) training
  analysis of, 266–268
  coaching in, 267
  debriefing in, 267
  interviews with instructors in, 267
  observation of instructional events in, 268, 269

Air Weapons Officer (AWO) Training System
  architecture of, 272–273
  AT&T text-to-speech engine, 272, 274
  coached practice in, 268–269, 270
  conclusions on, 280–281
  debriefing (After Action Reviews) in, 271–272
  Distributed Dynamic Decision-making interface in, 272, 273, 274
  early and late tutor in, 276–278
  evaluation study of, 276–278
  feedback on system concept, 279–280
  improvement in performance with, 279
  interpreter in, 272
  needs analysis in development of, 264–266
  OmarJ in, 272–273, 274

performance assessment by synthetic coach, 270–271
  performance changes with, 279
  simulation-based with synthetic agents in, 268–269
  speech recognition in, 272, 273, 274
  synthetic coach in, 269–270
  synthetic pilot in, 275
  synthetic tutor in, 272, 275–276
  Team Dimensional Training framework for, 264–265, 266
  training methods analysis for development of, 266–268, 269
  transferability of synthetic teams to synthetic–human teams, 280
  user performance in, 276–277

Ambient media, 235

Anderson, J. R., *27*

Anonymous contributions
  in electronic meeting rooms, 42
  in non-co-located group decision making, 43

Armstrong, D. J., *226–227*

Artifacts
  and activities, 108
  in distributed tactical operation, 94

Asynchronous communication, 194
  in group decision support, 46
  space flight teams and, 167

Asynchronous time, in virtual team operations, 217

Attitudes, of automated system vs. human, 248

Attribute Explorer, in MIND presentation, 99–101

Audio conversations, 44

Automated teammates
  attitudinal stability of, 248
  characteristics of, 247, 254, 255
  individual characteristics of, 248–250, 255
  limitations of, 254
  mental models of task in, 249
  task characteristics of, 251–252, 255
  team characteristics of, 250–251, 255

Automated teammates, *continued*
    team processes and, 252–254, 256
    trust of human teammate in,
      249–250
    work characteristics of, 252, 255
Automation
    definition of, 244, 245–246
    as team member, 286
Automation bias, 253–254
Autopilot
    as crew member, 245
    evolution of, 243, 244–245
    vs. human control, 244
AWACS. *See* Airborne Warning and
    Control System (AWACS)
AWO. *See* Air Weapons Officer (AWO)

Bader, P., *197*
Banks, D., *197*
Barber, H., *197*
Bias
    of automated vs. human team
      members, 248
    of human team members, 253–254
    reduction of, 39–40
    social categorization, 226
Bjorlo, T., *145*
Bordeleau, P., *28*
Breakdowns, between people and
    artifacts, 108
Brennan, L. L., *24*
Brodlie, K., *64*
Business rules
    for information sharing on Knowl-
      edge-Web, 123–124
    in Knowledge-Web, 121, 132, 134,
      135–136

Capsule communicator (CAPCOM)
    communication with crew, 172–173
    job description for, 172
Chat rooms, in virtual collaboration, 229,
    230
Chen, C., *51*
Claffy, K., *53*
Cognition
    in distributed teamwork, at individ-
      ual and team levels, 197–199
    team, 71

Cognitive performance
    advanced HSI effect on, 149
Cohesion
    lack in virtual collaboration, 225
    virtual team training for, 232
Cole, P., *226–227*
Collaboration
    collaborative workspace for shared
      tasks, 155
    in conventional control room of
      nuclear power plant, 143
    crew member-addressable frame-of-
      reference for, 155
    reduction of, in computer-based
      control rooms, 145
Command and control
    in distributed tactical operations,
      91–93
    generic definition of, 92
    linkage to communication process
      role, 93
Command and control team, military
    planning and coordination task of,
      113–114
Command and control teamwork, in
    Operation Enduring Freedom,
      113–137
Command and Information System, in
    military group support, 39
Communication
    in audioconferencing, 220–221
    between CAPCOM and flight crew,
      172–173
    characteristics of colocated and
      distributed environments, 193,
      194, 195
    in command and control of multiple
      teams, 108
    computer-mediated, benefits of, 218
    in context of distributed tactical
      operation, 94
    controller–crew in space flight,
      172–176
    distributed and face-to-face, charac-
      teristics of, 193–194, 195
    in distributed supervisory control
      system, 92
    in distributed teams, 193
    in establishing transactive memory
      in virtual teams, 198
    frequency of and distance, 222

inhibition of, in computer-based control rooms, 145
limitations of text-based, 219–220
synchronous and asynchronous, 194
synthetic Air Weapons Officer assessment of, 271
as teamwork dimension, 16, 18
text-based, 218
videoconferencing, 221–222
virtual team training for, 232
Communication analysis
context-driven, 104, 105
context in, 90, 93–94
distributed tactical operations and, 91–94. *See also* Distributed tactical operations
exploration and context in, 89–112
mission history model in, 90
needs in, 90
problems and potential solutions in, 89–90
reconstruction and exploration in, 94–101
reconstruction in, 90
Communication Explorer, 99
definition of, 99
in MIND presentation, 99–101
in subway emergency response, 104–105, 106, 107
Communication media
effect on temporal group processes, 45
task performance and, 44–45
Communities of practice, in reduction of social isolation, 192
Complexity
in distributed tactical operations, 91
Computer-based control rooms
distribution of information across team members, 149–150, 152
diversity of information sources in, 150–151
potential to impact communication patterns, 149–150
potential to reduce crew size, 148–149
problems with, 145
vulnerability to information compartmentalization in, 151
Computer-mediated communication
in group decision making, 43–44

Computer-supported cooperative work (CSCW)
definition of, 213
environments for, 216
groupware for, 215–216
key elements of, 153
loss of casual encounters with, 222
multidisciplinary development of, 214–215
objective of, 214
research in, 214, 227
teamware development goal of, 235
training for, 233–234
workplace layout, 153–154
Computer-supported cooperative work (CSCW) displays
administrative procedures for control of changes to, 156
collaborative workspace for shared task in, 155
common frame-of-reference in, for shared group situation awareness, 154
crew member-addressable frame-of-reference for, 155
design principles of, 153–156
facilitation of collaboration of operators and, 154
shared devices and, access to and identification of user of, 156
supervisor capacity to monitor operator displays, 155
tools in, 155
Computer-supported cooperative work (CSCW) team development, 227–234
adjustment time in, 228–229
chat rooms in, 229, 230–231
cross-training in, 232–233
face-to-face kick-off meetings for, 229
instant messaging in, 230–231
training in, 231–233
Computer-supported cooperative work (CSCW) team leaders
monitoring of group communication processes by, 233, 234
qualities of, 233
structured management approaches of, 234
in structuring of teamwork, 233, 234

Computer-supported, *continued*
    team performance and, 233
    training of, 233–234
Conditional trust. *See* Swift trust
Contextual moderator(s)
    distributed environment type, 20
    group size, 23
    high stress or high demand, 25–26
    status structure of team, 23–25
    task type, 20–22
    temporal context, 22
Control room of nuclear power plant
    conventional, 143, 144
    redesign of, 143
Coordination
    in context of distributed tactical
        operation, 94
    in human–automated environment,
        253
    as team function, 15
    as teamwork dimension, 16, 18
    virtual environments in develop-
        ment of, 202
Cue(s)
    in fostering social presence, 191
    recognition training for, 82
    in reduction of team opacity,
        192–193
    situational, and virtual teamwork,
        224
    virtual, absence of in virtual teams,
        223
    in virtual environments, 202

Data collection
    automated, for Knowledge-Web, 122
    for mission history, 96
Data visualization
    advantages of vs. traditional graphs,
        52
    benefits of, 54–56
    creation of compelling images with,
        54
    definition of, 52
    distortion of data in, 57
    effectiveness of, 53, 58–59
    good vs. poor, 64
    insight of, 54–55
    misinterpretation in, 58

navigation through information in,
    52–53
in numerical-based decision making,
    53
perception and cognition difficulties
    with, 57–58
pitfalls of, 56–57
predecessors of, 52
real-time information in, 52
requirements for effective use of, 64
revealing relationships in, 54, 55
speed of, 55–56
translation of data for nonspecialists,
    64
Data visualization in group decision
    making
    challenges of complex decision
        making, 60
    conditions for use of, 59–60
    cultivation of shared cognitive
        models and cohesion with, 60–62
    dispersal of information load with,
        60
    facilitation of communication in soci-
        otechnical environment, 62–64
    inclusion of specialists and non-
        specialists in, 60
Debriefing (After Action Review)
    in Air Weapons Officer training
        system, 271–272
Decision making
    group, 22, 59–64
    in human–automated environment,
        253
    as teamwork dimension, 16, 18
Digital Voice Intercommunications
    System (DVIS)
    for flight controller communications,
        173
Display panels
    group-view, 147
    Wall Panel Information System,
        147–148
Distance learning
    collaborative support tools for, 27
    conditions-of-learning approach to
        design of, 27
    declarative vs. procedural learning
        and, 28
    group support tools in, 26
    learner characteristics and, 28

learning outcome and, 27–28
task type and, 29
vs. traditional classroom learning
environment, 27
Distributed coordination space, team
opacity in, 72–73
Distributed environment
aspects determining communication
in teams, 193
communication media richness in,
20
computer-mediated, 20
increase in use of, 72
memory failures in, 81–84
memory theory and team cognition
in, 72
social presence and, 20
Distributed learning. See Distance
learning
Distributed supervisory control system,
definition of, 92–93
Distributed tactical operations
command and control in, 91–93
communication in, 93
complexity of, 91
context in, 93–94
contextual issues in, 94
distribution and complexity in, 91
domain of, 90
mission history model of, 90, 94–95
reconstruction and exploration of,
90
reuse of models in, 97
task force in, 91
uncertainty in, 91
Distributed team members
scenario-based training of, 200–201
virtual environments for development of, 201–203
Distributed teams. See also Team(s);
Virtual teams
challenges of, 62
definition of, 216
environment of, communication
over, 14
external environmental factors and,
72
failure of groupware to exploit, 29
personnel subsystem in, 72
supporting collaboration in, 14–26
technological subsystem in, 72

types of, 14–15
using data visualizations in, 63–64
and virtual teamwork, 216
Driskell, J. E., 26, 197

Electronic meeting rooms
anonymous contributions in, 42
brainstorming in, 39–40
group decision support in, 41–42
idea-generation in, 40–43
problem-solving and decision making in, 42
synchronous and parallel interaction
in, 42
Ellison, N. B., 191
E-mail
in brainstorming, 39–40
emoticons in, for facial cues, 219
Emergency response in subway
analysis and findings in, 102–106
casualty collection point in,
103–104
casualty models in, 102
Communications Explorer in, 104–
105, 106, 107
communication timeline and context in, 102–103
domain analysis in, 101–102
exploration of ambiguous casualty
collection point in, 103–104
Mind presentation in, 107–108
mission history in, 107
object models in, 102
reconstruction and exploration of,
101–106
Environment(s). See also Distributed environment; Virtual environment
command and control, 114
complex operational, 73–76, 79–81
in context of distributed tactical
operation, 94
human–automated, 251–252, 255
sociotechnical, 62–64
Event-based training. See Scenario-based
training (SBT)

Face-to-face groups
vs. non-colocated, in group decision
making, 43–46

Face-to-face interaction
    vs. text-based computer-mediated
        communication, 222
Face-to-face settings
    and communication in teams, 193
Fenner, B., 53
Fiore, S. M., 82, 192
Fleming, P., 197
Flight controllers
    capsule communicator, 172
    Digital Voice Intercommunications
        System support and, 173
    distributed supervisory coordination
        of, 172
    interaction with flight teams,
        171–176
Frames-of-reference
    crew member-addressable for collabo-
        rative activity, 154–155
    with group-view technology, 154
Fundamental attribution error, preven-
        tion of, virtual team training for,
        232

Griffith, T. L., 197
Group, developmental stages of, 22
Group decision making
    data visualization effect on, 59–67.
        See also Data visualization
    stages of, 22
Group decision support
    in electronic meeting rooms, 41–43
    non-colocated, 43–46
    synchronous and asynchronous, 46
Group performance
    moderators of, 40–41
    size and, 23
Group support systems
    advantages of, 47
    brainstorming and e-mail, 39–40
    definition of, 39
    facilitator in, 47
    ideal situation for, 41, 47
    implications for practice, 46–47
    interactive synchronous in problem
        solving, 47
    vs. manual groups, 46
        in face-to-face collaboration, 46
    settings for, 41–46
    teamwork and, 284

Groupware
    classification of, 215
    contextual model of development of,
        18–26
    contextual moderators and, 19–26
    conventions for sharing, 234
    current status of, 12–14
    definition of, 11
    for distributed team members, 215
    failure to achieve potential of,
        13–14
    and function supported by, 215–216
    for location of interaction, 215
    origin in product development for
        single-user applications, 13
    problems in, 227
    team functions and performance
        and, 18–19
    team performance outcomes and, 19
    team types, tasks, and contexts and,
        13–14
    in teamwork and communication,
        284
    timing of supported interaction and,
        215
    understanding of groups and, 13
Grudin, J., 12, 13
Gunawardena, D. N., 27

Hamming, R. W., 51
Hartley, A. P., 27
Haugset, K., 145
Hi-tech teams in action, 284–285
Hoffman, E., 53
Human–system interfaces (HSIs)
    in computer-based control room,
        144–145
    in conventional control room, 143
    effect on cognitive performance, 149
    evolution of, 156
    future, 157
    impact on situation awareness,
        149–150
    in nuclear power plant control
        rooms, 144–145
    tools for interaction with, 155

Idea generation, interactive synchronous
        communication in, 47

Immersion, in virtual environment, 203
Information
    business rules for sharing on Knowl-
        edge-Web, 123–124
    compartmentalization vulnerability,
        with diversity of sources, 151
    contextual, for communication
        analysis, 90
    distribution across team members,
        148–150
    diversity of sources for, and shared
        awareness, 150–151
    nuclear power plants and, 144,
        148–151
    organization and structure for Knowl-
        edge-Web, 135
    richness of, in face-to-face communi-
        cation, 44
    shared on Knowledge-Web, 133–134
Information exchange
    multi-echelon on Knowledge-Web,
        134
    synthetic Air Weapons Officer assess-
        ment of, 271
Instant messaging, in virtual collabora-
    tion, 230–231
Interaction, openness of, in workspace,
    144
Interdependency, in human–automated
    environment, 252–253
Interpersonal issues, in virtual teams,
    224–227
Interpersonal relations, as teamwork
    dimension, 16, 17–18
Involvement, in virtual environment,
    202–203

Jacobson, D., 203
Johnston, J. D., 26

Knowledge-Web (K-Web)
    adaptation of, to team configuration
        and tasks, 136
    business rules in, 121, 132, 134–135
    comparison of artificial war game
        and Operation Enduring Freedom
        use of, 131–133
    development in "Command 21"
        project, 114

enhancement of teamwork with,
    135–136
feedback about use of, 132–133
in information exchange with sub-
    ordinate teams, 137
initial use in Global 2000 War
    Game, 121
input, maintenance, and access to,
    115
multi-echelon information exchange
    in, 134
as new concept of operations,
    133–135
shared information in, 133–134
in support of information needs of
    other teams, 136–137
training for, 131
update rate differences in Global
    2001 and Operation Enduring
    Freedom, 132
Knowledge-Web (K-Web) design and
    development, 116–117
    core functional requirements for com-
        mand-level decision making, 116
    information requirements in,
        115–116
    requirements for guidance of, 117
    user-centered design approach to,
        115–116
Knowledge-Web (K-Web) in Operation
    Enduring Freedom, 121–124
    access to, concerns in, 129–130
    automated data collection on use of,
        122
    bandwidth and connectivity issues
        in, 130
    business rules for sharing informa-
        tion in, 123–124
    Commander, Carrier Group Three
        use of, 121, 123, 124, 125
    Destroyer Squadron Nine use of,
        121, 123, 124
    feedback about, 128, 129
    impact on teamwork and informa-
        tion exchange, 129–131
    information consumer perspectives
        on, 128–129
    information producer perspectives
        on, 125–128
    integration into organization and
        business processes of

Knowledge-Web (K-Web), *continued*
    Commander, Carrier Group
      Three, 130
    Knowledge Desks with, 131
    organization by functional areas cor-
      responding to team structure, 123
    perspectives on, 125–129
    post-deployment qualitative data
      collection on-line, 122–123
    time for updating of, 128
    training for, 123, 124
    update in near real time vs. Power-
      Point, 129
    use of and access to, 124–125
Knowledge-Web (K-Web) in war game
    and Operation Enduring Freedom
    differences in, 132–133
    similarities in, 131–132
Knowledge-Web (K-Web) tools, 115, 132
    changes to, 121
    Knowledge-Web Viewer and Knowl-
      edge Walls and Knowledge
      Desks, 120
    linking existing information/
      knowlege products to SumMaker,
      119–120
    SumMaker, 117–118
    TacGraph, 119
Kraut, R. E., *230*

Leaders
    of computer-supported cooperative
      work teams, 233–234
Leadership, synthetic Air Weapons Offi-
    cer assessment of, 271
Liang, D., *82*
Local actors, 92
Loss of engagement, in distributed
    groups, 44

McCann, C., *92*
McFarland, R. A., *244*
McIsaac, M. S., *27*
Memory
    in complex operational environ-
      ments, 73–74, 81
    factors influencing, 73
    prospective, 75–77, 80–81

retrospective, 75, 78
transactive, 197–198
Memory failure
    in air traffic control, 75–76
    classification of, 75
    in complex environments
      causes of, 80
      factors in, 78–79, 80, 81
    in complex operational environ-
      ments, 74–76
    in distributed environments, training
      interventions for, 81–84
    in prospective memory, 75, 77
    research on, 74–75
    in retrospective memory, 75, 78
    training for shared mental models
      and shared situation assessment
      and, 82
Memory failure framework, 78–81
    multimodal approach to memory
      and, 78, 79
    objectives of, 78
    practical implications of, 83–84
    theoretical implications of, 83
    in training, system design, and perfor-
      mance, 81–84
Metacognition
    development of, 201
    in distributed teamwork, 197
Microworld, creation by scenario-based
    training simulations, 200–201
Microworld simulation, in training astro-
    naut and flight controller, 169
MIND presentation
    architecture of, 97–98
    Attribute Explorer in, 99–101
    breakpoints in, 99
    Communication Explorer in, 99–101
    components in, 97–98
    coordination of multiple views in,
      98–99
    episodes in, 99
    managers in, 97–98
    of mission history, 97–101
    theme support in, 99
    time as navigation and coordination
      mechanism in, 99
Misattribution, virtual teams environ-
    ment and, 225
Miscommunication, during computer-
    mediated communication, 220

Mission Control Center (MCC)–crew
interactions, 171–176
Mission Control Center (MCC) environment
information flow and team performance in, 170
sensemaking in, 170
taskwork, teamwork, pathwork in,
170
Mission history
as cognition-aiding artifact, 108–109
exploration of, 108, 109
uses of, 108–109
Mission history model, 90, 94–95
in communication analysis, 90
data collection for, 96
exploration and reconstruction steps
in, 95–96
instrumentation goal in, 96
linkage analysis of data in, 96
presentation in, 96
purpose of modeling in, 96
timestamp in, 95
Mistrust, of automated system information, 250
Monitoring
of group communication processes,
233, 234
as team function, 15, 17, 18
Morris, N. M., 60
Motivation, as team function, 15
Munzer, T., 53
Mutual knowledge, achievement of in
distributed collaboration, 223

Nardi, B. A., 221, 234
Neale, M. A., 197
Nelson, W., 145
Non-colocated group decision making
advantages and disadvantages of,
43–44
Nuclear power plants
automation and intelligent agents
for operation, 157
backup support in, 140–141
behaviors important to teamwork in,
141
cognitively demanding situations in,
141–142

computer-based control rooms, openness and, 144–145
computer-based control rooms in,
problems with, 145
conventional control rooms, openness of, 144
coordination of multi-person teams
in, 139
decentralized functional groups
model for, 157
display panel re-design in, 146–147
distribution of information across
team members in, 148–150
evolution from analog HSIs to computer-based work stations, 156
example of re-design to improve
teamwork, 146–147
future of teams and technology in,
156–157
Generation IV design, identification
of new operational and staffing
models for, 156–157
HSI in future, 157
information in, 148–151
interaction skill in, 141–142
potential for closed workspaces in,
145
potential to re-create benefits of
open workspaces, 145–148
principles for technology use for
effective teamwork, 152–153. See
also Computer-supported cooperative work (CSCW)
roles and responsibilities in, 140
teamwork in, 140–142
tools in, 144

Observation, horizon of, in workspace,
144
Organization, in distributed tactical
operation, 94

Performance
group, 23, 40–41
monitoring and feedback for, 16, 17
reflection on in training, 108
Pigeau, R., 92
Plans and procedures, in distributed supervisory control system, 92

Power distribution, automated team members and, 251, 255
Presence. *See also* Social presence
    sense of, in distributed supervisory control system, 92
    in virtual environment, 203
Prospective memory
    directed search, 76, 77
    failure of, cue recognition training for, 82
    failures in, 75
    noticing in, 76–77
    relationship between intention and concurrent task, 77
    time-based vs. event-based tasks and, 80–81

Ragoonaden, K., 28
Reconstruction and exploration
    application to emergency response in subway, 101–106
    key idea in, 109
    summary of, 109–110
Reder, L. M., 27
Remote supervisor, 92, 93
Rossett, A., 192
Rouse, W. B., 60
Rubenstein, A. H., 24

Salas, E., 220, 224
Scenario-based training (SBT)
    creation of microworld in, 200–201
    definition of, 200
Schlumberger Information Solutions, 56, 67
Self-regulation, in distributed teamwork, 197
Sense-giving, by team leader, 199
Sense-making, by team leader, 199
Shared artifacts, virtual teams and, 223
Shared awareness
    in chat rooms and instant messaging, 230
    computer-supported cooperative work training for, 231–232
    in distributed collaboration, 223
    improvement in, with information source diversity, 150–151

limitation of, in computer-based control rooms, 145
    in nuclear power plants, 145, 150–151
    in virtual teamwork, 222–223
Shared cognitive models, data visualization in, 60–61
Shared information
    in command and control environments, 114
    on Knowledge-Web, 133–134
Shared leadership, organizational, in distributed teams, 199–200
Shared mental models
    data visualization in support or creation of, 61
    in distributed teamwork, 198–199
    face-to-face meeting in formation of, 199
    virtual environments in development of, 202
Shared situation awareness
    in conventional control room, of nuclear power plant, 143
    through common frame-of-reference display, 154
Shared understanding
    in nuclear power plant operation, 142
Shattuck, L. G., 92
Sheldon, K., 192
Simon, H. A., 27
Simulation technology
    microworlds and, 200–201
    in organizational operations, 202
    training in, 169
Situational awareness
    Air Weapons Officer enhancement of, 262, 263
    in command and control teams, 114
    shared as teamwork dimension, 16, 17
Situational cues, lack of and virtual teamwork, 224
Situation awareness
    advanced HSIs impact on, 149–150
    control room technology vs. conventional control room impact on, 148–149
    shared, in nuclear power plants, 143, 154
    shared group, 154

Wall Panel Information System and, 147
Social categorization bias, 226
Social isolation
    of distributed team members, 191
    reduction of, 191–192
Social presence. *See also* Presence
    chat rooms and instant messaging and, 230
    definition of, 191–192
    in distributed teams, 62
    synchronous communication for, 192
    in voice media communication, 220–221
Space flight
    controller–crew communications and task context, 175
    information flow and task coordination in controller–crew operations, 173, 174
    information flow requirements and paths for mission control–vehicle coordination, 173, 174
    in-group and out-group dynamics in, 171, 172
Space flight teams
    astronaut selection and assignment and, 168–169
    asynchronous communication and, 167
    breakdown in coordination and exchange of technical information and, 177
    challenge of extended support, 177
    Chinese space missions and, 176
    conflict with ground-based controller teams, 177–178
    context issues in, 164–165
    in continuous vs. discrete missions, 178
    delay tolerance in information transmission, 166–167
    flight controllers' interactions with astronauts and, 171, 172, 173, 174
    future space activity and NASA, 177
    group dynamics in, 165
    group issues in, 163
    impact of time on information sharing, 166–169
    information flow in, hierarchy of, 165–166
    information sharing problems in, 166–167
    interaction with flight controller teams, 171–176
    issues and contexts for, 163, 176–178
    long-term vs. short-term, 163
    models for information transmission delay, 166, 167, 168
    performance contexts of, 162–165
    performance of, 161–178
    simulation of training task and context in, 169
    synchronous communication and, 167
    task issues in, 163
    training and allocation of function in, 168–170
Status structure of team
    definition of, 23
    flat, 24
    hierarchical, 24
    team interaction and, 23–24
Stokke, E., *145*
Stressors, group decision making and, 25–26
Summary pages of K-Web, in Operation Enduring Freedom
    color for status indicators, 125, 129
    diamond shape for changed information status, 125, 126–127, 129
    linking and cross-linking of, 127
    update rates for, 127–128
Sundstrom, E., *205*
Supporting behavior, synthetic Air Weapons Officer assessment of, 271
Swift trust, 194, 196
Synchronous communication, 194
    for initial problem solving, 46
Synthetic teammates, 286, 287

TARGETS (Targeted Acceptable Responses to Generated EvenTs)
    in scenario-based training, 200
Task
    characteristics of, in human–automated team environment, 251–252
    classification of, 21
    difficulty of, 21

Task, *continued*
 group, 21
 interdependence or coordination of
  group members in, 21–22
 performance, media richness and, 44
 team member behaviors and, 21
 types of and team interaction, 20–22
 uncertainty and, 21
Team decision making
 brainstorming, 39–40
 Command and Information Systems
  (military), 39
 face-to-face vs. virtual teams, 40
 group biases and errors in, 36–37
 group size and, 40–41
 group support systems for, 39
 problems affecting, 36–39
 process facilitation, 41
 process losses in, 37–39
Team Dimensional Training (TDT)
 communication in, 264, 265, 266
 information exchange in, 264, 265,
  266
 leadership/initiative in, 264, 265,
  266
 support in, 264, 265, 266
Team effectiveness model (TEM), 5
 in analysis performance of human–
  automated member teams, 248
 individual characteristics and, 248–
  250, 255
 inputs in, 246, 247, 255
 member homogeneity and, 250–251
 outputs in, 247, 248, 256
 power distribution in, 251, 255
 team characteristics in, 250–251,
  255
 throughputs in, 246, 247–248
Team interaction
 in dynamic vs. ad hoc groups, 22
 stress and, 25
 task type and, 20–22
Team management, as teamwork dimension, 16, 17
Team opacity
 definition of, 73, 192
 in distributed coordination space,
  72–73
 as form of cognitive workload, 73
 and memory processes in distributed
  environments, 74, 81

reduction of, 193
 and virtual teamwork, 192–193
Team performance
 data visualization augmentation of
  verbal communication, 61–62
 distributed environment type and,
  20
 group size and, 23
 value of, 29
Team processes, in human–automated
  environment, 252–254, 256
Team(s). *See also* Distributed teams;
  Virtual teams
 activities and functions of, 15
 airborne transport, 243–244
 computer as teammate with reciprocal interdependence with person,
  246
 definitions of, 5, 245
 distributed vs. colocated, 5–6
 in future nuclear power plant design,
  157
 human and automated members of,
  245
 of human–machine, 6
 types of, 14–15
Teamwork
 commercial aviation accidents and,
  4
 dimensions of, 15–18
 evolution of, 3–4
 functions of, 15
 group decision-making support and,
  284
 groupware and, 284
 multidisciplinary contributions to, 4
 physical workspace contribution to,
  143–144
 science of, 3
 technological support of, 284
 technology as team member,
  285–286
Teamwork, in nuclear power plant operation
 conventional control room and, 143
 human–system interfaces and, 143
 impact of technology on, 142–152
 openness of physical workspace and,
  143–145
Technology
 adaptation to, 45

and changes in teams and teamwork, 283

Teledata, in distributed teams, 62

Temporal context, of teams, 22

Time. *See also* Asynchronous time;
Synchronous communication
elimination of, in virtual teamwork, 217
to gain experience using support tools, 47
impact of, on information sharing by space flight teams, 166–169
as navigation and coordination mechanism, 99

Tools
to enable user interaction with HSI or plant, 155
openness of, in workspace, 144

Training teamwork
for Airborne Warning and Control System Air Weapons Officer, 261–282
benefits of, 261

Transactive memory, in distributed teamwork, 197–198

Trust
distributed teams and, 194, 196
functions of, 194
swift, 194, 196
virtual environments in development of, 202
virtual teams and, 225

Tukey, J. W., 54

Uncertainty, in distributed tactical operations, 91

Verbal communication, data visualization and, 62

Videoconferencing, 44
communication failures with, 221–222

Video-mediated groups, 45–46

Virtual environment
absence of virtual cues in, 223

Virtual environment (VE)
absence of cues in, 223
collaboration problems in, 224
conflict in, 226

for distributed teams, 201–203
misattribution of team members in, 225

Virtual teams, 185, 186. *See also* Distributed teams; Team(s)
benefits of, 189–190
boundary spanning capability of, 188, 189
challenges of, 285–286
characteristics of, 188
cognitions in, individual and team, 196–199
collaboration problems in, 224
competencies and emergent states in training of, 196–200
cooperative behavior in, 225
definition of, 216
development of team members in, 200–203
differentiation from distributed teams, 188–189
distributed coordination space and, 186
distributed performance arrangements and, 187
individual, team, and organizational issues in, 193–196
lack of shared interpretative context in, 223
life cycle of, 188, 189
member roles in, 188–189
organizational shared leadership systems for, 199–200
problem summary, 226–227
relationship conflict in, 226
social isolation of team members and, 191–192
strategies for navigating distributive challenges in, 196–203
support technology for, 286
synchronous or asynchronous time operation of, 217
task complexity and work flow in, 189
team opacity in, 192–193
temporal distribution of, 188, 189
work of, 216–217

Virtual teamwork
benefits from use of computer-mediated communication, 218
challenges of, 190–196, 219–227

Virtual teamwork, *continued*
    characteristics of, 216
    communication quality and quantity
      in, 219–222
    diversity and novelty of members in,
      217
    elimination of time and space con-
      straints in, 217
    employee benefits of, 217
    employer benefits of, 217
    guidelines for, 203–205
    interpersonal issues in, 224–227
    shared awareness in, 222–224
Visualization systems, in device operation
    training, 61

Wall Panel Information System (WPIS)
    evaluation of, 148
    operator-configurable area in, 147

    plant overview area in, 147
    task state information area in,
      147–148
Walther, J. B., *229*
Weisband, S. P., *232*
Whittaker, S., *221, 234*
Woods, D. D., *92*
Work characteristics, in human–
    automated team environment,
    252, 255
Work environment
    characteristics that contribute to
      teamwork, 143–144
Workspace
    physical openness of, for teamwork,
      143–145
Workspace awareness, in distributed
    teams, 62

Zaccaro, S. J., *197*

ABOUT THE EDITORS

Clint Bowers, PhD, is professor of psychology and digital media at the University of Central Florida. He received his PhD in psychology in 1987 from the University of South Florida. He has worked in the area of team performance and training for the past 15 years.

Eduardo Salas, PhD, is trustee chair and professor of psychology at the University of Central Florida where he also holds an appointment as program director for the Human Systems Integration Research Department at the Institute for Simulation and Training. For 15 years, he was a senior research psychologist and head of the Training Technology Development Branch of the Naval Air Warfare Center Training Systems Division, where he focused on teamwork, team training, advanced training technology, decision making under stress, and performance assessment. He received his PhD in 1984 in industrial and organizational psychology from Old Dominion University.

Florian Jentsch, PhD, is director of the Team Performance Laboratory at the University of Central Florida. He obtained his PhD in human factors psychology in 1997. He received the 1998 George Briggs Dissertation Award and the 2002 Earl Alluisi Early Career Achievement Award in applied/experimental psychology. He studies team training, aviation human factors, cross-cultural research, and simulation.